THE DAY-STAR OF LIBERTY

The Day-Star of Liberty

WILLIAM HAZLITT'S RADICAL STYLE

Tom Paulin

faber and faber

First published in 1998
by Faber and Faber Limited
3 Queen Square London WC1N 3AU

Photoset by RefineCatch Limited, Bungay, Suffolk
Printed in England by Clays Ltd, St Ives plc

A CIP record for this book
is available from the British Library

ISBN 0-571-17421-3

2 4 6 8 10 9 7 5 3 1

For David and Eileen Hammond
who introduced me to
The Revd William Hazlitt

Contents

List of Illustrations ix
Acknowledgements xi
William Hazlitt: A Chronology xiii

Introduction 1
1 A State of Projection 17
2 Republican Poetics 47
3 Celebrating Hutcheson 64
4 Sheer Plod: Whig Prose 91
5 The Serbonian Bog 118
6 The Poetry in Prose 142
7 Southey's Organ of Vanity 171
8 Coleridge the Aeronaut 187
9 Blind Orion 205
10 Hazlitt *faciebat*: *The Spirit of the Age* 229
11 Vehemence versus Materialism:
    The Spirit in the Age 248
12 Great Plainness of Speech 271
    Epilogue 298

Biographical and Subject Appendix 303
Hazlitt's Publications 317
Bibliography 319
Notes 339
Index 371

List of Illustrations

1 William Hazlitt, early self-portrait
2 The Revd William Hazlitt (1732–1820)
3 Grace Hazlitt (1746–1837), from a painting by John Hazlitt
4 Margaret Hazlitt (1770–1837), by John Hazlitt
5 William Hazlitt, by John Hazlitt
6 John Thelwall, radical writer and editor, by William Hazlitt
7 Charles Lamb, essayist and critic, by William Hazlitt
8 Titian, *Young Man with a Glove*, c. 1520
9 The house in Wem, Shropshire, where Hazlitt lived from 1787 to 1795
10 19 York Street, Westminster: Hazlitt's home from 1810 to 1819
11 The building in Frith Street, Soho, where Hazlitt died
12 Joseph Priestley's apparatus, from *A Familiar Introduction to the Study of Electricity*, 1767
13 *The Illisos*, a fragment from the Elgin Marbles
14 The pugilist Tom Hickman
15 Manuscript of Hazlitt's essay 'The Fight'
16 Fives Court, Leicester Fields
17 Pugilists in the Fives Court
18 William Hazlitt by William Bewick, 1825

Acknowledgements

I am greatly indebted to the leading expert on Hazlitt, Stanley Jones. His biography, *William Hazlitt: From Winterslow to Frith Street*, is a remarkable piece of scholarship, and, along with his many scholarly articles, has been an inspiration to me. His friendship has also encouraged me greatly. The work of Jonathan Bate, David Bromwich, Roy Park, and Uttara Natarajan, as well as the readiness of these scholars to answer my queries, has helped me considerably. Over the years, many friends and admirers of Hazlitt helped me write this study. Roy Foster, Andrew Motion, and Duncan Wu read the completed typescript, and gave me enormous encouragement and assistance. Karl Miller, Uttara Natarajan, and Michael Neve read and commented on a number of chapters, and urged me on. Patrick O'Sullivan checked the typescript, drew up the bibliography, made many helpful comments and also helped to improve my prose. My editor at Faber, Christopher Reid, has been a constant support, and Jean van Altena has meticulously edited and shaped the text.

For their kindness and assistance, I would also like to acknowledge Toby Barnard, Liz Barry, David Bromwich, Charles Boyle, Bryan Burrough, Carmen Callil, Gillian and John Carey, Ciaran Carson, Jon Cook, David Chandler, Hoyt Duggan, Terry Eagleton, Peter Edwards, Marianne Elliott, Geoffrey Ellis, Matthew Evans, Jane Feaver, Michael Foot, Victoria Glendinning, Lavinia Greenlaw, Nick Groom, Clare Hutton, Alan Jenkins, Douglas Johnson, Gill Johnson, Paul Hamilton, Stephen Hull, Mick Imlah, David James, Valerie Kemp, Katherine Lambert, Grevel Lindop, Julian Loose, John Lucas, Joanna Mackle, John Manners, Blake Morrison, Ian McBride, J. S. McClelland, Robert McCrum, Gill McIntosh, Jamie McKendrick, Helen McNeil, Andrew McNeillie, Jonathan

Mee, Leslie Mitchell, David Norbrook, Bernard and Heather O'Donoghue, Roy Park, Barbara Paxman, Adrian Rice, Steven Roberts, Laura Roman, Xon De Ros, Michael Rosen, James Runcie, Edward Said, Christopher Salvesen, Andrew Sanders, Hugh Starkey, Oliver Taplin, Nigel Thompson, Thorlac Turville-Petre, Jenny Uglow, Tim Webb, Suzanne Webster, John Whale, David Womersley, and John Worthen.

I am deeply grateful to the British Academy for their award of a research readership in 1992. The readership released me from teaching a new modular syllabus, and gave me time to research and write as if I was once more a young graduate student sitting beneath the collected works of Thomas Hardy in the upper reading room of the Bodleian. I am grateful to the staff of that library, particularly to everyone on the reserve desk in the upper room. The librarians of the Hallward Library, University of Nottingham; Dr Williams's Library, London; Monticello, Virginia; Hertford College and Manchester College, Oxford, have been very helpful. Veronica Tonge, the Keeper of Fine and Applied Art at the Maidstone Museum, generously showed me the Hazlitt collection there. Georgiana Ziegler at the Folger Shakespeare Library in Washington arranged a photocopy and microfilm of Hazlitt manuscript T.b. 18, folios 17–36.

I am also grateful to Bruce Pollard, the Master of Eliot College, University of Kent, and to the Eliot committee and the staff of the English department there for inviting me to give the 1996 T. S. Eliot Memorial Lectures. Eliot's relationship with Hazlitt is one of the themes of this study, and the lectures I gave are at its core. I am also grateful to the Center for Cultural and Historical Studies, Columbia University, and to the John Hewitt Summer School for inviting me to lecture on Hazlitt.

Giti, Michael, and Niall have sustained me as I struggled with each chapter, and Surinderjiet, Jasvinder, Arvin, and Shaska have also cheered my labours.   T.P.

Spelling has been modernized throughout. As Hazlitt's use of italics is often contextual, I have not always retained italics in brief quotations.

William Hazlitt: A Chronology

1778 Born 10 April, in Maidstone, Kent, where his father, William, was the Unitarian minister. His mother, Grace, was from an English Dissenting family, his father from a family of Irish Presbyterians.

1780 The family moves to Bandon, Co. Cork. His father protests about the maltreatment of American prisoners of war. Gordon Riots in London.

1783 The Hazlitts move to the United States. The Revd William Hazlitt founds the first Unitarian church in Boston. Brief coalition government led by Lord North and Charles James Fox. Pitt's first ministry, 1783–1801.

1787 The family returns to England. Hazlitt's father becomes minister in Wem, Shropshire. American Constitution signed.

1788 Byron born.

1789 French Revolution. The Revd Richard Price's sermon 'On the Love of Our Country' draws Burke into the controversy over the Revolution.

1790 Burke's *Reflections on the Revolution in France* published. Replies to Burke by Mary Wollstonecraft, Joseph Priestley, and other radicals published by Joseph Johnson.

1791 Paine's *The Rights of Man* published. The *Observer* started.

1792 Percy Shelley born. Wollstonecraft's *A Vindication of the Rights of Woman* published. September Massacres in Paris.

1793 John Clare born. Hazlitt studies at Hackney New College. Godwin's *Political Justice* published. Hazlitt's brother John, a miniaturist and portrait painter working in London, becomes friendly with Godwin.

1794 Treason trials – Thomas Hardy, John Horne Tooke, and John

Thelwall acquitted. Sees Sarah Siddons act. Joseph Priestley emigrates to the United States. Godwin's *Caleb Williams* published. Blake's *Songs of Innocence and Experience* published.

1795 Hazlitt decides against becoming a Unitarian minister. Leaves the Hackney New College and lives in London with his brother, who introduces him to Godwin. John Keats born. Thomas Carlyle born.

1796 Death of Burns. Burke's *Letter to a Noble Lord* published. Hazlitt moves between London and Wem. Works on his philosophical essay, 'An Essay on the Principles of Human Action'.

1797 Burke dies. Wollstonecraft dies. Mary Wollstonecraft Godwin born. Naval mutinies at Spithead and The Nore. Hazlitt visits his mother's family in Peterborough.

1798 Hazlitt meets Coleridge when he comes to preach at the Unitarian chapel in Shrewsbury. Hazlitt visits Coleridge in Somerset and meets Wordsworth. Decides to become a painter. *Lyrical Ballads* published. Coleridge's 'Frost at Midnight' published by Joseph Johnson. United Irish uprising in Ireland. Death of United Irish leader Wolfe Tone.

1799 Hazlitt studies painting under his brother's tutelage. Travels to Manchester and Liverpool seeking portrait commissions. James Mackintosh renounces his support for the French Revolution in a series of lectures 'On the Law of Nature and Nations'. Napoleon becomes First Consul.

1800 Maria Edgeworth's *Castle Rackrent* published by Joseph Johnson. Irish Act of Union.

1801 Thomas Jefferson becomes third President of the United States.

1802 Hazlitt's portrait of his father in the Royal Academy exhibition at Somerset House. Peace of Amiens signed by Britain and France. Hazlitt commissioned by Unitarian businessmen to copy paintings in the Louvre. Catches sight of Charles James Fox and Napoleon in Paris.

1803 Hazlitt visits Wordsworth and Coleridge in the Lake District. War between Britain and France renewed. Addington becomes Prime Minister. Abortive uprising in Dublin. Robert Emmet executed.

1804 Hazlitt works on his philosophical account of disinterestedness, *An Essay on the Principles of Human Action*. Paints Charles Lamb's portrait (now in the National Portrait Gallery), but begins to doubt if he can become a painter. Joseph Priestley dies. Pitt becomes Prime Minister for the second time. Napoleon becomes Emperor.

1805 Joseph Johnson publishes Hazlitt's first book, *An Essay on the Principles of Human Action*. Battles of Trafalgar and Austerlitz. Jefferson begins second term as President.

1806 Hazlitt publishes political pamphlet, *Free Thoughts on Public Affairs*. Deaths of Pitt and Charles James Fox. Grenville becomes Prime Minister.

1807 Hazlitt publishes *An Abridgement of the Light of Nature Pursued by Abraham Tucker*. He also publishes an attack on Malthus, *A Reply to the Essay on Population*, and *The Eloquence of the British Senate*. Portland Prime Minister.

1808 Marries Sarah Stoddart. They leave London for Winterslow, near Salisbury. Peninsular War begins.

1809 Perceval becomes Prime Minister.

1810 Hazlitt publishes *A New and Improved Grammar of the English Tongue*. Coleridge lectures on Shakespeare. Perceval becomes Prime Minister.

1811 Hazlitt's son William born. Prince of Wales becomes Regent.

1812 Hazlitt lectures in London on English philosophy. Becomes parliamentary reporter for the *Morning Chronicle*. Byron publishes first two cantos of *Childe Harold's Pilgrimage*. Charles Dickens born. Perceval assassinated; Liverpool becomes Prime Minister.

1813 John and Leigh Hunt sent to prison for two years for libelling the Prince Regent. Hazlitt publishes drama criticism and essays in the *Morning Chronicle*. Southey becomes Poet Laureate. Liverpool becomes Prime Minister.

1814 Reviews Edmund Kean's performance of Shylock. Wordsworth publishes *The Excursion*, and Hazlitt reviews it in the *Examiner*. Leaves *Morning Chronicle*, starts writing for the *Champion* and the *Edinburgh Review*. Abdication of Napoleon.

1815 Hazlitt writes for the *Champion*, the *Edinburgh Review*, and the *Examiner*. Napoleon's 100 days. Battle of Waterloo. Hazlitt distraught for weeks after Napoleon's defeat.

1816 Hazlitt reviews Coleridge's 'Christabel'. A commissioned work, *Memoirs of the Late Thomas Holcroft*, published. Jane Austen publishes *Emma* anonymously.

1817 Hazlitt meets Keats. Publishes *The Round Table* and *Characters of Shakespeare's Plays*. Keats's *Poems* published. Hazlitt discusses monarchism and republicanism with the Shelleys and Leigh Hunt. Publisher William Hone imprisoned.

1818 Hazlitt gives two lecture series – on English poetry and the English comic writers – at the Surrey Institution in London. Publishes *A View of the English Stage* and *Lectures on the English Poets*. Hazlitt and Shelley attacked in the newly founded *Blackwood's Magazine*. Hazlitt sues *Blackwood's* for libel, Keats attacked in the *Quarterly Review*. Mary Shelley publishes *Frankenstein*. Byron publishes first two cantos of *Don Juan*. Karl Marx born.

1819 Hazlitt publishes *A Letter to William Gifford*, whose style Keats, in a famous remark, praised for 'the force and innate power, with which it yeasts and works itself up'. Hazlitt's genius as a prose stylist is now widely recognized. He publishes *Lectures on the English Comic Writers* and *Political Essays*.

1820 Death of the Revd William Hazlitt. Hazlitt elegizes him in 'On the Pleasure of Painting'. *Lectures on the Dramatic Literature of the Age of Elizabeth* published. Begins writing for the *London Magazine*. John Clare's *Poems Descriptive of Rural Life and Scenery* published. Shelley publishes *Prometheus Unbound*. Accession of George IV.

1821 Infatuated with Sarah Walker, with whose family he lodges

xvi

in London. Publishes *Table-Talk*. John Scott, editor of the *London Magazine*, killed in a duel following controversy with Lockhart and other writers for *Blackwood's Magazine*. Death of Keats; death of Napoleon.

1822 Divorces Sarah Hazlitt in Edinburgh. Sarah Walker refuses to marry him. Percy Shelley drowned.

1823 Publishes *Liber Amoris* and *Characteristics*. Briefly imprisoned for debt. Divides his time between London and Winterslow, where he stays at an inn called Winterslow Hut.

1824 Marries Isabella Bridgewater. Travels with her in France and Italy. Publishes *Sketches of the Principal Galleries in England*. Edits *Selected British Poets*. Byron dies.

1825 *The Spirit of the Age* published. Returns to England.

1826 *Notes of a Journey through France and Italy* published. Hazlitt's forgotten masterpiece *The Plain Speaker* published. Returns to Paris to work on his life of Napoleon. Death of Thomas Jefferson.

1827 Isabella leaves him. Returns to England and lives in Winterslow. Canning becomes Prime Minister.

1828 Contributes drama criticism to the *Examiner*. Publication of first volume of *The Life of Napoleon Buonaparte*. Wellington becomes Prime Minister.

1829 Hazlitt loses a substantial sum of money – £200 – through the failure of the publishers of *The Life of Napoleon*.

1830 Publication of *Conversations of James Northcote*. July Revolution in France overthrows the Bourbons. Hazlitt becomes ill in August, and dies in a lodging-house in Frith Street, Soho, on 18 September.

Introduction

At the turn of the stairs in an Elizabethan manor-house near the centre of Maidstone, there is a darkened, damaged self-portrait of the young William Hazlitt. To paint it, the apprentice artist used a brown bituminous pigment, which produced an instant Rembrandt-like effect, and helped create the chiaroscuro he was seeking. Unfortunately, this type of paint never dries completely, though eventually it produces a broken surface that looks like crocodile skin. In his cream, almost clamping neckcloth, the young Hazlitt stares at us with dark eyes, a little patch of sunlight on his right forehead. The cracks make him look strangely damaged – there is something raw, unformed, even dangerous, in his direct, but somehow vulnerably shrouded gaze. This is Hazlitt as he describes himself at the age of nineteen – 'dumb, inarticulate, helpless, like a worm by the wayside', and perhaps he was thinking of this early portrait when he went on to say that his soul has remained 'in its original bondage, dark, obscure, with longings infinite and unsatis-fied'. He is presenting himself as an eternal caterpillar or chrysalis. This is a portrait of the artist as a young prisoner – that bandaging neckcloth makes him look oddly convalescent. Above it, the studi-ous, brooding, gummily young face appears to be disappearing into the night.

Almost all the books and essays the young painter went on to write are now out of print. One of the very greatest masters of English prose, Hazlitt is almost never read or cited or studied. Read-ing my way through P. P. Howe's edition of the collected works in the Bodleian Library, I found that most of the pages in his *Life of Napoleon Buonaparte* were still uncut – I had to borrow a paper-knife and release the text. The three volumes had stood unvisited on

the open shelves for more than half a century. Recalling the bondage of those folded pages and looking at his self-portrait in the
Maidstone Museum and Art Gallery, I began to wonder would it be
possible to bring him back into the broad daylight his friend Lamb
identified the speaking voice of his essays with? What critic can
redeem him? How can his reputation be renewed?

He was born in Maidstone in 1778. His mother, Grace Loftus,
was from a Dissenting family in Cambridgeshire, and his father, the
Revd William Hazlitt, was an Irish Unitarian from Co. Tipperary.
His father was minister in Maidstone from 1770 to 1780, when
the controversy caused by his vocal support for the American
rebels forced him to return with the family to Ireland. Though
Hazlitt often beats the drum of his Britishness deliberately, we
must recognize that he was half Irish, and that his descendants
described the family as Irish. In *The Hazlitts: An Account of their
Origin and Descent*, the critic's grandson, William Carew Hazlitt,
says that the Revd Hazlitt was 'an Irishman, and my grandfather
after him'. The critic possessed a 'somewhat Celtic irritability', his
grandson suggests, and later in the same chapter he discusses
the friendship between Catherine Emmet – the niece of the Irish
revolutionary Robert Emmet – and Hazlitt's parents and sister,
who looked after her for the last five years of her life. The source of
the 'sympathy and tie between the two families ... is tolerably
obvious', Carew Hazlitt says: 'There was the common Irish blood
and the common republican leaning.' A family friend, the Revd
Joseph Hunter, confirms this in a brief memoir written shortly after
Hazlitt's death, when he says that the Revd William Hazlitt was 'an
ultra-Dissenter, and in politics a republican'. Hunter also mentions
Catherine Emmet, whom he calls the sister of the Emmet 'who was
executed for his share in the Irish rebellion'. The identification of
Hazlitt as Irish has not survived, though George Saintsbury, in a
history of English literature, notes that he was 'of Irish extraction'.

In her journal, Hazlitt's sister, Margaret, suggests that had the
family remained in Co. Cork, where her father was minister at Bandon from 1780 to 1783, he would not have survived the 1798 rebellion. His life, Margaret writes, 'would have been sacrificed to party

rage, and pretences would not have been wanting to destroy a man whose honest zeal for liberty gave so stern a rebuke to the slaves of power'. The Unitarian preacher, who was born in Shronell, Co. Tipperary, in 1734 and died in Crediton, Devon, in 1820, is described by his daughter as a fearless radical who inspired his children with a passionate political commitment. The minister 'never disguised his sentiments', and gave great offence 'by his freedom in writing and speaking at a time when the unbridled licence of the army (who took liberties in Ireland that they dared not do at home) made it dangerous to offend the haughty officers, who seemed to think wearing a sword entitled them to domineer over their fellow-subjects'.

During his ministry in Co. Cork, Hazlitt's father published a number of polemical letters about the maltreatment of American prisoners of war in Kinsale. In an introductory note to the letters, which were published in a Cork newspaper in 1782, he signed himself 'AN UNCHANGING WHIG'. His angry, compassionate letters of protest were written in a buttonholing polemical style and signed 'BENEVOLUS', meaning that he subscribed to the doctrine of benevolence common among Unitarians at this period, and rejected the doctrine of self-interest.

Through the Unitarian network, that élite of intellectuals and scientists, he was also able to communicate privately with the government in London, and to bring about an improvement in the prisoners' conditions. But, as Margaret Hazlitt noted in her journal, the plain-spoken minister became a marked man in a community that had already been angered by his forthright political views. With the ending of the American War of Independence, the family emigrated to the new United States, where they stayed for four years. Hazlitt Senior's outspokenness offended several of his fellow ministers, who nicknamed him 'Paddy', and dismissed him as a good-hearted but conceited man. The minister and his sons had a 'radical incapacity', Carew Hazlitt notes, for 'disguising what they felt'. This bold honesty and boisterous plain speaking was characteristic of what we might call the Whig *mentalité*, for the Hazlitts were what were known as 'Real Whigs'. Intellectually, they were

3

the descendants of the Commonwealth men who briefly made England a republic in the middle of the seventeenth century. They are in a line of descent from Milton, Harrington, and Algernon Sidney, and they carry proudly the scars of the battles those men fought, remembering in particular Sidney on the scaffold after his trial by Judge Jeffreys on a dubious charge of being an accomplice in a plot to assassinate Charles II. In *The Seasons*, Thomson calls Sidney the 'British Cassius' who 'fearless bled', and Sidney is often celebrated by Joseph Priestley, who taught Hazlitt history at Hackney College and was a friend of Hazlitt Senior.

In her study *The Eighteenth-Century Commonwealthman*, Caroline Robbins notes that Priestley, the Welsh Presbyterian minister, and economist Richard Price belonged to the third generation of English republicans – they were leading members of the extended radical family that shaped the young Hazlitt, who began as a philosopher and painter before becoming a copiously brilliant essayist in his early thirties. Priestley and Price were friends of his father, and it was through them that the Revd William Hazlitt met Benjamin Franklin during the 1770s and became a member of a club called the Honest Whigs, which Franklin set up during his residence in London. It was through his correspondence with Price and Priestley that the Revd William Hazlitt was able to communicate with the British Prime Minister Lord Shelburne about the treatment of American prisoners in Kinsale. Shelburne, who was briefly Prime Minister between July 1782 and February 1783, was friendly with Price and Priestley, and was sympathetic to the Dissenters.

Another Real Whig and intellectual heir of the English Commonwealth men was the third earl of Shaftesbury, whose study of aesthetics, *Characteristics*, is the volume which Hazlitt's father holds in the portrait his son painted in 1805. The portrait, which is in poor condition, is kept in a store-room in the Maidstone Museum. Dark, cracked, dusty, and unframed, it shows the old minister reading from a book, which dominates the foreground of the painting and functions as a Masonic symbol of openness, frankness, and Real Whig honesty. Like Jacob's ladder, which Hazlitt wanted to make a painting of, and which he employs as a symbol of the hopes inspired by the French Revolution, the open book is a Masonic symbol which belongs to the radical Enlightenment.

Hazlitt gives an account of painting his father's portrait in his essay 'On the Pleasure of Painting', where he tells us that the book 'was Shaftesbury's *Characteristics*, in a fine old binding, with Gribelin's etchings'. Though he had no affection for Shaftesbury's plush, rhapsodic prose, he chose to identify the text because he wished to make a deliberate connection between advanced Whig culture and his father in the tiny Unitarian meeting-house in Wem, the remote Shropshire village the Hazlitts moved to on their return from the United States. To mention Shaftesbury is inevitably to remind readers of the first earl, his grandfather, who is the model for Dryden's Achitophel. That character's restless energy is evoked by the association, so that Hazlitt has combined aesthetics with an implicit invocation of Whig political action – bold, turbulent, risk-taking, decisively intelligent.

Hazlitt develops the theme of historical action a few sentences later, when he says that he finished his father's portrait, 'or another afterwards', on the same day that the news of the Battle of Austerlitz reached Wem: 'I walked out in the afternoon, and, as I returned, saw the evening star set over a poor man's cottage with other thoughts and feelings than I shall ever have again.' In a moment of victory, Hazlitt's hero Napoleon completes this elegy for his outspoken father – an elegy that also celebrates and mourns his own youthful idealism, as well as catching the closeness shared by father and son while the portrait was in progress in the chapel at Wem.

The old, benevolent, bespectacled, craggy, doubly pocked face looks down at a book he seems almost to thrust towards us. Together, the portrait and Hazlitt's elegiac essay help to place the father, who began life as 'a poor Irish lad', the child of a Calvinist, North Irish family that had moved to Co. Tipperary. Abandoning his family's form of Presbyterianism, he studied under Adam Smith at the University of Glasgow, and became a veteran in the Unitarian cause. A forthright, argumentative, utterly unworldly man, his life was 'comparatively a dream'. His uncompromising nature and unshakeable principles meant that he didn't prosper in the Church.

Richard Price, in a letter to the earl of Shelburne, calls him 'a very honest man; but his great zeal as a liberty-man and his enmity to the late administration have sometimes brought him difficulties'. He calls him 'too open in his declarations and imprudent' – in many ways, he appears to have been a typical Irish Protestant.

His sermons appeared under the imprint of the celebrated Unitarian publisher Joseph Johnson, who published all of Priestley's works, and is remembered as the founder of the English book trade. Although Hazlitt Senior's devotional works are conventional expressions of Rational Dissent, they show very clearly those values of benevolence, reason, free enquiry, and energetic activity that are central to Dissenting culture. That cheerfully puritan culture is a developing structure of beliefs and strong political feeling which resists the pressure of traditional values by developing new ideas. In one sermon, Hazlitt's father takes a verse from Romans as his text – 'And be not conformed to this world, but be ye transformed, by the renewing of your mind' – and comments that we must be 'inviolably attached' to every principle of piety, righteousness, and truth. As children 'of the light and of the day', we must rise above all the 'maxims of the world'. In another sermon, 'On the Wisdom of God', he calls the sun a 'standing monument' of the Creator's wisdom, and says that it 'warms, refreshes, and enlightens' every corner of the earth – a phrase that expresses a combination of enlightened rationality and sensuous joy in the natural world which is typical of this strand of Dissenting culture. That light falls on the open book which the old minister proffers us in his forgotten portrait, and it is also present in Hazlitt's self-portrait.

Two years after painting his father, Hazlitt took a manuscript of his father's sermons to Joseph Johnson's publishing office in St Paul's Churchyard. The following year, 1808, *Sermons for the Use of Families* appeared, with a list of subscribers that includes a now-forgotten Unitarian called the Revd Thomas Belsham, whose address is given as Hackney.

There is a street named for Belsham in the London borough, a deprived area that in the late eighteenth and early nineteenth centuries was the seedbed of advanced educational ideas in

England. Hazlitt attended the Unitarian academy, Hackney New College, between 1793 and 1795. When Joseph Priestley emigrated to the United States in 1794, Belsham took over the ministry of the Gravel Pit Chapel in Hackney, and he was also the most senior tutor in the college, effectively its headmaster. Like Hazlitt Senior, and in common with most Unitarians, he believed in 'the gradual and increasing influx of intellectual and moral light', and he preached the necessity of removing 'all intellectual fetters from the mind'.

In a preamble to the rules of the Unitarian Society for Promoting Christian Knowledge and the Practice of Virtue, which he wrote for the meeting that founded the society in 1791, Belsham asserted the need to represent the doctrines of Christian revelation in 'their primitive simplicity', stating that the fundamental principles of the society were

That there is but ONE GOD, the Sole Former, Supporter, and Governor of the universe, the ONLY proper object of religious worship; and that there is one mediator between God and men, the MAN Christ Jesus, who was commissioned by God to instruct men in their duty, and to reveal the doctrine of a future life.

This is standard Unitarian doctrine, the energetic certainty which fuelled Unitarians' relentless intellectual curiosity and wish to make everything new. Unitarians, Belsham insisted, believed in freedom of enquiry, liberal discussion, the extrication of Christian doctrine from 'the mass of rubbish in which it has been for many centuries overwhelmed'. Unitarians insisted on the need for improvement, information (an important term in this culture), disinterested benevolence, and what Belsham terms 'sociality', a quality which he defines as the pleasure we take in 'the company and conversation of others', and which is attended with 'affability, complaisance and candour'. The voice of enlightened reason is 'the voice of God'.

God surveys his creation, views 'that infinite mass of happiness' which will be the ultimate result of his infinitely wise and benevolent operations, and is at all times 'infinitely happy'. Happiness – another key term with a strong societal application – is 'in the highest degree communicative'. Beneficence, as defined by

Richard Price, is the study of the 'good of others', which is 'public happiness', and Belsham believed, like Price and the Revd William Hazlitt, that the earth was in a state of 'gradual and accelerated improvement'. Drawing on Priestley's science, he notes that some philosophers are inclined to believe that matter should not be regarded as that 'inert and sluggish substance' which former systems of philosophy taught. This dynamism is present in both the Revd Hazlitt's sermons and his son's writings, most notably in the critical term 'gusto' which he coined.

Happiness, active energy, free rational enquiry, communication, liberty – these terms reverberate through Unitarian discourse, as Belsham and other preachers assert the need to change both society and the way people think. They are trying to shift the State and the established Church, and because they reject what is often viewed as the strange or crazy poetry of the Trinity, we may think that Unitarian doctrine is simply a form of liberal humanism, which retains a slight tincture of Christianity. But this is a culture with a principled faith in God, as well as in the power and goodness of humanity, and it's shaped by a historical memory of martyrdom and suffering. In a sermon, or 'discourse', preached at the fashionable Essex Street Chapel in 1813, Belsham remembers the Unitarian martyrs who were burnt at the stake or left to rot in prison. In particular, he singles out Thomas Aikenhead, a young Edinburgh student who was executed in 1697 for denying the Trinity. Aikenhead's trial and execution haunted John Locke, who was regarded by Unitarians as one of their greatest thinkers, but who was careful to conceal his rejection of Father, Son, and Holy Ghost. The anti-Trinitarian trinity of Locke, Newton, and Milton is constantly invoked by Unitarian preachers to underpin their faith and to express their pride in being advanced intellectuals. Though they are committed to progress and the future, they are always mindful of those who have suffered for their faith in free speech and free enquiry; they honour the dead, and keep the past alive by reciting the names of various heroes. There is a type of active piety in Unitarian culture which supports its rationalism. As a type of Christianity, it is what has been termed 'a process theology', which appears to explain material change.

8

During the 1790s, the government organized a campaign of persecution and harassment against Unitarian preachers and their congregations. Letters were opened at the post office, several prominent
Unitarians were imprisoned, and some were transported to Botany
Bay. At the beginning of the decade, Edmund Burke attacked Unitarians in *Reflections on the Revolution in France*, identifying these
middle-class reformers as dangerous English Jacobins who spoke a
'confused jargon' from their 'Babylonian pulpits'. Where the
reformers insisted on the 'diffusion' – a favourite term – of knowledge, liberty, peace, and virtue by 'the pious and useful Christian',
Burke portrays their faith in science as a type of arid, unsettling,
rash theory.

On 14 July 1791 a church-and-king mob burnt Priestley's house
and laboratory and the Unitarian Chapel in Birmingham. The mob
was called out by a number of country gentlemen who wanted to
intimidate the rising bourgeoisie in the city by attacking the Unitarians. The Hazlitts were living fifty miles away in Wem, and the
attack on Priestley and other Birmingham Unitarians – two other
chapels were also burnt down – inspired the thirteen-year-old
Hazlitt to write a letter of protest to the *Shrewsbury Chronicle*
which began:

'Tis really surprising that men – men, too, that aspire to the character of
Christians – should seem to take such pleasure in endeavouring to load
with infamy one of the best, one of the wisest, and one of the greatest of
men.

One of your late correspondents, under the signature of ΟΨΔΕΙΣ, seems
desirous of having Dr Priestley in chains, and indeed would not perhaps
(from the gentleman's seemingly charitable disposition) be greatly averse to
seeing him in the flames also. This is the Christian!

This the mild spirit its great master taught. Ah! Christianity, how art thou
debased! How am I grieved to see that universal benevolence, that love to all
mankind, that love even to our enemies, and that compassion for the failings
of our fellow-men, that thou art contracted to promote, contracted and
shrunk up within the narrow limits that prejudice and bigotry mark out.

This is a characteristically Unitarian effusion. The exclamatory
insistence on universal benevolence, the humane decency, and the

eulogy of a great man are routine features of the discourse which shaped the young Hazlitt, though we can see him beginning to relish the deeper structures of the language when he uses the word 'contracted', then kicks it back in the tougher sounding fricatives of the last clause.

Two years later, Hazlitt entered Hackney New College on a special grant to train for the Unitarian ministry. He was taught by Thomas Belsham, and attended Priestley's lectures. Gilbert Wakefield, a distinguished classicist who taught with Belsham at the college, was imprisoned for seditious libel in 1799, and died of gaol fever two years later. Wakefield, who influenced Coleridge and was particularly outspoken, attacked the Church of England as 'the muster-roll of ecclesiastical aristocracy ... the despicable trumpery of priestcraft and superstition'. Religion was employed, he said, as 'a state engine of despotism and murder'.

Hackney New College, where Wakefield taught from 1790 to 1791, was established by a group of Unitarians in 1787. Among the founders of this liberal institution was the Revd Richard Price, the Presbyterian minister and economist whose *Discourse on the Love of our Country* angered Burke and prompted his *Reflections on the Revolution in France*. Another founding tutor, the Revd George Cadogan Morgan, who was a nephew of Price was present at the storming of the Bastille, and is supposed to have been the first eyewitness to communicate the news to England.

Price's sermon celebrating the French Revolution was delivered at the Old Jewry meeting-house in November 1789. After sharing in the benefits of the Williamite revolution, Price says, he has been spared to witness two other glorious revolutions: 'I see the ardour for liberty catching and spreading; a general amendment beginning in human affairs; the dominion of kings changed for the dominion of laws, and the dominion of priests giving way to the dominion of reason and conscience.' This is one expression of the revolutionary consciousness which runs through Unitarian writing.

Two years later, Priestley delivered a discourse to the supporters of the college. In it he praises the public spirit of the primitive Christians – Unitarians were particularly attracted to the early Church –

and says that the students should never forget that they are not simply private citizens, but members of 'a larger society of mankind'. They should therefore take a real interest in whatever respects 'general truth, general liberty, and general happiness'. At one point, he says that all of his audience may perceive that 'we must be at the eve of great revolutions'.

Not long after, the Hackney students gave Tom Paine a republican supper, at which they sang 'Ça ira' and made revolutionary speeches (*The Rights of Man*, Paine's reply to Burke's polemic against the Revolution, was published in 1791, and broke all publishing records, selling 50,000 copies in two months). The school attracted a lot of hostile attention, particularly from the *Gentleman's Magazine*, and in 1793 a print was published which contained these lines attacking Priestley and Paine:

> Old Mother Church disdains
> Th'vile Unitarian strains
> That round her ring;
> She keeps her dignity,
> And scorning faction's lie,
> Sings with sincerity,
> God save the King.

Another print attacked the 'old Phlogistick the Hackney Schoolmaster', and the following year, in April 1794, Priestley and his family left for the United States. Many English Unitarians emigrated to the new republic during the 1790s.

In May of the same year, a former tutor at the college, the Revd Jeremiah Joyce, was arrested on a charge of 'treasonable practices'. Joyce, who was a favourite student of Price's, became tutor to Lord Stanhope's sons (Stanhope was a gifted scientist who was chairman of the Revolution Society, the reforming body to whom Price addressed his *Discourse on the Love of our Country*). Along with Thomas Hardy, Horne Tooke, John Thelwall, Thomas Holcroft, and a number of other radicals who belonged to the London Corresponding Society and the Society for Promoting Constitutional Information, Jeremiah Joyce was committed to the Tower. While a prisoner there, he was visited by the Revd William Shepherd of Gateacre, who is listed among the subscribers to Hazlitt Senior's *Sermons for the Use of Families*.

The chief defendant in the Treason Trials which began at the Old Bailey in the autumn of 1794 was the London shoe-maker Thomas Hardy (among Hazlitt's few surviving letters is a brief note to Hardy dated 1811, apologizing for not being able to pay for a pair of boots). His trial, which was dramatic, drawn out, and intense, attracted huge attention. The streets round the Old Bailey were crowded, and when Thomas Erskine, the brilliant barrister for the defence, whispered hoarsely to the jury at the end of his concluding speech, 'I am sinking under fatigue and weakness, – I am at this moment scarcely able to stand up', and then sank to his seat, the packed court-room applauded.

There had never been a case like this before. Almost all criminal trials during this period were completed in one sitting, even if the court had to continue into the early morning; but this trial lasted nine days. During it, Hardy was compared to John Hampden, and to the Whig martyrs Lord William Russell and Algernon Sidney. On 5 November 1794, the anniversary of William of Orange's landing at Torbay, the jury retired. An enormous crowd gathered outside the Old Bailey, where troops were deployed to protect the judge and jurors. After three hours the jury returned, and there were great shouts and applause when the foreman gave their verdict of 'Not guilty'. An ecstatic crowd drew a coach with Hardy in it through the streets of central London. Twelve days later, John Horne Tooke's trial began. It too caused a sensation – the attorney-general was hissed and booed by the crowd as he returned home each evening. After six days, Tooke was acquitted. The Lord Chief Justice then directed the jury to find Jeremiah Joyce and two other defendants not guilty, and the trial of John Thelwall commenced. He, too, was acquitted.

In the summer of 1795 the London Corresponding Society held a mass meeting in St George's Fields, and another in Islington in October, which 100,000 people attended. As an impressionable schoolboy in Hackney, Hazlitt was deeply affected by the Treason Trials, which, along with the attack on Priestley's house in Birmingham and his first meeting with Coleridge in 1798, were seminal events in his life. He refers to the trials and their leading defendants frequently in his writings, and later that decade he was commissioned by Thomas Holcroft's widow to compile a memoir of her husband, the third defendant to be acquitted. In his sketch of William Godwin in *The Spirit of the Age*, he remarks that a pamphlet which Godwin published in the *Morning Chronicle* just before Hardy's trial began in October 1794 influenced the outcome of the case, and 'possibly saved the lives of twelve innocent individuals'.

As a schoolboy, Hazlitt had access to radical circles through his brother, who was a successful portrait painter and miniaturist. He had a studio in Long Acre, and Hazlitt often met him and stayed in his house. John Hazlitt was friendly with Godwin (their families had been friendly for several generations). Godwin's pamphlet on the trial impressed William, because it was a successful intervention into the public world of law and politics. Like the Georgian polemicist Junius, and like Hazlitt Senior attacking the authorities in Ireland, the philosopher had won a decisive victory over the State.

Although Hazlitt felt that Junius was too trim and pointed a stylist to be a really great prose-writer, he identified him with his hero Napoleon – both figures have a hawk-like power of coming down 'souse' on their prey.* Hazlitt took the term from a speech of Burke's which refers to a particularly dangerous pamphlet of Junius's, and in considering Hazlitt's criticism, I have tried to analyse the way in which he makes links between his reading and contemporary figures and issues. His critical imagination depended on the vast number of quotations from the literary classics that were embedded in his memory.

That Hazlitt is so tenuously lodged in the cultural memory at the present time is saddening. Few readers – and still fewer places – claim him: the house beside the disused chapel in Wem where his father preached has a commemorative plaque on the wall, and

* Applied to hawks, 'souse' means to 'come down heavily with speed and force'.

so has the Maidstone chapel (Unitarians still worship there). The rooming-house in Frith Street, Soho, where he died on 18 September 1830, is now known as Hazlitt's Hotel, and writers are welcomed as guests. In St Anne's churchyard nearby there is a memorial tablet to mark where he is buried. In Winterslow, the Hampshire village to which he returned repeatedly, there isn't a trace of his presence.

Perhaps it's a pious mistake to try to make memories inhere in places and objects. Yet, over the five years I've been studying Hazlitt, the wish for some glimpse of the driven, fallible human being who created such ecstatically definite prose has prompted me to consider how piety must be part of the inspiration behind the attempt to write about a neglected author. During these years, I've come closest to a sense of his presence when I looked at that self-portrait and the portrait of his father reading. To see the Revd William Hazlitt's portrait, I had to go into a dark store-room in the Maidstone Museum, where I also saw Hazlitt's death-mask and a copy of the mask, both wrapped in tissue-paper. I also looked through a box of his brother John's miniatures – accomplished, rather slick works the size of large brooches: 'Mrs John Hazlitt', 'Lady with a Muff', 'James Boswell after Joshua Reynolds', John Hazlitt's daughter Harriet mourning over a dead starling. Then I found a miniature of Margaret Hazlitt, the sister who stayed at home to look after their parents. John's full-length portrait of Margaret hangs near Hazlitt's self-portrait in the main part of the museum, so I recognized her thoughtful, sensitive, strong-willed, rather Irish face. This miniature had more expression, more feeling, than the others in the box. Maybe that was why I looked at it for a bit longer, and then, on a sudden impulse, turned it over and found a bunch of plaited hair behind the glass back. Auburn, fresh, as though it had been newly cut, her hair looked just as it did in the portrait. For a moment, I felt in touch with the dead, with that family of painters and idealists, for Margaret painted too, and some of her work is in that store-room.

Another moment of apparent presence occurred when a friend gave me a copy of an unpublished letter which Keats's friend John

Hamilton Reynolds wrote to Mary Leigh on 28 April 1817. In it, Reynolds describes a long conversation he had with Hazlitt:

On Thursday last Hazlitt was with me at home, and remained with us till 3 o'clock in the morning! – full of eloquence, – warm, lofty, & communicative on everything imaginative & intelligent, – breathing out with us the peculiar & favourite beauties of our best bards, – passing from grand & commanding argument to the gaieties & graces of wit and humour, – and the elegant and higher beauties of poetry. He is indeed *great* company and leaves a weight on the mind, which 'it can hardly bear'. He is full of what Dr Johnson terms 'good talk'. His countenance is also extremely fine: – A sunken & melancholy face, – ; forehead lined with thought and bearing a full & strange pulsation, – on exciting subjects, – an eye, dashed in its light with sorrow, but kindling & *living* at intellectual moments, – and a stream of coal-black hair dropping around all. Such a face, so silent and so sensitive, is indeed the banner of the mind. 'It is as a book, in which men may read strange things.' He would have become the pencil of Titian, and have done justice to the soul-fed colours of that bold & matchless Italian. I fear you will be tired with this long *personality*, but I remember having read a few papers of his to you, and therefore imagine you will not be wholly un-interested in him.

This is very close to William Bewick's famous sketch of Hazlitt, and it catches the power of his personality, as well as the presence he held for his contemporaries.

One further moment of contact with the vanished writer was when I reread John Clare's autobiography, and found the passage where he describes how Hazlitt

sits a silent picture of severity if you was to watch his face for a month you woud not catch a smile there his eyes are always turnd towards the ground except when one is turnd up now and then with a sneer that cuts a bad pun and a young authors maiden table talk to atoms wherever it is directed I look upon it that it carries the conviction with it of a look to the wise and a nod to the foolish

he seems full of the author too and I verily believe that his pockets are crambd with it he seems to look upon Mr this and M Tother names that are only living on Cards of Morning calls and Dinner invitations as upon empty chairs as the guests in Macbeth did on the vacancy were Banquos ghost presided they appear in his eye as nothings too thin for sight and when he enters a room he comes stooping with his eyes in his hands as it were throwing under gazes round at every corner as if he smelt a dun or thief ready to seize him by the colar and demand his money or his life   he is [a] middle sizd dark looking man and his face is deeply lind with a satirical character   his eyes are bright but they are rather turned under his brows   he is a walking satire and you woud wonder were his poetry came from that is scatterd so thickly over his writings   for the blood of me I coud not find him out that is I should have no guess at him of his ever being a scribbler much more a genius

Like a hand-held shot, out of both time and sequence, or like one of those magic-lantern transparencies Hazlitt identified his intense prose with, this sketch of the dark-looking critic seems fortuitous and exact. The year is 1822, when Clare met Hazlitt at a dinner given by their publisher, John Taylor. This is the year in which Hazlitt divorced Sarah Stoddart, whom he had married in 1808 and by whom he had a son, William. It is the year he hoped to marry his landlord's daughter, Sarah Walker – his obsession with her is the subject of *Liber Amoris*, which was published in 1823. But she refused him, and the following year he married Isabella Bridgewater, a Scottish widow with a private income, who left him in 1827.

But Clare's 'silent picture of severity' needs to be allowed to float free of chronology. This is the haunted figure behind the prose style, and it is with that style – and with the search for a poetics adequate to it – that this study is concerned.

CHAPTER ONE

A State of Projection

History begins for Hazlitt with the big bang of the Reformation. In his opening lecture on Elizabethan literature, given to a London audience in the winter of 1819, he makes it clear that he has no interest in anything that happened before an event which gave a 'mighty impulse and increased activity' to intellectual argument and scientific enquiry by agitating the 'inert mass' of accumulated prejudices throughout Europe. Before the Reformation – really a convulsive series of events in different parts of Europe – all was gothic darkness and prejudice. Then the 'intolerable abuses' of centuries were toppled at a blow, and an unceasing roar of contrary opinions was unleashed. Germany was the first to break the spell of 'misbegotten fear', but then England 'joined the shout', and with her island voice echoed it back more loudly 'from her thousand cliffs and craggy shores'.

Because he's lecturing, and because innumerable inspirational sermons preached by his father and other Unitarian ministers have shaped his imagination, the style takes on a muscly declamatory urgency that at times anticipates Macaulay's confident rhetoric, or even the rant of Carlyle. His introduction to Elizabethan writing aims to renew a shared Protestant identity in his audience, as well as to reinvigorate his own sense of critical purpose. The year before, he had published *Political Essays*, a volume lacerated by his despair at the European order following Napoleon's final defeat in 1815. Retiring to Winterslow in the late summer of 1819, he goes to ground with the Elizabethan writers, and prepares his lecture series in about six weeks, then returns to London, to a house in York Street where Milton once lived.

He delivered the lectures in November and December, fell behind with the rent, and was evicted by his landlord, Jeremy Bentham. It was at this time that his marriage broke up, though he and Sarah remained friends until his death in a Soho rooming-house in 1830. After his eviction from York Street, he moved into lodgings in Southampton Buildings in Holborn, where he began a tortured affair with Sarah Walker, the daughter of the couple who were then his landlords. In February 1820, *Lectures Chiefly on the Dramatic Literature of the Age of Elizabeth*, a substantial, critical book of 350 pages, was published.

In the first lecture, the prose rhythm and imagery suggest that the critic is striking out in a new direction. Instead of attacking the corruption of contemporary Britain, as he had in *Political Essays*, he goes back to the Elizabethans, those 'old English' writers, as he called them, in order to rescue their work from obscurity and assert a renewed critical radicalism and patriotism. He insists that at this period our writers and 'great men' had something in them that 'savoured of the soil from which they grew'. They were 'truly English'. Calling them a bold, independent race of thinkers who were not the 'spoiled children of affectation and refinement', he draws a characteristically puritan contrast between the artificial and the natural which can still be heard in Presbyterian churches in Scotland and Ireland (the Revd Ian Paisley, for example, is fond of distinguishing rugged church reformers from contemporary 'putty paper' clerics). Hazlitt's tone in these literary sermons is direct, emphatically masculine, and simplistic in the almost gymnastic manner of evangelical sermons or keynote addresses, but they contain certain subtleties of allusion and imagery which are worth considering.

By layering his account of the Reformation with a series of historical allusions, he's able to compare that event both to the fall of the Bastille and to an explosion. The Reformation agitates inert prejudices, rather like Joseph Priestley conducting experiments with electricity, and it also produces a heroic race of writers. Remarking that public opinion in this period was 'in a state of projection', Hazlitt employs an alchemical term which means 'casting the powder of philosopher's stone (powder of projection) upon a metal in fusion to effect its transmutation into gold or silver'. Metaphorically, projection stands for the effect on public opinion of the translation of the Bible into English, as well as for the way in which that work helped to bring mass or popular opinion into existence. The vernacular Bible was the 'chief engine' of the Reformation: it threw open, 'by a secret spring', the rich treasure of religion and morality.

Hazlitt's use of the alchemical metaphor is cited in one definition of 'projection' in the *Oxford English Dictionary*: 'Change from one thing to another; transmutation.' The definition picks up his scientific image of accumulated prejudice as an inert mass, but the word is more slippery and complex, less easy to pin down, than its dictionary entry would suggest. It's connected with his interest in various forms of visual entertainment which were popular in London and Paris at the time – the phantasmagorias, dioramas, panoramas, fantascopes, thaumatropes, illuminated spectacles, and magiclantern shows which preceded the modern cinema. Punning on the idea of optical projection, he imagines public opinion as resembling an audience that is watching images projected by a fantascope (these displays of grotesque and macabre images were first brought to London in 1802 by a French showman called Etienne Robert). In saying that public opinion is in a state of projection, he's comparing it to a series of large moving images on a screen at one end of a darkened theatre, as well as referring to the way in which an object that is illuminated from behind stands out from its background in stark definition. Projection is his symbol for a revolutionary state of consciousness, and also, interestingly, a self-reflexive image for the type of quickfire, intense, often pictorial, literary journalism which he practised. This apparently straightforward term acquires a densely layered series of meanings that justify the artist William Bewick's description of Hazlitt as the 'Shakespeare prose-writer of our glorious country'.

He applies the term 'projection' to Shakespeare in a lecture delivered in 1818: 'The passions are in a state of projection. Years are melted down to moments, and every instant teems with fate.' Then in an essay 'On Application to Study', which he wrote five years later, he applied it to his own prose, explaining that critical journalism depends on 'rapidity of execution':

A number of new thoughts rise up spontaneously, and they come in the proper places, because they arise from the occasion. They are also sure to partake of the warmth and vividness of that ebullition of mind, from which they spring. *Spiritus precipitandus est.* In these sort of voluntaries in composition, the thoughts are worked up to a state of projection: the grasp of the subject, the presence of mind, the flow of expression must be something akin to *extempore* speaking.

The idea of a chemical process – its warmth and ebullition – is present here, so this may seem to be a simple reworking of the alchemical significance of the term; but when he immediately adds that such 'bold but finished drafts may be compared to *fresco* paintings, which imply a life of study and great previous preparation, but of which the execution is momentary and irrevocable', he is also drawing on the optical sense of 'projection' as an image on a wall – in this case a fixed image which has been created suddenly and completely in a single creative swoop. His commentary on the Reformation is therefore in part an expression of his own critical aesthetic, in that he's implicitly comparing the dynamic process of forming new ideas – breaking with inherited concepts – to the driven intensity of writing an essay to a deadline, or composing a series of eight substantial lectures on Elizabethan literature in six weeks. (Hazlitt would meditate on a topic, then, at the last moment, write an essay in a single draft with little or no revision.) Here, he's saying that his critical imagination is grounded in, and endlessly repeats, the Protestant experience of the Reformation. Like the vernacular Bible, he aims to give 'a *mind* to the people'.

Describing the projected state of opinion, he says that liberty was held out to all 'to think and speak the truth', then adds by way of concrete illustration: 'Men's brains were busy; their spirits stirring; their hearts full; and their hands not idle.' This sentence is deliberately staccato, concentrating his theme in a series of ringing, gestural phrases whose accompanying pauses might be marked by raps on the lectern or, in another context, thumps on the pulpit. What he designs here, as so often in his work, is an extemporized form of dramatic soliloquy that anticipates Browning's union of voice and consciousness in his monologues. It's a prose which can sometimes be broken up into a form of verse:

> Men's brains were busy;
> their spirits stirring;
> their hearts full;
> and their hands not idle.

This is inspirational rhetoric, prose as performance, a type of rough blank verse that's somehow oak-solid, but at the same time rather hollow or too general. At the end of the paragraph, his inheritance of anti-Catholic sermons and pamphlets overwhelms the prose: 'The death-blow which had been struck at scarlet vice and bloated hypocrisy, loosened their tongues, and made the talismans and love-tokens of Popish superstition . . . fall harmless from their necks.' This is routine evangelical oratory, Hazlitt in his woodland retreat bearing witness to the surge of English history as a way of renewing his political idealism and inspiring his audience. The style begins to become more concentrated in the next paragraph, where he imagines the Bible being suddenly and miraculously open to everyone, now that it has been translated. It's at this point that he describes the type of 'nervous masculine', imaginative intellect which, implicitly, he shares with the Elizabethans, whose 'conscientious severity of argument' is one of the period's distinctive features.

The term 'nervous', which nowadays signifies timidity and anxiety, at this time meant 'sinewy, muscular, vigorous, strong'. Applied to writing – almost always to prose – it meant that the style was vigorous, strong, concentrated, free from diffuseness. As a critical term, it often carries connotations of a lean, fit republicanism – an early editor of Algernon Sidney's *Discourses concerning Government* printed a preface to *Eikonoklastes* praising Milton's 'strong and nervous' style and Sidney's 'strong and masculine' prose style. Importantly for Hazlitt, who knew the *Discourses* and admired both Sidney and Milton, the term combines writing, oratory, and the healthy human body.

Similarly, he often uses 'masculine' and 'manly' to represent radical Whig boldness, a sometimes overwhelming cocksure certainty
that helps to texture his prose with a type of superfit muscularity.
When he remarked in 1816 that England was to reject the 'detestable doctrine' of the divine right of kings, which 'first tottered and
fell headless to the ground with the martyred Charles; which we
kicked out with his son James, and kicked back twice with two
Pretenders to the throne of their ancestors', the relished verbs enact
his enjoyment of English liberty as a sort of vigorous football game.
This is a sinewy, gestural prose that sings with a delighted confidence in its reach and stretch. It is dynamic, because its rhythms
express his unrelenting commitment to social change. He wants to
reshape society, and he believes that writing and printing are the
most powerful means of encouraging progress, or what was then
termed 'improvement'. We can see this in the metaphor of the press
as a siege-engine, when he says in 'The Influence of Books' that the
press is a powerful 'engine at the door', a remark that cleverly
interprets and applies the famous two-handed engine in *Lycidas*.
Like a siege-machine, the printing-press breaks open what is
obdurately closed, and, in an image that combines the long handle
on a traditional printing-press with Archimedes' hypothetical lever
for shifting the world, he states that the vernacular Bible was the
'one great lever' of English liberty. Marvell similarly calls the press
that 'villainous' engine which was invented 'much about the same
time with the Reformation'.

In *The Life of Napoleon Buonaparte*, he calls the French Revolution a 'remote but inevitable' result of the invention of printing.
Using an obvious image, of a building that has become 'crazy and
rotten', he celebrates the violent manner in which the diffusion of
knowledge breaks up traditional beliefs. What he delights in is the
collision of different opinions, a feisty or fermenting state of intellectual argument. This fascinated sense of yeasty ebullition is closely
connected with the philosophical view he held of matter and the
human mind. In 1812, right at the start of his literary career, he
affirms a belief in a Kantian notion of the mind's 'principle of cohesion', its 'pervading and elastic energy'. This philosophical idealism

is implicit in his remark that the translation of the Bible into English 'cemented' the English people's union of character and sentiment, and gave them a mind. Cohesiveness is also an expression of Unitarian culture, and Hazlitt's use of the term 'cement' issues from the experience of growing up as a member of a small body of Christian rationalists who prized communication, in part because they were scattered across England, often in tiny congregations that were subject to prejudice and persecution (Burke raged against them in his writings and speeches during the 1790s). For these Dissenters, communication meant not only sharing and promulgating ideas, but participating in a form of protective social bonding.

In a resolution attached to the printed version of a sermon preached at the Old Jewry in 1786 to celebrate the founding of Hackney New College that year, it is noted that if the resolutions which the college's assembled supporters had agreed on could be adopted in other parts of the country, they would have the desirable effect of 'cementing together a body of men at present too little known to one another, and too much unconnected'. When Hazlitt says that his father's visits to neighbouring Unitarian ministers in Shropshire established a 'line of communication' which nourished the flame of civil and religious liberty, he is expressing a similar belief in the cohesive, transforming effect of the exchange of ideas. In his account of the Reformation, when Germany gives the watchword and England echoes back the shout, fermentation follows.

It follows because, for Hazlitt, the mind is active like a chemical process. As he argues in his *Prospectus of a History of English Philosophy*, a very early work published in 1809, when he was thirty-one, the mind has laws, powers, and principles of its own, and is not the 'mere puppet' of matter. The mind is not a blank sheet on which sense impressions fall, and ideas are not 'more refined pulsations of matter'. All of Hazlitt's writing rests on this repudiation of Locke's empiricism.

In another early pamphlet, *Free Thoughts on Public Affairs*, which he published anonymously at his own expense in 1806, he casts the Prime Minister, William Pitt, as the political or institutional embodiment of Locke's mistaken view that the mind is passive in perception. Every subject presented to Pitt a simple *tabula rasa* on which he was free to place 'whatever colouring of language he pleased'. His style, with its merely mechanical passive eloquence, is monotonous, artificial, and faultlessly regular. He represents the denial of imagination, and Hazlitt rages against his devious greyness, the lack of anything 'far-fetched or abrupt' in his speeches.

Pitt's bad prose style epitomizes his mistaken Lockean epistemology. In *The Life of Napoleon Buonaparte*, Hazlitt states that Pitt writes in a cypher-hand that has neither beginning, middle, nor end; one that employs conventional, pompous phraseology which states nothing, proves nothing, and goes round and round in a circle 'of charges, committals, and equivocations'. In the flourishes and mazes of Pitt's contorted style – a style which contains 'a deadly purpose under a routine of hollow commonplaces' – England has lost 'her liberties, her strength, herself and the world'.

Although this is Hazlitt writing later, in the 1820s, the pamphlet he published in 1806 expresses the same view of Pitt's drearily passive mind. For Hazlitt, the mind is actively communicative and elastic – it isn't a mere receiver – and his whole career as a writer is founded on his early dismissal of Locke's epistemology. Taking up Locke's image of the mind as a blank sheet of paper, Hazlitt states that it has been used to prove that the mind is nothing in itself, 'nor the cause of any thing, never acting, but always acted upon'.

Using a typically physical verb, Hazlitt follows through Locke's analogy with a camera obscura, and states that the mind, 'being fairly *gutted* of itself' and of all positive qualities, has been made to resemble 'the bare walls and empty rooms of an unfurnished lodging'. This Bleaneyish cell of undwelling anticipates his subsequent criticism of utilitarianism, and it follows naturally from that emphatic, unexpected, even abrupt use of 'gutted'. Rejecting the view that the mind contains nothing more than what is brought into it through 'the doors of the senses', he affirms a belief in its 'active powers' and 'independent nature'. These powers shape, modify, and add feelings and ideas to the impressions which enter the mind. The critical act, expressed in a vigorous, flexible, fast-moving prose style, thus becomes analogous to the creative process by which every mind knows and understands.

Detailing all the qualities that Pitt does not possess, the young Hazlitt affirms the intellectual power and eloquence which is the spirit of criticism in action, stating that he 'had none of the profound, legislative wisdom, piercing sagacity, or rich, impetuous, high-wrought imagination of Burke; the manly eloquence, strong sense, exact knowledge, vehemence and natural simplicity of Fox; the ease, brilliancy, and acuteness of Sheridan'. The qualities which Hazlitt ascribes to Burke, Fox, and Sheridan – qualities that contrast with Pitt's grinding mediocrity – constitute stylistic aspirations for the young writer. He wants the virtues of these powerful men – they're heroic figures for him – to enter his own writing, and it's almost as though, by naming and praising them, he will acquire their gifts. His brief panegyric on the three politicians, who were friends until Burke broke with Fox and Sheridan over their attitude to the French Revolution, is in the nature of an invocation. As the young Hazlitt sets out on his epic journey, he's asking them to vouchsafe a combination of the several qualities that will help him achieve his ambition of becoming the leading prose stylist of the age. He wants to break through the 'fog and haze' of Pitt's style into light, liberty, equality. Alluding to a remark in Burke's *Reflections* – 'in the fog and haze of confusion all is enlarged, and appears without any limit' – he applies it not simply to Pitt's perceptions, but to a whole grungy mode of expression which infects other people. By taking a phrase from a counter-revolutionary polemic and turning it against Pitt's reactionary style, he liberates Burke and returns him to true Whig values.

Hazlitt makes copious allusions to Burke's pamphlets throughout his criticism, but he also has a technique of glancing back at his own writing – a habit that layers and inflects his critical vocabulary in a particularly subtle manner. Take the remark that there is nothing 'far-fetched or abrupt' in Pitt's speeches. Sixteen years after making it, Hazlitt picks up this phrase in a bravura passage in one of his critical masterpieces, 'On the Prose Style of Poets', where he again praises the picturesque, sublime qualities of Burke's style. Instead of soaring through the air like an eagle, Burke's prose stands upon a rocky cliff like the chamois, 'clambers up by abrupt and intricate ways, and browses on the roughest bark, or crops the tender flower'. Here 'abrupt' picks up its earlier use in the essay on Pitt, where he again praises the headlong qualities of Burke's style. Hazlitt's prose aesthetic assigns intense value to a type of romantic or gothic surprise – dissonance, unexpected imaginative leaps, breaks, lunges – qualities which he identifies in one of his essays on the Elgin Marbles, where he argues that transitions in prose must for the most part be 'gradual and pieced together'. But sometimes the most violent transitions are 'the most graceful', because when the mind is 'fairly tired out and exhausted with a subject', it's glad to leap to another topic as a relief from the first. There are many instances of such abrupt transitions in Burke's writings: his prose has a 'Pindaric' quality, a classical comparison which recognizes the fact that Pindar invented a new metrical pattern each time he composed an ode, as well as progressing by abrupt changes of subject (according to Maurice Bowra, the rhythm of the odes is unrivalled 'in variety, speed, and lightness'). By comparing Burke to Pindar, Hazlitt is suggesting that occasional prose can resemble a type of verse that was also written to celebrate specific events. Further, he's saying that a prose moment which is not beautiful in itself can be made so 'by position or motion' – motion, like nature, is a central critical value for Hazlitt. What he admires is an active, textured prose that is neither sonorous nor predictable. He wants ruggedness and difficulty combined with a gracefully flexible lightness, rather than polish or Pitt's 'faultless regularity'.

We see this in the second Elizabethan lecture, in which he praises the 'grand and daring' outline of Marlowe's *Dr Faustus*, stating that the execution is 'abrupt and fearful'. The thoughts are 'vast and irregular' – 'irregular' is an adjective he often associates with Burke – and the style 'halts and staggers under them'. Again, in the lecture on Beaumont and Fletcher he notes that the style of the first act of *Two Noble Kinsmen* has 'more weight, more abruptness, and more involution' than Fletcher's general style.

Placing these uses of 'abrupt' together, and noting that he elsewhere praises Swift's 'honest abruptness', we can see that they create a force field which transforms the adjective into a critical term that's almost electric with the energy of its application. There's also a punning wit in the essay on prose style, as he plays 'abrupt', in the sense of 'precipitous', against the earlier image of the chamois overlooking a precipice. And we can see that when he says elsewhere that the mind is sometimes 'glad to leap' to another subject, there's a faint image of the chamois moving nimbly up its abrupt Alpine cliff.

When he remarks in 'Personal Identity' that 'I have run myself out of my materials for this essay, and want a well-turned sentence or two to conclude with', he's being deliberately curt, abrupt and unpolished. And he produces a simile which gives a lovely, paradoxical lift to his admission of failure, saying that in this he resembles Benvenuto Cellini, who complained that 'with all the brass, tin, iron, and lead he could muster in the house, his statue of Perseus was left imperfect, with a dent in the heel of it'. An essayist, like a sculptor in metal, melts down not raw, but already processed material into a new and beautiful shape. This is a symbol of the essay as cento, as a *bricolage* of quotations, and it's part of the deep structure of Hazlitt's imagination, one of the means by which he seeks to transform criticism into an art-form.

We can see how his sensuous delight in an indented roughness shapes his prose style, when he remarks two pages earlier:

> / / × / × / × / × / × / / / \ ×
> Not so. The vital air, the sky, the woods, the streams – all these go for
>
> / × × / × × / × /
> nothing, except with a favoured few.

After the initial spondee, the prose relapses into a straightforward, and potentially limiting, iambic pentameter, before breaking suddenly at the dash into a different rhythm. Though he has complained earlier in the same essay about his manner of earning a precarious livelihood by indulging romantic sentiments and writing 'disjointed descriptions' of them, it's apparent that he values the disjointed and abrupt. Without it, prose would be too well-turned, too polished and Ciceronian, or too numbingly close to the opaque regularity of Pitt's style.

The name 'Pitt' is a critical term which condenses a whole system of values. Anticipating his criticism of a mind that is gutted of itself and unable to reshape impressions, Hazlitt says that nothing that passed through Pitt's mind ever assumed a 'new shape'. He recalled his ideas in exactly the form in which they were originally 'impressed' – the Lockean language is obvious, and it's developed in the next sentence, where those impressed ideas are described as being of that 'loose, general, unconnected' kind which are brought out and returned to their stations 'mechanically'. The image is partly military, but also draws on the moment in 'My First Acquaintance with Poets' when Coleridge tells Hazlitt's father that Burke's intellectual opponent, the Scottish jurist Sir James Mackintosh, was a 'ready warehouseman of letters, who knew exactly where to lay his hand on what he wanted, though the goods were not his own'. Here Mackintosh resembles Dickens's autodidact Bradley Headstone: his mind is a 'place of mechanical stowage' like a 'wholesale warehouse'. Pitt and Mackintosh are unimaginative logicians who speak in perfect, bookish sentences that never achieve a style that can properly be called good.

Coleridge's influence is strong here, because in 1800, two years after he told Hazlitt's father that Mackintosh was a literary ware-houseman, he published an article arguing that Pitt had 'no feelings connected with man or nature, no spontaneous impulses, no unbiased and desultory studies, no genuine science, nothing that constitutes individuality in intellect, nothing that teaches brother-hood in affection'. Hazlitt calls Coleridge's article 'masterly and unanswerable' in a footnote to his 1806 pamphlet *Free Thoughts on Public Affairs*, and thirteen years later he reprinted it in his *Political Essays* under the title 'Pitt and Buonaparte'.

Hazlitt's quarrel is with Pitt's intellectual inflexibility, his unbending steadiness, and lack of 'quickness or elasticity'. This quality, though it may appear to be personal to Pitt, is presented as an obdurately English failing, and this becomes a distinctive theme

in Hazlitt's writing. He works often by means of national stereo-
types – Scots, English, Irish, French – in order to imply a highly
sophisticated critical position which rises above the constrictions of
those cultures.

In a long reflective passage in *Notes of a Journey through France
and Italy*, one of his last books, he notes that there are two things an
Englishman understands: 'hard words and hard blows'. His symbol
for what he terms the 'matter-of-factness' of the English understanding is a Jack Tar who will bash his fist through a deal board to
show off his strength, give him a sensation, and prove his boasted
powers of endurance. Applying this symbol to the behaviour of
English spectators at a boxing match, he observes that the English
mostly perceive objects by their 'mere material qualities of solidity,
inertness, and impenetrability, or by their own muscular resistance
to them'. Like Dr Johnson refuting Berkeley by kicking a stone, they
want to collide with matter. They dislike the smell of a rose, the
taste of 'made dishes', soft music, fine pictures – but they will knock
down any man who tells them this. A 'drop of pleasure' is the most
difficult thing to extract from their 'hard, dry, mechanical, husky
frame'. Here, the adjectives appear to carry only a negative charge,
but elsewhere he praises the 'literal, dry, incorrigible tenaciousness'
of Swift's understanding in a manner that demonstrates that the
term 'dry' is flexible, and therefore capable, in particular contexts,
of being positive or ambivalent.

Praising Charles Macready's acting of Othello, he contrasts it
with Edmund Kean's, which is sometimes 'too wedgy and determined' – that is, too woodenly English. Elsewhere, he analyses a
failure in Macready's acting of the moment when Othello tells the
senators that custom has made 'the flinty and steel couch of war /
My thrice-driven bed of down'. Then Othello says that he can
'agnize' – recognize – in himself a 'natural and prompt alacrity / I
find in hardness'. Hazlitt compresses this into 'I do agnize a natural
hardness', and notes that Macready mistakenly delivers the line as if
he's impatient to exculpate himself from some charge. Othello is in
fact 'calm and collected' when he speaks the line about natural
hardness, so Macready, in rushing the words, fails to express

hardness transmuted into softness. It's a fine point, but what Hazlitt is saying is that the actor is too English in his address.

He is fascinated and repelled by the way in which the English imagination 'constantly clings to the concrete, and has a *purchase* upon matter'. This ability to draw inspiration from material reality makes English stage dialogue superior to French, and it makes Jack Tars into stubbornly heroic figures: 'Stung with wounds, stunned with bruises, bleeding and mangled, an English sailor never finds himself so much alive as when he is flung half dead into the cockpit; for he then perceives the extreme consciousness of his existence in his conflict with external matter.' In line with nineteenth-century melodrama, and like Hopkins, who mentions 'ill-visaged cursing tars' in one poem and blesses 'our tars' in another, he views English sailors as embodied symbols of the national imagination.

In an account of the Battle of the Nile which he wrote a few years after his celebration of English sailors, he asserts that the 'wooden walls of Old England' are nothing but this 'hard, obdurate character', which becomes expansive in the heat of battle. The thrawn, woody insularity of the English character, its toughness and resolution, as well as its gnarled limitations, is a significant theme in Hazlitt's criticism, and at times he writes like an exasperated foreigner. He admires fighting courage, compares the English national character to a bulldog and the French to a greyhound, but usually dislikes the qualities of 'hardness and setness' which he detects in Quakers and other Puritans.

The dislike is philosophical, because the mind is not a material puppet, but has principles of its own which cannot be expressed mechanically as Locke, or indeed Pitt, suggest. Their reductive, materialistic concept of mind stems from Hobbes, whose work Hazlitt revered and accused Locke of plagiarizing, but which he nevertheless characterizes in this formidably materialist passage:

His strong mind and body appear to have resisted all impressions but those which were derived from the downright blows of matter. All his ideas seemed to be 'like substances in his brain': what was not a solid, tangible, distinct, palpable object was to him nothing. The external image pressed so close upon his mind that it destroyed all power of consciousness, and left no room for attention to anything but itself. He was by nature a materialist.

This is from a letter which Hazlitt later incorporated in his prospectus for a new history of philosophy, and it's curiously similar to his accounts of the hardy, obdurate Jack Tars. With its insistence on 'downright blows', and those echoing packed dentals in 'solid, tangible, distinct, palpable object', it seems appropriate that Hazlitt should have sent his prospectus to William Windham, a politician whose devotion to pugilism he pays tribute to in his famous essay about boxing, 'The Fight'. In that essay – it's really a symbolist prose poem pretending to be simple, fresh-air reportage – the contest is on one level between two views of matter. Hickman, the Gas-man, is 'light, vigorous, elastic', while his opponent, Bill Neate, is a huge, knock-kneed English materialist, a Jack Tar who triumphs in the end. By association – or opposition – this makes Hickman French. Hazlitt compares the French national character to the greyhound in his description of the superior fighting powers of English sailors, and Hickman's elastic lightness evokes the supple shimmer of a greyhound's movements. Notice, too, that the boxer possesses an elasticity which Pitt's mind lacks, for this is an epistemological battle as well.

When Hazlitt asserts that all Hobbes's ideas appear to be 'like substances in his brain', he is alluding to a passage in *The Excursion* which he heard Wordsworth recite when he visited him in the Lake District in 1803. The poem was published in 1814, five years after Hazlitt quoted it in his account of Hobbes. In book 1, Wordsworth describes how the 'foundations' of the Wanderer's mind were laid:

> In such communion, not from terror free,
> While yet a Child, and long before his time,
> He had perceived the presence and the power
> Of greatness; and deep feelings had impressed
> Great objects on his mind, with portraiture
> And colour so distinct, that on his mind
> They lay like substances, and almost seemed
> To haunt the bodily sense.

Here, Wordsworth is using a partly Lockean language – 'impressed' – in order to deny that this learning process derived ideas simply from experience. The Wanderer's bodily sense is confused by the emotional power of his mental images, until he attains an active power to fasten them upon his brain. Hobbes's philosophy therefore resembles the Wanderer's early, 'perplexed' stage of physical knowledge. Locke's philosophy is similarly in thrall to material reality, because he founded his *Essay concerning Human Understanding* on the supposition that ideas are mere copies of sense impressions.

In a work published the year before his philosophical prospectus, Hazlitt also alludes to *The Excursion*, in order to characterize the genius of seventeenth-century prose. He does so in a heartfelt introduction to a speech by the Commonwealth politician and diplomat Bulstrode Whitelocke which he included in *The Eloquence of the British Senate*, an anthology of parliamentary speeches he compiled in his late twenties:

men's minds were stored with facts and images, almost to excess; there was a tenacity and firmness in them that kept fast hold of the impressions of things as they were first stamped upon the mind; and 'their ideas seemed to lie like substances in the brain'. Facts and feelings went hand in hand; the one naturally implied the other; and our ideas, not yet exorcised and squeezed and tortured out of their natural objects, into a subtle essence of pure intellect, did not fly about like ghosts without a body, tossed up and down, or upborne only by the ELEGANT FORMS of words, through the *vacuum* of abstract reasoning, and sentimental refinement.

This is the 'old English intellect', as he terms it, and it's a quality celebrated throughout his work. The body is central to this concept of the intellect, though he doesn't imply that ideas are produced by physical sensation. As a critic, he exults in sensuous adjectives and active, concrete verbs, but he will not allow the senses to determine ideas. Similarly, his admiration for Jack Tars is countered by the view that every sailor is a stupid materialist: 'Pain puts life into him; action, soul: otherwise, he is a mere log.'

Hazlitt's prospectus for a history of English philosophy, of which only the copy he sent to William Windham survives, was preceded by a long letter he published the same year in the *Monthly Magazine*. The letter, entitled 'Proposal for the Basis of a New System of Metaphysical Philosophy', was published anonymously in 1809, but wasn't recognized as Hazlitt's until 1953. In it he says that he will try to show that 'the mind itself is not material', or that the common properties of what is called 'matter' are not the origin of mental phenomena or the 'thinking principle'.

For Hazlitt, the real foundation of knowledge is general, as he explains in the lectures on English philosophy which he delivered in London early in 1812. Discussing the way in which knowledge is founded, he says that we have always the general idea 'of something extended'. We never know its exact length, and cannot conceive what sort of distinction or individuality can be found in any visible image or 'object of sense'. It is like seeking certainty 'in the dancing of insects in the evening sun, or for fixedness or rest in the motions of the sea'. This perceptual dance is a figure for the mind's complex intellectual structure, its active understanding of reality, and also expresses what Hazlitt means when he speaks in his letter to the *New Monthly Magazine* of 'setting our ideas to quarrel with one another'. He values buzz, movement, activity, gusto, as against fixed concepts.

This is the atomic dance of the free spirit, the vital centre of the aesthetic which Hazlitt is formulating in his early writings and lectures. As he argues in his introductory lecture on Elizabethan literature, the vernacular Bible created 'endless diversity and collision of opinion'. What he values is argument, as a continuous process which embodies what he terms 'free play'. This concept he explains in a revealing polemic, *A Letter to William Gifford*, which he published in August 1819, the month he left for Winterslow to write his lectures on Elizabethan literature. Attacking the critic William Gifford, who edited the conservative *Quarterly Review*, Hazlitt sketches the argument he outlined in his first book, *An Essay on the Principles of Human Action*, which Joseph Johnson published in 1805. Defending and explaining his philosophical system in the polemical letter he wrote to Gifford, he says that in *The Principles of Human Action* he aimed to explode the notion that the human mind is innately selfish. His object was to leave 'free play' to the social affections and to the cultivation of the 'more disinterested and generous principles of our nature'. Those principles are imaginative, because if we consider the future as a concept, we have to admit that it exists only in the mind: it is not grounded in the exclusive, absolutely selfish faculties of memory and sensation, but belongs instead to the imagination, which is not a limited, narrow faculty.

In a phrase that might have come from Francis Hutcheson, he calls the imagination 'common, discursive, and social'. We cannot project our self-interest into the future – this is Hazlitt's youthful philosophical discovery, the lever that enabled him to move the world as he found it. Now, angrily addressing his enemy Gifford, he lovingly recasts that discovery in his mature prose:

Everything before us exists in an ideal world. The future is a blank and dreary void, like sleep or death, till the imagination brooding over it with wings outspread, impregnates it with life and motion. The forms and colours it assumes are but the pictures reflected on the eye of fancy, the unreal mockeries of future events. The solid fabric of time and nature moves on, but the future always flies before it. The present moment stands on the brink of nothing. We cannot pass the dread abyss, or make a broad and beaten way over it, or construct a real interest in it, or identify ourselves with what is not, or have a being, sense, and motion, where there are none.

The imagination is like the dove of the Holy Spirit brooding over the void before creation, while we, as potentially self-interested philosophers, are like a baffled Satan who cannot make a bridge from hell into the future. The concrete metaphors and allusions to Genesis, Milton, and Shakespeare make this passage read like a piece of dramatic verse. That last phrase, 'being, sense, and motion', picks up Claudio's agonized plea to be spared execution in *Measure for Measure*: 'This sensible warm motion to become / A kneaded clod'.

When Hazlitt uses the term 'motion', he means not only that principle of natural movement which is such a notable feature of his aesthetic, but its Elizabethan meaning of an animate body's capacity for moving. The idea of blood pulsing is a strong component of this definition. Textured by allusion, 'motion' has a more than denotative significance in Hazlitt's use of it. Like Milton's 'Devoid of sense and motion', or Wordsworth's 'No motion has she now, no force', the noun is less a synonym for movement than a specially weighted, strongly accented term.

Attacking the doctrine of self-interest, Hazlitt says that our interest in the future, our identity with it, cannot be substantial. The self which we 'project' before us into the future is 'like a shadow in the water, a bubble of the brain'. In becoming 'the blind and servile drudges of self-interest, we bow down before an idol of our own making, and are spellbound by a name'. The whole weight of Unitarian culture, as well as Francis Hutcheson's philosophy, which views benevolence as the paramount moral sense, shapes this rejection of Hobbesian selfishness. This inheritance from Rational Dissent shows in the way he adheres to ideas of disinterestedness, communicativeness, and that benevolent 'social joy' which Hutcheson recommends.

Accompanying his belief in an imagination that's essentially and benignly social is a definition of wit which is at the foundation of the philosophical quarrel he has with a theory of knowledge that reduces perception to 'simple sensations'. This concept of simple sensations and single, discrete impressions prevents us from understanding those *'mixed modes* and various clusters of ideas' which almost all language refers to.

In an apparently extempore demonstration of his argument, he says in 'Definition of Wit' that if we regard wit as something resembling

a drop of quicksilver, or a spangle from off a cloak, a little nimble substance, that is pointed and glitters (we do not know how) we shall make no progress in analysing its varieties or its essence; it is a mere word or an atom: but if we suppose it to consist in, or be the result of, several sets and sorts of ideas combined together or acting upon each other (like the tunes and machinery of a barrel-organ) we may stand some chance of explaining and getting an insight into the process.

He then develops this idea of interaction by arguing that if all our ideas were 'literal, physical, confined to a single impression' of an object, then wit could not exist. This is because wit consists in two things: perceiving the 'incongruity' between an object and the class to which it is generally thought to belong and pointing out, or making more obvious, this incongruity by transposing it to a totally different class of objects in which it is 'prescriptively found in perfection'.

Describing the 'rapid, careless decomposition and recomposition' of our ideas, he again argues for process, movement, activity, as against passively received, inertly separate impressions. His definition of wit, which is basically philosophical, brings it close to metaphysical wit, and it further aligns him with those seventeenth-century, or 'old English', writers who practised it.

When he speaks in his *Letter to William Gifford* of 'the force of a reasoning imagination', he adds that this is the same faculty that carries us out of ourselves, as well as beyond the present moment. It pictures other people's thoughts, passions, and feelings. It clothes the 'whole possible world with a borrowed reality', and breathes into all other forms the 'breath of life'. It 'diffuses' the soul of morality through all the 'relations and sentiments' of our social being.

Though this account of imaginative reason is less vivid than the Miltonic passage that precedes it – God creating the world out of nothing – the reference to God breathing life into Adam is a way of giving body to disinterestedness and communication as universal values. Protestantism and scientific enquiry – 'the good which is communicative', as Bacon terms it – shape this belief in the wide circulation of ideas. Francis Hutcheson, in *A Short Introduction to Moral Philosophy*, affirms the belief characteristic of liberal Ulster Presbyterianism that there is 'scarce any cheerful or joyful commotion of mind' which does not 'naturally require to be diffused and communicated'. Many societies and public bodies for circulating books and ideas were formed in the eighteenth century, among them the Southwark Friends of the People for the Diffusion of Political Knowledge and the Linen Hall Library for the Promotion of Knowledge, founded by Belfast Presbyterians. The term 'diffuse' should be read as a significant part of the vocabulary of reform. Thomas Belsham, one of Hazlitt's tutors at Hackney, said that the Unitarian Society for the Promoting of Christian Knowledge 'diffused the doctrines of uncorrupted Christianity, by the extensive circulation of books', and the term appears frequently in Dissenter publications.

Communication is one of the primary values in the belief system of Rational Dissenters. They recommend it with an insistent excitement, because they see freedom of enquiry and 'liberal discussion' as the means by which a wholly enlightened society will be established. In *The Life of Napoleon*, Hazlitt writes enthusiastically that society is an 'electrical machine' which communicates good and bad ideas with 'instantaneous rapidity'.

Where Mary Shelley dramatizes the dangers of passing electrical currents through dead bodies in *Frankenstein*, Hazlitt is fascinated by electrical energy, and employs it metaphorically as a positive critical term. Mary Shelley, writing in 1816, in the aftermath of the ultimate failure of the revolutionary experiment, is ironizing the legacy of the scientists whom Priestley celebrates. She distrusts new ideas, and believes that their diffusion can be dangerous. Hazlitt, though he had an acute sense of personal, as distinct from social, evil – something which marked him off from many reformers – shows no such reservations about electrical experiment. He often draws on the new science, observing of Sir Joshua Reynolds that there are certain minds that appear to be formed as 'conductors' to truth and beauty, then adding, by way of explanation, 'as the hardest metals carry off the electric fluid'.

This is his way of reconciling hardness – that distinctively English value – with motion, so that the two opposites complement each other. In an elegiac essay written in the last year of his life, 'The Letter-Bell', he places the bell's particular timbre among those sounds which are '*conductors* to the imagination', before eulogizing mail coaches and the semaphore telegraphs that had recently communicated intelligence of the July Revolution 'to all France within a few hours'.

In a review of Godwin's novel *Cloudesley*, he observes that when the philosopher-novelist sits down to write, it's then that the electric spark begins to unfold itself – 'to expand, to kindle, to illumine, to melt, or shatter all in its way'. Similarly, when he describes Edmund Kean as an electrical performer, he associates him, as Jonathan Bate shows, with Franklin and Priestley, as well as with Jean-Paul Marat, who also wrote a treatise on electricity (Priestley and Marat both taught at the Unitarian academy at Warrington, which closed in the year that Hackney New College opened). Nowadays we think of electricity as a simple, very obvious metaphor, but for Hazlitt and Mary Shelley it had profound social meanings. Writing alone in his study, Godwin – Mary Shelley's father – is like Priestley and Frankenstein experimenting in a laboratory. Who knows what new creature they will animate or invent? Where Hazlitt is actively knowledgeable about electricity and excited by its power, the author of *Frankenstein* expresses a particularly haunting scepticism about its effects. Her parable reworks the traditional ghost story to express the terror of modernity. Frankenstein's artificial monster is on one level that creature of the Revolution, Napoleon, who led the *Grande Armée* on a European rampage.

Where Mary Shelley appears to have an essentially conservative instinct for anticipating certain unintended consequences of idealistic political theory and of the scientific experiment which often accompanied it – consequences which are evil, though not deliberately so, not matters of volition – Hazlitt in much of his writing exemplifies a confident assurance about the beneficial results of certain social reforms. Less naïvely assured than Percy Shelley, whose work he criticized for its over-excited idealism, his prose nevertheless rides on the tide of Whig history.

Yet, if Hazlitt's writings often appear to be buoyantly progressive, there is a countervailing movement in his criticism that tries to make his readers contemplate the irrational. Think of a regular contributor to a left-wing journal such as the *New Statesman* in its heyday, trying to interest readers in the nature of evil, and you get some idea of the way Hazlitt is challenging the sunny benevolism of Rational Dissent. He believes in benevolence and disinterestedness, but this does not mean that he adheres to a simple ethic of progress. He knows what it is to be subject to self-destructive urges, to hate passionately, to harbour murderous grudges and desires, and he understands that people admire the exercise of plenary power.

His most famous expression of radical doubt – the one passage everyone knows – is that moment in his essay on *Coriolanus* when he remarks that the cause of the people is 'but little calculated' as a subject for poetry:

The language of poetry naturally falls in with the language of power. The imagination is an exaggerating and exclusive faculty: it takes from one thing to add to another: it accumulates circumstances together to give the greatest possible effect to a favourite object. The understanding is a dividing and measuring faculty: it judges of things not according to their immediate impression on the mind, but according to their relations to one another. The one is a monopolizing faculty, which seeks the greatest quantity of present excitement by inequality and disproportion; the other is a distributive faculty, which seeks the greatest quantity of ultimate good, by justice and proportion. The one is an aristocratical, the other a republican faculty. The principle of poetry is a very anti-levelling principle. It aims at effect, it exists by contrast. It admits of no medium. It is every thing by excess. It rises above the ordinary standard of sufferings and crimes. It presents a dazzling appearance. It shows its head turretted, crowned, and crested.

This excited, desperate, tormented passage is like an agonized soliloquy, and if we remember that Hazlitt wrote this essay in the aftermath of Napoleon's defeat and exile to St Helena, then its clear-eyed recognition of reforming republicanism's limitations takes on an almost tragic gaiety.

Hitting the word 'it' like an unbudging fence post, he says that the principle of poetry has a 'gilt and blood-stained' front: 'Before it "it carries noise, and behind it leaves tears." It has its altars and its victims, sacrifices, human sacrifices. Kings, priests, nobles, are its train-bearers, tyrants and slaves its executioners. – "Carnage is its daughter." – Poetry is right-royal.' This is dashed off like a review, extemporized like a speech – 'sacrifices, human sacrifices' is a perfectly spontaneous oral amplification which the logic of printed prose should reduce to 'sacrifices and human sacrifices'. Adapting a new-minted Wordsworthian phrase 'Carnage is thy

Daughter', he tersely confronts the former republican's celebration of the Allied victory.

In his 'Thanksgiving Ode', dated 18 January 1816, Wordsworth says:

> But thy most dreaded instrument,
> In working out a pure intent,
> Is Man – arrayed for mutual slaughter, –
> Yea, Carnage is thy Daughter!

By alluding to this passage, Hazlitt is recognizing just how completely Wordsworth has rejected his earlier commitment to the people's cause. The poet has followed the 'logic' of the imagination and the passions, which seek to 'aggrandize what excites admiration and to heap contempt on misery'.

The essay on *Coriolanus* was first published in the *Examiner* on 15 December 1816, the same year as Wordsworth's poem celebrating the Allied victory at Waterloo. It was subsequently reprinted in the study of Shakespeare which was published in September 1817, and the following year Hazlitt published it again in *A View of the English Stage*. The brief publisher's advertisements which open *Characters of Shakespear's Plays* contain one which explains that the *Edinburgh Annual Register* for 1815 includes 'that memorable series of military and political events, which terminated with the Battle of Waterloo, and the final downfall of Buonaparte's Dominion'. Viewed in this context, there's an almost Nietzschean exhilaration as Hazlitt rages against his hero's defeat by following the logic of the imagination through, and describing the history of mankind as a 'romance, a masque, a tragedy, which is built on the principles of poetic justice'. In this noble or royal hunt, the spectators 'halloo and encourage the strong to set upon the weak'.

The exultant relish in the prose dramatically reflects his impatience with what he was later to call, in an essay on Guy Fawkes, 'mitigated, sceptical, liberalized, enlightened belief'. Such belief, based on the distributive idea of the greatest happiness of the greatest number, is the opposite of blind idolatrous bigotry and intolerant zeal. Rejecting a smug optimism, he remarks that 'downright, rooted, rancorous prejudices are honest, hearty, wholesome things'. He has his doubts about liberal scepticism, partly because he believes that such an attitude blocks off the irrational and the prejudiced, as well as denying the heroic, which he terms 'the fanaticism of common life'. It denies the imagination, and is self-interested. Praising the disinterestedness of Fawkes's motives, he confesses: 'I like the spirit of martyrdom.'

This may seem a safely standard expression of admiration for a courageous Catholic whose principles he disagrees with, but whose brutal torture and execution disgust him, except that it issues from the darker recesses of his imagination. He makes a joke out of his interest in defeated Catholics when he says that to be 'a lord, a papist, and poor, is the most enviable distinction of humanity . . . It is just the life I should like to have led'.

In 'Capital Punishments' he discusses how criminals can go to the gallows 'with the resolution of martyrs in the cause of justice'. Noting that there is a 'determination' in the human mind to defy untoward consequences, or even to court them where they appear inevitable, he states:

This is what is understood by the power of *fascination*. Thieves are subject to this power, like other men, as they are to that of gravitation. Objects of terror often haunt the mind; and, by their influence in subduing the imagination, draw the will to them as a fatality. Persons in excessive and intolerable apprehension fling themselves into the very arms of what they dread, and are impelled to rush upon their fate, and put an end to their suspense and agitation. These are said to be 'the toys of desperation': and, fantastical as they may appear, Legislators ought to pay more attention to this than they have done; for the mind, in those extreme and violent temperaments which they have to apply to, is not to be dealt with like a mere machine.

This passage reworks a passage in 'Mind and Motive' where he again speaks of the 'power of fascination', and tells what he suggests is the well-known story of a young girl who is locked in a room with a corpse in order to cure her of her fear. She is found senseless the next morning, embracing the corpse. And he again quotes the phrase 'toys of desperation' from a speech in *Hamlet* in which Horatio warns the Prince against being deprived of his 'sovereignty of reason'.

Hazlitt's sense of the pull which the imagination exerts – that urge, in Horatio's speech, to jump over the 'dreadful summit' of a cliff – and his impatience with liberals who take a mechanistic view of mental processes prompt these psychological insights. In the manuscript of the essay on capital punishment, under a reference to a leading liberal, Bentham, Hazlitt has added a note to himself in darker ink, which says simply: 'Remember gibbets.' This double reminder is the source of a curious passage in the published essay which follows his dismissal of those legislators who, like Bentham, treat the mind as if it were a simple machine:

Gibbets, which have now become very uncommon, may, we think, have produced equivocal effects in this way. They belong to the class of what are called interesting objects. They excite a feeling of horror, not altogether without its attraction, in the ordinary spectator, and startle while they rivet the eye. Who shall say how often, in gloomy and sullen dispositions, this equivocal appeal to the imagination may not have become an ingredient to pamper murderous thoughts, and to give a superstitious bias to the last act of the will? To see this ghastly appearance rearing its spectral form in some solitary place at nightfall, by a wood-side or barren heath – to note the wretched scarecrow figure dangling upon it, black and wasted, parched in the sun, drenched in all the dews of Heaven that fall cool and silent on it, while this object of the dread and gaze of men feels nothing, knows nothing, fears nothing, and swings, creaking in the gale, unconscious of all that it has suffered, or that others suffer – there is something in all these circumstances that may lead the mind to tempt the same fate, and place itself beyond the reach of mortal consequences!

Hazlitt then turns to 'simple hanging', which, in an astonishingly laconic phrase, he says has 'nothing inviting' in it and is an entirely disagreeable prospect:

The broken slumbers that precede it – the half-waking out of them to a hideous sense of what is to come – the dull head and heartache – the feverish agony, or the more frightful deadness to all feeling – the weight of eyes that overwhelm the criminal's – the faint, useless hope of a mockery of sympathy – the hangman, like a spider, crawling near him – the short helpless struggle – the last sickly pang: – all combine to render this punishment as disgusting as it is melancholy.

Taken together, these passages tell us something about Hazlitt's deepest fears and obsessions. He was fascinated by self-destructive behaviour, by an irrationalism which negates a rational, calculating self-interest. This is the type of desperation he sketches in a footnote to the essay on Guy Fawkes: 'There is a common inversion of this opinion, which is *desperation*; or the becoming reckless of all consequences, poverty, disease, or death, from disappointment in some one thing that the mind is set upon.' That murderous sexual possessiveness which he exposes in *Liber Amoris*, and the vicious reviews the work provoked, exemplify the confessionalism which runs through a certain kind of Puritan writing like a temptation. His account of his affair with Sarah Walker shows the autobiographer as scarecrow. To write in haste and then publish immediately, without revision, checking, second thoughts, or the advice of friends, is to court damnation by repudiating all that's calculated and rational. It's almost as though he wanted to murder her in order to be judicially murdered in public. The next best thing was to gibbet himself by publishing his account of their affair. Yet the self-immolation appears to be calculated, because it is clear from the manuscript that Hazlitt read through *Liber Amoris* before publication, as he annotated the fair copies made by his friend Patmore.

Because disinterestedness is the opposite of self-interest, it is close to, or even identical with, martyrdom and self-destruction. This is why he makes the Catholic rebel Fawkes into a torn icon of disinterested imagination, and it is also why there is a narrow – even abrupt and intricate – path that leads from this subject to his fascination with the criminal mind. Here, imagination – the right-royal principle of poetry which he often associates with murder – tempts someone of a gloomily sullen disposition to commit a crime which will turn him into an obscene scarecrow, or 'stuffed straw figure', as he calls Guy Fawkes. This interest in the psychopathology of criminals anticipates Dickens and Dostoyevsky, and is one of the sources of *Liber Amoris*.

As an account of unrequited love, sexual idealism, failure, and humiliation, *Liber Amoris* has been admired for its embarrassingly honest narrative of Hazlitt's obsession with a young woman who walked with a gliding motion like a snake and, by his account, teased, tempted, and enchanted him. The problem is that the style is stilted, paradoxically so. Right from the beginning, he calls her 'my charmer', a phrase that deliberately echoes Lovelace's patronizing compliments in *Clarissa*. He praises her 'sovereign grace and beauty', saying in an obnoxiously overblown, self-consciously Satanic manner: 'Thou art an angel of light, shadowing me with thy softness.'

But where Richardson reveals the cheap, nasty vulgarity of these encroaching terms of endearment, Hazlitt merely assumes the persona of the aristocratic rapist whose name is taken from the Cavalier poet Richard Lovelace, and who is meant to resemble Milton's Satan. Richardson based Lovelace partly on another court poet, Rochester, and partly, I suspect, on Henry St John, Viscount Bolingbroke, the brilliant Tory politician and Jacobite sympathizer who fled to France after the accession of George I. By sounding like Lovelace – 'enchanting little trembler', 'adorable creature' – Hazlitt aims to make these phrases sound ominously hackneyed. The ironic current in certain forms of male sexual flattery turns desire into the threat of imminent control, as well as being a form of almost disdainful bullying – a bullying which contemptuously acknowledges its linguistic banality while at the same time challenging the recipient to demand a more authentic compliment and so become more deeply entrapped. By adopting such language, Hazlitt has transgressed very seriously. He has joined the royalist enemy and adopted its kitsch language. For him, women are either whores or angels who are 'reserved and modest, so soft, so timid'. He wants to prove that Sarah is a 'common lodging-house decoy', a 'wanton' (here he casts himself as Othello), and a poisonous serpent in the place of a woman. In one particularly nasty moment, he bids farewell to Sarah's mother: 'I took her wrinkled, withered, cadaverous, clammy hand at parting, and kissed it. Faugh!'

This is the obsessive, dangerous side of the male Protestant imagination. The passage in his introduction to Elizabethan literature in which he remarks on the 'talismans and love-tokens of Popish superstition' similarly employs this combination of sexual and theological disgust. Alluding to Spenser in *Liber Amoris*, he calls Sarah the 'false Florimel'. In a parody of Rousseau's style of operatic puritan autobiography – it's a form of emotional pornography – he exclaims to his correspondent:

Ah! my friend, it was not to be supposed I should ever meet even with the outward demonstrations of regard from any woman but a common trader in the endearments of love! I have tasted the sweets of the well-practised illusion, and now feel the bitterness of knowing what a bliss I am deprived of, and must ever be deprived of. Intolerable conviction!

Like a type of postmodernist writing, there is a nihilistic, self-flagellating desperation, a having-it-all-ways irony, a masturbatory, taut flaccidity, in the recycled clichés which comprise *Liber Amoris*. This is an exploration of imaginative extremity which never in all its sequence of dead surprises achieves an authentic image or cadence even for a moment.

There is a confessional desperation in Hazlitt which is well caught in Thackeray's account of the Walker affair:

Proctor told us about Hazlitt being in love with Nancy [*sic*] Walker, about whom he wrote the *Liber Amoris*. He was quite wild about her and talked of his passion to everybody. One day he met Basil Montagu's son: seized upon him and in a walk of many miles told the story to him. Montagu left him near Haydon's. Haydon was not at home: but his man & model was. Hazlitt unbosomed himself to the model. By God Sir says he I couldn't help it so I told him. He then went to look for lodgings; and the woman of the house remarking his care-worn appearance asked the cause of it – By God Sir he said she seemed a kind soul and so I told *her*!

Thackeray made this diary entry in 1846, sixteen years after Hazlitt's death. He knew some of the surviving members of Hazlitt's circle – as did Dickens, who was also friendly with Hazlitt's son.

In approaching the disjointed epic autobiography – a kind of prose *Prelude* – which Hazlitt's writings comprise, we need to picture him in the defects of his 'naked shivering nature', as Burke put it in one of his favourite quotations. Malicious though it is, Carlyle's sketch of Hazlitt in 1824 captures something of the fallible human being who created such confident prose:

William Hazlitt takes his punch and oysters and rackets and whore at regular intervals; escaping from bailiffs as he best can, and writing when they grow unguidable [unmanageable] by any other means. He has married (for the second time, his first spouse and the taylor's daughter being both alive): I never saw him, or wished to.

The second wife to whom Carlyle refers was Isabella Bridgewater, a Scottish widow with an income of £300 a year, whom he married in 1824. She left him after three years of marriage, and died in 1869.

In trying to account for the genius of Hazlitt's work, we need to remember the seemingly willed chaos of his personal life. Spendthrift, lonely, obsessed, unable, as he admitted, to love any woman, he walks a dangerous edge in his writings. In part this is an expression of the driven nature of reviewing – its exposed existential commitment – and in part it is the usually invisible heed his writing pays to those forces which liberal views – mitigated, enlightened belief – will never tame. This emerges in the last paragraph of the essay on Guy Fawkes, where he says that 'mental courage' is the only courage he pretends to: 'I dare venture an opinion where few else would, particularly if I think it right. I have retracted few of my positions.' Whether this is the result of obstinacy, strength, or indifference to other people's opinions, he doesn't know, but in little else does he have 'the spirit of martyrdom'.

Reading his prose, we watch Hazlitt Agonistes. His essays dramatize consciousness as a form of combative self-exposure, and they exult in the pelt of the storm. Deep down he knows that the critic who is afraid of looking like a fool is bound to shirk the mission to be honest which energizes the critical act. But his repeated references to the scarecrow figure of Guy Fawkes, that strange evocation of a gibbeted corpse, and the way he describes his passion for Sarah Walker all suggest that even deeper than the assertion of principle was a wish to be transformed into 'poor Guy – that miserable fifth-of-November scarecrow, that stuffed straw figure, flaunting its own periodical disgrace'. Hazlitt, too, endured his own form of 'periodical disgrace' at the hands of hostile reviewers and government hacks, and we must recognize that at some level he sought such punishment, because he needed to vex his readers and provoke their anger.

CHAPTER TWO

Republican Poetics

There is another form of violence in Hazlitt's writing which is historic and which also deliberately courts punishment, though in saying this, I don't mean to reduce its aggressiveness to the personal and neurotic – his admiration for Guy Fawkes, his gibbet fantasies – but rather to notice the prose style's extremity, its harsh, confrontational daring. As Stanley Jones insists, Hazlitt showed remarkable courage in the years after Waterloo, when he made violent attacks on the government and its supporters, venting his spleen and disappointment on numerous powerful figures. That courage, 'barely acknowledged' by his previous biographers, was probably sustained, Jones argues, by his memory of the Treason Trials which took place in 1794, when he was at school in Hackney, and were still celebrated every year at the Crown and Anchor Tavern. Now middle-aged, Hazlitt was in danger of imprisonment and transportation, and this increased his rage at Napoleon's victors.

Hazlitt's angriest and most provocative book, *Political Essays*, was published on 14 August 1819, just before he left London for Winterslow to begin writing the lectures on Elizabethan literature. It was a time of industrial depression, high food prices, and mounting popular discontent. On 16 August, more than 60,000 people attended a highly disciplined rally on St Peter's Fields in Manchester. It was the culmination of a series of demonstrations which often involved military drilling carried out by Waterloo veterans. The demonstrators were violently dispersed by cavalry, who killed eleven people and wounded about five hundred. The deserted field, with its hewn flagstaffs and torn banners, is obliquely present in the last, subtly queasy stanza of 'To Autumn', which Keats wrote the following month:

While barred clouds bloom the soft-dying day,
  And touch the stubble-plains with rosy hue;
Then in a wailful choir the small gnats mourn
  Among the river sallows, borne aloft
    Or sinking as the light wind lives or dies;
And full-grown lambs loud bleat from hilly bourn;
  Hedge-crickets sing; and now with treble soft
  The red-breast whistles from a garden-croft;
    And gathering swallows twitter in the skies.

Influenced by Poussin and by Hazlitt's admiration for Poussin's paintings, this is an image of a battlefield which offers a coded elegy for the dead reformers and which mourns the defeat of the large army of radicals struck down by the yeomanry. The singing hedge-crickets in this stanza derive from classical elegy, and are a benign choric version of Burke's jacobin grasshoppers with their 'importunate chink' in the pastoral prose poem on the British oak-tree in *Reflections on the Revolution in France*.

On 17 August, the day after Peterloo, Hazlitt gave a copy of *Political Essays* to Godwin, inscribing it 'Mr Godwin / with the Author's best respects'. Then he left London to prepare his next critical intervention, the Elizabethan essays.

His inscription to Godwin obviously expresses and affirms the bond between these two opponents of the government. They had first met in John Hazlitt's studio in London in 1794, when Hazlitt was a pupil at Hackney New College. As an expression of admiration from one friend to another, the inscription is private, but the book's printed dedication to John Hunt, Leigh Hunt's brother, is a public affirmation of his friendship with one of London's leading liberal reformers. The dedication has the effect of concentrating the miscellaneous pieces on the two contents pages which precede it into a single utterance:

To JOHN HUNT, Esq.

THE tried, steady, zealous, and conscientious

advocate of the liberty of his country, and the rights
of mankind; ——

One of those few persons who are what they would
be thought to be; sincere without offence, firm but
temperate; uniting private worth to public principle;
a friend in need, a patriot without an eye to himself;
who never betrayed an individual or a cause he pre-
tended to serve – in short, that rare character, a man
of common sense and common honesty,

This volume is respectfully and gratefully
inscribed by

THE AUTHOR

As well as giving unity to the collection, Hazlitt's dedication chimes
wittily with the imprint on the title-page:

LONDON
PRINTED FOR WILLIAM HONE,
45, LUDGATE HILL.

——

1819.

Readers in 1819 would have been quick to spot the link between
John Hunt and William Hone, and they would have understood
how a particular political victory, as well as a collaborative radical
network, are being affirmed in the volume's preliminary pages.

The connection between Hone and John Hunt, which, like the
memory of both men, is almost invisible now, works like this. With
his brother Leigh, Hunt launched the *Examiner* in 1808, eleven
years before the publication of *Political Essays*, which contains
nineteen pieces Hazlitt wrote for that famous weekly. Very rapidly
the *Examiner* established itself as Britain's leading liberal journal,
and by 1812 was selling more than 7,000 copies a week, as well as
reaching thousands more readers through reading-rooms and other
circles. In February 1813, the Hunt brothers were sentenced by the

Lord Chief Justice, Lord Ellenborough, to two years' imprisonment and a fine of £500 each for libelling the Prince Regent. They were offered their freedom if they agreed not to publish any further attacks on the Prince Regent, but they refused. Leigh Hunt's imprisonment in Surrey Gaol is particularly well known, partly because the numerous visitors who came to pay their respects to him and his family included Byron, Shelley, Tom Moore, Hazlitt, and the Lambs. They were comfortably housed there, and in his autobiography Hunt describes the rose-trellised wallpaper and baroque ceiling he designed for their quarters.

In 1817, two years after the Hunt brothers were released, the radical writer and publisher William Hone was prosecuted for blasphemy. Hone had angered the government in various ways, most recently by publishing the weekly *Reformist's Register*, between February and October 1817. His periodical was praised by Cobbett, who had given up publication of the *Political Register* when he fled to the United States in March 1817 in order to avoid a second imprisonment. Hone was held in gaol for several months in 1817, and in December he was brought to trial for publishing blasphemous libels. To the government's anger, he was acquitted after the jury had deliberated for a mere fifteen minutes. He was then sent for trial on a second charge of blasphemous libel, and in order to secure his conviction, the Lord Chief Justice took over from the previous judge. Four years earlier, Lord Ellenborough had sentenced the Hunts, and he was determined to send Hone to gaol.

As Stanley Jones shows in his account of Hone's three trials in December 1817, the publisher defended himself with a 'stubborn, rude skill and courage' that deeply moved the packed court-room. Ill, domineering, and ineffective, Lord Ellenborough was rendered a ridiculous figure by the determined publisher, whose courage, learning, sense of drama, and instinct for publicity made him a popular hero. Humiliated by the acquittals which followed Hone's second and third trials, Ellenborough could never hold up his head in public afterwards. He retired, and died a year later.

Later that month – 29 December 1817 – a public meeting was held at the London Tavern to promote a subscription for Hone. The sum of £3,000 was collected, and Hone moved to a large shop at 45 Ludgate Hill, the address on the title-page of *Political Essays*. Later in 1819, after Peterloo, Hone published his satire *The Political House that Jack Built*, which contained woodcuts by his friend the caricaturist George Cruikshank, and ran to fifty-four editions. Angry, rough, vigorous, wild, Hazlitt's *Political Essays* draws sustenance from its identification with Hone. Though Hone was viewed as an opportunist, ruffian journalist, Hazlitt obviously welcomed the association with him, and enjoyed his and Cruikshank's company. E. P. Thompson correctly points out that Hazlitt would have thought less of Hone's audience when he was writing the essays than of his hope of embarrassing Southey, who had recently become Poet Laureate, but the collected pieces gain a popular energy from the book's identification with the shop on Ludgate Hill and from the many passionate outbursts in the essays. Hazlitt often drops his 'patrician drawl', as Thompson terms it, and hits out like a street-fighter.

When the cause of liberty triumphed with the election of the Whigs in 1830, Leigh Hunt was rewarded with a Civil List pension. John Stuart Mill wrote to him in 1837 regretting that he had missed an opportunity of putting on the record 'my sense of your great merits as a political journalist, & of what you have done & suffered in the cause'. Hunt, Hazlitt, and Cobbett, as well as Godwin, Bentham, and Mill's father, had 'laboured for radicalism' during the 'badness' of the Regency period, and society was no doubt benefiting from the battles that were fought then. This sense of historical continuity, with its accompanying cast of heroes and villains, is a significant feature of any radical culture, and Mill's praise of Hunt, Hazlitt, and Cobbett makes a living link with the early Victorian period. Hone's printing shop on Ludgate Hill, paid for by public subscription, stands as a beacon of liberty on the title-page of *Political Essays*.

Usually, we think of liberty as a value argued for in polemics against an oppressive government, but one of the most distinctive features of English radical journalism is the way writers like Cobbett and Hazlitt give liberty an aesthetic dimension by displaying an absolute confidence in the range and vigour, the sheer pull, of their prose styles. These are wild native wood-notes they're singing as they write, and their affirmation is both joyous and almost off-hand in its concentrated spontaneity, rather casual but firmly spoken. At certain moments, reading them is like observing a skilled cellist plucking the strings on the instrument before starting to play it. This confidence – 'each tucked string tells', in Hopkins's phrase – is a type of mastery that relishes the subtle acoustic textures of English prose. Leigh Hunt noticed this tactile quality when in 1816 he published a verse letter to his friend which began: 'Dear Hazlitt, whose tact intellectual is such / That it seems to feel truth, as one's fingers do touch.'

We can feel that thrumming, cat-gut quality in the opening sentence of the preface to *Political Essays*, which immediately follows the dedication to John Hunt: 'I am no politician, and still less can I be said to be a party-man: but I have a hatred of tyranny, and a contempt for its tools; and this feeling I have expressed as often and as strongly as I could.' In these terse, direct statements, Hazlitt announces himself and his theme. His style is the decisive expression of a value which in a later essay on Londoners and country people he terms the 'plenary consciousness' of the citizen of London. Such a decisive, founding style depends on the intense activities of urban life, on what Algernon Sidney calls 'turbulent contentious cities'. It aims to represent 'this free writing and free speaking', as Milton defines the culture of revolutionary London in *Areopagitica*.

Take the first part of Hazlitt's sentence – 'I am no politician, and still less can I be said to be a party-man' – it's casual, modest, almost thinking aloud or marking time before the real performance starts. In choosing to begin in this apparently unstudied manner, he's obeying an injunction in a textbook he would have studied at Hackney: Joseph Priestley's *A Course of Lectures in Oratory and Criticism*, a work which shows how closely Unitarians studied the art of public speaking and the poetics of prose composition. In the eleventh lecture Priestley advises his pupils to give the appearance of 'present thought, and extempore unprepared address' when they are writing or speaking. This deliberate spontaneity will make them appear to be 'in earnest'.

Free and plain-spoken as Hazlitt's prefatory sentence seems, its natural enunciation and its implicit insistence – I am not a biased, an *interested* writer – have been worked hard for. There are many varieties of writing and speaking, Priestley states, which derive power from their resemblance to 'unpremeditated discourse' – discourse in which the sentiments are supposed to be natural and sincere, 'proceeding directly from the heart'. St Paul, Priestley notes, is the master of 'these abruptnesses', or effects which lack the least appearance of design (this is probably Hazlitt's source of 'abrupt' as a critical term). We can tell from these slightly jagged effects that Paul dictated his real thoughts and sentiments 'at the time of their composition', and we can also recognize that the apostle was a 'warm man, of a quick apprehension, of great ardour and vehemence in whatever he engaged in', and that he was inclined to be 'hasty'. 'Vehemence' for Priestley, as for Hazlitt, isn't simply a descriptive noun; it's a critical – an aesthetic – term as well. To describe a passage in a literary work as possessing 'vehemence' or 'momentum', 'alacrity', or 'communicativeness', is to identify and praise an aesthetic quality. For Hazlitt, it's associated with Burke's writing, and with the phrase 'sacred vehemence' in Milton's *Comus*. Behind Hazlitt's opening sentence we begin to see that there is a theology and a style which derive, through Priestley, from St Paul's insistently plain-spoken epistolary form. This vehement directness, or *verba ardens*, is a way of appearing to override or supplant print by suffusing it with the energetic directness of speech.

For Hazlitt, a written style must effervesce like unpremeditated conversation or an unrehearsed address to an audience. Lecturing on English comic writers in 1818, he remarks that Shakespeare's humour 'bubbles, sparkles, and finds its way in all directions, like a natural spring', while Ben Jonson stagnates in a leaden cistern, and is enveloped in 'the crust of formality', a phrase taken from one of Milton's attacks on superstition. In the passage in which it occurs, Milton is insisting on the quickening power of the spirit to break external signs, so Hazlitt is responding to this characteristically puritan distinction between dynamic spirit and dead letter. He grounds his critical aesthetic in the natural yeastiness, the uncontrollable bubbliness, of the mind in its creative processes. Joseph Priestley, the republican scientist who invented soda-water, helped the young Hazlitt to this image of free imaginative play, just as he taught him that an offhand directness was one of the secrets of effective prose and public speaking. Keats's famous line 'With beaded bubbles winking at the brim' may have been influenced by this image pattern of effervescence in Hazlitt's criticism.

Priestley's poetics of prose style is outlined in his lecture 'Of Harmony in Prose', where he states that if a long syllable which marks a pause is preceded by short syllables, then the pause is 'lively'. Hazlitt breaks his opening sentence at the semicolon with an anapaest: 'and a / contempt / for its tools'. And examining the sentence structure, we can see that the liveliness of its movement is braced by the strong 't' sounds introduced in 'but I have a hatred of tyranny and a contempt for its tools'. As Hazlitt remarks in 'On Familiar Style', a writer's meaning is clenched, or clinched, by the adaptation of the expression to the idea, just as it isn't the size or 'glossiness' of the building materials that gives strength to an arch, but the materials being 'fitted each to its place'. Similarly, in the dedication to John Hunt, the rising 't' in 'liberty' reverberates with several other words – *tried country rights* – to make the prose sing its affirmation of English freedom.

Hazlitt draws on Priestley's lessons on the poetics of republican prose when in 1809 he remarks in one of his first publications, *A New and Improved Grammar of the English Tongue*, that a vowel or a syllable is long when what he calls the 'accent' is on the vowel – it is then 'slowly' joined to the following letter. A syllable is short when the accent is on the consonant – it is then 'quickly' joined to the following letter.

In his lecture on harmony in prose, Priestley advocates in considerable analytic detail a set of rules which govern prose composition. Those single words which are most agreeable to the ear, he writes, are those in which the long and short syllables are 'the most remarkably distinguishable', because such words contain the greatest variety of sounds. This 'excellence' we perceive in many polysyllables, such as *rapidity impetuousity independent*. Analysing the use of pauses in Bolingbroke's style, he states that the last pause is weak and bad in this sentence: 'If the heart of a prince be not corrupt, these truths will find an easy ingression through the under- standing to it.' The three final short syllables enfeeble the sentence, though Bolingbroke, Priestley suggests, can write gracefully and solemnly on other occasions (here he's also demonstrating to his pupils the Unitarian candour and disinterestedness which enable him to admire Bolingbroke's prose style, while disagreeing with his treacherous Jacobite politics). Explaining that when a short syllable which precedes a pause is itself preceded by a long syllable, it makes the close of a sentence 'easy and graceful', Priestley rather suddenly asserts the doctrine of the association of ideas.* No one who has any notion of the analogy there is between 'intellectual ideas and those of sense', he says, will be at a loss to explain the propriety of the distinctions he's been making. And he reminds his listeners that this analogy has often been mentioned in his lectures.

The idea that there is a connection between sense experience and the formation of ideas is based on Locke's epistemology and Hartley's doctrine of association. Although Hazlitt rejected Locke's idea of the understanding – and recognized the limitations of associationism – he believed strongly in the relationship between the body and the understanding, the senses and the intellect. So intense was his critical monism that he uses both 'body' and 'unctuous' as terms of the highest aesthetic approbation. Defending his friend and fellow Unitarian Charles Lamb against the charge of being an old-fashioned – even antiquarian – stylist, he states that there is an 'inward unction', a marrowy vein in both the thought and the feeling of Lamb's prose, which carries off any quaintness or awkwardness. This greasy, nutritive value is much celebrated by Rabelais, who loves marrow-bones and 'most juicy books', and Hazlitt sets it against any perceived dryness in Lamb's style. He also contrasts the biscuity dryness of Swift's understanding with

* Priestley's scansion should read 'easy and graceful'.

Rabelais's language, which is 'of marrow, unctuous, dropping fatness'.

Elsewhere Hazlitt praises Scott and Cobbett for their 'strong, vivid, bodily perception', but criticizes Priestley, despite his insistence on the significance of the body, for a lack of co-ordination in his physical movements: there was nothing 'to induce you to say with the poet, that "his body thought", it was merely the envelope of his mind'. This concept of perfect mental and physical integration is the very foundation of Hazlitt's critical method. He remarks that at the outset of our life the imagination has 'a body to it', and he notices that Shakespeare's particularly felicitous manner of employing adjectives ensures that every prominent word in the 'bold happy texture of his style' cannot be torn 'limb from the body'. The Irish comic actor John Liston is praised for his 'oily richness of expression', his 'lubricated brogue', while the artist David Wilkie is said to have failed in an attempt to sketch Liston: 'his pencil was not oily and unctuous enough'. The erotic charge which oiliness has for Hazlitt is obvious, and, as Virginia Woolf perceptively remarks, the body has a 'large share' in everything he writes. It does so because he wishes to unite sense experience and, importantly, expressive physical movement with imagination and understanding. He wants his prose to have the tone, the silky ripple, the perfect ease and confidence of the human body exultant at a peak of health and fitness. He wants it to glisten like the boxer Hickman's skin, to unite grace and grease in a pun similar to the phrase 'strong toil of grace' – the gladiatorial vaginal net in which Cleopatra catches Antony. Prose style is therefore a mode of being for Hazlitt: it isn't simply descriptive, or a vehicle for ideas, or a means to an end. Like a boxing match, it is a 'complete thing', a glossy, perfectly articulated body in energetic action.

For Hazlitt, seventeenth-century English prose – notably Bacon's and Jeremy Taylor's – displays a completely unified sensibility. This emerges most startlingly in his note on Bulstrode Whitelocke which I quoted in the previous chapter, a note which states that his aim in compiling *The Eloquence of the British Senate* is to illustrate the successive changes that have taken place in 'the minds and characters of Englishmen' within the last 200 years. He argues that the distinctive character of the period during which Whitelocke lived was that the understanding

was invigorated and nourished with its natural and proper food, the knowledge of things without it; and was not left, like an empty stomach, to prey upon itself, or starve on the meagre scraps of an artificial logic, or windy impertinence of ingenuity self-begotten. What a difference between the grave, clear, solid, laborious style of the speech here given, and the crude metaphysics, false glitter, and trifling witticism of a modern legal oration!

The passage from which this is taken immediately brings to mind T. S. Eliot's 'dissociation of sensibility', and we can only conclude that Eliot happened on Hazlitt's anthology in the course of his researches into seventeenth-century literature. The Revd William Hazlitt founded the Unitarian church in Boston in which Eliot's family became prominent. Like Henry Adams, with whose ancestors the Hazlitts claimed kinship, the Eliots belonged to the small, but extremely influential culture of Rational Dissent. Eliot was a cousin of Henry Adams's, and he may well have regarded Hazlitt as a distant great-uncle whom he could first rob and then repudiate.

Comparing Donne and Lord Herbert of Cherbury with Browning and Tennyson, Eliot says that the difference between them is not a simple difference between poets: it is caused by something which happened 'to the mind of England' between the two historical periods in which these writers lived. The passage is familiar, at least to those who were brought up on its critical gospel, but in its feline intelligence and ruthless critical upstaging it is worth quoting at length.

Praising Chapman for his 'direct sensuous apprehension of thought', a Donne-like transposition of thought into feeling, Eliot states that it is the difference

between the intellectual poet and the reflective poet. Tennyson and Browning are poets, and they think; but they do not feel their thought as immediately as the odour of a rose. A thought to Donne was an experience; it modified his sensibility . . . We may express the difference by the following theory: the poets of the seventeenth century, the successors of the dramatists of the sixteenth, possessed a mechanism of sensibility which could devour any kind of experience. . . . In the seventeenth century a dissociation of sensibility set in, from which we have never recovered; and this dissociation, as is natural, was aggravated by the influence of the two most powerful poets of the century, Milton and Dryden.

The theory enables Eliot to begin reshaping the literary canon by dislodging Milton and Dryden, and it is cruelly ironic that he should have been handed this theory in an almost-forgotten work by an earlier Unitarian critic who revered the anti-Trinitarian Milton and keenly admired Dryden, neither of whom he viewed as being agents of dissociation. Interestingly, in his review of *The Education of Henry Adams* Eliot uses the word 'sensuous' obsessively, as a way of defining what late nineteenth-century Unitarianism lacked: 'It is probable that men ripen best through experiences which are at once sensuous and intellectual; certainly many men will admit that their keenest ideas have come to them with the quality of sense perception; and that their keenest sensuous experience has been "as if the body thought".' Like Hazlitt on Priestley, Eliot goes to Donne's erotic lines in 'The Second Anniversary':

> her pure, and eloquent blood
> Spoke in her cheeks, and so distinctly wrought,
> That one might almost say, her body thought.

Eliot may have read Hazlitt on Whitelocke and Priestley in the Waller and Glover edition of the collected works, but he hid his tracks very carefully; and although he must have been attracted by the passionate – the strongly sensuous – intelligence of Hazlitt's writing, which recognizably belongs to the cultural family he was in the process of repudiating, he still retained certain Unitarian values – notably an interest in science and economic theory. That famous, apparently modernist moment in 'Tradition and the Individual Talent', when Eliot describes what happens when 'a bit of finely filiated platinum is introduced into a chamber containing oxygen and sulphur dioxide', is actually the expression of a religious upbringing which saw science as central to social life, not as the enemy of the imagination. Joseph Priestley, who gave a series of lectures on experimental philosophy when Hazlitt was a pupil at the Hackney Unitarian academy, says that 'platina' is a perfect metal which suffers 'no change by fusion, or the longest continued heat'. There is no reason to suppose that Eliot, who dismissed Hazlitt as possessing 'perhaps the most uninteresting mind of all our distinguished critics', also felt the need to patronize Priestley. What links the poet to the Unitarian imagination is the relish with which he introduces experimental science into his criticism. He is drawing on the modernizing energies which are part of their shared culture.

Though it would be stretching the point to argue that the sensuousness which Eliot detects and admires in Chapman's writing is a quality whose recognition owes much to his upbringing (William Greenleaf Eliot, his Bostonian grandfather, was a distinguished Unitarian minister), it is none the less something which many Puritans and Rational Dissenters valued very highly. When Milton remarks, in a pamphlet Hazlitt knew, that poetry is 'more simple, sensuous and passionate' than logic, he draws attention to a term which is given significant weight in Unitarian writings.

Addressing God and the supporters of Hackney New College at its opening in 1787, Thomas Belsham composes a prayer which expresses gratitude for 'the liberal provision which thou hast made for the gratification of the senses'. This easy and unembarrassed idea of sensuous gratification is one expression of the republican cast of mind which Milton, Priestley, and Hazlitt all share, and which the monarchist, often squeamish Eliot repudiates. In his *Essay on the First Principles of Government*, Priestley argues that a man who lacks political and religious liberty has 'no perfect enjoyment of himself', while a sense of such liberty, even though there need be no great occasion to act on it in the course of his life, gives him 'a constant feeling of his own power and importance', and is the foundation of his indulging 'a free, bold, and manly turn of thinking, unrestrained by the most distant idea of control'. It's this free, bold manliness that Hazlitt expresses in the opening sentence of his preface to *Political Essays*, where he announces his contempt for those who become the tools of tyranny.

Priestley rejects the complaint that an 'evil tendency' inheres in matter, and he dismisses the traditional division between a 'sluggish body' and the liberty of the 'immortal spirit'. This is one expression of the mortalism which Priestley shares with Hobbes and Milton, and which Hazlitt inherits as part of their common language.

A key word in that discourse is 'happiness', a term which does not simply refer to personal, private gratification, but also has a public, civic reference that is most notably present in the phrase 'the greatest happiness of the greatest number', which Bentham adapted from Francis Hutcheson's 'the greatest happiness for the greatest numbers'. In Western political theory, the happiness of the individual was originally identified with the functioning of a well-conducted state, but the term has now lost its civic meaning and applies only to personal life. Thomas Jefferson, who was even more deeply influenced by Hutcheson than Locke, offers the most famous formulation of the republican ideal of civil liberty and sensuous pleasure in the American Declaration of Independence's phrase 'life, liberty, and the pursuit of happiness'; while in an admiring letter to Priestley he remarks that climate is one of the sources 'of the greatest sensual enjoyment'. This hedonistic belief also informs the poetry of Keats, whom Hazlitt befriended and decisively influenced, and it is significant that Keats was also educated in a Dissenting academy.

Though Eliot aimed to minimize the power of the republican imagination in the literary canon, he drew on Hazlitt's nativist vision of a unified sensibility, and was drawn, like him, to the cadences of seventeenth-century prose. Both writers would have recognized how Bacon's statement in *The Advancement of Learning* that reason 'doth buckle and bow' the mind into the nature of things is an example of that undivided, or Old English, sensibility at work in its use of concrete, physical process to express thought.

Bacon possesses a 'pomp and copiousness of style' which Hazlitt also finds in Sir Thomas Browne and Jeremy Taylor. At times, Bacon's prose has a Rabelaisian verbal prodigality and plenitude, as when he describes the footsteps of diseases as 'imposthumations, exulcerations, discontinuations, putrefactions, consumptions, contractions, extensions, convulsions, dislocations, obstructions, repletions'. Hazlitt admired Bacon's manner of uniting 'the powers of the imagination and understanding', and in this passage from one of his lectures on Elizabethan literature he sings Bacon's singularly unified sensibility:

Reason in him works like an instinct: and his slightest suggestions carry the force of conviction. His opinions are judicial. His induction of particulars is alike wonderful for learning and vivacity, for curiosity and dignity, and an all-pervading intellect binds the whole together in a graceful and pleasing form. His style is equally sharp and sweet, flowing and pithy, condensed and expansive, expressing volumes in a sentence, or amplifying a single thought into pages of rich, glowing, and delightful eloquence. He had great liberality from seeing the various aspects of things (there was nothing bigot-ted or intolerant or exclusive about him) and yet he had firmness and decision from feeling their weight and consequences.

Instinctive reason, vivacity, grace, firmness, decision, and 'pleasing form' – these constitute both an ideal composite of related values and a quality which Hazlitt seeks to incorporate in his own prose by offering a type of invocatory praise. For him, aesthetic form is an embodied ideal – Diomed in the guise of an English pugilist. Prose isn't static, but must have an active, decisive energy that binds reason and instinct together. Bacon, in his account, has a founding, or plenary, intellect that's highly sensitive to concrete particulars, as well as being categorical, discriminating, and formally graceful.

But the body, though it can feel and look beautiful, is a perishable thing, and here Hazlitt introduces a cleverly condensed quotation from *Holy Dying*, by the seventeenth-century Anglican divine Jeremy Taylor, both to catch an ephemeral physical beauty and to draw that glossy, ever so brittle, and fragile motion into his own prose:

A man is a bubble. He is born in vanity and sin; he comes into the world like morning mushrooms, soon thrusting up their heads into the air, and con-versing with their kindred of the same production, and as soon they turn into dust and forgetfulness; some of them without any other interest in the affairs of the world, but that they made their parents a little glad, and very sorrowful. Others ride longer in the storm; it may be until seven years of vanity be expired, and then peradventure the sun shines hot upon their heads, and they fall into the shades below, into the cover of death and darkness of the grave to hide them. But if the bubble stands the shock of a bigger drop, and outlives the chances of a child, of a careless nurse, of drowning in a pail of water, of being overlaid by a sleepy servant, or such little accidents, then the young man dances like a bubble empty and gay, and shines like a dove's neck, or the image of a rainbow, which hath no substance, and whose very imagery and colours are fantastical; and so he dances out the gaiety of his youth, and is all the while in a storm, and endures, only because he is not knocked on the head by a drop of bigger rain, or crushed by the pressure of a load of indigested meat, or quenched by the disorder of an ill-placed humour; and to preserve a man alive in the midst of so many chances and hostilities, is as great a miracle as to create him; to preserve him from rushing into nothing, and at first to draw him up from nothing, were equally the issues of an Almighty power.

Hazlitt and his first wife, Sarah Stoddart, lost a baby son early in their marriage, so there is an unspoken personal grief that bonds him with the airy beauty and doctrinal wisdom of this remarkable passage. Writing ecstatically about Taylor's style, he characterizes it as rapid, flowing, endless, a choral song and hymn to the spirit of the universe which displays a 'transparent brilliancy' in the working out of an idea that is more like 'fine poetry than any other prose whatever'.

It is this quality of pure poesis, of effortless creativity in Taylor's subtly rhapsodic prose which lets us glimpse Hazlitt's critical intention here. He wants to identify and characterize a prose style (both Taylor's and his own) which is more than prose – at least as prose is commonly understood to exist as an efficient medium for communicating ideas or information clearly and directly. He's drawing attention to Taylor's intricately beautiful cadences and patterns of imagery, and, in describing their immediacy as having a transparent brilliancy, he's identifying them with two symbols which express the nature of his own critical prose – the glass-blower's bubble, and the magic lantern's illuminated transparency.

Notice the bubble metaphor which Taylor very nimbly pats throughout the passage; it has the living gleam of an eye smiling or a glistening complexion, the transient bulge of an early mushroom. It also has the rather metallic, rainbowy shimmer of a stockdove's

neck feathers. But the shimmery, iridescent, light-as-a-feather bubble is also connected intertextually with that moment in an earlier
lecture in the same series in which Hazlitt praises the way Shakespeare's humour bubbles and sparkles like a 'natural spring'. This is
a delighted image of movement, and the word 'motion', as we have
seen, is a central, dynamic critical term for Hazlitt, one that he often
links with the term 'expression'. This bubbliness appears again in
his comment on the sociable way in which Shakespeare's ideas react
upon each other 'as the blower's breath moulds the yielding glass',
an image which, significantly, he also applies to the art of literary
journalism, as he does the term for a magic-lantern slide, 'transparency'. That effervescent image is also present in one of those brief
epiphanic moments which are meant to be taken as more than
anecdotal illustrations in Hazlitt's essays:

If a drizzling shower patters against the windows, it puts me in mind of a
mild spring rain, from which I retired twenty years ago, into a little public-
house near Wem in Shropshire, and while I saw the plants and shrubs
before the door imbibe the dewy moisture, quaffed a glass of sparkling ale,
and walked home in the dusk of evening, brighter to me than noon-day
suns at present are!

Rather like the moment when the waiter holds young David
Copperfield's glass of ale to the light, this sentence seeks to embody
a formative memory, one of those spots of time that appear buoyant
with meaning, instinct with the flowing, light-filled openness of
youth. These beaded bubbles are symbols of youthful sensations
that Hazlitt terms 'all glossy, spruce, voluptuous'.

This delighted joy in movement has its source in the expressive
plasticity of the free individual conscience combined with an intense
observation of natural phenomena. It is an intellectual joy that is
central to the philosophy and aesthetics of Francis Hutcheson, one
of the most powerful intellects to shape Unitarian culture.

CHAPTER THREE

Celebrating Hutcheson

Although Hazlitt refers directly to Hutcheson only twice in his writings, noting in an essay on self-love that Hutcheson rejected the idea that morality is 'an affair of the five senses', and elsewhere calling him the 'celebrated' author of an elegant treatise on beauty and virtue, it is essential to understand how Hutcheson's ideas shaped the culture of Rational Dissent. I have mentioned him several times already, but it's necessary to try and place Hazlitt's critical writings in relation to the philosopher who is known as the father of the Scottish Enlightenment.

In *A System of Moral Philosophy*, Hutcheson observes that small children have a 'constant propensity to action and motion . . . grasping, handling, viewing, tasting every thing'. He argues that their ceaseless experimental activity stems from an impulse to action and 'an implanted instinct toward knowledge', even – and this point is crucial – 'where they are not allured by any prospects of advantage'. Children therefore resemble disinterested experimental scientists; they are not selfishly motivated, and they live in a flurry of perpetual activity, like nature's first Presbyterians.

For Hutcheson, as for Hazlitt, the impulse towards knowledge is unselfish and disinterested:

Nay we see almost all other animals, as soon as they come to light, exercising their several powers by like instincts, in the way that the Author of Nature intended; and by this exercise, though often laborious and fatiguing, made happier than any state of slothful sensuality could make them. Serpents try their reptile motions; beasts raise themselves and walk or run; birds attempt to raise themselves with their wings and soar on high; water-fowl take to the water as soon as they see it. The colt is practising for the race, the bull is butting with his horns, and the hound exercising himself for the chase.

This primal scene is utopian and primitivist. It employs exultantly pleasurable physical activity not as a symbol for the impulse towards knowledge, but as the actual embodiment of knowing. This is a prose which draws on Genesis and on Milton, in order to anticipate a republic of active knowledge, a natural polity which later finds expression in Whitman's free verse. Hutcheson is one of the founders of the American Enlightenment, and his exuberant benevolence also influenced Hazlitt's father.

The eager intense directness of children fills Hutcheson with wonder:

Children are ever in motion while they are awake, nor do they decline weariness and toil: they show an aversion to sleep till it overpowers them against their wills: they observe whatever occurs, they remember and enquire about it; they learn the names of things, enquire into their natures, structures, uses, and causes; nor will their curiosity yield to rebukes and affronts. Kind affections soon break out toward those who are kind to them; strong gratitude, and an ardour to excel in any thing that is praised; in vying with their fellows they are transported with success and victory, and exceedingly dejected when they are outdone by others. They are soon provoked to anger upon any imagined injury or hurt; are afraid of experienced pain, and provoked at the cause of it; but soon appeased by finding it undesigned, or by professions of repentance. Nothing do they more resent than false accusation or reproach. They are prone to sincerity, and truth, and openness of mind, until they have experienced some evils following upon it.

As an image – a fluid moving image – of Hutcheson's critical vision, this passage is crucial. With its benign, undisappointed cherishing of experience, his philosophy has at its centre a delighted admiration for children's principles: those values of sincerity, truth, and openness of mind to which they are naturally 'prone'. Observing them play and learn, he argues that there is 'an immediate pleasure in knowledge'. And we can observe a similar delight in Hazlitt, when he comments that the boy playing in Murillo's painting *Spanish Beggar Boys* is 'done with a few dragging strokes of the pencil, and with a little tinge of colour; but the mouth, the nose, the eyes, the chin, are as brimful as they can hold of expression, of arch roguery, of animal spirits, of vigorous, elastic health'.

It is this concept of sensuous immediacy – the leaps, the kingfisher darts of aesthetic recognition – that is one of Hutcheson's great contributions to critical practice. Hazlitt inherits it and the accompanying value of motion, as part of his Dissenting heritage. Indeed, the word 'immediate' is a significant term in Hazlitt's aesthetic: he comments on how Cobbett relies on his own acuteness and 'immediate evidence'.

Hutcheson argues that there is a superior power of perception which is 'justly' called a sense, and which does not arise from any knowledge of principles, proportions, causes, or the 'usefulness of the object'. This natural power strikes us at the very first 'with the idea of beauty'. And, crucially, these aesthetic perceptions are antecedent to any prospect of personal advantage – that is, to self-love. Thus disinterestedness, which is a central value in the culture of Rational Dissent, is synonymous with the perception of the beautiful.

As Peter Kivy shows in his study of Hutcheson, aesthetic awareness is perceptual or emotive, rather than rational – hence the emphasis Hutcheson places on children's tactile experience and on their open-minded sincerity. Children have active principles, though this doesn't mean that they are rational beings. Importantly, Kivy notes that Hutcheson was convinced by an analogy between sense perception and critical judgement: sense perception leaps, reason plods. From this, he argued that the ability to recognize the beautiful and other aesthetic qualities is innate, not under the control of the will. Hazlitt usually assigns a negative value to the term 'plodding', and he prefers a direct, immediate intuitiveness. The value Hutcheson places on what he terms 'intenseness', which in *A System of Moral Philosophy* he denotes as 'the degree in which any perceptions or enjoyments are beatific', is close to the critical term 'gusto' which Hazlitt invented.

Hutcheson's *An Inquiry into the Original of our Ideas of Beauty and Virtue*, the treatise Hazlitt praises, is the founding text in

English of the subject we now term 'aesthetics'. More than any other philosopher of his generation, Hutcheson is responsible for establishing aesthetics as a philosophical discipline. And aesthetics, as Kivy shows, became an autonomous discipline by marking out a unique realm of experience for itself. As we have seen, Hutcheson's concept of disinterestedness was the means by which that experience was marked out. His ideas – indeed, the whole generous and radical outlook, or *mentalité*, to which they belong – represent a distinctive critical address to art and society that finds its most perfect expression in Hazlitt's writings. Hutcheson's connection with Hazlitt is briefly noted by David Bromwich in his very distinguished study of the critic, but it's necessary to define more closely the intellectual culture to which both men belonged.

As H. McLachlan shows in his study of English Unitarianism, Hutcheson helped shape the thought of Unitarians through a succession of students who went to Glasgow University from the liberal Dissenting academies. Hutcheson, who was an Ulster-Scot, was born in Co. Down in 1694 and died in 1746. He attended Glasgow University, and was professor of philosophy there from 1727 until his death. He pioneered the use of English rather than Latin in the lecture-room, and was a charismatic and passionately committed teacher whose influence on Dissenting culture is celebrated in a speech which the Ulster Presbyterian radical William Drennan prepared when he was tried for sedition in 1794.

In the speech, Drennan praises his father, who was a Presbyterian minister and 'the friend and associate of good, I may say, great men; of Abernethy, of Bruce, of Duchal, and of Hutcheson'. Drennan's father was Hutcheson's assistant in the private academy he headed in Dublin for several years, and was also a Unitarian. The link with Hazlitt is less direct; but it is nevertheless a strong one, because William Drennan married a member of his father's congregation, Sarah Swanwick, whose brother Joseph was a close friend of Hazlitt and attended Hackney New College with him. Drennan went on to become one of the founders of the United Irishmen, the revolutionary society which failed to establish an Irish Republic after the uprising in 1798.

What we can begin to trace, I believe, is a particular Dissenting counter-culture which embraces among others Hutcheson, the Drennans, and the Hazlitts. Thus Hutcheson's influence on William Hazlitt, the critic, is not mediated simply through his books, but through the extended family that was Unitarianism. For example, Hutcheson's most distinguished pupil, Adam Smith, taught Hazlitt's father at Glasgow. The culture of the university was classically republican, and its large body of Irish – particularly Ulster-Scots – students was at the forefront of the arguments against aristocracy which took place there during the early decades of the eighteenth century.

Without wishing to detract from Hazlitt's originality as a critic, or from Bromwich's distinction as a scholar, I think it necessary to reconsider Bromwich's discussion of Hazlitt's concept of the disinterested imagination. In *Hazlitt: The Mind of a Critic*, he states that Hutcheson sought to refine Shaftesbury's ethic of 'private virtue, public benefits' by arguing for the disinterestedness of the benevolent affections. But he still regarded benevolence 'primarily as a social good, derived from habit, and desirable as it promoted the harmony of the "system" of affections'. Hazlitt, Bromwich states, wanted to prove the natural disinterestedness of the mind, rather than its artificial benevolence. This principle of natural disinterestedness, which Hazlitt succeeded in establishing, was 'a serious departure from what had preceded it in moral philosophy'. But in the *Inquiry* Hutcheson distinguishes this internal sense, the faculty which perceives the beautiful, from an innate idea, stating that the internal sense is a 'natural' power of perception. It is 'a passive power of receiving ideas of beauty from all objects in which there is uniformity amidst variety'. Therefore it is not artificial.

One of the most important aspects of Bromwich's discussion of Hazlitt is the rescue operation he mounts on this concept of the disinterested critical imagination. Bromwich shows that 'disinterested' is not the same as 'detached' or 'impartial'. For Hazlitt, it was a test of the 'sense and candour' of anyone belonging to the opposite party 'whether he allowed Burke to be a great man'. This is to say that the disinterested imagination is capable of an empathy with a position it does not share – indeed, which it opposes. Tragically for the practice of literary criticism, Hutcheson's and Hazlitt's concept of disinterestedness was reinterpreted by Matthew Arnold in a very influential essay, 'The Function of Criticism at the Present Time', so as to give a new meaning to disinterestedness. As Bromwich shows, it is now the characteristic virtue not of the member of the opposite party who nevertheless recognizes Burke's greatness, but of the member of 'no party at all'. This has the effect of removing culture from the world of passions, so that it 'returns upon itself'.

This idea of a free-floating impartiality would have been incomprehensible to Hutcheson and Hazlitt, but its essential conservatism and bland unimpassioned limitedness were until relatively recently a pervasive feature of British literary criticism. If the pre-Arnoldian meaning of 'disinterested' could be revived, then an altogether subtler concept of the critical imagination might emerge. This would involve recognizing that all critical writing is essentially polemical, but at the same time stripping away many of the negative qualities which are so often associated with the term 'polemic'. The disinterested imagination takes a position, but it is not entrenched, obdurate, or rigid; rather, it is based on an active and flexible way of knowing that is essentially dialogic. It doesn't talk to itself.

For Hutcheson, a child's 'impulse to action' is 'an implanted instinct toward knowledge', and often in Hazlitt we find that action – sensuous physical activity – is greatly valued. The term 'gusto' refers to aesthetic expressiveness – 'power or passion defining any object' – and it can be linked to Hutcheson's concept of 'intenseness' and to his image of children being always in motion. Thus Hazlitt praises Thomson's descriptions of nature for the way they are seen 'growing around us'. Thomson describes 'not to the eye alone, but to the other senses', the whole person. Discussing Wordsworth, Hazlitt notes that Wordsworth cares nothing for any landscape painting that does not express 'the time of day, the climate, the period of the world it was meant to illustrate, or had not this character of *wholeness* in it'. Poetry, for Hazlitt, puts a spirit of 'life and motion' into the universe. It describes 'the flowing, not the fixed', and drama represents 'not only looks, but motion and speech'. Each feature of the human face is 'in motion every moment'. As Roy Park shows in his study of Hazlitt, the 'kinetic vocabulary' he employs is a vast network of terms that are all expressive of the need for action and movement: 'motion', 'life', 'workings', 'fluctuations', 'play', 'flexibility', 'malleability', 'movement', and many other cognate words. This is an attempt to be true to the experiential and revelatory nature of art. Hazlitt's kinetic vocabulary also embodies – gives almost literal flesh to – the idea of pleasure in art, and here he follows Hutcheson's argument that there is an immediate pleasure in knowledge. Hazlitt emphatically values writing that has an 'immediate appeal to the senses', and in his essay on the Elgin Marbles says that the 'communication of art with nature is here everywhere immediate, entire, palpable'. Usually, though, he prefers painting to sculpture, because it gives one view of an object at a particular time.

This idea of immediacy, which is so much a feature of the puritan imagination, is connected with the idea of 'intenseness', and, as we have seen, Hutcheson states that intenseness is the degree to which any perceptions are 'beatific'. It's this emphasis on happiness or perceptual 'enjoyments', this directly passionate involvement with the subject that's being discussed, which makes me think there's a New York quality in both Hutcheson and Hazlitt. The direct immediacy of Susan Sontag's aesthetic response and the pleasure she so evidently takes in the critical act make her seem the embodiment of their idea of the disinterested critic. Together, Hutcheson and Hazlitt help us to glimpse a critical imagination that is mobile, sensuous, immediate, direct, performative, and happy.

As Roy Park argues in his study of Hazlitt, the critic is like an actor who doesn't analyse his role in terms of 'rules and formulae'. The actor 'grasps the central feeling behind the character that alone determines the weight to be given to particular aspects of its portrayal. Like the actor, the critic must eliminate the personal in grasping the dominant feeling of the work as a whole.' As an active participant in the text, the critic is by definition a performer who creates an occasion. And that sense of occasion ought to give us pleasure as an audience. This plasticity of thinking and feeling and this dramatic empathy are the mobile expressions of disinterestedness, a value that is articulated not as a fixed detached observation of any object or idea, but as the dynamic embodiment of mental process. That process and the perception of it are not separable; together they continuously, immediately, expressively shape a reality that isn't made up of sluggish, inert matter. Here, 'motion' isn't simply a quality of the phenomenal world, but a value that for Hazlitt, as for Wordsworth, interfuses spirit, matter, and perceptual processes.

The term 'motion' is employed by Hazlitt's revered friend, the Unitarian poet and preacher Joseph Fawcett, whose synthesis of Priestley's concept of vital matter with a type of Christian Platonism significantly influenced Wordsworth in the 1790s, when he attended Fawcett's sermons at the Old Jewry. Fawcett is an almost forgotten figure now, but he was widely respected during his lifetime. He died in 1804, and the following year Hazlitt considered writing his biography. He was friendly with Godwin, who may have based Mr Clare in *Caleb Williams* on him. The solitary in *The Excursion* is in part a distorted view of Fawcett which repudiates the influence of his writings and sermons on Wordsworth.

As Leslie Chard pointed out in an important discussion of Rational Dissent's impact on Wordsworth, the young republican was attached to the Unitarian network through friends, relatives, and his first publisher, Joseph Johnson. Fawcett employs the term 'living soul' in a sermon which is central to the inspiration of 'Tintern Abbey' where:

> we are laid asleep
> In body, and become a living soul:
> While with an eye made quiet by the power
> Of harmony, and the deep power of joy,
> We see into the life of things.

In a sermon entitled 'Reflections Drawn from the Consideration that God is our Creator', which was published in 1795, three years before 'Tintern Abbey', Fawcett tells the sophisticated, middle-class congregation of Rational Dissenters gathered in the Old Jewry that the Creator is the great spring and impulse that actuates all things. He is in himself the attracting power that holds the particles of all bodies together, and combines all bodies into the beautiful systems we see them compose. He is himself the living soul that inhabits and animates every living thing; that propels every drop through every vein; that produces every pulsation of every artery, every motion of every limb, every action of every organ, throughout the whole animal kingdom. Every operating principle, through the ample compass of things, is God, that moment willing, God, that moment acting. He is the life of the world: at once the maker, the inspector, and the mover, of all things. Water we call the element of one animal; air, we say, is the element of another: the vital presence of God himself is the universal element, in which all living creatures 'live and move and have their being'.

As Chard shows, this Priestleyan rhapsody to motion caught the young Wordsworth's imagination, and is invoked in 'Tintern Abbey'. Wordsworth's lines in turn became a touchstone for Hazlitt, who quotes them frequently.

Writing an essay on a portrait by Van Dyck in the winter of 1824, he asserts that 'expression' – each feature being in motion every moment – is the great test and measure of a painter's genius, and that a still life can never give sufficient proof of the highest skill:

for there is an inner sense, a deeper intuition into nature that is never unfolded by merely mechanical objects, and which, if it were called out by a new soul being suddenly infused into an inanimate substance, would make the former unconscious representation appear crude and vapid. The eye is sharpened and the hand made more delicate in its tact,

> While by the power
> Of harmony, and the deep power of joy
> We see into the life of things.

We not only *see*, but *feel* expression, by the help of the finest of all our senses, the sense of pleasure and pain.

And Hazlitt develops this by stating that the greatest painter is he who is able to put the 'greatest quantity of expression' into his works.

What we can trace here is the central thread of Unitarian discourse in Hazlitt and in Wordsworth, with the publisher Joseph

Johnson as a key figure. It was he who published Wordsworth's first volumes of verse, *An Evening Walk* and *Descriptive Sketches* in 1793, and in 1795 he published Fawcett's sermons (ten years later, Hazlitt's first book appeared under Johnson's imprint: 'Printed for J. Johnson, no. 72, St Paul's Church-Yard'). In the 1790s, Wordsworth became part of Johnson's circle, and he also made Unitarian friends in Halifax and Norwich. The influence of Rational Dissenting culture at this period was strong, and as Chard shows, it helped Wordsworth towards the view that poetic language doesn't differ essentially from the language of prose. The high value which Dissenting culture placed on perfecting prose style also made Hazlitt affirm the power and beauty of prose as a distinct medium that should often aim to be tactile, direct, engaged, active.

When Wordsworth testifies to having felt

> a sense sublime
> Of something far more deeply interfused,
> Whose dwelling is the light of setting suns,
> And the round ocean and the living air,
> And the blue sky, and in the mind of man:
> A motion and a spirit that impels
> All thinking things, all objects of all thought,
> And rolls through all things,

he is celebrating the combined motion of consciousness and natural objects. The collocation of *thinking things thought through things* makes the Priestleyan identification of matter and spirit assonantly forceful. The special force which Wordsworth gives to the verb 'roll' here and in a line from a poem written the following year – 'Rolled round in earth's diurnal course' – makes clear that it is not inert matter which is being contemplated. As Hazlitt said in his letter on philosophy to the *Monthly Magazine* in 1809, we need to consider the existence of an 'entirely unknown and undefined principle, which may be called spirit as well as matter'. This undefined principle pervades his critical writing. It is the 'new soul' being suddenly infused into inanimate substance in the essay on Van Dyck in which he quotes 'Tintern Abbey'. We can see it being given a dynamic aesthetic form when he contrasts the 'fixed repose' and 'harmony' of Claude Lorraine's landscapes with Rubens's paintings, where everything is 'fluttering and in motion, light and indifferent, as the winds blow where they list'.

This imagery is also employed by D. H. Lawrence in the essay 'Poetry of the Present' which he wrote for the American edition of *New Poems*. There he outlines his poetics by praising free verse's 'wind-like transit', and then contrasts it with finished, or measured, verse which belongs to 'the stable, unchanging eternities'. He cries out like an inspired preacher:

Give me the still, white seething, the incandescence and the coldness of the incarnate moment: the moment, the quick of all change and haste and opposition: the moment, the immediate present, the Now. The immediate moment is not a drop of water running downstream. It is the source and issue, the bubbling up of the stream. Here, in this very instant moment, up bubbles the stream of time, out of the wells of futurity, flowing on to the oceans of the past.

Lawrence's Congregational background helps shape this statement of a Dissenting Protestant aesthetic which also draws on industrial processes and on science for its metaphor of incandescent melt-down. The Lawrence who employed the chemical term 'allotropic' to identify various states of consciousness belongs, like Wordsworth and Hazlitt, to the radical Enlightenment. When Thomas Belsham, one of Hazlitt's tutors at Hackney, says that some scientists view the laws of nature as being 'the immediate energy of God', he's identifying the scientific with the divine, as well as drawing attention to that emphasis on immediacy which we see in Hutcheson and which Lawrence would have recognized.

Hazlitt runs Wordsworth's lines from 'Tintern Abbey' into his prose in his lecture 'On Liberty and Necessity', where he disagrees with those theologians who argue that God is the sole agent in the universe, arguing that if this is so, then 'all second causes are parts of the divine essence, and in all that we see or hear or feel, we must conceive of something far more deeply interfused, a spirit and a motion that impels all thinking things, all objects of all thought, and breathes through all things'. This, he remarks, is the doctrine of Spinoza. But Wordsworth's lines, as Chard shows, are also shaped by his contact with the ideas shared by the Unitarians he met socially. Norwich, Halifax, London, and other cities helped produce this rhapsodic vision of nature. There is a line which stretches from the woods in the Wye Valley to middle-class activism and to Priestley's scientific experiments and writings. Wordsworth's early poems take nature as their subject, but their treatment of nature as movement and process also makes them radical documents. Praising nature as an energetic amalgam of matter and spirit, they reject traditional views of matter as inert.

The related concepts of immediacy, process, energy, and suffusion all shape Wordsworth's vision of nature, and, as Chard shows in his account of Dissenting culture's influence on the poet in the 1790s, there was a social base to those ideas. Wordsworth heard Fawcett preach to an enlightened, sophisticated, middle-class congregation. He mixed with Rational Dissenters, absorbed their ideas, and this helped him bring experimental science and republican ideology into his account of his feelings in the woods around Tintern Abbey. How removed the poem seems today from the eager push towards reform and revolution in Britain in the 1790s, but in his many citations of its central lines Hazlitt must always have identified it with that decade.

Wordsworth's lines shape the cadence of Hazlitt's prose in his account of Spinoza's doctrine, as they also shape an earlier lecture in which he states that Locke breaks human perception into an infinite number of 'microscopic impressions and fractions of ideas'. But there is nothing to unite them, because by this argument 'the most perfect grace and symmetry would be only one mass of unmeaning, unconscious confusion. All nature, all objects, all parts of all objects would be equally "without form and void".' Here, Wordsworth's lines are combined with a famous phrase from Genesis to give power and authority to Hazlitt's refutation of Locke's theory of knowledge. And the authority he is enforcing is immediately consolidated by an italicized statement from Kant in the next sentence:

The mind alone is formative, to use the expression of a great German writer; or it is that alone which by its pervading and elastic energy unfolds and expands our ideas, that gives order and consistency to them, that assigns to every part its proper place, and fixes it there, and that frames the idea of the whole.

This concept of the plastic energy of mind and matter is at the centre of Hazlitt's critical project. Wordsworth's lines serve as a plenary inspiration – an inspiration which is amplified by the allusion to a dead universe before God says 'Let there be light', and then further strengthened by the deliberately unnamed, and therefore more mysterious and powerful, 'great German writer'.

The metaphor in the sentence is architectonic or pictorial, but its combination of expansive flow and decisive closure is self-referential, in that Hazlitt is thinking of the distinction between good and bad prose styles. Thus Locke writes his *Essay Concerning Human Understanding* without saying a word about the nature of the understanding, treating it dismissively as a 'convenient repository for the straggling images of things'. Hazlitt intends that the faint image of untidy handwriting in the adjective 'straggling' will support his criticism of what he terms the 'prolixity and ambiguity' of Locke's prose style. There is 'a sort of heaviness' about the philosopher's writing, a lack of 'clearness and connection', which, in spite of all his effort and the 'real plodding strength' of his mind, he was never able to overcome (here 'plodding' is subtly ambivalent, not wholly negative). Locke's style and thought are like dense, inert, unenergized matter. Where Hobbes is gifted with a concise, masterly style, Locke's inability to formulate a creative and formative concept of the mind means that, in the absence of such an organizing principle, all our ideas are 'decomposed and crumbled down'. For Hazlitt, ideas issue from the understanding, not the senses, and the mind is emphatically not a sheet of paper scribbled over with sense impressions. The understanding is the common principle of thought, the superintending faculty which alone perceives the relations of things.

In expressing the limitations of an epistemology that is built on an absent or unclear idea of the understanding, Hazlitt's verbs –

'straggling', 'scribbled', 'decomposed', 'crumbled down' – are carefully chosen, and in their savoured concreteness are reminiscent of Bacon's prose. In a bravura passage repudiating the originality of Locke's system, Hazlitt furiously asserts that the same system

came from the mind of Hobbes, not hesitating, stammering, puling, drivelling, ricketty, a sickly half-birth, to be brought up by hand, to be nursed and dandled into common life and existence, but just the reverse of all this, full-grown, completely proportioned and articulated, compact, stamped in all its lineaments with the vigour and decision of the author's mind, is what we now have to show.

This is the physical body writing the thinking body. Hazlitt's prose is intensely physical as he articulates literally what he wants to say, while at the same time drawing on the passage in *Areopagitica* where Milton states that truth's 'body is homogeneal, and proportional'. In this way Hazlitt reveals the mortalist theology which Hobbes shared with Milton and which Priestley also held.

Hazlitt was drawn to Hobbes's combination of decisive terseness with a type of almost wistful rumination. That famously dismissive adjectival finale – 'solitary, poor, nasty, brutish, and short' – is one example of his muscular style, and Hazlitt's adjectival chain-shot accuracy owes something to his admiration of Hobbes. To quote a phrase from Bacon, whom he also admired, such adjectives are 'magistral and peremptory, and not ingenuous and faithful'. But we should also note that because he's drawn to a type of philosophic indolence which is the opposite of downright plenary consciousness, there's a counter-momentum in Hazlitt's critical imagination, which works to offset this type of absolute finality. Hume's intellect, he suggests, was one of the subtlest, because Hume was an 'easy, indolent, good-tempered man'. Though he was a Scotsman, he lacked the hard, rigid purposiveness which Hazlitt saw as distinctively Scottish and which takes away from 'that tremulous sensibility to every slight and wandering impression'. This makes Hume sound rather like Shelley, and as his philosophy influenced the poet significantly, the comparison is apposite.

In Hobbes, this tone of philosophic indolence can be caught in his interest in the 'secret thoughts of man', his fascination with mental associations – 'this wild ranging of the mind', he calls it – and also in this passage whose style has a quietly spoken, chirring texture, like a mind ticking over very quietly and subtly and gently:

As it is necessary for all men that seek peace, to lay down certain rights of Nature; that is to say, not to have liberty to do all they list: so is it necessary for man's life, to retain some; as right to govern their own bodies; enjoy air, water, motion, ways to go from place to place; and all things else without which a man cannot live, or not live well.

The subtle fragrance of Hobbes's style depends on his ability to vary iambic decision with anapaestic and amphibrachic ease and fluidity:

× / × × / × × / × × / × / × / × ×
The heaven, the ocean, the planets, the fire, the earth, the winds, were so
/ × /
many gods.

This contrasts, to take a random example, with the overly decisive iambic rhythm of Hazlitt's

× / × / × / × / × / × / × /
These giant sons of genius stand, indeed, upon the earth,

which he has to loosen by adding

/ × / × × / × / × / × / / × × × / ×
but they tower above their fellows, and the long line of their successors
/ \ / × / / × / × × / × / × / × ×
does not interpose anything to obstruct their view, or lessen their
/ ×
brightness.

In addition to employing subtly varied prose rhythm, Hobbes has a knack of using what Priestley terms 'sensible images', as when he remarks how myopically bookish people, 'not mistrusting their first grounds, know not which way to clear themselves; but spend time in fluttering over their books; as birds that entering by the chimney, and finding themselves enclosed in a chamber, flutter at the false light of a glass window, for want of wit to consider which way they came in'. Like Hobbes, Hazlitt is committed to employing this type of tactile image, which illustrates an idea with a shrewd, quiet, concrete precision.

His most brilliant use of this device is in the essay 'On Genius and Common Sense', where he argues that genius and taste are not strictly reducible to rules: that in art, taste, life, and speech we decide from feeling, not reason. Common sense is what he terms 'tacit reason', and conscience is the same unspoken sense of right and wrong.

The source of this idea is the Roman coin passage in *Leviathan*, where Hobbes analyses unguided thoughts which wander and 'seem impertinent to one another as in a dream'. And yet, he says, in this wild ranging of the mind,

a man may oft-times perceive the way of it, and the dependence of one thought upon another. For in a discourse of our present civil war, what could seem more impertinent, than to ask (as one did) what was the value of a Roman penny? Yet the coherence to me was manifest enough. For the thought of war, introduced the thought of the delivering up the king to his enemies; the thought of that, brought in the thought of the delivering up of Christ; and that again the thought of the 30 pence, which was the price of that treason: and thence easily followed that malicious question; and all this in a moment of time; for thought is quick.

Drawing on this passage, Hazlitt argues that any impression in a series can recall any other impression in that series without running through the whole in sequence, so that the mind 'drops the inter-mediate links' and passes on with rapid stealth to the 'more striking' effects of pleasure or pain which have 'naturally taken the strongest hold of it'. And he deduces this type of instantaneous, subconscious, mnemonic short-cutting from an account he gives of the radical writer and political activist John Thelwall, who made a wandering journey through Wales after he had been imprisoned in the Tower of London for five months in 1794, then kept in the 'dead-hole' in Newgate with the corpses of those who had died of gaol fever. Thelwall was acquitted at the Treason Trials in December 1794, one of the great public events which shaped the young Hazlitt.

Thelwall left London to recover from the government's attempt on his life, and Hazlitt describes how one morning he arrived at an inn (always a favourite location for an epiphany in the essays), ordered breakfast, and sat down cheerfully at the window. Then a face passed which he took no notice of at that moment:

but when his breakfast was brought in presently after, he found his appetite for it gone – the day had lost its freshness in his eye – he was uneasy and spiritless; and without any cause that he could discover, a total change had taken place in his feelings. While he was trying to account for this odd circumstance, the same face passed again – it was the face of Taylor the spy; and he was no longer at a loss to explain the difficulty. He had before caught only a transient glimpse, a passing side-view of the face; but though this was not sufficient to awaken a distinct idea in his memory, his feelings, quicker and surer, had taken the alarm; a string had been touched that gave a jar to his whole frame, and would not let him rest, though he could not at all tell what was the matter with him. To the flitting, shadowy, half-distinguished profile that had glided by his window was linked unconsciously and mysteriously, but inseparably, the impression of the trains that had been laid for him by this person; – in this brief moment, in this dim, illegible short-hand of the mind he had just escaped the speeches of Attorney and Solicitor-General over again; the gaunt figure of Mr Pitt glared by him; the walls of a prison enclosed him; and he felt the hands of the executioner near him, without knowing it till the tremor and disorder of his nerves gave information to his reasoning faculties that all was not well within.

From this exceptionally succinct example, which he cites in his essay on genius and common sense, Hazlitt deduces that the same state of mind – a deep nervous horror – was evoked by one circumstance in the series of associations that had been produced by the whole set of circumstances at the time of Thelwall's trial. In explaining a philosophical point, he also lodges a highly significant time-spot in the historical memory and makes a political statement. The result is a sensible image – concrete and anecdotal, not abstract – which functions as a type of poem in prose, as well as an illustration of his theme.

Hazlitt also employs the principle of association to set up two important paired associations in his essays: Johnson and Goldsmith, Burke and his political disciple William Windham, a friend of Cobbett's. Johnson typifies for Hazlitt the fixed, the formal, the dead, in prose style. His moral constitution has a 'sluggish moroseness', while his style has a too measured, regular, singsong effect. It's a species of rhyming prose without discrimination or variety. Goldsmith, who is a talismanic figure for Hazlitt, is, on the other hand, angelically superior to the purblind, materially heavy Johnson 'in the fine tact, the airy, intuitive faculty with which he skimmed the surfaces of things, and unconsciously formed his opinions'. This binary linking of Johnson and Goldsmith in the essay on genius and common sense is reproduced in the contrast he draws between Claude Lorraine and Rubens, or Ben Jonson and Shakespeare. It is a contrastive means of expressing that quality of airy motion which is one of his favourite critical concepts. Thus Johnson/Goldsmith is a type of associative counter which sets in play the aesthetic difference between a cautiously conservative imagination and one which skims easily and joyously like a swallow. For Hazlitt, the imagination in general is 'an *associating* principle' which has an instinctive perception of when a thing 'belongs to a system, or is only an exception to it'.

For example, the casual mention of Windham in 'The Fight' is intended to remind us of both Burke and Cobbett, the other members of an associative system we might designate as 'Windham'. In a footnote to his *Life of Holcroft*, Hazlitt describes Windham, who was War Secretary throughout Pitt's first administration, as an imitator of Burke, but one whose whole political style was borrowed, artificial, set like plaster in a mould. The ablest speaker in the House of Commons after Sheridan, he possessed an 'infinite fund' of wit and information, but lacked force and originality. Hazlitt, who respected Windham's character and pursuits – he was a renowned pugilist – says in 'The Fight' that an old gentleman in the coach back to London looked 'very like Mr Windham'. It turns out that as a boy the old man had been to a boxing match with Windham, who is mentioned a total of three times in the closing paragraph. This is a deliberate strategy on Hazlitt's part, which works like this.

Windham knew Fox and Cobbett, as well as being a favoured friend of Samuel Johnson. As Minister for War from 1795 to 1801, he improved the efficiency of the British Army, and vigorously prosecuted the war with revolutionary France. In 1803, he said that Cobbett 'merited a statue of gold' for his polemical journalism in the United States, and invited him to dine in his house with Pitt and Canning. Earlier in 'The Fight', Hazlitt compared the English yeoman's conversation to Cobbett's prose, and, by the principle of association, he's also ghosted Burke's presence by mentioning Windham. Following the same principle, the boxing match is a symbol of warfare, as it is also, much less obviously, a violent image of political action and pamphleteering. Moreover, when Hazlitt says that the boxer Neate displayed 'none of the *petit maîtreship* of the art' – he didn't spar cautiously – he's using a term which he often employs in a literary context to characterize a mere professional competence that lacks real force and originality. For example, in his 'Character of Mr Burke' he contrasts Burke's style, which has the 'stalk of a giant', with Junius's, which is 'the strut of a *petit-maître*'.*

The boxing match is a spectacle of total immediacy – Hazlitt writes of being swallowed up in the 'immediate interest of the scene'. The fight is the literal embodiment of that crucial critical term which Hazlitt employs to capture the whap of pure presence. Like a primitive painting, like the fight itself, this study in popular culture aims to be 'a complete thing'. It is a symbolic unity which shows us the deepest sources of Hazlitt's inspiration. Where the paragraph in which he recounts Thelwall's ruined breakfast is a carefully shaped cameo moment that decisively illustrates an intellectual argument, 'The Fight' is a completely unified work with a studied, throw-away casualness that aims at a journalistic immediacy, a low-life jossing urban haste combined with the atmosphere of a Cobbett-like rural ride.

Fighting and journalism are identified in this perfectly poised moment in the letter which Cobbett wrote to his countrymen in March 1817 on his way to Liverpool to catch a boat for the United States, in order to escape government persecution. Addressing the charge that he is a coward for going into exile, Cobbett tells this anecdote:

A few years ago, being at Barnet fair, I saw a battle going on, arising out of some sudden quarrel between a butcher and the servant of a west country

---

* Junius's style is thin, balanced, correct: 'Corruption glitters in the van; – collects and maintains a standing army of mercenaries, and, at the same moment, impoverishes and enslaves the country.'

grazier. The butcher, though vastly superior in point of size, finding that he was getting the worst of it, recoiled a step or two, and *drew out his knife*. Upon the sight of this weapon, the grazier turned about and ran off till he came up to a Scotchman who was guarding his herd, and out of whose hand the former snatched a good ash stick about four feet long. Having thus got what he called *a long arm*, he returned to the combat, and in a very short time, he gave the butcher a blow upon the wrist which brought his knife to the ground. The grazier then fell to work with his stick in such a style as I never before witnessed. The butcher fell down and rolled and kicked; but, he seemed only to change his position in order to ensure to every part of his carcase a due share of the penalty of his baseness. After the grazier had, apparently, tired himself, he was coming away, when happening to cast his eye upon the *knife*, he ran back and renewed the basting, exclaiming every now and then, as he caught his breath, 'Dra thy knife *wo't!*' He came away a second time, and a second time returned and set on upon the caitiff again; and this he repeated several times, exclaiming always when he recommenced the drubbing, '*Dra thy knife wo't!*' Till, at last, the butcher was so bruised, that he was actually unable to stand, or even to get up; and yet, such, amongst Englishmen, is the abhorrence of *foul fighting*, that not a soul attempted to interfere, and nobody seemed to pity the man thus unmercifully beaten.

Applying the story, Cobbett states that it is his intention to 'imitate the conduct of this grazier; to resort to a *long arm*, and to combat Corruption, while I keep myself out of the reach of her knife'. The application is direct, immediate, and unassailable. Cobbett's readers become the onlookers approving the grazier as he punishes the butcher for his un-English cowardice and treachery, his foul fighting. It is all wonderfully matter of fact.

By contrast, the sensible images or cameos which Hazlitt introduces into his essays are often charged with intense philosophical and political significance, rather like Eliot's broken king at nightfall, though from the opposite end of the ideological spectrum. This, I think, is what he means when he tells the government critic William Gifford that at the start of his career he found a popular mode of writing 'necessary to convey subtle and difficult trains of reasoning'. Sometimes a fabular anecdote or luminously unexpected *petite histoire* of the kind that Miroslav Holub employs in his poetry will be repositioned in the cultural memory or revivified by the essayist, like this story about the first earl of Shaftesbury which concludes 'On Genius and Common Sense', the essay in which he describes Thelwall's breakfast:

He had been to dine with Lady Clarendon and her daughter, who was at that time privately married to the Duke of York (afterwards James II) and as he returned home with another nobleman who had accompanied him, he suddenly turned to him, and said: 'Depend upon it, the Duke has married Hyde's daughter.' His companion could not comprehend what he meant; but on explaining himself, he said: 'Her mother behaved to her with an attention and a marked respect that it is impossible to account for in any other way; and I am sure of it.' His conjecture shortly afterwards proved to be the truth. This was carrying the prophetic spirit of common sense as far as it could go.

A point about intuition, tact, tacit reason, or prophetic common sense is being illustrated here; but it is interesting that Hazlitt should introduce this anecdote by mentioning that the first earl of Shaftesbury was the grandfather of the author of *Characteristics*. It's a slightly odd way of placing that political genius, but it is important for Hazlitt to pair the Whig politician with an influential volume of essays in aesthetics which he significantly gives his father to read when he paints his portrait. He is setting up a system of associations which works like this.

'On the Pleasure of Painting' appears in the collection *Table-Talk* close to 'On Genius and Common Sense', the essay in which Hazlitt recounts Thelwall's inn breakfast and the first earl of Shaftesbury's realization that the duke of York had married Hyde's daughter. In the closing elegiac paragraph of the essay on painting, written in 1820, the year of his father's death, Hazlitt describes how he painted the old Dissenter's portrait:

One of my first attempts was a picture of my father, who was then in a green old age, with strong-marked features, and scarred with the smallpox. I drew it with a broad light crossing the face, looking down, with spectacles on, reading. The book was Shaftesbury's *Characteristics*, in a fine old binding, with Gribelin's etchings.

The Whig line stretches from the first earl of Shaftesbury through his close associate Locke to Locke's pupil the third earl. It includes viscount Molesworth who, during his lord-lieutenancy of Ireland, was friendly with Locke, with the third earl of Shaftesbury, and with Francis Hutcheson, and it lives on in the moment of Hazlitt writing. In effect, he's designing an iconic image which still survives in the vaults of the Maidstone Museum. This Whig line combines political action with disinterested aesthetic appreciation, and Hazlitt chooses to represent it in an account of a portrait being painted, a work in progress, or, rather, a work that was once in progress. Hazlitt's fondness for Titian's signature – *Titianus faciebat*, 'Titian was working on this' – is a way of evoking an expressive creativity that exists most fully and completely both when it is happening and, paradoxically, in the process of completion. The bloody excitement of a boxing match is another version of this creative intensity, or 'the moment, the immediate present, the Now', as Lawrence terms it.

William Hazlitt Senior, his essayist son writes, would 'as lieve' read any book other than *Characteristics*, and he adds this comment because Shaftesbury's book is another planted clue, like the mention of Windham in 'The Fight'. Shaftesbury's essays explore the concept of disinterestedness, and affirm a dynamic, sensuous appreciation of beauty. They were highly regarded by Viscount Molesworth's Dublin circle, to which Francis Hutcheson belonged, and they also influenced Priestley.

This is the Whig Unitarian line that Hazlitt is elegizing in *Table-Talk*'s opening essay on the pleasure of painting, and in another associative plant in the same paragraph he concludes by saying:

I think, but am not sure, that I finished this portrait (or another afterwards) on the same day that the news of the Battle of Austerlitz came; I walked out in the afternoon, and, as I returned, saw the evening star set over a poor man's cottage with other thoughts and feelings than I shall ever have again.

So he affirms his hero Napoleon victorious, before moving to the essay's emotional conclusion:

Oh for the revolution of the great Platonic year, that those times might come over again. I could sleep out the three hundred and sixty-five thousand intervening years very contentedly! – The picture is left: the table, the chair, the window where I learned to construe Livy, the chapel where my father preached, remain where they were; but he himself is gone to rest, full of years, of faith, of hope, and charity!

This is an exultant confrontation with the defeat of Hazlitt's dearest hopes, and it draws together Whig aesthetics, his radical father, the art of painting, and recent European history into one final exclamatory composite which could have been part of a sermon, a sermon his dear father would have liked him to write, instead of painting like 'Rembrandt or like Raphael'. It's a triumphant elegy for the devout Unitarian minister and his culture, an elegy whose theme and aim are inspiration. As Chistopher Salvesen has shown, the composite event – star, battle, cottage, father reading – is what Hazlitt elsewhere calls a 'standing resource', a permanent impression or Wordsworthian spot of time.

As Salvesen also notes, the Christian pastoral overtones of the star above the manger symbolize the promise of better things, but I think the image also condenses other meanings, because it alludes to Portia's speech in *The Merchant of Venice*: 'If to do were as easy as to know what were good to do, chapels had been churches, and poor men's cottages princes' palaces.' Remembering the winter of 1805 and the defeat of Napoleon ten years later, Hazlitt layers his wish that poor men's cottages might become palaces with the recognition that just as his father's small chapel never became a large church – just as his ideals were never realized – so the cottage remained unchanged. And in an earlier use of the cottage trope in a letter to the *Morning Chronicle*, he joins it to a slightly adapted quotation from Wordsworth's 'Immortality Ode' to express the radiance of that moment and the enduring reverence for the feeling of hope it inspired in him:

He who has seen the evening star set over a poor man's cottage, or has connected the feeling of hope with the heart of man, and who, though he may have lost the feeling, has never ceased to reverence it – he, Sir, with submission, and without a nickname, is the *true Jacobin*.

> What though radiance which was once so bright,
> But now for ever taken from his sight.

Though nothing ever can bring back the hour
Of splendour in the grass, of glory in the flower;
He does not grieve, but rather find
Strength in what remains behind,
In the primeval sympathy,
Which having been must ever be;
In the soothing thoughts that spring
Out of human suffering;
In years that bring the philosophic mind.

Hazlitt is writing in January 1814, shortly after Napoleon's abdication, and he is recalling his elation, nine years earlier, at the news of Austerlitz. By quoting Wordsworth, he emphasizes the visionary permanence of the moment, its crucial significance in the growth of his own mind.

The problem with journalism is that, by its very nature, it's occasional, not permanent in the manner that poetry such as Wordsworth's aspires to be. To overcome this problem, and to redress his own sense of inferiority as a writer, Hazlitt, as we have seen, identifies prose with the active human body. Thus the Irish racket-player Cavanagh, whom he celebrates in an elegy appended to 'The Indian Jugglers', is a symbol of polemical prose in action: 'Cobbett and Junius together would have made a Cavanagh.' Like painting, racket-playing is presented as an activity that is superior to the act of writing, because it is not a sedentary employment. Painting requires 'not indeed a strong, but a continued and steady exertion of muscular power'. The precision and delicacy of the manual operation, Hazlitt says, makes up for the want of 'vehemence', just as the rope-dancer must strain 'every nerve' to balance himself. This resembles the 'sensual and practical' part of the painter's art, and he wants it to belong to our experience of reading prose. The body, its physical motion, its glow and shapeliness, has a gusto and an enjoyment of itself, but is also subject to decomposition. Locke's prose style decomposes and crumbles, as do the bodies mentioned in the man-is-a-bubble paragraph from Taylor's *Holy Dying* – isn't all prose transient and subject to decay? Political journalism, which is glued to the bubble reputations of transient politicians; literary journalism, which similarly follows charismatic ephemera; drama criticism, which addresses last night's melted spectacle – all these prose forms are bound to disappear, surely? Prose as a medium – not just Locke's crumbly style of writing – actively 'decomposes', because its critical function is to break up set ideas. Where poetry equals 'composition', prose is identified with 'decomposition' in the lecture 'On the Living Poets'. It is as though prose is doomed never to achieve lasting form because, by its very nature, it is iconoclastic. It is a destructive element.

Hazlitt identifies poetry with composition in his discussion of the living poets, shortly after a passage in which he praises the Unitarian writer Anna Laetitia Barbauld, whose stories he had known since early childhood (later, as a schoolboy, he read her poems in Enfield's anthology *The Speaker*, which was a standard textbook in Dissenting academies). He also at this point calls Joanna Baillie a 'Unitarian in poetry', before balancing his apparently partial praise of Dissenting writers with an attack on the Unitarian banker Samuel Rogers's 'elegant, but feeble' poetry. In a particularly vehement expression of the style-as-body metaphor, he characterizes Rogers's verse as 'tortuous, tottering, wriggling' – that is, as a kind of maggot-dance. Thomas Campbell's volume *The Pleasures of Hope* is then aligned with Rogers's work, and criticized for substituting the 'decomposition' of prose for the 'composition' of poetry.

But the subject is more complex than this. Discussing the act of writing prose in an important passage in 'Whether Genius is Conscious of its Powers?', Hazlitt insists that the act of writing is like being intoxicated:

While we are engaged in any work, we are thinking of the subject, and cannot stop to admire ourselves; and when it is done, we look at it with comparative indifference. I will venture to say that no one but a pedant ever read his own works regularly through. They are not *his* – they are become mere words, waste-paper, and have none of the glow, the creative enthusiasm, the vehemence, and natural spirit with which he wrote them. When we have once committed our thoughts to paper, written them fairly out, and seen that they are right in the printing, if we are in our right wits, we have done with them for ever. I sometimes try to read an article I have written in some magazine or review – (for when they are bound up in a volume, I dread the very sight of them) – but stop after a sentence or two, and never recur to the task. . . . I do not think that even painters have much delight in looking at their works after they are done. While they are in progress, there is a great degree of satisfaction in considering what has been done, or what is still to do – but this is hope, is reverie, and ceases with the completion of our efforts.

And he goes on to mention Titian's signature – *Titianus faciebat* – which implied that his works 'were imperfect', even though he was the greatest portrait painter the world has ever seen. A parallel here might be with action painting: the prose-writer is inside his medium, ever in motion, like Hutcheson's vision of children playing. Once he or she steps out of that creative process, it chills into a series of fixed letters, because it no longer possesses the 'vehemence' with which it was composed.

This intense concept of prose writing is developed in an answering passage in 'On Application to Study', in which Hazlitt first explains how thoughts are worked up into a state of projection in prose composition and then rebuts the argument that 'rapidity of execution necessarily implies slovenliness or crudeness'. On the contrary, writing prose in a rush makes for 'sharpness and freedom'. Though there is less formal method, there is more life, spirit, truth: 'In the play and agitation of the mind, it runs over, and we dally with the subject, as the glass-blower rapidly shapes the vitreous fluid.' This is another version of his favourite bubble image, and he underlines the connection when he says that proper expressions rise spontaneously 'to the surface from the heat and fermentation of the mind, like bubbles on an agitated stream'. Like the poor man's cottage, this is a pastoral image, and one which is a version of Milton's development of the biblical comparison of truth to a 'streaming fountain' in *Areopagitica*: 'if her waters flow not in a perpetual progression, they sicken into a muddy pool of conformity and tradition.' And in his pamphlet Milton similarly uses an image of a hot, busy workshop to express the formation of new ideas:

Behold now this vast city; a city of refuge, the mansion-house of liberty, encompassed and surrounded with his protection; the shop of war hath not there more anvils and hammers waking to fashion out the plates and instruments of armed justice in defence of beleaguered Truth than there be pens and heads there, sitting by their studious lamps, musing, searching, revolving new notions and ideas wherewith to present, as with their homage and their fealty, the approaching Reformation; others as fast reading, trying all things, assenting to the force of reason and convincement.

Hazlitt's image of molten glass and bubbling water are his equivalent of the various hymns to motion and rapid action in Hutcheson's philosophy. Sophisticated skills and urban technology are implicit in the glass-blower's molten swelling bubble. The patient concentration of a workman, who wears a protective mask with a glass visor as he blows through a thin metal pipe that looks like an elongated flute which he twists and turns, is a naturally pregnant symbol of the *engagé* journalist writing vehement prose to a deadline. But we must now consider why Hazlitt should wish to invent such an image for the process of prose composition.

CHAPTER FOUR

Sheer Plod: Whig Prose

Hazlitt's description of the vehemence of prose composition and his comparison of journalism to the manufacture of glass are two of his most sustained accounts of his chosen art-form. But is it an art-form? Can the perishable medium of prose achieve composition? Or is the prose-writer not condemned to work in a medium which reeks of decomposition? Aren't such writers just plodders forcing themselves over the flatlands? They may stick to their principles like Godwin, Bentham, and, he implies, himself, but this means that they're committed to a long march that often feels tedious and unending. Poets, by contrast, are fickle meddlers who aren't tied down and who can change their opinions.

The poet and the prose-writer are exact opposites, as William Shenstone argues in a passage which haunted Hazlitt:

As for politics ... I think *poets* are *Tories* by nature, supposing them to be by nature poets. The love of an individual person or family, that has worn a crown for many successions, is an inclination greatly adapted to the fanciful tribe. On the other hand, mathematicians, abstract reasoners, of no manner of attachment to persons, at least to the *visible* part of them, but prodigiously devoted to the ideas of virtue, liberty, and so forth, are generally *Whigs*. It happens agreeably enough to this maxim, that the Whigs are friends to that wise, plodding, unpoetical people the Dutch.

Hazlitt quotes this passage from one of Shenstone's letters in his essay 'On Paradox and Common-Place'. It lies behind his famous distinction in the essay on *Coriolanus* between the imagination, which he defines as royalist, and the understanding, which he calls republican. Shenstone's ambivalent adjective 'plodding' is one which Hazlitt significantly applies to Locke, and the section of

Shenstone's letter which he omits does not give any comfort to the radical prose-writer:

The Tories, on the other hand, are taken mightily with that shewy, ostentatious nation the French. Foxhunters, that reside amongst the beauties of nature, and bid defiance to art, in short, that have intellects of a poetical *turn*, are frequently Tories; citizens, merchants, &c. that scarce see what nature is, and consequently have no pretensions to a poetical taste, are, I think, generally argumentative and Whiggish.

Hazlitt's prose, then, is 'argumentative and Whiggish', an instrument of civic virtue that can never be poetic, and which can be aligned with the shaping force of mercantile endeavour and political commitment in Defoe's prose. When Hazlitt applies the adjective 'plodding' to Locke – 'the real plodding strength of his mind' – the words either side of it stretch it into a complex term which encompasses both a slow, negative dullness and a positive identification with those bourgeois Whig values; similarly, Shenstone gives the same adjective a lift when he refers to the Dutch as 'wise'.

Hazlitt's sense of inferiority as a prose-writer emerges in his lecture 'On Poetry in General', where he speaks of the 'jerks, the breaks, the inequalities, and harshnesses of prose', which destroy the flow of the poetic imagination, as 'a jolting road or a stumbling horse disturbs the reverie of an absent man'. He is saying that there is something gauche, thrawn, lumpish, dissonant – even downright annoying – about prose; but at the same time he's relishing the fricatives that insist on the roughness of prose as a medium, and he's also introducing a vehement and eruptive moment to compensate for the abstract language of the sentence which precedes it. But if prose and plodding are linked, Hazlitt is capable of giving significant twists to both words when he uses them as critical terms elsewhere.

In his essay 'On the Knowledge of Character' he comments on the French people's 'everlasting prosing tragedy', notes that the English are considered as being by comparison 'a slow, plodding people', but then goes on to suggest that while the French may be 'quicker', they are also more plodding. Here, the term is negative, though when he praises Jonathan Edwards, the New England philosopher and divine, for the 'plodding, persevering, scrupulous accuracy' of his prose style, and then contrasts it with Priestley's 'easy, cavalier, verbal fluency', the term is given a positive force. It would seem that, like Hopkins in 'The Windhover', he must enlist 'sheer plod' as an important prose virtue. And Hopkins believed that written – written as opposed to conversational – prose had its own 'belonging technic' and 'proper eloquence'. He believed that prose was 'a positive thing', not simply the absence of verse forms, and that it had potentially more beautiful effects than verse. And we can find scattered in his notebooks and letters the materials for an aesthetic of prose style which insist on its autarkic nature, its sophistication and absolute otherness.

But this sense that prose is essentially boring and limited emerges in Hazlitt's remark that Bentham had struck 'the whole mass of fancy, prejudice, passion, sense, whim, with his petrific, leaden mace, that he had "bound volatile Hermes", and reduced the theory and practice of human life to a *caput mortuum* of reason, and dull, plodding, technical calculation'. This is scarcely a recognition of the plodding virtues. Quoting the lines from *Paradise Lost* in which philosophers bind volatile Hermes by their 'powerful art', Hazlitt combines them with the phrase 'petrific mace' from a passage in which Death smites the 'aggregated soil' with his mace 'petrific, cold and dry'. He also applies the word 'petrific' to Crabbe, who is said to wield a 'petrific pencil', and is therefore less poet than prose-writer. In an early philosophical essay, he describes Locke as a plagiarist who staggered under Hobbes's 'petrific mace'. Deep in Hazlitt's critical imagination there appears to be an associative cluster – *plodding petrific prose Locke English Dutch decomposition* – which makes the element of prose look very like the flat aggregated soil of hell or the level plains of the Dutch state (Crabbe is associated with 'Dutch interiors, hovels, and pig-styes'). Applied to Hobbes, this means that within Hazlitt's admiration for the philosophy and the prose style are a reserve, a scepticism, a perhaps subconscious resistance to its empirical epistemology that is clarified by the source in Milton of the 'petrific' and the manner in which Hazlitt attaches it to Crabbe and Bentham.

When we examine the associations which gather round the adjective, we can see that this cluster carries real pain for Hazlitt, and that he's desperate to break out of its deadening clutches. But how can he? His medium is prose, only prose, and with every sentence he writes, the mace's stony shadow strengthens its hold on him. He feels trapped, subdued to what he works in, and anguished by the knowledge that prose can never receive the esteem and adulation that poetry attracts.

His solution to this dilemma is brilliantly intertextual, because 'petrific mace' is both a quotation from *Paradise Lost* and a borrowing from another text which Hazlitt knew in the same detail as he knew Milton's complete works – Burke's *Reflections on the Revolution in France*. There Burke attacks the politician Jean-Sylvain Bailly for a speech he made in the National Assembly praising the inhabitants of Paris. But Bailly, Burke says, 'will sooner thaw the eternal ice of his Atlantic regions, than restore the central heat to Paris, whilst it remains "smitten with the cold, dry, petrific mace" of a false and unfeeling philosophy'.

As Hazlitt employs Burke's Miltonic phrase, it applies both to Bentham's utilitarianism and more widely to French philosophy – the work of Condillac and Helvétius, for example – which he strongly disagreed with because it grounded knowledge in sensation, not understanding. And because the petrific mace combines both Milton and Burke, it joins what he calls the 'rich, impetuous high-wrought imagination of Burke' with a technique he especially admires in Milton – a technique of multiple quotation that inspires his own critical method.

In 'Shakespeare and Milton' he ringingly asserts that

Milton has borrowed more than any other writer, and exhausted every source of imitation, sacred or profane; yet he is perfectly distinct from every other writer. He is a writer of centos, and yet in originality scarcely inferior to Homer. The power of his mind is stamped on every line. The fervour of his imagination melts down and renders malleable, as in a furnace, the most contradictory materials.

Where the petrific mace freezes and kills, Milton's imagination

94

melts his many different sources into a new malleable material –
metal in this symbolic figure, not glass. His learning has 'the effect
of intuition', his imagination 'the force of nature'. And this is more
than a type of belle-lettrist rhetoric, for it also describes the critical
process as Hazlitt practises it: the critic is a creative artist who
assembles rapidly and intensely a prose argument which draws into
its molten flux quotations, single allusions, and multiple or layered
or intertextual allusions like Burke's Miltonic mace. Here he is also
following Burke, who, like a truly cultivated eighteenth-century
gentleman, has a genius for quoting the canonical authors. The
furnace image, as we've seen, is also one which Hazlitt uses to
describe the reviewer's art when he compares it to Cellini's dramatic
account of how he melted down all the metal objects in his house to
cast his statue of Perseus.

In Hazlitt's particular type of critical prose – a prose that's a
version of Milton's poetic centos – there is a redemptive life, a new
quickening spirit which melts down or decomposes quotations,
sources, and subjects in order to recompose. Anyone who practises
literary journalism, with its rapid, heated bursts of energetically
assembled quotations, interpretative paraphrase, and related commentary all funnelling towards a deadline and pressured by the
social moment – anyone who practises that driven art must recognize that the related images of furnace, cento, new-minted coins,
and Homeric originality are a means of both praising Milton and
drawing attention to critical writing as it is practised by the supreme
master of the reviewer's art. The assonantal keeping* of *centos
originality Homer* makes the point about quotation as a form of
creativity by melding those words together, then reflecting that
composite sound in the strong 't' sounds in the two sentences that
follow. This acoustic patterning expressively renders the direct,
emphatic inspiration which Hazlitt draws from Milton.

* 'Keeping' is one of Hazlitt's favourite critical terms. It derives from painting, and
refers to the 'proper subserviency of tone and colour in every part of a picture, so that
the general effect is harmonious to the eye'. Applied to poetry or prose, it means
'agreement, congruity, harmony'. Hazlitt was the first to use it as a term in literary
criticism, and his application of the term to Blifil's character in his discussion of *Tom
Jones* (H VI. 113) is cited in the *OED*.

But if he seeks to give purpose and dignity to critical practice by linking it to the epic imagination and to Cellini in his workshop, he also wants to identify it with Shakespeare's dramatic imagination, which differs, he argues earlier in the same lecture, from the type of imagination that Chaucer possessed. Chaucer shows us a 'fixed essence of character', while in Shakespeare there is a 'continual composition and decomposition of its elements, a fermentation of every particle in the whole mass'. Every particle – there is a Priestleyan experimental observation at work here – ferments through its 'alternate affinity or antipathy to other principles' which are brought into contact with it. Hopkins also uses the term 'decomposition', noting that the 'savagery' of Whitman's verse resembles his own poetic rhythm in its 'last ruggedness and decomposition into common prose'.

The painter Northcote, in *Conversations with James Northcote*, picks up Hazlitt's chemical terminology when he remarks on 'a chaos of elementary particles'. And in an echo of Priestley's argument that matter is not '*inert*' because '*powers of attraction* or *repulsion*' are necessary to its very being, Hazlitt in his account of Shakespeare adds that until the experiment is tried, we do not know the result, 'the turn which the character will take in its new circumstances'. Prose as a decomposing medium is implicitly identified with Shakespeare's drama here, because reviewing and the theatre – most especially theatre reviewing – are totally social arts that happen in the moment. Shakespeare is therefore characterized as a completely social being who 'mingled with the crowd, and played the host, "to make society the sweeter welcome" '. The effect of these implicitly self-reflexive comparisons to Shakespeare and Milton is to give Hazlitt's critical prose a form of autonomy. Just as we read, say, Eliot's literary criticism for the access it gives us to his poetic imagination, so we must read Hazlitt's prose as if it is the work of a creative writer – Hazlitt on Milton is also Hazlitt on Hazlitt.

What Hazlitt is searching for is a means of giving prose an embodied natural grace and beauty, so when he compares racket playing (at which he excelled) to prose writing, he rather disingenuously admits to having a much greater ambition to be the best racket-player than the 'best prose-writer of the age'. This remark links with his references to the body in the same essay, 'On the Qualifications Necessary to Success in Life', where he praises and delights in the physical accomplishments of the body, defining a constitutional talent as the 'warmth and vigour' imparted to someone's ideas and pursuits by their 'bodily stamina, by mere physical organization'. We can feel his prose tendons stretch when he remarks:

Let a man have a quick circulation, a good digestion, the bulk, and thews, and sinews of a man, and the alacrity, the unthinking confidence inspired by these; and without an atom, a shadow of the *mens divinior*, he shall strut and swagger and vapour and jostle his way through life, and have the upper hand of those who are his betters in everything but health and strength.

This sentence exults, slightly too emphatically, in the manly physical constitution it seeks literally to embody, and it's just one among many examples of the rude good health he wants his prose to possess.

The Whig exception to this, though he does not say so here, is the first earl of Shaftesbury, whose puny, diseased body is shaken and transcended by his political passions. Hazlitt is fond of quoting Dryden's lines on Shaftesbury:

> A fiery soul, which, working out its way,
> Fretted the pigmy-body to decay,
> And o'er inform'd the tenement of clay.
> A daring pilot in extremity;
> Pleas'd with the danger, when the waves went high
> He sought the storms; but for a calm unfit,
> Would steer too nigh the sands to boast his wit.

He quotes these lines because they express with a dramatic and disinterested bounce those argumentative Whig values of restlessness, magnanimity, quickness, buoyancy of feeling, daring. These are values which he also associates with Jeffrey, the editor of the *Edinburgh Review*, and with Godwin, who is characterized in *The Spirit of the Age* as 'the bold and adventurous pilot, who dared us to tempt the uncertain abyss'. Jeffrey is a critic whose pen 'is never at a loss, never stands still, and would dazzle for this reason alone, like an eye that is ever in motion'.

How perfectly that image of the moving eye communicates the value of 'motion', an aesthetic term that is as significant as 'nature' for him. It is profoundly rooted in Hazlitt's imagination, and appears, for example, in a definition of 'grace' as 'the natural movements of the human body, heightened into dignity, or softened into ease, each posture or step blending harmoniously into the rest'. There is grace in the waving of a tree and in the bounding of a stag, because there is 'freedom and unity of motion'.

This passage from *Notes of a Journey through France and Italy* arises directly out of a remark Hazlitt makes in a footnote a few pages earlier, where he expresses the wish that French sculptors would come to London and look at the Elgin Marbles. The footnote reads like an extemporized addition to the main text, and it contains Hazlitt's solution to the petrific pen, that stultifying symbol in whose shadow, he suggests elsewhere, prose-writers are caught. Praising the Parthenon sculptures, he says there is

a flexibility and sway of the limbs and of the whole body. The flesh has the softness and texture of flesh, not the smoothness or stiffness of stone. There is an undulation and a liquid flow on the surface, as the breath of genius moved the mighty mass: they are the finest forms in the most striking attitudes, and with everything in its place, proportion, and degree, uniting the ease, truth, force, and delicacy of Nature. They show nothing but the artist's thorough comprehension of, and entire docility to that great teacher. There is no *petit-maîtreship*, no pedantry, no attempt at a display of science, or at forcing the parts into an artificial symmetry, but it is like cutting a human body out of a block of marble, and leaving it to act for itself with all the same springs, levers, and internal machinery. It was said of Shakespeare's dramas, that they were the *logic of passion*; and it may be affirmed of the Elgin Marbles, that they are the *logic of form*. – One part being given, another cannot be otherwise than it is. There is a mutual understanding and reaction throughout the whole frame. The Apollo and other antiques are not equally simple and severe. The limbs have too much an appearance of being cased in marble, of making a display of every recondite beauty, and of balancing and answering to one another, like the rhymes in verse. The Elgin Marbles are harmonious, flowing, varied prose.

This is the central, sudden, critical epiphany, because here a petri-fied substance – marble – has been made to flow by the sculptor's art, a process emphasized by the repeated 'o' sounds. His chisel, a tool which is analogous to Hazlitt's pen or to the blowing iron used by glass-makers, challenges the deathly authority of the petrific mace. By identifying other classical sculptures with rhyming verse, and then comparing harmoniously varied prose to the aesthetic illusion in the Elgin Marbles of flowing stone, liquid stone, Hazlitt has let his own prose run free, and has united classical form with nature. Melting into and out of the Parthenon frieze, he has asserted the unique dignity of his chosen art, prose.

We can see this identification with the sculptor's art in a late essay on Flaxman's *Lectures on Sculpture*, in which he again praises the figure of Theseus, calling it 'the perfection of style', and then explains the term by saying that as poets and engravers used a '*stylos*, or style' to execute their works, the name of the instrument was metaphorically transferred to the art itself. Style properly means 'the mode of representing nature' – it's essential that he introduces the crucial term 'nature' at this point – and this identification of nature and sculpture is also present in the very apposite remark elsewhere that Thomson paints in colours which seem 'yet wet and breathing, like those of the living statue in *The Winter's Tale*'.

In his essay on Flaxman, he then mentions how his first sight of the Elgin Marbles forced him to revise his opinion of other classical sculptures which, until that moment, he'd thought entirely perfect. Now he recognized a new principle at work: 'a principle of fusion, of motion, so that the marble flows like a wave'. Instead of being perfect forms composed of exquisite parts which answer to models of themselves in the artist's mind, the whole is 'melted into one impression like wax'. In the fragment of Theseus, there is all the 'flexibility, the malleableness of flesh'. The idea of a miraculous transformation into living flesh, as in Shakespeare's statue scene, informs this statement.

The Elgin Marbles caused a sensation in London when they were made accessible to selected visitors starting in the summer of 1807. Mrs Siddons was reported to have been moved to tears; the painter

Benjamin West spent hours sketching the marbles; and Hazlitt's friend Benjamin Haydon said he felt as if a 'divine truth' had blazed upon his mind, and knew that they would at last 'rouse the art of Europe from its slumber of darkness'. Keats and Hazlitt, who both appear in Haydon's painting *Christ Entering Jerusalem*, were similarly inspired by these masterpieces of classical civic republicanism, sculptures which were regarded as a decisively beautiful challenge to the gothic imagination of Europe and to monarchist art.

Hazlitt wrote two short pieces on the Elgin Marbles for the *Examiner* in June 1816, the year they were moved from Burlington House to the British Museum. Six years later he published two substantial essays on them in the *London Magazine*, discussed them again in the footnote on flowing varied prose in *Notes of a Journey*, and analysed them further in his 1829 review of Flaxman's lectures.

In that review he discusses the reclining figure now identified as Dionysus or Herakles, but who was misidentified as Theseus at the time, and says that instead of a block of marble there is the internal machinery of nerves and muscles, so that there can be felt 'every the slightest pressure or motion from one extremity to the other'. This, he argues, is 'the greatest grandeur of style', because the idea of the whole has the greatest simplicity, with no ostentation, no stiffness. It combines the greatest power with the greatest ease; there is the 'perfection of knowledge' along with the total absence of a conscious display of that knowledge.

At various moments from 1816 onwards, Hazlitt praises the Marbles' undulation and liquid flow, their 'negligent grandeur'. Despite their enormous weight and 'manly strength, they have the buoyancy of a wave of the sea, with all the ease and softness of flesh'. They are not vapid abstractions, but forms that profess to imitate 'the entire, undoubted, concrete object', a phrase whose crisp dentals resonate like the passage about Milton's centos, and give incontrovertible body to the statement. The sculptures are like casts of the finest, living forms in the world 'taken in momentary action'. By being put on public display, the Marbles are associated with the Louvre for Hazlitt, and in the first *Examiner* article, written the year after Napoleon's defeat, he says that in the Gallery of the Louvre, 'Art lifted up her head and was seated on her throne, and said, All eyes shall see me, all knees shall bow to me . . . The crown she wore was brighter than that of kings.' It's as if, for a fantasy moment, the Marbles in the British Museum have been transported to France under Napoleon, so that they embody the triumph of the Enlightenment struggle against monarchy and gothicism. Again, his poignant, ecstatic prose seems to become one with Greek sculpture.

When he says in 'The Prose Style of Poets' that every word should be 'a blow' and grapple with its fellow, his concept of an indented, rigorously assonantal style is implicitly underpinned by the lapiths and centaurs locked in combat on the Parthenon friezes. Prose is like an undulating series of fighting bodies; it is motion in the moment, a series of breaks, jerks, inequalities. By contrast, bland prose, like Addison's, fails to 'project' from the surface. In this way, Hazlitt elevates and dignifies critical prose writing by identifying it with the external pulsing skin of the great temple to art and civic life. Prose is therefore a type of ideal classical form which combines the permanence of character with action and expression. What he's celebrating is a continuously moving force that should never become static or stand still. Prose must have bustle, energy, momentum, vehemence, boldness, texture, and force, but with ease and grace and natural freshness.

These are all obsessive critical terms for Hazlitt, and so are 'communication', 'immediate', 'flexible', 'expression' – qualities he also finds in the Elgin Marbles. They prompt him to make a significant comparison when he remarks that Burke's writings have 'something Pindaric' in them. Explaining how grace in writing relates to the transitions which are made from one subject to another, he remarks that transitions must in general be 'gradual and pieced together'. But sometimes, when the mind is 'fairly tired out and exhausted with a subject', the most violent transitions are 'the most graceful'. In this way he dignifies prose abruptness by identifying it with classical form and classical poetry.

He wants his readers to make the connection with his own prose, yet the image of prose as a frieze around the temple – critical commentary as encasing great art – is rather less seamlessly perfect than at first appears. We read Hazlitt on the Parthenon frieze, admire the 'living moving body' of his writing, and imagine the ideal sculptures to which it refers. Yet to contemplate the Marbles in the British Museum is to realize that Hazlitt's prose identifies itself with a series of damaged and eroded objects that have survived by luck and accident, are seriously incomplete, and have been battered by two and a half millennia of weather and history.

The Parthenon Marbles were badly damaged in 1687 when a gunpowder store placed in the Parthenon by the occupying Turkish garrison was hit by a shell fired by a besieging army. When the Turks later recaptured the Acropolis, the Parthenon was a ruin. Lime-burners, stone-robbers, tourists helped to further destroy or scatter the fragments. What the visitor to the Duveen Gallery in the British Museum sees is a combination of flowing classical perfection – billowing cloaks, flickering horses' manes, tossing heads, bodies in action, all kinds of crinkly active detail and flying shapes – with an effect that appears unfinished, provisional, decomposed, flawed, and confused, like a series of unfinished sketches in stone. As Hazlitt remarks, they are more impressive because of their 'mouldering, imperfect state'. We are forced to imagine how they might have appeared originally, then to try and appreciate a composition which is in actual material terms decomposed and fractured. There are uniquely graceful transitions on the metopes, for sure, but there are also violent, jagged breaks that Hazlitt must have identified with Burke's prose. So the friezes and the sculptures are both classical forms and a type of gothic ruin. Brighter than the crown of kings they certainly are; but they also embody war, defeat, and failure. Here perfect bodies jostle with imperfect bodies; here the ideally pure and the impurely actual are eternally entangled. Classical Greece and post-Napoleonic Europe are thrown together in a series of fighting marble figures that were shaken and broken by actual modern battles. No wonder Hazlitt identified them with Napoleon's Louvre, because just as he illustrates the power of Burke's prose by paradoxically quoting Milton's republican account of creation, so here he cannot disentangle the classical from the gothic, the ideally perfect from the historically ruined, or what his friend Keats in one of his sonnets on the Marbles terms the mixture of 'Grecian grandeur with the rude / Wasting of old Time'.

Strictly, the statues and frieze figures appear to be unfinished – damage and weather have undone their perfection. This would have been important to Hazlitt, because he shared with his friend the painter Northcote an admiration for works which appear to be still in process. Interestingly, this point is picked up by Ruskin thirty years later in his famous account of the nature of gothic architecture, when he adds a footnote on the Marbles to the sentence in which he asserts that only bad work can be perfect: 'In the most important portions they indeed approach perfection, but only there. The draperies are unfinished, the hair and wool of the animals are unfinished, and the entire bas-reliefs of the frieze are roughly cut.'

Whether Ruskin was thinking of Hazlitt, I am not sure, but it's interesting that he adduces glass blowing, one of Hazlitt's figures for prose composition, a few pages earlier, arguing that Venetian glass is beautiful in part because we never see 'the same form in it twice'. Ruskin knew Hazlitt's art criticism, and was probably more influenced by him and more in dialogue with him than his few slighting, inaccurate references suggest. He was also friendly with Northcote, knew the *Conversations*, and would have read the passage in which Northcote says that stray, unfinished sketches by Reynolds are now more sought after than ever. Those imperfect hints and studies

seem to bring one more in contact with the artist, and explain the process of his mind in the several stages. A finished work is, in a manner, detached from and independent of its author, like a child that can go alone: in the other case, it seems to be still in progress, and to await his hand to finish it; or we supply the absence of well-known excellences out of our own imagination, so that we have a two-fold property in it.

This idea of a 'two-fold property' in many ways describes how Hazlitt re-creates Theseus sitting 'in form like a demi-god, basking on a golden cloud'. But the actual reclining statue is a handless, footless, scarred, pitted figure with a damaged nose who looks helpless and vulnerable, so we may deduce from this early, random, almost postmodern conjunction that Hazlitt is implicitly arguing that prose, unlike verse or drama, must carry – and even seek out – the burden of history and discontinuous actuality. Like war, weather, and the action of acid, prose is a decomposing critical medium as well as a form that resembles liquid marble.

The weathered figure of Theseus is thrown back rather like a boxer reclining on an animal skin. Interestingly, Hazlitt published 'The Fight' in the same month – February 1822 – as the first of his paired essays on the Marbles, and when he compares the boxer Hickman to Diomed, and his opponent Neate to a 'modern Ajax', he must have associated them with the Parthenon frieze. Hickman is 'light, vigorous, elastic', and as he moves about, his back glistens in the sun 'like a panther's hide' – again, there may be a reminiscence of the animal skin in the statue of Theseus here. The semi-naked boxers easily assume classical form, and they do so because Hazlitt intends them to act as natural symbols for polemical prose writing, in which every word should be a blow.

The associative bridge with polemic is signalled by the inn conversation with the tall English yeoman earlier in 'The Fight'. The yeoman has 'a hearty body and a joyous mind', and talks 'just as well' as Cobbett writes. And Cobbett, we remember from Hazlitt's often reprinted sketch of the master, is like a pugilist who possesses 'absolute intuition'. Samuel Johnson, though he is a costive prose stylist, becomes a 'thorough prize-fighter' when he talks – a solid patriotism and populism are invested in this comparison.

In 'The Fight', Hazlitt intends his readers to activate the reference to Cobbett's style, and to see the two boxers as living symbols of vehement prose in action. The whole of Cobbett's writing bears down on this celebration of English values; the yeoman he meets in the inn is 'free-spoken, frank, convivial – one of that true English breed that went with Harry the Fifth to the siege of Harfleur – "standing like greyhounds in the slips" '. What we can discern here is a complex of associations: Shakespearean patriotism, classical figures, forms of political and imaginative writing, the active glistening male body, the highly cultured politician Windham, who was also famous for his love of boxing. This associative complex aims to create a symbolic unity that takes the ephemeral, jobbing nature of journalistic or conscientious, expository prose on to a different level of refinement. An essay or review bursts into print, stirs up interest and excitement, then is suddenly over like a boxing match. Prose needs to represent the swell, the stretch, the imprint of the moment. Every word should strike like a fist, while continuous prose should have a flexible crinkling sweep like muscular action as it's represented in the Marbles.

'Let anyone', Hazlitt says,

> look at the leg of the Ilissos or River-God, which is bent under him – let him observe the swell and undulation of the calf, the intertexture of the muscles, the distinction and union of all the parts, and the effect of action every-where impressed on the external form, as if the very marble were a flexible substance, and contained the various springs of life and motion within itself, and he will own that art and nature are here the same thing.

Sinuous like the name Ilissos, prose is like a cat's paw of wind blowing over water; it is perfect expressive motion, but it also has a concrete embodiment in newspapers and journals which come and go, before it's later excerpted and collected in books of essays which can never – and *should* never – escape the random and accidental. To read about Indian jugglers, Kean playing Shylock, Hogarth's prints, Wordsworth's latest volume, is to encounter a random assortment of subjects. What connects and creates them is their prose medium. Hazlitt is both sculptor and hack, a Phidias driven by self-disgust and the knowledge that his chosen medium, prose, is common or garden. After all, every member of the reading public can, and often does, write prose. It's an impermanent, discardable medium; writing it and at the same time wishing it could stay in the cultural memory is like trying to bequeath snow sculptures.

The solution is to figure prose as Ilissos 'floating in his proper element . . . firm as a rock, as pliable as a wave of the sea'. The artist's breath may be said to mould and play upon the 'undulating surface'. The whole is expanded into noble proportions, and heaves 'with general effect'. What then?, Hazlitt asks. Are the parts 'unfinished', or are they 'not there'? No, he replies, they are there

THE DAY-STAR OF LIBERTY

with the 'nicest exactness', but in due subordination. That is, they exist as they are 'found in fine nature', and float upon the general form 'like straw or weeds upon the tide of ocean'. But the crucial image for Hazlitt is the figure of Ilissos, which represents a stream that has its source on Mount Hymettus – famous for its honey and marble – and descends through the stony plain of Attica past Athens on the south. It is mentioned in Plato's *Phaedrus*, where Socrates suggests walking along the Ilissos, and Phaedrus says it will be easy to wade in the stream, 'which is especially delightful at this hour of a summer's day'. This sense of relaxed pleasure shapes Hazlitt's treatment of Ilissos.

But he knew that the figure of Ilissos is unfinished in the sense that the twisting body has damaged limbs and no head. His prose has completed and perfected it. This is one of the functions of critical prose: it re-creates, re-imagines, goes beyond the boundaries of the aesthetic given. So the beautiful broken figure is the occasion for the perfect body of the prose statement. This is like the image Hazlitt uses in his lecture on Locke to explain the difference between Locke's view of the mind and Leibniz's. Opposing the doctrine of innate ideas, Locke argued that the mind was like 'a piece of free stone, which the mason hews with equal ease in all directions, and into any shape', while according to Leibniz it resembles a piece of marble 'strongly ingrained', with a human or animal figure enclosed in it, 'which the sculptor has only to separate from the surrounding mass'. By analogy and association, the critic as artist brings out of a damaged sculpture the perfect figure it originally represented, and in so doing he gives form to the doctrine of innate ideas.

Though Hazlitt's praise of them has been little commented on, the Elgin Marbles held a symbolic value for his prose that's similar to that of the Grecian urn or urns which Keats admired. The *London Magazine*, in which Hazlitt's two essays appeared, included an engraving of the Ilissos statue on a separate sheet, and this clearly made it the central essay in that issue. The magazine was published by Taylor and Hessey, and contained a tiny flyer insert advertising several of Hazlitt's books – *Characters of Shakespear's Plays*, *Lectures on the English Poets*, and *Lectures on the English Comic*

Writers – as well as Keats's *Lamia* and *Endymion* and Clare's *Village Minstrel* and *Poems Descriptive of Rural Life and Scenery*. In a clever piece of editorial placing, the opening page of Hazlitt's second essay (in the May issue) is on the recto facing Clare's poem 'To the Cowslip'. Clare's line 'Blest flower, with spring thy joy's begun' is directly opposite Hazlitt's quotation from *Paradise Lost*:

> So from the ground
> Springs lighter the green stalk, from thence the leaves
> More airy, last the bright consummate flower!

Placed together, Clare, Hazlitt, and Milton support and comment on each other, while the essay's theme of the union between nature and art – marble flowing like a stream – is beautifully amplified by this conjunction. The effect is to foreground Hazlitt's identification with Ilissos and to make the river-god into the spirit of critical prose. We arrive, then, at a symbolic figure for prose style, and recognize that this is the moment when it sheds its gritty, plodding nature and swims free. Instead of a nightingale or an urn, the headless, graceful, muscular body of Ilissos represents inspiration for the critic.

This is apparent in the passage in which he celebrates interrelated, varying, muscular texture, and compares Hogarth's art to the Marbles in order to emphasize another of his central critical values – communication. In Hogarth:

If the mouth is distorted with laughter, the eyes swim in laughter. If the forehead is knit together, the cheeks are puckered up. If a fellow squints most horribly, the rest of his face is awry. The muscles pull different ways, or the same way, at the same time, on the surface of the picture, as they do in the human body. What you see is the reverse of *still life*. There is a continual and complete action and reaction of one variable part upon another, as there is in the Elgin Marbles. If you pull the string of a bow, the bow itself is bent. So is it in the strings and wires that move the human frame. The action of any one part, the contraction or relaxation of any one muscle, extends more or less perceptibly to every other:

'Thrills in each nerve, and lives along the line.'

Thus the celebrated Iö of Correggio is imbued, steeped, in a manner in the same voluptuous feeling all over – the same passion languishes in her whole frame, and communicates the infection to the feet, the back, and the reclined position of the head. This is history, not carpenter's work.

The line about muscles thrilling in each nerve is from Addison's poem in praise of Milton's style ('nervous', we know, was a prominent stylistic term at this time), so that once again the crucially significant value which Milton's epic imagination represents is being reintroduced. This is the body warm and electric, as Whitman would say.

The most important verb in this passage is 'communicates', a term that is closely linked to Rational Dissent's concept of free speech and the diffusion of knowledge through books, newspapers, educational societies, and academies. In *The Ready and Easy Way to Establish a Free Commonwealth*, Milton praises the Athenian commonwealth, and then recommends the establishment of schools and academies which would spread knowledge, civility, and religion through all parts of the land 'by communicating the natural heat of government and culture more distributively to all extreme parts, which now lie numb and neglected'. This would soon make the whole nation more industrious, 'more ingenuous at home, more potent, more honourable abroad'. To this a 'free Commonwealth' will easily assent, because a commonwealth, more than any other form of government, aims most to make the people 'flourishing, virtuous, noble and high-spirited'.

Milton's underlying image is corporeal, a version of the body politic being massaged into perfect fitness by the spread of knowledge. In the twentieth century, D. H. Lawrence drew on this physical manner of expressing ideas in order to offer a final puritan defiance of disembodied, Cartesian rationality. The decayed or decomposed rationality which Hazlitt detects in Locke's philosophy is a constant target for the sexually tortured idealist who dreamed, like Milton in *The Ready and Easy Way*, of a free commonwealth of flourishing citizens. And, like Milton, he is fond of employing classical imagery to express the republican values of free speech and communication.

Describing the Unitarian network in Shropshire to which his

father belonged, he says that the ministers' practice of exchanging visits established a 'line of communication' by which the flame of civil and religious liberty 'is kept alive, and nourishes its smouldering fire unquenchable, like the fires in the *Agamemnon* of Aeschylus, placed at different stations, that waited for ten long years to announce with their blazing pyramids the destruction of Troy'. The Salopian signal-fires are the natural heat of liberty spreading through a numbly monarchical culture, and they reappear with the classical reference to the *Agamemnon* in the conclusion to his posthumous essay 'The Letter-Bell', where they are linked with the 'telegraphs that lately communicated the intelligence of the new revolution to all France within a few hours'. Celebrating the revolution of July 1830 which ended the Bourbon regime in France, the dying Hazlitt designs a poem in prose that is structured around the letter-bell's 'importunate clamour' (a glance at the grasshoppers' 'importunate chink' in Burke's *Reflections*). That sound, which wakes him 'from the dream of time', is given a Priestleyan, electrical embodiment as one of those '*conductors* to the imagination' which becomes a means of gaining access to his whole life and to that unified understanding which he has consistently opposed to sensationalist philosophy.

The term 'conductor', we should note, was popularized by Benjamin Franklin and Sir Humphrey Davy. It replaced the term 'non-electric', and is used by Hazlitt when he says that the English imagination is a 'non-conductor'. In his essay on poetry in general, he speaks of 'conductors to the imagination', and he would also have associated the term with Priestley's experiments (Joseph Johnson marketed mail-order electrical machines designed by Priestley). As an aesthetic term, 'conductor' is firmly based in advanced republican science – the type of attitude Mary Shelley questions in *Frankenstein*.

The term belongs to the ethic of communication which Hazlitt, like Milton, insistently values. He calls the mail coaches setting off from Piccadilly the finest sight in London, saying that each coach is a winged chariot, because there is a 'peculiar secrecy and despatch, significant and full of meaning, in all the proceedings concerning them'. Calling Napoleon 'frank, communicative, unreserved and free in the highest degree' in his conversations with scientists, he again emphasizes the value of active, open communication. This is one expression of Unitarian culture, with its literary and scientific societies, libraries, critical and theological journals, and interest in canals, telegraphs, improved roads, and electrical instruments. Noting the Hellenism of Rational Dissent, John Seed calls Hazlitt Senior 'a remarkable example of the channels of information and influence among Rational Dissenting ministers'. Hazlitt's father was friendly with Priestley, Richard Price, and Andrew Kippis, who, as we have seen, were linked to some of the leading Whig politicians. In the 1770s and 1780s these Dissenting ministers provided 'a network of social communication through which politically significant information was transmitted between governing circles and groups of Dissenting merchants: from Rockingham's cabinet through Lindsey to Turner and on to Wakefield merchants; from Hazlitt in an Irish village through Price to Shelburne, the Prime Minister'. In this period, to say that someone had 'information' was to praise them for possessing good general knowledge as well as a keen awareness of contemporary issues (we would now term them an 'informed' person). Both 'communication' and 'information' figure strongly in Dissenting discourse.

Discussing the substantial numbers of Irish students who came, like Hazlitt's father, to the University of Glasgow, Ian McBride argues in an essay on eighteenth-century Dissenting culture that these Scottish-trained schoolmasters, ministers, and physicians formed an important part of the 'communications network of the Enlightenment', not only in Ulster but also in colonial America, where Francis Hutcheson's philosophy had a significant influence. What we begin to see is a powerfully intelligent, actively networking culture which had real access to, and influence on, the centre of political power.

If we examine both the concept and the practice of communication in Rational Dissent, we can see that Hutcheson as teacher and philosopher is widely and deeply influential. In *A Short Introduction to Moral Philosophy*, which was published the year after his death in 1746, he observes that by means of sympathy and 'of some disinterested affections', 'it happens, as by a sort of contagion or infection, that all our pleasures, even these of the lowest kind, are strangely increased by their being shared with others. There's scarce any cheerful or joyful commotion of mind which does not naturally require to be diffused and communicated.' The idea of communication is represented, for example, by the Society for the Diffusion of Knowledge and by several other societies, and it's closely connected with the concepts of disinterestedness and benevolence or good will. Human beings do not hug their ideas and emotions selfishly to themselves – they are not Hobbesian primitives suspiciously competing with each other; rather, they manifest a 'sincere, ingenuous, candid temper' of which we 'immediately approve'. And in his posthumously published lectures, A *System of Moral Philosophy*, Hutcheson argues that mankind's 'curiosity, communicativeness, desire of action, their sense of honour, their compassion, benevolence, gaiety, and the moral faculty, could have little or no exercise in solitude'. We all share a 'natural immediate dislike of a selfish sullen dark taciturnity', while 'an immediate approbation' naturally attends both 'this communicativeness, and the steadfast purpose of speaking according to our sentiments'. Hutcheson identified himself as a classical republican, and aimed to refute Hobbes's concept of a gloomy, selfish state of nature.

The values of immediacy, candour, and emotional honesty are part of the value system which communication draws on, and, as we've seen, so is 'happiness' as both a private and a public value. Thomas Belsham, the Unitarian divine who influenced Hazlitt, as we have seen, and was head of Hackney New College, stated that to 'communicate knowledge is to communicate happiness', and that the most active and disinterested happiness is 'in the highest degree communicative'. Priestley, who also taught briefly at the college, succinctly described one of his purposes in writing as 'a cheap and extensive circulation'.

Despite the severe government persecution which they suffered in the 1790s, Unitarians contributed significantly to the emergence of what John Seed in his study of the culture terms 'a liberal public sphere outside the control of the state or church', and this contributed to the development of democracy. The Greek signal-fires in Hazlitt symbolize both Rational Dissent's classical élitism and its concept of communicativeness. The Shropshire ministers, Seed notes, were isolated figures who viewed popular culture with its 'unchristian rituals, festivals and symbolic universe' as 'simply disorderly and ignorant'. Hazlitt's interest in popular culture – prize fighting and racket playing, for example – is a conscious attempt to redress that limitation, to enter common life and turn bodily movement and physical action into participatory values (his essay 'Merry England' is a loving celebration of the variety of English popular pastimes, games, and sports – boxing, blind-man's buff, hunt the slipper, hot cockles, snapdragon, quarterstaff). Even so, there is an exclusive, or patrician, idea of leadership in his imagination which makes him sometimes write like a Whig general or Napoleonic marshal rallying his army against the corrupt, stupid forces facing them. The celebratory, muscle-flexing tone of his writing, the insistence on unshakeable principle, is formed by the activism of Dissent, and it looks to images of heroically noble fortitude – Algernon Sidney on the scaffold – to reaffirm its deepest principles and values.

Like his admired Bacon, he is driven by a need to 'exalt the good which is communicative'; and this is echoed in the preface to the Irish Unitarian romance, *John Buncle*, which was first published in 1770 and which Hazlitt is fond of citing for its Rabelasian freedom. There the author, Thomas Amory, recommends 'a sincerity and benevolence of temper, a disinterestedness, a communicativeness'. The terms are listed routinely, because they are the linked expressions of Unitarian science, philosophy, and political theory. In the culture of Rational Dissent, free information meant full, active citizenship.

Part of the idea of communicativeness involves the admiration of expressive physical movement and emotional volatility. The disinterested affections, Hutcheson writes, are either 'calm, or turbulent and passionate', and in that beautiful passage in which he notes children's 'constant propensity to action and motion' – children grasping, handling, viewing, testing – he hymns the sensuous pleasures of discovering knowledge. Hutcheson's civic republicanism, his influence on Hume and Adam Smith, as well as on the educational system which formed Hazlitt's father, are most completely expressed in the accounts which survive of his teaching methods. An outstanding teacher, who lectured in English rather than Latin – an innovative idea at the time – Hutcheson would walk up and down the lecture-room while delivering his ideas extempore. His 'dynamic hortatory classroom style', Ian McBride shows, introduced 'an activist, didactic strain' into the culture of enlightened Scotland. He spoke, an admirer noted, with 'an animation of countenance, voice, and gesture, which instantly went to the heart'.

This ease, animation, and joyful vivacity is the expression of Hutcheson's rational republicanism, a republicanism which is based on a strong pleasure principle and on an intuitive immediacy which leaps where reason 'plods'. Hazlitt, as we have seen, often uses 'plodding' as a negative critical term, and he is also shaped by the concept of expressive motion which Hutcheson articulates in his writings. This is because he fears a petrified prose flatness, so he must always struggle to redeem his own writing from the kind of 'serious, plodding, minute prolixity' he dislikes in Jonson's *The Silent Woman*, or the 'plodding tenaciousness' he mentions in 'Merry England'.

Yet, like any serious prose-writer, he knows that the medium cannot be viewed as a mixture of privileged moments and flat discursive passages. The prose-writer has to cover the ground, not simply prepare it for visions or for moments in and out of time to break over its dreary, workmanlike sameness. This is because the prosing pen is guided by the principle of 'truth, not beauty – not pleasure, but power'. The prose-writer works the most unpromising materials 'by the mere activity of his mind'. So when he praises Jonathan Edwards's plodding accuracy, refers to painting as a 'dry, plodding art', or calls the Dutch and the English 'plodders', he is identifying a quality of active, unimaginative, practical perseverance, a kind of necessary droniness or deliberate, enforced doggedness – like digging ditches – which is part of the actual living experience of prose writing. If you write prose, you must face up to the fact that it is a recalcitrant medium that's gritty with facts and references.

He approaches this subject – the actual physical slog demanded by the creative act – in 'The Letter-Bell', where his ostensible subject is his early career as a painter. This is a late essay, a memory and a farewell; so, when he describes the dim embers in the little back painting-room, he is setting a Hobbesian symbol of imaginative memory – decaying sense – within a puny, remembered workshop that was the scene of his early failure in the dry art of painting.

In that workshop, he brooded

over the half-finished copy of a Rembrandt, or a landscape by Vangoyen, placing it where it might catch a dim gleam of light from the fire; while the Letter-Bell was the only sound that drew my thoughts to the world without, and reminded me that I had a task to perform in it. As to that landscape, methinks I see it now –

> The slow canal, the yellow-blossomed vale,
> The willow-tufted bank, the gliding sail.

There was a windmill, too, with a poor low clay-built cottage beside it: – how delighted I was when I had made the tremulous, undulating reflection in the water, and saw the dull canvas become a lucid mirror of the commonest features of nature!

Dutch painting, effort, the airiness of Goldsmith's lines on the canal, undulating natural light – he is building an image of hard work and intense inspiration here. But what also interests him is the inspired painter before he becomes successful and has a capacious studio and a liveried servant to clean his brushes. There is no part of a painter's life in which he enjoys himself and his art more than when, with 'furtive, sidelong glances' at what he has done, he is employed in washing his brushes and cleaning his palette for the day. What fascinates Hazlitt here is the production process in which the young impoverished artist is totally immersed. The artist will not be so wholly 'in his art', nor will his art have so much hold on him, as in the period of his life when he was too poor to transfer 'its meanest drudgery to others'. When he is above 'this mechanical part' of his business, his art will no longer be 'the delight of his inmost thoughts' – the idea of art as pure still being is particularly strong here. Physical, mechanical drudgery – the plod plod of the workshop – is an essential component of the dynamic of creativity. Prose writing and painting as physical activities are associated and identified in this concentrated, tactile evocation of the aesthetic process as hard work – a developed sensation which is expressed in his account of Salvator Rosa's landscapes, in which he says that the strength of the impression is confirmed 'even by the very touch and mode of handling'.

Praising the bold firmness of Rosa's art, he says that the artist brings us into physical contact with the objects he paints: 'the sharpness of a rock, the roughness of the bark of a tree, or the ruggedness of a mountain path'. This passage resembles the account of the leaping chamois in 'The Prose Style of Poets'. The lithe deer stands upon a rocky cliff, clambers up by abrupt and intricate ways, and browses on the roughest bark, or crops the tender flower. And it is hard not to imagine that he is thinking of Burke when he says that Rosa is drawn to whatever snaps the chain that binds us to humanity: 'the barren, the abrupt, wild sterile regions, the steep rock, the mountain torrent, the bandit's cave, the hermit's cell'. This sense of jagged texture and dizzying height is a quality he wishes to transfer to the actual act of prose writing, and it's there in those moments when Hazlitt reminds his readers that he is writing 'this' at Winterslow or some other place.

Rosa and Burke are closely associated, and when we examine the primary associative cluster in 'The Letter-Bell' – Rembrandt and Wordsworth – we can begin to discern the philosophical structure which underpins this seemingly casual reminiscence. In *The Spirit of the Age*, Hazlitt remarks that Wordsworth admires the way in which Rembrandt works something out of nothing and transforms 'the stump of a tree, a common figure, into an *ideal* object by the gorgeous light and shade thrown upon it'. Wordsworth's admiration, Hazlitt points out, springs from the analogy with his own mode of investing the minute details of nature with 'an atmosphere of sentiment', and in pronouncing Rembrandt to be a man of genius, 'feels that he strengthens his own claim to the title'. In 'The

Letter-Bell' Hazlitt underscores his point that painting gives one a strong interest in nature and humanity by quoting from 'Tintern Abbey':

> While with an eye made quiet by the power
> Of harmony and the deep power of joy,
> We see into the life of things.

Here Hazlitt is implicitly strengthening his own claim to the title of genius. His prose also makes something out of nothing by taking us to the very heart of the creative process, while at the same time he presents himself as a humble copyist, the equivalent of the critic who assembles a series of admired quotations. But Hazlitt is the impresario of the images and quotations he inserts, and he draws the Greek signal-fires at the essay's close out of the dying remembered fire. We can feel him actively relishing his medium here, as he employs the ringing sound of the letter-bell to activate a vision of his life and beliefs.

The essay is structured through a series of movements, sounds, 'shifting objects', and images of fixity – the bell's clear ring, the perfect chrysolite,* the unbroken republican integrity of early opinions. This insistence on a unified integrity is also there in a remark Hazlitt makes elsewhere about the man who resists tyranny with Hampden or who worships 'the ONE GOD AND FATHER with the Christian philosopher Locke'. Hazlitt happily combines these opposites in an assertion of unflinching personal integrity: 'What I have once set my hand to, I take the consequences of.' Initially he means that he never attempts to retrieve personal letters once he has written and posted them, but he is also thinking of how Wordsworth, Southey, and Coleridge changed their opinions, and of how Southey tried to use the law to prevent the re-publication of his youthful Jacobin drama *Wat Tyler*.

---

* Near the end of *Othello*, Othello tells Emilia that had Desdemona been true to him, and 'If heaven would make me such another world / Of one entire and perfect chrysolite, / I'd not have sold her for it' (v. ii. 144–6). In 'The Letter-Bell', Hazlitt applies the image to 'the habitual feeling of the love of life' which 'if analysed, breaks into a thousand shining fragments' (H XVII. 377). The broken fragments are an image of the Lockean idea of the mind – an idea he rejects.

In a late dialogue essay, Hazlitt attacks Burke's lack of integrity, and asserts that there was a 'rotten core', a 'Serbonian bog', in his understanding, in which all that 'modern literature, wit and reason' had done for the world 'sunk and was swallowed up in a fetid abyss for ever!' By associating Burke with Milton's imagery of hell, he evokes both his tortured imagination and the shifting – even shifty – qualities of his soul. Burke's understanding is therefore not a perfect chrysolite, but an unstable aggregate of particles in a state of perpetual Lockean decomposition. Philosophically, the understanding ought to be a unified structure of knowing; politically, it should be republican, and express itself in an unflinching style and manner. The problem for Hazlitt is that Burke was both a great prose stylist and a monarchist. Hazlitt wants somehow to reconcile an admiration of his style with the detestation he feels for Burke's politics. From his first reading of Burke when he was eighteen, he began a lifelong, even obsessive intellectual relationship with a writer whose defection to the Tory cause was mourned by the Dissenters whose civil rights he had championed. Like Milton and Shakespeare, Burke is part of the deep structure of Hazlitt's critical imagination, but, because of their shared Irish background, he is even more personally part of his soul and identity.

CHAPTER FIVE

The Serbonian Bog

In *Reflections on the Revolution in France*, Burke denounces the new governors of France:

attornies, agents, money-jobbers, speculators, and adventurers, composing an ignoble oligarchy founded on the destruction of the crown, the church, the nobility, and the people. Here end all the deceitful dreams and visions of the equality and rights of men. In 'the Serbonian bog' of this base oligarchy they are all absorbed, sunk, and lost for ever.

By employing the phrase 'Serbonian bog', Burke aims to remind his readers of a passage in *Paradise Lost* where Milton draws on Dante to build an achingly personal image of revolution and counter-revolution in which war, terror, and torture are unleashed to pitiless extremes:

> A gulf profound as that Serbonian bog
> Betwixt Damiata and Mount Casius old,
> Where armies whole have sunk: the parching air
> Burns frore, and cold performs the effect of fire.
> Thither by harpy-footed Furies haled,
> At certain revolutions all the damned
> Are brought: and feel by turns the bitter change
> Of fierce extremes . . .

This is a mythic version of a civil conflict that peace can never end or redeem.

Seared by the impact of French revolutionary politics on Europe, and immersed in a lifelong argument with Burke's writings, Hazlitt seizes on the counter-revolutionary application of the phrase 'Serbonian bog' in *Reflections* and turns it back against him. He tells Northcote in 'The Court Journal – A Dialogue': 'With regard to Burke, there was a rotten core, a Serbonian bog in his understanding, in which not only Gay's masterpiece [*The Beggar's Opera*] but the whole of what modern literature, wit, and reason had done for the world, sunk and was swallowed up in a fetid abyss for ever!' By glossing that bog as the 'rotten core' in Burke's understanding, Hazlitt makes a witty – even a racist – hit, which plays on the malicious perception of him as a sinister Irish Jacobite and secret Papist who was educated by the Jesuits (his mother was Catholic, but Burke was in fact an Irish Anglican who was educated at a hedge-school, before going to a Quaker school and then Trinity College, Dublin). In fingering Burke as an Irish Catholic, Hazlitt is both ministering to a particular prejudice and recognizing that *Reflections* is on one level a diatribe against the advanced Whiggish Protestantism which Burke espoused for most of his career. It is a diatribe occasioned by Richard Price's *Discourse on the Love of our Country*, a sermon given on 4 November 1789 at the Old Jewry, the Unitarian meeting-house where Wordsworth would hear Fawcett preach the sermon which helped to inspire the central lines of 'Tintern Abbey'.

In the sermon, Price referred to a 'diffusion of knowledge' which had undermined superstition and error, and he concluded:

Tremble all ye oppressors of the world! Take warning all ye supporters of slavish governments, and slavish hierarchies! Call no more (absurdly and wickedly) REFORMATION, innovation. You cannot now hold the world in darkness. Struggle no longer against increasing light and liberality. Restore to mankind their rights; and consent to the correction of abuses, before they and you are destroyed together.

This rhapsodic passage is the culmination of Price's celebrations of the Glorious Revolution, as well as the French and the American revolutions. The ardour for liberty, he asserts, is 'catching and spreading'. His rhetoric of advancing light is similar to Hazlitt's favourite image of Greek signal-fires for the communication of Dissenting rationalism. The rule of kings is being exchanged for the dominion of laws, while priestly rule is being supplanted by 'the dominion of reason and conscience'.

Price's sermon was published by the Revolution Society, which was founded in 1788 to commemorate the centenary of the Glorious Revolution. It incensed Burke, who disliked the Society's anti-popery, which he associated with Lord George Gordon's Protestant Association (Gordon made a series of inflammatory speeches to an angry crowd in June 1780, and singled out Burke for his support of the Catholic Relief Act, which the Protestant Association was petitioning the House of Commons to repeal). As Conor Cruise O'Brien points out in *The Great Melody*, his idiosyncratic study of Burke, Price's pamphlet placed the British welcome for the French Revolution firmly in 'a context of anti-popery'. Price, like Priestley, was a protégé of the powerful Whig politician Lord Shelburne, who was keenly interested in science. Burke hated Shelburne (he's an unnamed target in *Reflections*), and suspected him of having helped to incite the Gordon Riots, which followed the rejection of the Protestant Association's anti-Catholic petition in June 1780.

Burke read Price's sermon in January 1790, and he used it to bolster his opposition to any further progress in allowing religious toleration by repealing the Test Acts. In a speech delivered in the House of Commons on 2 March 1790, he attacked Priestley, and produced one of Priestley's open letters, in which the Unitarian leader 'talked of a train of gunpowder being laid to the church establishment, which would soon blow it up'. He also raised the spectre of the Gordon Riots. Two years later, in a debate on Charles James Fox's motion for the Repeal of Certain Penal Statutes Respecting Religious Opinions, he attacked the Unitarians' petition as being against 'the general principles of the Christian religion, as connected with the state'. The Unitarians were the 'avowed enemies' of the Anglican Church, and it was well known that Dr Priestley was 'their patriarch'. Burke then attacked Paine, and linked the Revolution Society to the Jacobin Club in Paris.

Burke was therefore an enemy of the Unitarian culture which shaped Hazlitt, whose relationship to Burke's writings must be partly understood in this light. In *Reflections* Burke attacks Price and Priestley vehemently, mobilizing anti-Semitic prejudice against Unitarians by ringing changes on the name 'Old Jewry'; and in a gloating, particularly nasty moment comparing Price to the Revd Hugh Peters, the parliamentary chaplain who was executed for treason at the Restoration.

The chairman of the Revolution Society was Earl Stanhope, a radical Member of Parliament who was also a notable scientist and the inventor of printing and calculating machines. Burke's hatred of science is a deeply personal hatred of these scientifically minded reformers:

When I see the spirit of liberty in action, I see a strong principle at work; and this, for a while, is all I can possibly know of it. The wild *gas*, the fixed air is plainly broke loose: but we ought to suspend our judgement until the first effervescence is a little subsided, till the liquor is cleared, and until we see something deeper than the agitation of a troubled and frothy surface.

By 'fixed-air' – carbonic acid gas – he signifies Priestley's invention of soda-water, which becomes a symbol of a modernity that is chaotically dangerous and driven by intellectual sophists, economists, and statisticians, or 'calculators'. Picking up the image of bubbling gas, he says that these radical theorists act by the 'organic *moleculae* of a disbanded people'. They are drunken, violent, highly intelligent barbarians who want to create an entirely atomized society which is the product of what, later in the polemic, he calls 'this new-sprung modern light', a rationalist outlook which he contrasts with the 'inborn feelings' of his nature.

In a sprawling series of related images, he damns Rational Dissent, scientific enquiry, and economic theory – everything geometrical, arithmetical, abstract. What Burke particularly detests is the feistiness of Rational Dissent, and it is notable that on several occasions he deliberately and provocatively hurls the unlovely adjective 'sluggish' at these modern activists. Thus property as an interest is 'sluggish, inert, and timid', while we – Burke is ventriloquizing for the English here – are supposed to be 'a dull sluggish race'. Our resistance to innovation, he later adds, is thanks to 'the cold sluggishness of our national character'.

This last statement is linked to the famous passage in *Reflections* where the importunate chinking of a mere half-dozen grasshoppers is contrasted with the silent, cud-chewing thousands of 'great cattle reposed beneath the shadow of the British oak'. Sluggishness is therefore a quality that is part of the national preference for the unwritten, the intuitive, the ancient, and the concrete, as against the abstract and theoretical. But it is more than this.

Burke's use of the adjective is a challenge thrown back to Dissenting science because the term 'sluggishness' was rejected by Priestley as representing a quality that reinforces a traditional and false distinction between body and spirit. Priestley opposes the view that matter has an evil tendency, arguing that this idea is the result of a dualism which divides reality into a sluggish body and an immortal spirit. He wants to 'remove the *odium* which has hitherto lain upon matter, from its supposed necessary property of *solidity, inertness,* or *sluggishness*'. As we have seen, Hazlitt's poetics of bubbling motion follows Priestley's energized materialism, while Burke rejects such a view of matter, because he is opposed to the release of energy in both social and material terms. In a sense, soda-water is the physical symbol of Priestley's dynamic concept of matter.

Rejecting the radical Whig idea of liberty which suffuses that concept – it is the substance of Wordsworth's vision in 'Tintern Abbey' – Burke favours the idea of what he calls 'a liberal descent', which inspires us with a sense of 'habitual native dignity' and prevents

that upstart insolence almost inevitably adhering to and disgracing those who are the first acquirers of any distinction. By this means our liberty becomes a noble freedom. It carries an imposing and majestic aspect. It has a pedigree and illustrating ancestors. It has its bearings and its ensigns armorial. It has its gallery of portraits; its monumental inscriptions; its records, evidences, and titles.

The rhetoric here is nervous and forced, the tone unconvinced.

Though he revered Burke's style, Hazlitt would have recognized the hollow, kitschy instability of this nervous, rather blustery passage, which desperately repeats *it its it* as though trying to breathe life into a fake institution. This is what Hopkins means when he asserts that Burke has no style: that because his writing is oratorical, it shows 'the strain of address'. The copious, profligate, teeming, exaggerated, angrily personal manner in which *Reflections* addresses its readers reduces ideas to the heat of performance, to the vanished intimacy of a particular occasion, so that if we choose to hear, rather than coldly read, this and many other eruptively imaginative passages, what we catch is less their rockiness and strain than the lazily confident nonchalance of expressive vocalization which only really famous or assured actors permit themselves. Like Stormont, the neo-classical 'Protestant' parliament erected earlier this century on a green hill outside Belfast, this passage of monumental prose is an empty shell, a rickety and pretentious stage-set. Something – tradition? heritage? – appears to be melting here, so fraudulent are Burke's words at this point, while the voice that shapes them is resonantly hollow, pompously hammy. The passage is unconvincing, because Burke is subconsciously unimpressed by these rather ersatz images of Protestant ascendancy. Their ricketiness anticipates Maria Edgeworth's *Castle Rackrent*, a novel which Hazlitt admired and alluded to in one of his many attacks on Burke (he compares Judy Quirk's rejection of the impoverished Sir Condy to Burke turning 'his back upon liberty').

Castle Rackrent was published in 1800, ten years after the publication of Burke's *Reflections*, and in this seminal novel Maria Edgeworth's narrator, the profusely loyal servant Thady, runs the independent, business-like voice of his lawyer son Jason into the narrative. Jason's efficiently modern voice contrasts with Thady's feudal emotion and Sir Condy's panic:

So Jason with much ado was brought to agree to a compromise – 'the purchaser that I have ready (says he) will be much displeased to be sure at the incumbrance on the land, but I must see and manage him – here's a deed ready drawn up – we have nothing to do but to put in the consideration money and our names to it. – And how much am I going to sell? – the lands of O'Shaughlin's-town, and the lands of Gruneaghoolaghan, and the lands of Crookaghnawaturgh, (says he, just reading to himself) – and – "Oh, murder, Jason! – sure you won't put this in" – the castle, stable, and appurtenances of Castle Rackrent – Oh, murder! (says I, clapping my hands) this is too bad, Jason.'

Jason, who is referred to as an attorney, is like one of Burke's 'attorneys, agents, money-jobbers, speculators', and he eventually acquires all the Rackrent property. His garrulous father, who, like Iago, continually describes himself as 'honest', and who insists, unconvincingly, on the 'most ancient' lineage of the Rackrents, undermines his own narrative with an increasingly ironic tone which resembles the unconscious falsity of Burke's windy images of 'ensigns armorial'.

If we remember that Edgeworth's novel was first published by Joseph Johnson, the influential radical bookseller who published most of the pamphlets attacking *Reflections*, it is hard not to read Thady as a parody of Burke:

Oh Jason! Jason! how will you stand to this in the face of the county, and all who know you, (says I); and what will people think and say, when they see you living here in Castle Rackrent, and the lawful owner turned out of the seat of his ancestors, without a cabin to put his head into, or as much as a potato to eat?

This is the lawyer as revolutionary, and Edgeworth intends it to serve as a warning to her own class, the Anglo-Irish. It's as though she has intuitively perceived that Burke's sentences on the imposing, majestic aspect of English liberty are not convincing because subconsciously he's ironizing what he recommends. Both texts are unstable, highly theatrical, almost drunkenly various and alarmed. Like Edgeworth's infinitely subtle novel, the diffuse, febrile, eruptive, or campily spontaneous style of *Reflections* could be viewed as buoyed up by, or surging on, a series of unstable contradictions. This is partly because Burke is a ferociously driven and unsluggish exponent of the type of intellectual ability which he contrasts with placidly propertied existence.

Burke is the wild gas on the loose, a barbarian romantic battering down the enlightened, rational, Hellenic structure of Dissent. Employing emotive, thrilling language drawn from the gothic novel, Burke throws reasoned argument aside in order to persuade his readers through sentiment, pathos, and moments of warm, terrified or violent feeling. With his new style of argument, he rampages through the 1790s like a man who is at last free to indulge in a total verbal riot. The element of sheer release from all control cannot be underestimated: it whoops out from his exaggerations like the collective cry of a rushing mob. His prose style enacts a type of apocalyptic melt-down as it participates in the destructiveness it attacks.

This is what Hazlitt means when he describes the hawk-like qualities of Burke's prose, which drops in 'one fell swoop'. Look, Burke is telling his English audience, I understand mob violence the way none of you ever will, for I am of it, blood and bone. I know what – dare I say it directly? – Protestant violence has done in Ireland. I was threatened on the streets of London by the Gordon rioters. I've seen their bigoted comrades in Ireland. All those great houses are ricketty shams. And I'm a sham, but it's my love of chaos that goads me into authenticity. This isn't a letter; it's an anguished monologue from out the forests – the felled forests – of the night. I'm the tiger burning bright in my denunciations of all those other tigers, terrorists, and Jacobin projectors.

Hazlitt recognizes the wild, the roller-coaster element in Burke's style when he attacks Southey's reply to William Smith, the Unitarian MP who opposed Burke in the debates on toleration for Dissenters in the early 1790s. Commenting on Burke's *Letter to a Noble Lord*, Hazlitt says that the attack made on Burke's pension,

by rousing his self-love, kindled his imagination, and made him blaze out in a torrent of fiery eloquence, in the course of which his tilting prose-Pegasus darted upon the title of the noble duke like a thunder-bolt, reversed his ancestral honours, overturned the monstrous straddle-legged figure of that legitimate monarch, Henry VIII, exploded the mines of the French Revolution, kicked down the Abbé Sieyès's pigeon-holes full of constitutions, and only reposed from his whirling career, in that fine retrospect on himself, and the affecting episode of Admiral Keppel.

Calling Burke an 'apostate', a malignant 'renegado' like Southey, he angrily turns against his admiration for the quixotic polemicist whose 'whirling career' he has punningly characterized as concealing a shrewd self-interest behind the antique bluster.

It's the anarchic nature of Burke's imagination, its hidden Catholic fury – the way he overturns Henry VIII – that appeals to Hazlitt, and here he affectionately portrays this modern Quixote as a loose cannon whose gifts as a polemicist are altogether superior to Southey's. Burke's knockabout, street-fighting tactics, the polemical urgency which makes him what the historian Alfred Cobban calls 'a pleader for oppressed peoples, and in three or four cases a defender of rebels', speak to Hazlitt out of their shared, but opposed, Irish backgrounds. There is a historic rage in Burke which stems from his identification with Irish Catholicism and English Catholics, especially at the time of the Gordon Riots, when he was singled out as an enemy by the virulently Protestant rioters. There is also a resentment against those Whig oligarchs, especially Shelburne, who had hindered his career. As Conor Cruise O'Brien imaginatively argues, *Reflections* is the work of an atavistic Catholic who hates and dreads Whig triumphalism.

Burke's expressive wildness enraptured Hazlitt when he first read *Letter to a Noble Lord* at the age of eighteen. Recalling this crucial epiphany in the essay on reading old books, one of his portraits of the critic as a young man, he writes:

I said to myself, 'This is true eloquence: this is a man pouring out his mind on paper.' All other style seemed to me pedantic and impertinent. Dr Johnson's was walking on stilts; and even Junius's (who was at that time a favourite with me), with all his terseness, shrunk up into little antithetic points and well-trimmed sentences. But Burke's style was forked and playful as the lightning, crested like the serpent. He delivered plain things on a plain ground; but when he rose, there was no end of his flights and circumgyrations – and in this very Letter, 'he, like an eagle in a dove-cot, fluttered *his* Volscians' (the Duke of Bedford and the Earl of Lauderdale) 'in Corioli'.

Dissociating himself from Burke's doctrines, he states that if there are greater prose-writers than Burke, they either lie outside his field of study or are beyond his sphere of comprehension (Junius, whose polemics he admired in his youth, and who was closely associated with Burke, lacks the master's wildness). In another essay on the periodical press, he returns to this early moment of discovery, remarking that he instantly became a convert to Burke's 'familiar, inimitable, powerful prose-style'. The richness of his invective contrasted with the meagreness of the ordinary style of the paper in which it was 'thrown'. This is the aesthetic of vehement prose writing, the glass-blower's molten bubble, its all-in-the-moment expressive heat.

Burke's style is electric, forked like lightning, and therefore associated with the new science it condemns. There is a rage in his writings against the boredom and dullness of workaday prose, against what he calls in *Letter to a Noble Lord* 'the dull English understanding'. This emotion, which has its historical base in Irish Catholic experience, combines with the rage of an ambitiously intelligent immigrant to fuel his supremely exasperated prose, so that he appears to be breaking out of its limitations. Burke pushes himself well beyond the pale of civilized gentlemanly utterance, because he knows that he is on an imaginative journey back to base camp, back to a mass rock in the hills where his ancestors wait to receive and honour him. He writes in a fury of expiation, as though desperate to impress a ghostly confessor. After all, he has spent most of his life in a foreign country, acting on a public stage like a travelling player.

Yet, in the very copiousness of his mental outpourings, Burke knows there is an obvious contradiction, one which he attempts to face in *Reflections* when he speaks of indulging himself in the freedom of 'epistolary intercourse' and begs leave to 'throw out my thoughts, and express my feelings, just as they arise in my mind, with very little attention to formal method'. This informality – the thoughts thrown on paper – is identical with that rapid, bubbling, extempore spontaneity which Hazlitt saw as essential to good prose style, and it naturally and continually unsettles Burke's stated belief in bearings and ensigns armorial. It is the daylight flow of English liberty, as the Whigs defined it, and it runs above the hurried scrambling desire to appease the *dei inferni*, the dark unconscious gods of kinship. This is the powerful counter-current in his prose. It's as though Creon and Antigone fuse into a single energy within the tragic fury of Burke's style.

How can this type of scribal freedom – Milton's free writing and free thinking – how can this fulsome informality express the highly constrained and monumental inscribings which Burke recommends so passionately? Don't these traditional values bob and duck on the swirling surface of his active prose style? Isn't Burke's invective against modernity like a river trying to flow backwards? His style races forward into the future even as it attempts to cling to the past. His fury is self-lacerating, boundless, unfixed, and terrifying, because it's so personal, and so historically and culturally bound. Swift, Shaw, Yeats, Joyce, all share this type of rage, however different the styles in which they choose to express it. Contemplate the contradictions that tear through Burke's style, and you see the next two centuries of Irish history impatient to be born (as I write, a Sinn Fein leader is walking down the steps outside Stormont).

In the passage from his essay 'On Good-Nature', which culminates in the comparison between Burke and Judy Quirk in *Castle Rackrent*, Hazlitt says that the Irish

have wit, genius, eloquence, imagination, affections: but they want coherence of understanding, and consequently have no standard of thought or action. Their strength of mind does not keep pace with the warmth of their feelings, or the quickness of their conceptions. Their animal spirits run away with them: their reason is a jade. There is something crude, indigested, rash, and discordant, in almost all that they do or say. They have no system, no abstract ideas. They are 'everything by starts, and nothing long'. They are a wild people. They hate whatever imposes a law on their understandings, or a yoke on their wills. To betray the principles they are most bound by their own professions and the expectations of others to maintain, is with them a reclamation of their original rights, and to fly in the face of their benefactors and friends, an assertion of their natural freedom of will. They want consistency and good faith. They unite fierceness with levity. In the midst of their headlong impulses, they have an undercurrent of selfishness and cunning, which in the end gets the better of them. Their feelings, when no longer excited by novelty or opposition, grow cold and stagnant. Their blood, if not heated by passion, turns to poison. They have a rancour in their hatred of any object they have abandoned, proportioned to the attachment they have professed to it. Their zeal, converted against itself, is furious.

It would be wrong to dismiss this as simply expressing the essentialist prejudice that the Irish are emotional and destructive. There is an understanding here of a particular *mentalité* that appears to draw on inside knowledge, possibly on inherited family prejudices, perhaps on his friendship with the Irish journalist Peter Finnerty. Gibbon said that Burke was the 'most eloquent and rational madman' he ever knew, and Hazlitt is saying something similar, adding that Burke 'abused metaphysics, because he could make nothing out of them, and turned his back upon liberty, when he found he could get nothing more by her'. As an exemplary, representative Irishman, Burke lacks 'coherence of understanding', which clearly implies that Hazlitt feels superior to him, as well as secure in his possession of the perfect chrysolite – his image for an integral, irrefragable, coherent understanding (Philip Larkin's 'cube of light' is an almost identically Protestant trope gleaming with a similar self-esteem). Then, in a lengthy footnote, Hazlitt abuses Burke as a 'half poet and a half philosopher' who has done more 'mischief' than perhaps any other person in the world.

The footnote, which was even longer on first publication, breaks off – 'This man, – but enough of him here' – in a dramatic Burkean manner that deliberately, even self-consciously aggrandizes the figure whom Hazlitt is ostensibly seeking to belittle so vehemently. This studied contradiction aims to catch the contradiction at the heart of Burke's counter-revolutionary polemic. The creative flaw in his style – a flaw that is preferable by far to the void behind Gibbon's composure – exercises a kind of familial fascination, because at some level Hazlitt knows he is kin to this 'half-English, half-Irish prose poet'.

For all his robust British Whiggishness, Hazlitt appears to have identified with a personal pantheon of Irish writers – Swift, Burke, Goldsmith, Sheridan – and in his admiration for his father's Shandyish letters, as well as in his frequent citations of Tristram Shandy, he adds Sterne, that affectionate mocker of Whig values, to a group that invisibly includes his own father, who was devoted to the novelist's work.

When the unbeatable racket-player Cavanagh is elegized in the conclusion to 'The Indian Jugglers', an interesting literary metamorphosis takes place as the London Irishman is transformed into a type of polemicist: 'Cobbett and Junius together would have made a Cavanagh.' Noting that Goldsmith consoled himself that there were places where he was admired, Hazlitt moves from this casually deliberate associative link with the Irish writer and with Junius to mention that Cavanagh could not show himself on any ground in England, but 'inquisitive gazers' would try to find out

in what part of his frame his unrivalled skill lay, as politicians wonder to see the balance of Europe suspended in Lord Castlereagh's face, and admire the trophies of the British Navy lurking under Mr Croker's hanging brow. Now Cavanagh was as good-looking a man as the Noble Lord, and much better looking than the Right Hon. Secretary. He had a clear, open countenance, and did not look sideways or down, like Mr Murray the bookseller.

Like a figure in a naïve painting, Cavanagh is given the status of a noble hero, who rises out of the common people to challenge Castlereagh, the Foreign Secretary, and John Wilson Croker, the prolific literary journalist who attacked Keats and was for thirty years Chief Secretary to the Admiralty. Cavanagh thus confronts two powerful Irish reactionaries, and he becomes an emblem of the dashing, sporty writer who is designing his memorial and has made him into a living symbol of literary style: 'His blows were not undecided and ineffectual – lumbering like Mr Wordsworth's epic poetry, nor wavering like Mr Coleridge's lyric prose.'

Behind this portrayal of Cavanagh may stand Hazlitt's friend the radical Irish journalist Peter Finnerty, who in 1797 was sentenced to the pillory and then gaoled for two years for exposing the scandalously rigged trial of the United Irishman William Orr, who was hanged that year. When Hazlitt first met him, Finnerty had just served another prison sentence – eighteen months in Lincoln Gaol for libelling Castlereagh in an article charging him with cruelty in Ireland. Finnerty, who was a reporter on the *Morning Chronicle* with Hazlitt, is described by Stanley Jones as a martyr in the cause of press freedom.

Cavanagh is thus an ideal type of the polemical journalist, and I believe that he is also associated with Finnerty, who was a member of the United Irishmen and, interestingly, a friend of Sheridan, whom Hazlitt greatly admired. The association of Cavanagh with Goldsmith is strictly unnecessary, but Hazlitt has a fund of Goldsmith anecdotes which he often draws on to express his admiration for his prose style. One of them is of Goldsmith rebuking Johnson for being unable to write a fable for little fishes without making them speak 'like great whales'. Goldsmith/ Johnson, as we have seen, is one of his associative critical double acts which help define the nature of prose style, so the reference is in fact highly appropriate. Hazlitt is citing an imaginative talisman, and attaching him to Cavanagh, another Irish immigrant.

The conflation of Cavanagh with Cobbett and Junius follows from the passage some sentences earlier where Hazlitt excitedly makes the pure whap of fives-playing into a kinetic figure for the experience of launching polemics at those in power:

He who takes to playing at fives is twice young. He feels neither the past nor future 'in the instant'. Debts, taxes, 'domestic treason, foreign levy, nothing can touch him further'. He has no other wish, no other thought, from the moment the game begins, but that of striking the ball, of placing it, of *making* it!

This resembles the passage in 'Whether Genius is Conscious of its Powers?' where Hazlitt contrasts the intoxication of the writing process – writing in and to the moment – with the waste-paper of the published article. On a symbolic level, it's an enactment of the concentrated, blind, sloggering, disciplined fury of the prose-writer at work, in wild but highly trained action like the boxers he also celebrates.

Hazlitt's admiration of Cavanagh, like his friendship with the journalist Finnerty, is woven in with those shadowy Irish affiliations which are most complexly expressed in his relationship to Burke, where he is responding to an interstitial, an in-between quality – half-Irish, half-English, part poet, part prose-writer – which also blurs the distinction between imaginative and polemical prose, and makes the Irish writer a secret sharer with Hazlitt the London journalist who was friendly with the Irish revolutionary Finnerty. This affiliative underworld works to complicate the confident in-your-face directness of various robust Whig certainties, as well as to leaven and sophisticate the Dissenting imagination. If we trace his critical

131

inspiration to its deepest sources, we will find that Burke is identified with the plenary creative act which produces Hazlitt's criticism.

Discussing Burke's counter-revolutionary polemics in the essay
on Fox which he published in 1807, when he was twenty-nine and
just beginning his writing career, Hazlitt says that we can 'conceive'
– significant verb – of Burke as

the genius of the storm, perched over Paris, the centre and focus of anarchy,
(so he would have us believe) hovering 'with mighty wings outspread over
the abyss, and rendering it pregnant', watching the passions of men grad-
ually unfolding themselves in new situations, penetrating those hidden
motives which hurried them from one extreme into another, arranging and
analysing the principles that alternately pervaded the vast chaotic mass,
and extracting the elements of order and the cement of social life from the
decomposition of all society.

On one level this is a symbolic figure for the decomposing nature of
prose, as against poetic style, which he calls 'composition'. The
image of Burke as the genius of the storm draws on Addison's
triumphalist Whig poem 'The Campaign', which celebrates the duke
of Marlborough's victories in the War of the Spanish Succession,
and describes how

> Calm and serene he drives the furious blast;
> And, pleas'd th'Almighty's orders to perform,
> Rides in the whirl-wind, and directs the storm.

Hazlitt dismisses Addison's poem elsewhere as a 'Gazette in rhyme',
but here he adapts his image of the general who was essential to the
success of the Glorious Revolution, in order to dramatize Burke's
attempts to influence the course of the French Revolution and shape
British domestic politics during the unstable 1790s.

Burke's 'whirling career' is a version of Marlborough's whirlwind
– this is the Whig idea of history strangely applied to the polemical
prose that Hazlitt held responsible for the Allied opposition to the
Revolution, an armed intervention which then brought about the
Terror. To this image of angel in a storm he adds Milton's invocation at the beginning of *Paradise Lost*, in which he asks God to aid

his adventurous song as it pursues things unattempted yet in prose or rhyme, and then prays to the Holy Spirit for instruction:

> thou from the first
> Wast present, and with mighty wings outspread
> Dove-like sat'st brooding on the vast abyss
> And madest it pregnant.

By applying these lines to Burke's counter-revolutionary polemics, Hazlitt is saying that this is the dawn of creation for his critical prose. Fusing Milton and Burke as the twinned sources of his critical inspiration, his citation is a creative act – more properly *the* creative act. The tense, unstable linking of these seminal writers features again in the perhaps suspiciously neat autobiographical moment which Hazlitt designed many years later in 'Reading Old Books', where he remembers bringing back from Shrewsbury in 1798 a copy of *Paradise Lost* and another of *Reflections*. This 'double prize' is still in his possession, he says. In that year of insurrection in Ireland and political panic in England, the two texts seem appropriate to the times and to his discovery of his literary vocation. His manner of combining the two writers in his character of Fox is epic: under Fox's aegis he is offering his own invocation to Clio by celebrating Burke's genius within the framework of Milton's opening invocation to the Holy Spirit. As Milton seeks to justify God's historical design, so Hazlitt seeks to build an account of a pattern in history which can be shaped by writing. This is his *fiat lux*.

When Hazlitt says in 'My First Acquaintance with Poets' that the figures which make up the date 1798 resemble 'the dreaded name of Demogorgon', he is linking that historical period to the lines which immediately follow Milton's mention of the name:

> Rumour next and Chance,
> And Tumult and Confusion all embroiled,
> And Discord with a thousand various mouths.

And it is the same numerals that make up 1789, the year of the

French Revolution. The image of a nervous, seething political situation is attached to 1798, the year he met Coleridge, whose 'Frost at Midnight', dated early the same year, enacts the tightening power of the state apparatus within the now common metaphor of a political freeze. By giving the same date to the acquisition of his treasured copies of *Paradise Lost* and *Reflections*, Hazlitt intends his readers to imagine him at the age of twenty beginning his journey towards the epic poem in prose that his scattered books and essays never quite compose. They fall short of a state of composition, I'd suggest, because from that random, sometimes ephemeral – in any case, unstable and decomposed – mass of energized molecules, we need to draw out the shape of an ideal work which is not in twelve books, or in any readily accessible material form.

The year 1798 has left few traces in the English historical memory, but in Ireland it is shorthand for an attempt to establish a united, indivisible republic. Hazlitt's sister, Margaret, mentions the date in her journal, and suggests that, had they stayed in Cork, her father would have been murdered by loyalists. The 1798 uprising clearly had a powerful significance for the Hazlitt family, lonely in Shropshire, reminding them of their ties to Ireland and linking them to the United Irishmen. This was the year of an unsuccessful French invasion of Ireland and of the United Irish leader Wolfe Tone's capture and suicide before his execution (Thomas Holcroft, in the diary which Hazlitt reproduced in his early biography of Holcroft, notes Tone's 'manly behaviour').

When they lived in Co. Cork, the Hazlitts were close to several members of the Irish Volunteers, the militia whose leaders brought about a partial and short-lived form of Irish independence between 1788 and 1800. Burke opposed this Protestant force, and no doubt Hazlitt held this against him. But in 1807, describing Burke as the genius of the historical storm, he transforms him into the Creator. Burke is the dove of the Holy Spirit brooding on the abyss of history; but he is that originary spirit as conceived by Milton, which means that Burke's monarchism is to some extent contained by the poet's republicanism, and by the allusive link to the Whig general Marlborough. Notice, too, how Burke in Hazlitt's essay on Fox is compared to one of the scientists he hated – he analyses, extracts, and arranges materials in a process that resembles a laboratory experiment. He is joining the molecular particles of a decomposing society into a composition.

By associating Burke with God and Milton within a metaphor drawn from the experimental science that is such an influential part of Unitarian culture, Hazlitt obviously makes him central to his entire purpose as a writer. Though he held no religious beliefs, deep in his imagination he, like Milton, is offering an invocation to a force which will aid and sustain his epic argument. 'Old father, old artificer', Stephen Dedalus writes when Joyce has reduced inherited literary style to rubble, 'stand me now and ever in good stead.' Like Joyce, Hazlitt is invoking spiritual aid as he draws the glowing metal of his art from out the burning furnace of the soul in history. With Burke's help he will then be able to raise the imperishable fabric of his critical prose from the social chaos of contemporary British and European history. This is his consuming ambition: to put the disinterested critical spirit so profoundly and so intelligently in the service of liberty that his perfected prose style will achieve lasting composition. Hazlitt's manner of both embracing and repudiating Burke is crucial to this ambition, because in a sense he aims to hug that febrile writer's irregular, brilliant style to death. Constantly reiterated praise of the same figure can eventually sound hollow, because, like the moon, Burke ends up reflecting the light his admirer casts on him. As a stylist, Hazlitt wants to colonize Burke, to eat him up or subsume him in his own Cavanagh-like 'power of execution'.

He alludes again to Milton's opening invocation to the heavenly muse in his *Letter to William Gifford*, where the future is characterized as a 'blank and dreary void like sleep or death' until the imagination, 'with wings outspread, impregnates it with life and motion'. In the passage in which he characterizes him as the conceptualizing genius of the storm, Burke, too, is the dove of the imagination mating with chaos, though there is another symbolic figure which is equal and opposite to the dove image. This symbol is concentrated in the hawking term 'souse', which Burke employed in a parliamentary speech in which he considered the effect of Junius's pamphlets on contemporary politics. Junius was the pseudonymous author of a series of powerful political letters which appeared in the *Public Advertiser* between January 1769 and January 1772. These Whig invectives sided with Wilkes, and attacked George III, the duke of Grafton, and Lord Mansfield, among others. They caused an enormous stir, but so successfully did their author conceal his identity that he achieved, Hazlitt says, a 'posthumous fame' while still alive.

Sir Philip Francis, who was a clerk in the War Office from 1762 to 1772, then received an important Indian appointment, and later helped Burke prepare the charges against Warren Hastings, was the author of the letters, but for many years Burke and Wilkes, among others, were suspected of being Junius. Hazlitt's *Lectures on the English Poets*, which was published in 1818, the year Philip Francis died, contained this advertisement:

THE IDENTITY OF JUNIUS with a DISTINGUISHED LIVING CHARACTER established. Including the SUPPLEMENT; consisting of Facsimiles of Hand-writing, and other Illustrations. The Second Edition, corrected and enlarged. Printed uniformly with Woodfall's edition of Junius, and accompanied with a fine Portrait, and five Plates of Hand-writing. 8vo. price 14s. bds.

'That it proves Sir Philip Francis to be Junius we will not affirm; but this we can safely assert, that it accumulates such a mass of circumstantial evidence, as renders it extremely difficult to believe he is not; and that, if so many coincidences shall be found to have misled us in this case, our faith, in all conclusions drawn from proofs of a similar kind, may henceforth be shaken.'

Edin. Rev. 57.

Hazlitt speculates on Junius's identity in *The Eloquence of the British Senate*, where he argues that Burke's style does not fit, because Junius's compositions are not characterized by 'grandeur'. But he nevertheless links the two men by including in his anthology a speech which Burke gave in 1770 during the excitement caused by Junius's letters.

Looking at the effect of those letters, Burke asks:

How comes this Junius to have broke through the cobweb of the law, and to range uncontrolled, unpunished, through the land? The myrmidons of the court have been long, and are still pursuing him in vain. They will not spend their time upon you or me. No; they disdain such vermin, when the mighty boar of the forest has broke through all their toils – is before them. But what will their efforts avail? No sooner has he wounded one than he lays another dead at his feet. For my part, when I saw his attack upon the king, I own my blood ran cold: I thought he had ventured too far, and that there was an end of his triumphs. Not that he has not asserted many truths. Yes, sir, there are in that composition many bold truths, by which a wise prince might profit. It was the rancour and venom by which I was struck . . . But while I expected from this daring flight his final ruin and fall, behold him still rising higher, and coming down souse upon both houses of parliament. Yes, he did make you his quarry, and you still bleed from the wounds of his talons. You crouched, and you still crouch, beneath his rage.

This passage describes polemical prose intervening violently and decisively in political affairs, and Hazlitt evidently admired it, because he employed the term 'souse' in a pamphlet, *Free Thoughts on Public Affairs*, which he published in 1806, the year before the anthology that includes Burke's speech. Discussing French strategy, he says that Napoleon was going to occupy Malta, cross to Egypt, and then 'at another vast stride, to come down *souse* upon our possessions in India'. The associative composite is clear: Burke, Junius, Napoleon. For Hazlitt, 'souse' conflates the geniuses of the three men.

Burke employs 'souse' more than twenty years after his speech on Junius, when he reworks a passage from Dryden's translation of the *Aeneid* to attack the revolutionary harpies of France who 'flutter over our heads, and souse down upon our tables, and leave nothing unrent, unrifled, unravaged or unpolluted with the slime of their filthy offal'. As Hazlitt employs it, 'souse' is a concentrated expression of polemical power which equates writing with military victory. Burke is both hawk and dove: he is the Old and New Testament deities combined, the tiger and the lamb that somehow issue from the same furnace. And, by applying the term to Napoleon, Hazlitt aims to cleanse it of the negative, scatological associations which it's given in *Letter to a Noble Lord*.

What we observe in Hazlitt's immensely assured early writings is a particular type of creative preparation which is analogous to the laying out of writing materials, the delivery of an invocation to the Muses, or to the old artificer. The young writer is both setting out his stall and designing a unique personal shrine, in which a series of talismanic texts and figures are placed carefully and lovingly. Burke is a crucially important figure here; so is the Whig leader Charles James Fox and the 'Great Commoner' Lord Chatham. Hazlitt also pays his respects to John Pym, 'one of the great leaders of the republican party', to Lord William Russell, who is 'generally looked upon as one of the great martyrs of English liberty', and to Algernon Sidney, who was condemned on the same charge of treason. William of Orange he praises for his 'great abilities'. As the reiterated adjective insists, these are his revered heroes, who belong in a personal pantheon with Defoe, whom he also admired as a champion of liberty.

That Hazlitt is a true Whig is clear – his first name bears that Williamite ancestry. But he also insists on the disinterested nature of his principles, asserting in that famous remark in his character sketch of Burke that it has always been with him a test of the 'sense and candour' of anyone on the Whig side 'whether he allowed Burke to be a great man'. Adding that he has not met more than one or two people who would make this concession, he then proceeds to outline Burke's belief that society must attend to more than bare physical necessities. Burke knew that human beings have 'affections and passions and powers of imagination', as well as hunger and thirst and a sense of heat and cold.

Reprinting his 1807 character sketch of Burke twelve years later in *Political Essays*, he explains that he wrote it originally in a 'fit of extravagant candour', at a time when he thought he could do an enemy 'justice or more than justice, without betraying a cause'. This youthful display of the prized value candour – disinterested but forceful truth-telling – is a remarkable example of assured stylistic analysis which makes a plenary address to the subject and possesses a quality of incontrovertible intelligence. Reading this early essay is like watching a categorical, entirely coherent intellect spring out at us fully armed, perfectly healthy, and completely confident.

In describing Burke, Hazlitt at the age of twenty-eight says that he will speak of the 'whole compass and circuit of his mind'. He was the 'chief boast and ornament of the English House of Commons', and the only public figure who can compete with him is the earl of Chatham, William Pitt the Elder. Chatham's eloquence was 'popular', his wisdom 'altogether plain and practical' – the alliteration is deliberately limiting – while in more expansive adjectives, Burke's wisdom is 'profound and contemplative'. The power which governed Burke's mind was his imagination, and it is clear that Hazlitt is using his commentary on Burke's parliamentary speeches to put forward his own concept of imaginative eloquence, as opposed to the kind of theological or philosophical definition of imagination formulated by Coleridge. Thus Burke is the master of the inventive and refined style. He unites the two extremes of 'refinement and strength' to a higher degree than any other writer. Answering the charge that Burke was a 'florid' writer who was without understanding, he addresses the philosophical position that underlies his criticism of Locke's passive theory of the mind. Burke's opponents make the mistake, he argues, of confounding reason with judgement, and supposing that it is the province of the understanding merely to 'pronounce sentence', rather than to give evidence or argue the case. They view the understanding as a 'passive', not an 'active', faculty.

Here Hazlitt points out that he is speaking of Burke as an author: he would not take issue with anyone who argued that the effects of his writings as 'instruments' of political power have been 'tremendous, fatal, such as no exertion of wit or knowledge or genius can ever counteract or atone for'. Yet his writings are to be admired for their union of grace and beauty with reason, their way of combining imagination with the understanding. Far from being a 'gaudy or flowery writer', Burke is one of the 'severest' writers we have:

His words are the most like things; his style is the most strictly suited to the subject. He unites every extreme and every variety of composition; the lowest and the meanest words and descriptions with the highest. He exults in the display of power, in showing the extent, the force, the intensity of his ideas; he is led on by the mere impulse and vehemence of his fancy, not by the affectation of dazzling his readers by gaudy conceits or pompous images. He was completely carried away by his subject. He had no other object but to produce the strongest impression on his reader, by giving the truest, the most characteristic, the fullest, and most forcible descriptions of things, trusting to the power of his own mind to mould them into grace and beauty. He did not produce a splendid effect by setting fire to the light vapours that float in the regions of fancy, as the chemists make fine colours with phosphorus, but by the eagerness of his blows struck fire from the flint, and melted the hardest substances in the furnace of his imagination. The wheels of his imagination did not catch fire from the rottenness of the materials, but from the rapidity of their motion.

This praise of the prose's union of 'untameable vigour and originality' anticipates the passage in his essay on Shakespeare and Milton in which he states that the fervour of Milton's imagination melts down and makes malleable 'as in a furnace, the most contradictory materials'. Like Milton, Burke has the ability to produce an effect by blending together harmoniously 'the most opposite and unpromising materials'. Once again we see how Hazlitt is fusing the monarchist with the republican writer in order to shape his own concept of the imagination. This means that *The Eloquence of the British Senate*, in which his essay on Burke first appeared, is an early, exploratory, concealed statement of his own poetics. No wonder Eliot secretly drew on this forgotten anthology when, at the age of thirty-two, he outlined his own poetics in 'Tradition and the Individual Talent'.

In order to define Burke's style more closely, Hazlitt contrasts him with a favourite example of dull pompous writing – Samuel Johnson's monotonously polished syntax. With his teeming, multiplying lexis, Burke rejects the '*set* or formal style, the measured cadence, and stately phraseology' of Johnson and most modern writers. This style is '*artificial* . . . all in one key'. Its false, levelling, masking medium completely destroys 'all force, expression, truth, and character' by arbitrarily confounding the differences between things, and so reducing everything to the same 'insipid standard'. Making the, to him, essential comparison with a living human body, Hazlitt says that to suppose that his 'stiff uniformity' can add anything to real grace or dignity is to suppose that, in order to be perfectly graceful, the human should never 'deviate from its upright posture'. But Burke's discriminating style is altogether free from this type of pedantry:

His style was as original, as expressive, as rich and varied, as it was possible; his combinations were as exquisite, as playful, as happy, as unexpected, as bold and daring, as his fancy. If anything, he ran into the opposite extreme of too great an inequality, if truth and nature could ever be carried to an extreme.

What draws Hazlitt so strongly to Burke's style is its quality of excess, its dangerous wildness, its brilliant fancy. Contrasting his style with Cicero's, he shows how Burke's intellect is destructive of classical order. Though he lacks 'the polished elegance, the glossy neatness, the artful regularity, the exquisite modulation' of Cicero, he has a thousand times more richness and originality of mind, 'more strength and pomp of diction'. Burke is a Romantic genius whose high, enthusiastic fancy challenges both the classical order and eighteenth-century neo-classicism. His prose, the implication is, has a spectacularly destructive quality that is uniquely and distinctively modern. The ancients, Hazlitt notes, had no word for genius, and so there is no room for a figure like Burke within a world-view which kept ideas 'too confined and distinct', and did not allow them to be 'melted down in the imagination'.

CHAPTER SIX

The Poetry in Prose

The idea of melt-down – hot liquid metal or glass – forms the basis, if basis is the correct term, of Hazlitt's critical imagination. Rather like Cellini throwing blocks of copper, bronze scraps, and lumps of pewter into a furnace, memory feeds quotations from a wide range of authors into his imagination where they're melted down before emerging as, literally, a finished article. Blake, who held a more exalted notion of the imagination as divine and transcendental, said it was not a daughter of memory, while Hobbes viewed imagination as just another term for memory or 'decaying sense'. Hazlitt is close to Hobbes, yet, paradoxically, by aligning Burke with Milton's lines on the Holy Spirit of dove-like creativity, he introduces the idea of divinity in a mnemonic, second-hand form. And, by implicitly comparing his method of composing a critical article to the art of that master goldsmith and sculptor Cellini, he elevates it far above mnemonic hack work, even though both he and Cellini use second-hand materials.

This paradox is central to his fascination with Burke, whom he views in his 1807 'Character' as being a poet only in the 'general vividness' of his fancy and the richness of his invention, arguing that the finest parts of his writing are illustrations of 'dry abstract ideas'. The union between the idea and the illustration is not, he points out, of that pleasing and perfect kind which constitutes poetry. He then takes up a friend's remark that the sound of Burke's prose is 'not musical', that it lacks cadence, and admits that this may be true compared with some poets or even some early prose-writers. But it is not true if we compare Burke with any other political writer or parliamentary speaker. Burke, as we've seen, has a grandeur which no one else – certainly not the *petit maître* Junius – can attain.

This is an evasive answer, because it does not face up to the argument that there is something curiously *styleless*, or, in Seamus Deane's phrase 'dishevelled', about Burke's writings. As Hopkins argued, Burke has 'no style properly so called: his style was colourlessly to transmit his thought'. His unique, distinctive manner isn't so much informed by the cadences of speech as a means of representing speech in an oratorical manner that's always rushed or rushing:

It is now sixteen or seventeen years since I saw the queen of France, then the dauphiness, at Versailles; and surely never lighted on this orb, which she hardly seemed to touch, a more delightful vision. I saw her just above the horizon, decorating and cheering the elevated sphere she just began to move in – glittering like the morning star, full of life, and splendour, and joy. Oh! What a revolution! and what a heart must I have, to contemplate without emotion that elevation and that fall! Little did I dream when she added titles of veneration to those of enthusiastic, distant, respectful love, that she should ever be obliged to carry the sharp antidote against disgrace concealed in that bosom; little did I dream that I should have lived to see such disasters fallen upon her in a nation of gallant men, in a nation of men of honour and of cavaliers. I thought ten thousand swords must have leaped from their scabbards to avenge even a look that threatened her with insult. – But the age of chivalry is gone. – That of sophisters, economists, and calculators, has succeeded; and the glory of Europe is extinguished for ever. Never, never more, shall we behold that generous loyalty to rank and sex, that proud submission, that dignified obedience, that subordination of the heart, which kept alive, even in servitude itself, the spirit of an exalted freedom. The unbought grace of life, the cheap defence of nations, the nurse of manly sentiment and heroic enterprise is gone! It is gone, that sensibility of principle, that chastity of honour, which felt a stain like a wound, which inspired courage whilst it mitigated ferocity, which ennobled whatever it touched, and under which vice itself lost half its evil, by losing all its grossness.

Like Gar O'Donnell, who obsessively quotes this passage in Brian Friel's *Philadelphia Here I Come*, Hazlitt cites those sixteen or seventeen years so frequently that he reduces Burke's chivalric vision to the hoariest of dead quotations, to an exhausted fantasy. By repeating it so mercilessly, he shows that it's somehow loose, flaccid, impetuous, and forced, yet still maddeningly and unarguably *there*, like a royalist banner flying against the republican understanding.

Overdone and cavalier, at moments specific in an ugly, vulgar, oddly mercantilist manner – 'unbought grace', 'cheap defence' – this passage forces the reader to recognize uneasily that there is a queasiness in the prose which is part of its excitement. This type of aesthetic embarrassment stems from Burke's ambition to offer relished moments of maximum excitement: reading him is like watching a prize-fighter dancing round the ring, then landing a blow – *splat*! – on his opponent's nose. It's opera, political pantomime, fairground stuff. There is a sweaty seaminess – even a seediness – in the energetic body of his kinetic prose, which makes it splendidly, coarsely entertaining. And how we love to watch him rise up like a learned cabin-boy to impale the grand duke of Bedford for his huge inherited wealth, calling him the Leviathan among all the creatures of the Crown, then moving into this vision of his enormous, so very happy and privileged, blubbery tubbiness:

He tumbles about his unwieldy bulk; he plays and frolics in the ocean of the Royal bounty. Huge as he is, and whilst 'he lies floating many a rood', he is still a creature. His ribs, his fins, his whalebone, his blubber, the very spiracles through which he spouts a torrent of brine against his origin, and covers me all over with spray – everything of him and about him is from the Throne. Is it for *him* to question the dispensation of the Royal favour?

Burke's primitivism, his lunging physical language and theatrical flourishes – that conclusive, resonantly italicized *him* – are compelling, but his constant, absolute sense of audience means that this is a prose which wears like the sound of nearby traffic sluffing past. It never dwells; it is never, in Hazlitt's phrase, 'indolent', but always on display. It's too completely self-conscious and performative. In a word, it is camp – brilliant, inspired camp, certainly, but as a style it can only in various eruptive moments break through the worn carapace of its used glossiness.

Even the 'proud Keep of Windsor' passage, which Hazlitt admired as one of Burke's greatest achievements, is arguably like the fading reproduction of a living voice. It's a talismanic prose passage for him, a personal icon he always cites lovingly, except that oratory printed is like the smell of a dead, communal dinner when the hall has emptied – something processed and spent hangs in the air. The creative urgency of the prose is gripping and exciting, but the effect is slurred or slippery, like a receding echo. What we hear is not the big bang, but the faint, scuzzy ripples produced by the original moment of creation, the actual occasion on which the words were delivered (Burke writes as if he is speaking aloud). He therefore presents himself as an entertainer: ostentatious, spectacular, occasionally outrageous, he's his audience's creature. His verbal largesse is self-indulgent, a type of stylistic overkill that at times has a pantomimic, almost smelly vulgarity. As a performer, Burke may be brilliant – he often is – but he also addresses us in a used, megaphonic public voice that's often too delighted by its own eloquence. There's something consuming and consumed about his violently historical style.

James Joyce distinguishes between art, which does not aim to produce an immediate effect, and pornography, or 'improper art', which excites 'kinetic emotions'. Similarly, this immediate style aims almost physically to enlist the emotions. Its lunging, plunging, sousing physicality entrances Hazlitt. For him, Burke is both eagle and dove; the momentum of his style is an explosive, murderous disturbance that also contains a detached artist's irenic gentleness. By comparing his style to Coriolanus on the battlefield, Hazlitt suggests that Burke's prose polemics are behind the famous observation in the essay on *Coriolanus* that the language of poetry 'naturally falls in with the language of power'. The imagination, he says in that essay, is 'an exaggerating and exclusive faculty' which must always excel against the prosy republican understanding; and though he doesn't say so here, it's the Irish prose-poet that he's thinking of. The force of imaginative writing – poetry in particular – is a source of anxiety for the radical critic, who feels intimidated by its irrational drive, its emotional and destructive logic. Fox remarked, Hazlitt notes, that Burke mistakenly made politics into a 'question or department of the imagination', and Hazlitt employs this idea in the contrast he draws between Fox's plain, straight-forward understanding and Burke's romantic, fanciful view of the French Revolution. In effect, this acts as a gloss on the distinction he makes between imagination and understanding in the essay on *Coriolanus*, a play he likes to quote when he wants to characterize Burke's style. Drawing on Fox, he says that politics treats of the 'public weal and the most general and wide-extended con-sequences', while the imagination can be appealed to only by 'individual objects and personal interests'.

The view of Fox which he presents in his *Life of Napoleon* is characteristically consistent, because two decades earlier, in his brief sketch of the politician, he remarks that it is difficult to describe his character without running into insipidity or extravagance:

there are no splendid contrasts, no striking irregularities, no curious dis-tinctions to work upon; no 'jutting frieze, buttress, nor coigne of vantage' for the imagination to take hold of. It was a plain marble slab, inscribed in plain legible characters, without either hieroglyphics or carving. There was the same directness and manly simplicity in every thing that he did.

This seems a straightforward explanation, though its faintly cur-tailed tone – an uneasy defensiveness beneath the direct praise – goes right to the depths of Hazlitt's relationship with Burke, Fox's friend and, later, opponent. The adjective 'plain', applied to Fox twice in the same sentence and again in the later remark on Fox's plain, straightforward understanding, means not only that the Whig leader isn't showy, but that he belongs to the past. Unlike Macbeth's castle, he has no jutting frieze for swifts to nest in, for the imagination to take hold of. Where Burke, by implication, is irregular and gothic, Fox is regular, symmetrical, and neo-classical. The comment is reminiscent of his remark that Horne Tooke, with his lack of imagination and 'plain, downright English honesty', resembles a 'finished gentleman of the last age'. Fox is similarly dated, alas, Hazlitt is suggesting.

Interestingly, he employs the same quotation from *Macbeth* later in the *Coriolanus* essay:

No jutty, frieze,
Buttress, nor coign of vantage, but this bird
Hath made his pendent bed and procreant cradle.

Shortly after mentioning Burke's *Reflections*, he remarks that the cause of the people is 'but little calculated' as a subject for poetry (even that verb 'calculated' is Burkean, for it alludes to the 'age of sophisters, economists, and calculators' denounced in *Reflections*). The popular cause admits of rhetoric, Hazlitt says, but it presents 'no immediate or distinct images to the mind, "no jutting frieze, buttress, or coigne of vantage" for poetry to make its "pendent bed and procreant cradle in"'. Once again the poetic imagination is figured as a bird: this time a swift whose nest under the eaves is an emblem of good luck in folklore. That snug, textured nest embodies for Hazlitt the gothic, the unpolished and non-classical, as well as being a sexual symbol that possesses a kind of wondering or religious innocence. Fox's direct plainness, which contrasts with the indented, projecting wall and corbel-like nest, is a version of Cicero's 'glossy neatness', his ultimately unsophisticated smoothness and 'artful regularity', as it's described in 'Character of Mr Burke'. The 'procreant cradle' is also, paradoxically, a symbol of modernity which exceeds or advances beyond the flat, traditional, regular values which Fox represents. Like Burke's style, the nest is rough-textured and irregular in its surface. It's tactile and exciting, or, as we might now say, sexy, like the image of a wasps' nest which Elizabeth Bishop uses.

Hazlitt also attaches this eminently adhesive quotation directly to Burke in his essay on prose style, where he praises the 'proud Keep of Windsor' passage in a manner that fuses the two complementary bird images:

how finely, how nobly it stands out, in natural grandeur, in royal state, with double barriers round it to answer for its identity, with 'buttress, frieze, and coigne of vantage' for the imagination to 'make its pendent bed and procreant cradle', till the idea is confounded with the object representing it – the wonder of a kingdom; and then how striking, how determined the descent, 'at one fell swoop', to the 'low, fat, Bedford level!'

For Hazlitt, Burke's imagination is a procreant cradle, like a swift's nest, like Milton's dove brooding on the abyss, and it is also a hawk plunging, like Coriolanus or Macbeth. Here, the second quotation in this critical cento – 'at one fell swoop' – makes the comparison with Macbeth explicit. The phrase summons Macduff's agonized cry of grief at the news of the murder of his wife and children:

> All my pretty ones?
> Did you say all? O hell-kite! All?
> What, all my pretty chickens and their dam
> At one fell swoop?

For Hazlitt, Burke is a hell-kite that souses down on its prey and destroys his dearest, most cherished hopes. He knows that the classicism of Rational Dissent and of high Whig politics is *passé*, as well as tame or insipid. Burke is associated with the dark murderous power of the gothic: bloody castles, churches, organized religion, murderous statecraft, a kind of heritage modernity. He is both a murderer and a seminal writer, whose darting, playful, tortured, powerful, magnificent prose style differs from poetry 'like the chamois from the eagle'.

This image, which is inevitably brushed associatively by the poetic eagle it denies, is an adaptation of the temple-haunting martlet, because the chamois is a creature that in its supple lightness of being also avails itself of jutties and coigns of vantage: it stands upon 'a rocky cliff' and clambers up 'by abrupt and intricate ways' – the language becomes gothic here. In a sense, Hazlitt is denying that Burke's prose is poetic, while imaging his denial in a manner that gives it the quality of *poesis*, or pure creative originality.

Yet his critical subconscious is more complex still, as we can see at the beginning of the paragraph in the essay on prose style where he introduces the chamois image:

It has always appeared to me that the most perfect prose style, the most powerful, the most dazzling, the most daring, that which went the nearest to the verge of poetry, and yet never fell over, was Burke's. It has the solidity, and sparkling effect of the diamond: all other *fine writing* is like French paste or Bristol-stones in the comparison. Burke's style is airy, flighty, adventurous, but it never loses sight of the subject; nay, is always in contact with, and derives its increased or varying impulse from it. It may be said to pass yawning gulfs 'on the unsteadfast footing of a spear': still it has an actual resting-place and tangible support under it – it is not suspended on nothing.

Eagerly admiring though this passage is – it's another version of the prose-writer as tightrope-walker – there is something not quite right about the images that Hazlitt employs. Just as an unexpected pause or quaver in the voice can alter a straightforwardly affirmative statement or stymie some routine words of welcome, so Hazlitt's prose takes on a kind of counter-colouring that partly inhibits or complicates his praise of Burke's style. That style is 'dazzling' and 'sparkling' like a diamond – predictable adjectives and simile that begin to crumble when the contradistinction which makes all other fine writing like French paste or Bristol-stones somehow attaches itself to the diamond trope. The style now resembles sparkling cos-tume jewellery, which is a perfectly reasonable way of expressing the view, as it were subliminally, that Burke's prose can possess a kitschy theatrical quality at times. ('Mr Burke was much of a theat-rical man', Hazlitt remarks elsewhere.) Subconsciously – at least at this point in the essay on prose style – this is what Hazlitt believes, and in 'Arguing in a Circle', a long discussion of Burke's mad theatrical genius, he says: 'The light of his imagination, sportive, dazzling, beauteous as it seemed, was followed by the stroke of death.' Malign and treacherous like Iago, he strews 'the flowers of his style over the rotten carcase of corruption'.

Hazlitt's critical doubts rather complicate his praise of Burke. But why is other fine writing like a transparent rock-crystal found in the Clifton limestone near Bristol, and once fashionably known as 'Bristol diamonds'? Such a comparison conveys qualities of strength, integrity, and clarity, like the 'one entire and perfect chrysolite' to which Hazlitt likens his consistency and unyielding personal integrity in 'The Letter-Bell'. And those qualities are strengthened if we know, as Hazlitt would have, that Burke lost his Bristol seat over a famous issue of principle in which he argued that MPs weren't their constituents' delegates, but must instead act according to conscience. In this case, Burke's principles and his nationality made him support free trade with Ireland, while his constituents wanted English trade protected. On the other hand, Bristol-stone functions primarily as an image of costume jewellery, cheap jewellery, not as an image of shining integrity. Burke's style is being contrasted with Bristol-stone, almost as though it is capable of being evaluated against both itself and writing that is not itself. A vertiginous paradox opens here.

The critical moment is complicated, because if we accept that Burke's prose is fine writing, then the pejorative term 'French paste' catches the theatrical, the opportunist queasiness in, say, his prose aria on Marie Antoinette. Except that we are then immediately thrown up against the sterling English image of Bristol stone, which acts as a contradictory brake on the ostensible argument. Burke's style is meant not to resemble Bristol stone; yet, if we also remember that the city of Bristol was stubbornly royalist during the Civil War, then there is a further complication. There is a tension – more, an antipathy – between French paste and Bristol-stone. They are opposites that cannot be paired or matched. Yet they are both meant to represent writing which is inferior to Burke's. More than this, Hazlitt must have associated Bristol with three poets – Wordsworth, Southey, and Coleridge – who deserted the republicanism they professed in that city during the 1790s, and became devout monarchists and Tories.

What we begin to see here is the way a critical argument can either take on the contradictory qualities in a text or itself become radically ambiguous like a work of art. Sometimes this enactment of a complicated critical judgement can be achieved by reproducing a vocal tone, as in Hazlitt's essay on Hogarth's *Marriage à la Mode*, in which he praises the artist for putting life and motion everywhere in his pictures: 'every feature and muscle is put into full play; the exact feeling of the moment is brought out, and carried to its utmost height. . . . The expression is always taken *en passant*.' Carrying this expressive aesthetic over into his critical style, Hazlitt extemporizes, saying: 'Just – no, not quite – as good, is the joke of the woman overhead.' Rather like a moment in a Browning monologue, the spontaneous tone of voice conveys the immediate formation of an idea, and it's interesting that George Saintsbury, in his exhaustive account of English prose style, should compare Hazlitt's style to Browning's verse. Nourished in English Dissent, both artists are drawn to an infinitely flexible vernacular expressiveness that's far subtler in its effects and range than anything in Johnson's style. They dramatize consciousness in process, and for this they need a syntax and a system of punctuation in which gaps, breaks, shifts, and unexpected changes in vocal texture fluidly embody thinking, feeling, and speaking.

Hazlitt's imagery of furnaces and molten metal derives from his love of process and his detestation of all that is fixed, dry, concrete, or literal. He must communicate ideas and aesthetic pleasure as motion and fluidity, and these in turn express his own delight in the creative act of communication, its compulsiveness and necessity. This is the living root of Dissenting culture, a belief in growth and process that breaks through the institutional fixity which a style like Johnson's consolidates. In his essay on prose style, Hazlitt employs allusion and symbolic ambiguity to express the slipperiness of Burke's writing and his own shifting responses over more than twenty years. This is the critic as actor embodying the hermeneutic process in a manner that is democratic, rather than authoritarian and *ex cathedra*, like Johnson's. The performative nature of Hazlitt's criticism plunges us into living, moving, interpretative action as it happens here and now. This is the motion in the moment which he embodies literally in a quick adjectival sketch of Hogarth's servant-girl with her 'plump, ripe, florid, luscious look'. This type of critical writing is something we don't simply observe or register: we participate in it fully as audience, rather than existing separately and autonomously as private readers addressed by the critic. Such critical judgements are dynamic, not static, and they are passionately and unashamedly erotic.

The essentially dramatic impulse behind his account of prose style is underscored by a passage I quoted earlier that follows the comparison to Bristol stones:

Burke's style is airy, flighty, adventurous, but it never loses sight of the subject; nay, is always in contact with, and derives its increased or varying impulse from it. It may be said to pass yawning gulfs 'on the unsteadfast footing of a spear': still it has an actual resting-place and tangible support under it – it is not suspended on nothing.

Here, he catches the style's headlong momentum by alluding to Worcester's speech to the angry Hotspur early in *Henry IV, Part 1*:

WORCESTER   And now I will unclasp a secret book,
And to your quick-conceiving discontents
I'll read you matter deep and dangerous,
As full of peril and adventurous spirit
As to o'erwalk a current roaring loud
On the unsteadfast footing of a spear.

HOTSPUR   If he fall in, good night, or sink, or swim!
Send danger from the east unto the west,
So honour cross it from the north to south,
And let them grapple. O, the blood more stirs
To rouse a lion than to start a hare!

So Burke is vehement, impatient, combative, headstrong, morally passionate, and wildly impolitic like Hotspur. His prose style is a weapon unstably bridging the current of history. He, too, is a doomed, chivalric anachronism, loud and noisy and undeviating like the river. The single, quoted line of Shakespeare catches the propulsive, balancing-by-keeping-moving, and there-fore potentially unbalanced nature of Burke's armed style. Placed in context, the line keys a whole composite of qualities, chief among them the noise, the rush, the danger, in the historical process.

There is a similar image in Hazlitt's 1817 character sketch of Burke, in which he argues that it is Burke's impatience

to transfer his conceptions entire, living, in all their rapidity, strength, and glancing variety, to the minds of others, that constantly pushes him to the verge of extravagance, and yet supports him there in dignified security –

Never so sure our rapture to create,
As when he treads the brink of all we hate.

What he's stressing is the current of existential danger in Burke's style, the way he is for ever on the brink of transgressing boundaries, and the excitement this creates in the reader, through the animation of his language, its direct intensity.

Anticipating his remark that prose works its most striking effects out of 'the most unpromising materials', Hazlitt immediately offers an image of its self-delighting airiness in another cliff-hanging passage from which I quoted earlier:

It differs from poetry, as I conceive, like the chamois from the eagle: it climbs to an almost equal height, touches upon a cloud, overlooks a precipice, is picturesque, sublime – but all the while, instead of soaring through the air, it stands upon a rocky cliff, clambers up by abrupt and intricate ways, and browses on the roughest bark, or crops the tender flower. The principle which guides his pen is truth, not beauty – not pleasure, but power.

He has applied the image of the Coriolanian eagle to Burke's style elsewhere, but here he denies it, in order to offer the more interesting figure of the chamois, whose Alpine habitat immediately introduces the idea of the Romantic poet, an idea which also counters his argument that this prose is not quite poetry (the assonance and full rhyme *browses flower power* assists the contradiction).

There is a similar moment in a novel Hazlitt admired, Godwin's *St Leon*, where the central character climbs up into the Alps:

The wildness of an untamed and savage scene best accorded with the temper of my mind. I sprung from cliff to cliff among the points of the rock. I rushed down precipices that to my sobered sense appeared in a manner perpendicular, and only preserved my life, with a sort of inborn and unelective care, by catching at the roots and shrubs which occasionally broke the steepness of the descent. I hung over the tops of the rocks still more fearful in their declivities, and courted the giddiness and whirl of spirit which such spectacles are accustomed to produce.

This passage consciously reproduces Rousseau's phony sensitivity, and if it is the source of Hazlitt's comparison of Burke's style to a

chamois, then we can notice how that image brings, through Godwin, the idea of Rousseau, one of his early heroes. It also kicks up
and away from Godwin's stiff sentences to revel in the sensation of
giddiness and danger.

The statement that prose is directed toward truth not beauty,
power not pleasure, is contradicted by the very beautiful image of
the small shy deer browsing on the roughest bark, or cropping 'the
tender flower'. Burke's savouring of his style – in the 'proud Keep of
Windsor' and 'rolling Leviathan' passages – is perfectly figured
here, before Hazlitt explains that the nature of Burke's task pre-
cluded 'continual beauty', but not continual 'ingenuity, force,
originality'. Because Burke had to treat of political questions and
abstract ideas, there was necessarily a 'resistance in the *matter* to the
illustration applied to it'. Using a term drawn from physics, he
warms to the struggle between a resistant materiality and imagination, because he wants to emphasize the element of sheer difficulty
in writing prose.

He then states that poets are in general bad prose-writers, an
argument that forms the subject of his essay on style, in which he
argues that the prose-writer always 'mingles clay with his gold' and
often separates truth from mere pleasure. This is because prose aims
to impart conviction, and therefore no ornament or relief can be
admitted that does not add 'new force or clearness to the original
conception'.

The effect of this is to mark out prose style as an especially difficult and taxing aesthetic genre which poets can never fully comprehend or practise. It is at this point in his critique of poets' failure
to write true prose that he quotes Burke on the proud Keep of Windsor and in his commentary introduces the 'coign of vantage' passage
from *Macbeth* with its associated image of the temple-haunting
martlet. This picks up the earlier image of the chamois clambering
up a cliff by those 'abrupt and intricate ways' which not only figure
the difficult texture of prose argument, but also introduce a gothic
texture to this dynamic image. As we have seen, by quoting
Macbeth, Hazlitt transforms the chamois into the temple-haunting
martlet. He raids Shakespeare's verse for an image that expresses

the absolute nature and identity of true prose by likening it to the martlet's weaving flight and sacral, summery associations. In allowing poetic imagery, especially Shakespeare's, to serve as an illustration of the *haecceitas*, the thisness, of prose, he makes that medium appear even more difficult and unique than poetry. We're travelling deep into his imaginative interior here, and can begin to glimpse the secret springs of his critical art.

Hazlitt's images and quotations are therefore incremental. They are not isolated flowers of rhetoric gummed to his argument, but dynamic figures which work in this particular essay to contradict his assertion that prose, even Burke's, is not poetic. Or is this too simple, too clear-cut, a way of approaching this subject? After all, part of the excitement in reading Burke lies in the recognition that he went 'the nearest to the verge of poetry, and yet never fell over'. His prose depends on his being always about to lose his unsteadfast footing on that horizontal spear. If he lost it, he'd be dead – that is, he'd be a poet writing prose like Scott's or Byron's. Poets, when they abandon verse, tend to adopt a prose style which 'halts, totters, is loose, disjointed, and without expressive pauses or rapid movements'.

By keeping poets and true prose style strictly apart, Hazlitt aims to mark out a separate, distinct category for prose which does not make it the poor relation of poetry. Thus poets who write prose either do so badly, or are never quite good enough. They are self-indulgent and emotional, because they crave 'continual excitement', while that 'severity of composition' which the medium requires damps enthusiasm, as true prose-writers recognize, and this cuts off the poet's resources.

Criticizing Scott for the 'desultory vacillation and want of firmness in the march of his style', he explains that there is neither '*momentum* nor elasticity in it'. The critical terminology which Hazlitt employs here and elsewhere in the essay ('expressive pauses', for example) naturally invites us to apply it to his style – a style whose momentum and elasticity we immediately recognize and approve of, even as we perceive that a new poetics of prose style is being unfolded before our eyes:

Poets either get into this incoherent, undetermined, shuffling style, made up of 'unpleasing flats and sharps', of unaccountable starts and pauses, of doubtful odds and ends, flirted about like straws in a gust of wind; or, to avoid it and steady themselves, mount into a sustained and measured prose (like the translation of Ossian's *Poems*, or some parts of Shaftesbury's *Characteristics*) which is more odious still, and as bad as being at sea in a calm.

True prose is neither desultory nor rhapsodic, neither falsely synco-pated nor – really momentous prose would break the cadence here – nor too suavely complete like Shaftesbury's velvety rhapsodies.

Of course, in making the case for prose, Hazlitt is also making the case for criticism to be recognized as an art-form, and he does this by introducing a series of images and quotations – French paste, Bristol stone, procreant cradle – which enrich his arguments to the point of contradiction, or at least ambiguity. With its steep cliff, makeshift spear-bridge, twisting paths, and plunging noise, this essay's dizzying sense of difficulty and lift-off catches the vertigin-ous, existential contradictions of prose as a medium; and this expresses Hazlitt's puritan commitment to its sudden, apparently ephemeral existence as writing to the moment. Thus, if Addison had argued at his club or spoken in public, his ear would have caught the necessary 'modulations of sound arising out of the feeling of the moment'. He didn't, so he missed the different intonations and 'lively transitions' of speech – his style was not 'indented, nor did it project from the surface'. The implication is that Addison's smooth, equable uniformity sought no coign of vantage – no indentation or projection – and so could neither leap like the chamois nor dip and circle like the swift. Addison's style, unlike Burke's, had no texture to savour. The 'poetical prose-writer', Hazlitt argues, stops to describe an object, if he admires it or believes it will bear dwelling on, while the genuine prose-writer alludes to the object rapidly or else characterizes it in passing, and then only with reference to his subject. The prose-writer is 'master of his materials: the poet is the slave of his style'. This is a decisive contrast which presents the prose-writer as autonomous, fully empowered, active, like the citi-zen of a republic, while at the same time exposing the poet as a slave of style, like a member of a royal court. Poets are Tories; prose-writers, the best of them, are radical Whigs. Shenstone's distinction holds. Or does it?

Though Hazlitt agrees with Fox's remark that it would 'never do' to make politics a department of the imagination, he knows that the question of whether or not Burke should have aestheticized politics is irrelevant. His transgressive prose has entered the public arena. Very visibly and influentially, that prose exists, and has to be grappled with. It has rejected the republican faculty of the under-standing in favour of the aristocratic 'exaggerating and exclusive' faculty of the imagination. It seeks, as Hazlitt says of the monarchist or poetic imagination, the greatest quantity of 'present excitement by inequality and disproportion'. And Hazlitt loves the immediacy, the suddenness and excitement, of Burke's prose poetry. When he says that every word 'should be a blow', and every thought should 'instantly grapple with its fellow', he's representing those values as the equivalent of this passage in 'The Fight': 'There was little cautious sparring – no half-hits – no tapping and trifling, none of the *petit maîtreship* of the art – they were almost all knock-down blows.'

As surely as Neate wants to pulverize the Gas-man, Hazlitt wants to diminish Burke. Contrasting him with Rousseau, who overthrew the French monarchy 'by the force of style', he remarks that Burke was jealous of Rousseau's enormous influence, and wrote his tracts against the Revolution out of violent pique. By patronizing Burke in this way, Hazlitt is expressing the negative, competitive attitude which is so profoundly part of his lifelong relationship to this tragic, self-dramatizing, hugely contradictory figure.

When Hazlitt mentions a friend's criticism of the absence of cadence in Burke's prose, he introduces a doubt which hovers over the admiration he expresses elsewhere. We are meant to wonder if there may not be something jagged, dissonant, forced, and strained in the prose. But is this necessarily a bad thing? Might it not be a virtue? And when Hazlitt remarks that Burke's frequently violent transitions have 'something Pindaric' in them, he is recognizing the jumps and breaks in the style, even though its lack of cadence isn't really addressed by the comparison to Pindar. Burke has a 'great, but irregular mind', and this idea of the unhinged genius allows Hazlitt both to admire his writing and to keep him at arm's length. He is not going to allow the force of Burke's exuberance, originality, and irregular genius to overwhelm him. Though Hazlitt blames Burke's polemics for bringing about British interference in France – a disastrous intervention that produced the Terror – he presents him as an eloquent apostate and brilliant sophist, a genius whose madness seconded the madness of the court. His 'flaming imagination' was the torch that kindled 'the smouldering fire in the inmost sanctuary of pride and power', and spread havoc, dismay, and desolation throughout the world: 'I myself have played all my life with his forked shafts unhurt, because I had a metaphysical clue to carry off the noxious particles, and let them sink into the earth, like drops of water.'

The mixed metaphor is initially that of a lightning conductor, which draws off the electricity generated by Burke's imagination, and this Priestleyan, or Franklinian, scientific image signals the concept of natural disinterestedness which Hazlitt outlines in his *Essay on the Principles of Human Action* (that concept of disinterestedness is the metaphysical clue, the lead). The problem is that the English are 'not a nation of metaphysicians', or they would have detected the 'glittering fallacies of this half-bred reasoner' who was also the 'most accomplished rhetorician that the world ever saw'.

Hazlitt's habit of sometimes putting a critical distance between himself and the English is immediately complicated by his surely racist, snobbish description of Burke as 'half-bred'. Burke, as he says elsewhere, is 'our half-English, half-Irish prose poet'; but the dismissive adjective 'half-bred' is puzzling. Could it not more accurately refer to Hazlitt, the child of an Irish father from Co. Tipperary and an English mother from Cambridgeshire? Or is he simply scorning Burke's social station? It certainly isn't a simple moment, because it articulates, I think, the complex self-disgust which can afflict those who exist on the interface between two cultural identities. Is there a doubt surfacing here as to the nature of his own enterprise? Isn't this a rather camp, over-the-top moment, one which might have been penned by Wilde and voiced by Lady Bracknell? The dramatic tone of Hazlitt's style, which he learnt in part from Burke, permits a type of rhetorical overstatement designed to catch his audience's attention. This is a moment of comic repartee, unlike his frustrated diatribe against the unphilosophic English, who are 'perplexed by sophistry, stupefied by prejudice, staggered by authority'.

The attack begins to modulate into a very different key when Hazlitt states that Pitt, with his 'deep-mouthed commonplaces', was able to follow in the same track as Burke, 'and fill up the cry', but could not have led the 'chase' against the revolution with 'so musical a discord, such sweet thunder'. Here, the Shakespearean allusion is particularly apt, because it implicitly rebuts the view that Burke's prose is not musical, by picking up the speech from *A Midsummer Night's Dream* in which Theseus invites Hippolyta to mark 'the musical confusion' caused by the way the noise of the hounds' barks is multiplied by the mountain's echo. In a lyric speech, Hippolyta replies:

> I was with Hercules and Cadmus once,
> When in a wood of Crete they bayed the bear
> With hounds of Sparta. Never did I hear
> Such gallant chiding; for, besides the groves,
> The skies, the fountains, every region near
> Seemed all one mutual cry. I never heard
> So musical a discord, such sweet thunder.

Hazlitt cites this passage in his lecture on the play, commenting that even Titian 'never made a hunting-piece of a *gusto* so fresh and lusty, and so near the first ages of the world as this'. It is a remark whose reference to Titian and whose prose keeping – *gusto fresh lusty first* – richly insist on the passage's magnificence.

In his remark about Pitt and Burke, the quotation keys Hippolyta's whole speech, and allows us to peer into Hazlitt's imaginative subconscious, a region in which Burke's reactionary madness and unmusical rhetoric are softened, uplifted, classicized, and utterly transformed by Shakespeare's stately lines. The sweetness of the verse, along with Hazlitt's delighted sense of its primal, painterly beauty and gusto, resolves all dissonance and conflict into 'one mutual cry', so that Burke is wafted out of the noise of political argument into the divine element of art and leisure. His prose becomes poetic, even consensual, at least at this particular moment of critical appreciation – I say 'particular moment', because Hazlitt finds the style indefinable. It is easy to describe second-rate talents, he says in his character sketch of Cobbett, but first-rate powers defy calculation, because they are defined only by themselves:

I have tried half-a-dozen times to describe Burke's style without ever succeeding – its severe extravagance; its literal boldness; its matter-of-fact hyperboles; its running away with a subject, and from it at the same time – but there is no making it out, for there is no example of the same thing anywhere else. We have no common measure to refer to; and his qualities contradict even themselves.

Where Yeats, for his own strategic purposes, discerns a 'great melody' in the prose, Hazlitt finds something slippery, self-contradictory, and unclassifiable, an abyss of violent irony from which he draws his own exasperated inspiration. Burke's historical imagination is the procreant cradle, the deep womb which feeds Hazlitt's writing, and he can best express its oratorical power through phrases and images drawn from verse drama. If Hazlitt seems to be elevating the prose by trying to define its essential qualities through images taken from Shakespearean verse, we should not ignore the fact that he is also grounding prose in the eloquence of active bodies moving on an illuminated stage, where they express the absolute social moment of their performance. When he quotes Shakespeare, he must often be remembering how a particular actor delivered a particular speech.

By attaching Burke's prose to Hippolyta's lines, Hazlitt aims to characterize his style almost as a type of melodic dissonance that is raised above the antagonisms which its political content breathed and generated during the last decade of the eighteenth century. As with the hounds' cries, distance soothes its blood-lust. Hippolyta's speech is the generous judgement of posterity on Burke's style, a judgement we need to deduce from the quotation, because it runs counter to the attack which Hazlitt is making on Burke. What draws him to Burke's style, and makes him want to mount his prose Pegasus, is the perception that this writing is actively imaginative. It shifts boundaries, moves goal-posts, uses unfair tactics – partly because it's in revolt against the constrictions which separate prose from verse. Thus Burke may be the great apostate from liberty, but he wins out against an opponent like Sir James Mackintosh, who had nothing but a 'dry, cold, formal' understanding with which to challenge Burke's swingeing Coriolanian imagination. When Burke speaks of France being 'hackled and torn to pieces', for example, he relishes an unusual verb which he probably took from North's Plutarch, where, appropriately for this citation, Caesar is 'hackled & mangled' by his republican assassins, 'as a wild beast taken of hunters'. Among Hazlitt's innumerable allusions to Burke, I haven't discovered this passage, but it exactly expresses the lunging, cutting, physical intelligence of Burke's allusive style – the way he appears to participate physically in the dismembering that he so furiously repudiates. As Hippolyta's speech shows, it is the hunter's instinct which fuels a prose whose radically unstable, ironic doubleness is most famously expressed in the conclusion to *Reflections*, where Burke, quoting Addison's *Cato*, says that before the Revolution's 'final settlement' France may be obliged to pass ' "through great varieties of untried being", and in all its transmigrations to be purified by fire and blood'.

In his edition of *Reflections*, Conor Cruise O'Brien links this remark with another passage in Burke's prose, one which was perceptively praised by Matthew Arnold, who wrote that he knew of nothing more striking and more 'un-English' than Burke's manner of turning back upon himself. For Arnold, the passage from *Thoughts on French Affairs* which O'Brien compares to the end of *Reflections* embodies what he termed 'living by ideas', and it is the sheer intellectual drive and self-exposure which Hazlitt valued in the style. Riding the molten rapids of that prose, he couldn't fail to cheer the burning fiery furnace from which it flows. Burke's imaginative leaps and way of doubling back on himself put Hazlitt in touch with the un-English side of his own upbringing, invigorating him and making him as ready for any opponent as the racket-playing genius Cavanagh. Where a writer this century might quote Yeats to elevate and enhance an occasion, Hazlitt cited Burke. His prose is the pure drop, the thing itself.

Immediately after Hippolyta's musical reply, Hazlitt would have heard the guttural spondees in Theseus's vigorous lines, which he also quoted in his lecture on the play:

> My hounds are bred out of the Spartan kind,
> So flewed, so sanded; and their heads are hung
> With ears that sweep away the morning dew;
> Crook-kneed, and dew-lapped like Thessalian bulls;
> Slow in pursuit, but matched in mouth like bells.
> Each under each.

The hound-cry of Burke's style is both dissonant and harmonious, like a type of early modernist music, but it is also muscular, glossy, ringing, and classical – and intent on trapping its prey.

Burke is a truth-teller, and Hazlitt takes his side against the modern 'Panoptic and Chrestomathic School of reformers' whose logical Benthamite diagrams concede all taste, fancy, and sentiment to admirers of *Reflections*. In this virtually unknown essay, 'People of Sense', he expresses impatience with *Prometheus Unbound*, describing Percy Shelley as a sophist indulging in rhapsodies of words, and characterizing the philosophic radicals' social ideas as 'bare walls and skeletons of houses'. Destitute of comfort, as of 'outward show', their system wants 'house-warming'. They make man with a 'quadrant', and although they can distinguish the hard edges and 'determinate outline of things', they banish pleasure. Bentham has no style: his language is a mere 'logical apparatus'.

Burke's writings embody an ontological idea of beauty for Hazlitt – house-warming *and* elegance – and this is connected with their emotionalism. In a passage from *Reflections* which Hazlitt is fond of citing, Burke rejects 'our pert loquacity', and states:

In England we have not yet been completely embowelled of our natural entrails; we still feel within us, and we cherish and cultivate, those inbred sentiments which are the faithful guardians, the active monitors of our duty, the true supporters of all liberal and manly morals. We have not been drawn and trussed, in order that we may be filled, like stuffed birds in a museum, with chaffs and rags, and paltry, blurred shreds of paper about the rights of man. We preserve the whole of our feelings still native and entire, unsophisticated by pedantry and infidelity. We have real hearts of flesh and blood beating in our bosoms.

Hazlitt admires this passage, because he is critical of Protestantism's captious nature, its 'dry, meagre, penurious imagination'. Blood, being liquid, flows, and for Hazlitt it represents a passionate emotion, an indwelling quality and sense of the sacred that Rational Dissent often lacks (Burke's imagery appears to be a disguised version of the Sacred Heart).

The word 'dry', as we've seen, is a significant critical term in Hazlitt's writing, where it is often linked allusively to Burke, particularly to his dismissive reference in *Reflections* to preachers who 'at present beautify the *hortus siccus* of Dissent'. Applying the phrase to Coleridge's Unitarian period – he falls ten thousand fathoms into 'the *hortus siccus* of Dissent' – Hazlitt says that the poet pared religion down to 'the standard of reason, and stripped faith of mystery'. This is similar to the judgement elsewhere in *The Spirit of the Age* that there was in the 'very texture' of Horne Tooke's understanding a 'hard, dry materialism'. Hazlitt is drawing on Burke's social vision, his sense of mystery, his reverence for what, in a proleptically Yeatsian phrase, he calls 'the ancient permanent sense of mankind', in order to challenge a parched, unimaginative ratiocination. Just as Godwin makes man into a 'logical machine', so Bentham's panopticon is like a 'glass bee-hive' which will effect no permanent reform in the criminal who is imprisoned in it. The charm of criminal life, Hazlitt argues in his profile of Bentham, is like that of savage life, and consists in 'liberty, in hardship, in danger, and in the contempt of death: in one word, in extraordinary excitement'. It is this type of wild excitement which, we may deduce, he finds in Burke's prose. And when he contrasts the reformer Robert Owen's *New View of Society* with a book called *Captivity among the North American Indians*, he introduces a Burkean passage in which he asks if Owen has anything to show in all the 'apparatus' of New Lanark's desolate monotony 'to excite the thrill of imagination like the blankets made of wreaths of snow under which the wild wood-rovers bury themselves for weeks in winter'. It's the imaginative thrill in Burke that refutes the earnest logical paradigms of the reformers, and haunts Hazlitt. He wants to redeem those blurred sheets by transforming their arid prose into passionate emotion.

But isn't Hazlitt responding to the attractions of Burke's romantic irrationalism? Or is he instead following him and Coleridge in opposing a despotic, abstract, Jacobin reason? His contradictory emotions are expressed in a passage in *Political Essays* where he says that Burke's lamentations over the death of the age of chivalry, and his projected crusade to restore it, are about as wise as someone becoming a pickpocket after reading *The Beggar's Opera*, or, after admiring the landscapes of Salvator Rosa, wishing to convert the abodes of civilized life into 'the haunts of wild beasts and banditti'. The charm of criminal life and Rosa's brilliant, erratic genius are associated with Burke's imagination. Rosa was also an actor, and this ties in with Burke's theatricality, which the reference to Gay's opera glances at. And Rosa's wild, picturesque, mountain landscapes helped shape the image of Burke's style as a chamois.

When Hazlitt writes in his essay on the prose style of poets that Burke's execution, like that of all good prose, 'savours of the texture of what he describes, and his pen slides or drags over the ground of his subject, like the painter's pencil', this consciously echoes his remark on the bold, firm freedom of Rosa's painting. Burke combines rigid fidelity with fanciful extravagance, and in Hazlitt's praise we can savour the sensuous texture of his own enjoyment of prose as a medium. Burke's style has all the 'familiarity' of conversation combined with all the 'research' of the most elaborate composition. For the most part, he gives 'loose reins' to his imagination, and follows it as far as the language will carry him. He is the 'most poetical' of all our prose-writers, while at the same time never degenerating into the 'mere effeminacy' of poetry. This is because he always aims at 'overpowering rather than at pleasing', and consequently sacrifices beauty and delicacy to 'force and vividness'.

Such a masculinist concept of style, as a weapon wielded by a writer whose only object is to 'strike hard, and in the right place', is connected, for Hazlitt, with the struggles of the centaurs and lapiths on the Elgin Marbles. It also expresses his fear of poetry as female, and an essentially puritan hostility to ornament and artifice. In certain important respects, the poetics of prose, which he spontaneously sets out in the essay on style, is an anti-aesthetic that depends emphatically on *not* possessing certain qualities. In poetry, the increasing sense of beauty and grandeur, he says, is the 'principle of composition'; while in prose writing, the professed object is to impart conviction, and no ornament or relief can be admitted that does not add 'new force or clearness to the original conception'. Founding itself on certain gritty, recalcitrant refusals, prose style constitutes itself as *not* beautiful, *not* delicate, leaving readers to discover beauty in what has been designed with altogether other aims in mind. Where every word should be a 'blow', and every thought should instantly 'grapple with its fellow', there must necessarily be a 'weight, a precision, a conformity from association in the tropes and figures of animated prose to fit them to their place in the argument, and make them *tell*, which may be dispensed with in poetry'.

There is an instrumental concept of accuracy here – trueness – which is concentrated in the way the emphasized verb 'tell' means to utter, announce, be visibly effective, and emphatically spot-on. This insistence on making tropes and figures *tell* emphasizes animated conversation and direct speech. Like Hopkins's instressing of 'each tucked string tells', Hazlitt's idea of what fits and utters itself has an exacting precision, which communicates his sensuous vision of the English language's might and power. When Burke praises the 'simplicity of our national character . . . a sort of native plainness and directness of understanding', he similarly affirms the value of what Hazlitt in *The Eloquence of the British Senate* terms 'good sound English sense'. Good prose has a downright, common-sense exactness: it hits nails on their heads, and allows us to enjoy the hammer-bang of its certainties. Like Dryden's prefaces, it must be a model of 'simplicity, strength and perspicuity'; but where Dryden's critical prose is 'perfectly unexceptionable', Hazlitt aims to write a prose that is exceptional, in a class of its own.

Identifying prose style with violent conflict, Hazlitt seeks to identify its medium as world-historical, and to present Burke as a universal genius rooted in a decade of war and political conflict. Here he ran counter to the view of Burke which prevailed in British, French, and Irish radical circles, because some early reviewers of his essays suggested that he was mistaken in his view of Burke's prose style. Criticism of Burke was widespread, and when, for example, a member of the French National Assembly described his visit to Hackney New College in 1791, he wrote that Burke's imagination was full of '*paladins et prodiges*' and that he had raised a shameful, brilliant monument to the glory of French chivalry and the servitude of nations. This extravagant rhetorician had called down the fury of the mob on Priestley's head.

If we look at Priestley's reply to Burke – a series of fourteen letters – we find that his prose breathes a placidly sorrowful sense of having been betrayed by a politician whom the Dissenters had always imagined was someone 'on whom we could depend'. They lamented his fall as that of a friend and a brother. Priestley's tone is coolly rational and decorously unimaginative. He describes *Reflections* as 'this most intemperate publication', and tells its author that his imagination is 'evidently heated, and your ideas confused'. He argues that if Burke will 'please to change' his style and assume the character of a philosopher, not that of a 'mere rhetorician', then it will be very agreeable to the Dissenters to have him 'of the party'. You are now of an age, he admonishes Burke, when the powers of imagination should have been 'more checked' by those of reason, because on this subject imagination should, like the passions, 'be absolutely silent, and the friends and enemies of church establishments would then be enabled to simply *reason together*'.

Hazlitt was not impressed by what he termed the 'numerous and respectable' replies to Burke ('respectable' is a synonym for middle-class Dissenters, as well as meaning that they put up a reasonable, but not overwhelming, show of argument). Paine's *The Rights of Man* was the best reply to *Reflections*, Hazlitt says, but all Burke's opponents evaded his 'recondite meaning', while no one could match his 'colours of style'. Standing on the prow of the ship of state, he had harpooned the Leviathan of the French Revolution.

In the first reply to Burke, *A Vindication of the Rights of Men*, published by Joseph Johnson in 1790, Mary Wollstonecraft attacks his irrational, imaginative language, and finds him rhetorical, romantic, theatrical, bombastic. Man preys on man, she concludes, 'and you mourn for the idle tapestry that decorated a gothic pile, and the dronish bell that summoned the fat priest to prayer'.

Another radical, Christopher Wyvill, defended Price and the reformers against Burke's 'false and fraudulent eloquence'. The *Analytical Review*, a periodical edited by the Unitarian Thomas Christie and published by Joseph Johnson, attacked him for 'looseness of style', and suggested that many passages were inflated. Another Unitarian, Richard Sharp, praised Burke's style, but found it 'too undisciplined' to be a model. The question of style, not simply content, clearly exercised the reformers who challenged Burke, and this was because they belonged to a culture which set a high valuation on prose style. It was therefore important to attack not just what Burke said, but how he said it.

Hazlitt identifies another reason for the breadth of this critical reception when he says that Burke changed 'our style of thinking'. Here he is saying that Burke changed political discourse, as we would now term it, and that by so doing he dictated terms to everyone who tried to discuss the issues he raised. Priestley half recognizes this when he suggests that Burke should change his style, but the fair-minded Unitarian's rational coolness and Sunday-school manner was no match for the vivid bundle of flashy images, dirty tricks and inspired declamation that make up *Reflections*. Hazlitt's quarrel with Burke is a lifelong, smouldering, incandescent argument which he can never extinguish, because he's powerless to turn our style of thinking – the discourse we're now trapped in – back to its former direction or into a different mode. Like Punch and Judy, or Tweedledum and Tweedledee, he and Burke are condemned – at least in Hazlitt's writing – to be either at loggerheads or negotiating a truce. Hazlitt calls Irish oratory 'a sort of aeronaut' – an image thrown back from the close of *Reflections*, where the firm ground of the British constitution is contrasted with the desperate flights of the 'aëronauts of France'.

The extensiveness of Hazlitt's citations from Burke means that he cannot escape from the definition of political reality which the Irish aeronaut's polemics have shaped. He praises Burke copiously, but might this not be a strategy for escaping his dominance by provoking his readers into resisting the praise he so lavishly and obsessively heaps on him? Perhaps not, but there are times when he appears to be as chained to Burke as he is to Napoleon, that unchanging object of his compulsive hero-worship. Contrasting the 'capricious caricature' of Windham's imitative style with his master Burke's 'bold, natural, discursive manner', he notes that Burke conversed as he spoke in public, in a manner that was 'communicative, diffuse, magnificent'. This is not too different from Napoleon's conversation, which was 'frank, communicative, unreserved and free in the highest degree', and it counts as the highest possible praise. Again, *Letter to a Noble Lord* is praised for being 'rapid', 'impetuous', the most 'sportive' of all his writings. Very importantly, Burke's mind never became 'set': it was always in 'further search and progress'. Where Samuel Johnson, the implication is, exemplifies a set style, Burke is for ever thinking things through.

Such praise of a member of the opposite party also shows Hazlitt's supremely confident disinterestedness, and he obviously knew that his audience would give him credit for his display of that Dissenting value. But when he asks what living prose-writer would think of comparing himself to Burke, we can feel him willing his readers to make the comparison with his own prose. Hazlitt wants to more than equal him – he wants to excel him. Behind his disinterested admiration we can discern an interested but noble ambition to become the supreme prose stylist of his age. Fighting a long critical war with Burke, he aims to put permanent critical pressure on his style. He cites and parodies the aria on Marie Antoinette many times: 'It is now seventeen years since I was studying in the Louvre,' he tells us in a passage of autobiography which rebounds off the famous opening sentence of Burke's eulogy.

Earlier in the same essay, he relives the moment when he was admitted to the Louvre:

It was *un beau jour* to me. I marched delighted through a quarter of a mile of the proudest efforts of the mind of man, a whole creation of genius, a universe of art! I ran the gauntlet of all the schools from the bottom to the top; and in the end got admitted into the inner room, where they had been repairing some of their greatest works. Here the Transfiguration, the St Peter Martyr, and the St Jerome of Domenichino stood on the floor, as if they had bent their knees, like camels stooping, to unlade their riches to the spectator. On one side, on an easel, stood Hippolito de Medici (a portrait by Titian) with a boar-spear in his hand, looking through those he saw, till you turned away from the keen glance: and thrown together in heaps were landscapes of the same hand, green pastoral hills and vales, and shepherds piping to their mild mistresses underneath the flowering shade. Reader, 'if thou hast not seen the Louvre, thou art damned!' – for thou hast not seen the choicest remains of the works of art; or thou hast not seen all these together, with their mutually reflected glories. I say nothing of the statues; for I know but little of sculpture, and never liked any till I saw the Elgin Marbles. . . . Here, for four months together, I strolled and studied, and daily heard the warning sounds – '*Quatre heures passées, il faut fermer, Citoyens,*' – (Ah! why did they ever change their style?) muttered in coarse provincial French; and brought away with me some loose drafts and fragments, which I have been forced to part with, like drops of life-blood, for 'hard money'. How often, thou tenantless mansion of godlike magnificence – how often has my heart since gone a pilgrimage to thee!

The phrase '*un beau jour*' picks up a passage which occurs just before the evocation of Marie Antoinette, where Burke laments the events of 6 October 1789, when the King and Queen were removed from Versailles to Paris. Then Burke suggests that, notwithstanding the 'applauses' of the Revolution Society in Britain, a majority of the French National Assembly must be 'silently scandalized with those of their members, who could call a day which seemed to blot the sun out of Heaven, "*un beau jour*"!'

Burke's double blow – at the Revolution Society in London and the progress of the Revolution in France – is caught up in Hazlitt's allusion. But he does not stop there. He marches delightedly through the Louvre, like Napoleon after a victory, glorying in the collection which his hero created there. To Hazlitt's intense anger, many of the works of art in the Louvre were returned by the duke of Wellington after Waterloo. Art, military victory, defeat, youthful hope, and a refusal to relinquish that hope all combine in a prose version of several passages in Wordsworth's then unpublished *Prelude* which portray his experience of revolutionary France. Hazlitt knew that epic poem, and must have designed the Louvre passage partly in imitation of Wordsworth's spots of historical time. It can also be linked with another autobiographical prose poem – with the evening star above the poor man's cottage after Austerlitz, which concludes the first of these paired essays, 'On the Pleasure of Painting'. The attendant's republican announcement fuses with this concentrated combination of Titian, Napoleon, the Revolution, and its wars. The Elgin Marbles, those symbols of perfect prose style, as well as the packed artistic treasures in the people's palace and his own personal memory of having twice seen Charles James Fox there, cram the prose to bursting-point. He is writing after the dismantling of the Louvre's collection; but in remembering his three months in Paris during the brief Peace of Amiens in 1802, he aims to raise an imperishably unchanged style above the historical events that followed. Hazlitt represents his style as heir to Napoleon – it bashes Burke to one side, and marches on undefeated. It is an occupying army that fuses great art with great power.

This is a triumphalist style, which in its assertive boldness is not dissimilar to Yeats's poetic manner of raising the stakes, elevating his subject so that every detail appears charged and permanently important. Like Yeats – like Burke too – Hazlitt is writing out of a wish to assert historic rights on behalf of a people with a history of being beaten down. The achievement of a lasting, self-delighting, beautiful, and beautifully armed style is the politically engaged artist's answer to oppression – or it is sometimes. The bare logical diagrammatic bones of reformist prose angered Hazlitt, who rejected its parched rationalism, and instead aimed to write well by ceaselessly invoking and pummelling Burke. Marching through the Louvre, he is saying that he has the Irish sophist on the run at last.

CHAPTER SEVEN

Southey's Organ of Vanity

Where Hazlitt's triumphalist style aims to conquer historical disappointment by dazzling his readers with the verbal equivalent of a republican victory parade, his harsher polemical mode seeks to reduce Burke and other counter-revolutionary writers to ignominious figures motivated by envy and malice. In 'Arguing in a Circle', he again remarks that Burke was not invited by the French national assembly to advise on a new republican constitution. Unlike the duke of Marlborough in Addison's 'The Campaign', Burke was not called upon to 'ride in the whirlwind and direct the storm' – a remark which picks up the more generous allusion to Addison's Whig panegyric in Hazlitt's 1807 sketch of Burke directing the counter-revolutionary storm. Characterizing him in 'Arguing in a Circle' as piqued and jealous, the polemicist is seen in a prose version of a political cartoon as a 'malicious hag' trying to shipwreck the new republic. Linking Burke to the Poet Laureate, Southey, Hazlitt states that deserters are never 'implicitly trusted', and in a comic put-down remarks that it is impossible not to travesty Southey's odes on kings into lampoons against monarchy.

Southey is a favourite target – no fewer than eight pieces in *Political Essays* are devoted to this strenuous, but in certain ways somewhat complex reactionary. We follow Hazlitt's long quarrel with him in a comic sub-plot to the main drama of his engagement with Burke. The Irish monarchist is a tragic figure, but the former English republican is a misguided, decent, uptight human being whose inept political verse Hazlitt quotes for the amusement of the anti-Tory readers of the *Examiner* and the *Morning Chronicle*. Unlike Burke, Southey is neither subtle nor wildly imaginative; he's an unreconstructed Jacobin who is just as fanatical in the service of his new political creed. His extreme monarchist sentiments every-where betray his deeply rooted Jacobin principles, a fixed and cal-low ideology which makes him appear in Hazlitt's prose as a rigid, mechanically active figure. A writer who passes from verse to prose, history to poetry, he seems to work by the clock, and is as stiffly definite as the umbrella he always carries on his visits to London.

What angers Hazlitt is that Southey's celebrations of the Allied victory over Napoleon's army fly in the face of Whig history and culture, and also deny the struggles of British Protestantism against European Catholicism. Furiously, he returns in *Political Essays* to the Royalist massacres of Protestants in southern France in 1816, to the brutal treatment of Spanish patriots by the Allies, and to the obscenity of Britain's new-found closeness to the Bourbons. England has embraced the enemies of all that it used to stand for as a nation, but Southey's patriotic muse is silent before this betrayal. In the period that followed Napoleon's defeat, a wild populist Protestant atavism howls through Hazlitt's prose. He is devastated by Waterloo, and wanders through London inconsolably miserable. As his polemical powers return, he shouts loud abuse, and runs riot in print. It's as though Napoleon's defeat and the massacre of French Protestants in the White Terror which followed the restor-ation of the monarchy have merged into a single apocalypse.

In a series of articles on the history of the French monarchy, which he published in the *Examiner* during April 1817, Hazlitt's anguish at times transforms him into a persecuted Huguenot, so complete is his identification with the sufferings of French Protestants. Rapidly paraphrasing, Howe suggests, a French ori-ginal, he calls the French Huguenot leader Admiral de Coligny 'one of our greatest men' (Coligny was murdered at the start of the St Bartholemew's Day Massacre in 1572), and then rounds on the British Foreign Secretary Castlereagh for saying 'That in the mas-sacres at Nîmes, there were ONLY a thousand people killed!' In his bitter historical sketch 'The Good Old Times before the French Revolution', Hazlitt describes how Francis I massacred 6,000 Protestants:

But their cries still sound in the ears of humanity; they ride upon the rack of history and roll down upon the tide of time; they, the dead, speak to us, the living, with the voice of warning, amidst the slavering cant of Coleridge, and the pert gossiping of Southey with shrill eunuch's voice.

Not the rustling of venal pens shall drown this noise, Hazlitt says, because it is the voice of 'outraged humanity' which philosophy, released from the 'bondage of priestcraft', has heard and echoed back:

Voltaire heard it, Rousseau heard it, Milton heard and gave it back in that noble sonnet to 'our slaughtered Piedmontese brethren'; but Mr Wordsworth, though he must have heard of the massacres at Nîmes, has not yet made them the subject of a sonnet to the King, nor has Mr Southey whispered the case of the Spanish Patriots in the ear of the Prince Regent!

This is a desperate vindication of the radical Enlightenment, which cries out passionately from the tragic agony of bearing witness to England's shameful repudiation of its Protestant history (Hazlitt alludes frequently to Spenser during this period).

By its actions in sending Wellington and his army to crush France back into monarchy, England has sided with a reactionary, punitive Catholicism. The government's indifference to the massacres sends Hazlitt into a violent historical fury, and the atmosphere of his prose lours with tribal memories of persecution:

> Their martyred blood and ashes sow
> O'er all the Italian fields where still doth sway
> The triple tyrant.

Milton's sonnet on the massacre of the Waldensians in Piedmont in 1655 is invoked by Hazlitt. This is the hectic, lacerated, atavistic ground of the Protestant conscience. Milton, be with us now and ever in this hour of trial, the secular Hazlitt is saying as his grief takes on the texture of an embattled, committed faith that affirms solidarity with the living and the dead. And in an extravagant passage that belongs to sectarian tracts or to stage melodrama, he calls the Catholic Church a harlot, and says that the English government wants to give her back 'her fires, her mummeries, her holy oil, her power over the bodies and the minds of men'. Has John Bull nothing better to do nowadays, he exclaims, than to turn 'bottle-holder to the Pope of Rome'?

Desperate, wounded, furious, and inspired, his historical witness hurls itself against the knowledge of defeat; and though he writes in these articles with an embittered urgency, it's entirely characteristic of his dedication to the republican ideal of beautiful and effective prose style that he should also include a long note attacking the ways in which writers for *The Times* misuse the English language. These hack polemicists employ an impotent, inflated style packed with routine slang phrases and nicknames – 'Corsican Upstart', 'Fiend', 'Monster' – to abuse Napoleon. Such phrases are 'petrific even to behold', and the result is rubbishy abuse arranged according to the rules of Lindley Murray's *English Exercises*, with all 'the ridiculous pedantry of subjunctive moods and adverbial expletives'.

Hazlitt is writing in December 1816 just after the violent demonstrations and riots which followed the Spa Fields meeting at the beginning of the month. A frightened government intensified its measures against radicals and dissidents. It was a time of 'double darkness' which made Hazlitt feel like Milton enduring the repression of a restored monarchy. And, like Milton's Samson, he gives rein to a destructive, very Protestant violence. There is an extremity in his journalism at this period, as he savages Southey for his political treachery, sometimes writing hastily and slackly out of an enormous, driven anger – in a rather glib zeugma he mentions that the government has 'suspended Cashman and the Habeas Corpus'.

The suspension of the Habeas Corpus Act took place in March 1817, and the government took control of all reading-rooms in a move to block circulation of the *Political Register*. The climate of repression was intense, with Southey attacking the influential Unitarian MP William Smith, and calling for the libel laws to be extended to cover Hazlitt's and Cobbett's writings. In March, Cobbett fled to the United States, to avoid being arrested.

Among the rioters arrested after the Spa Fields meeting on 2 December 1816 was an impoverished Irish sailor John Cashman, whose execution Hazlitt is referring to when he mentions the

1 William Hazlitt, early self-portrait: 'dumb, inarticulate, helpless, like a
worm by the wayside'

2 The Revd William Hazlitt (1732–1820), by William Hazlitt
3 Grace Hazlitt (1746–1837), from a painting by John Hazlitt

4 Margaret Hazlitt (1770–1837), by John Hazlitt
5 William Hazlitt, by John Hazlitt

6 John Thelwall, radical writer and editor, by William Hazlitt
7 Charles Lamb, essayist and critic, by William Hazlitt

8 Titian, *Young Man with a Glove*, c. 1520

9 The house in Wem, Shropshire, where Hazlitt lived from 1787 to 1795

10 19 York Street, Westminster: Hazlitt's home from 1810 to 1819
11 The building in Frith Street, Soho – then a lodging-house, now a hotel – where Hazlitt died

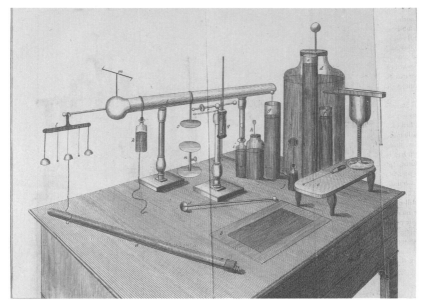

12 Joseph Priestley's apparatus, from *A Familiar Introduction to the Study of Electricity*, 1767. The letters are explained in Priestley's text: 'To make the nature of charging and discharging a jar the easier to young electricians, *k* … represents a jar hanging by its wire from the prime conductor, while a chain connects the outside with the table.'

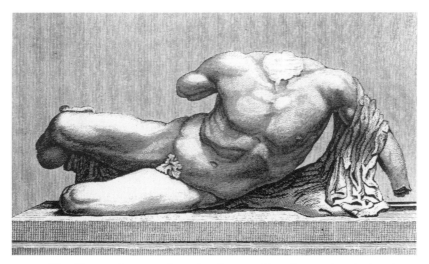

13 The Illisos, a fragment from the Elgin Marbles, illustrated in the *London Magazine*, February 1822: 'harmonious, flowing, varied prose'

14 The pugilist Tom Hickman: 'light, vigorous, elastic'
15 Manuscript of 'The Fight', Hazlitt's essay
published in the *London Magazine*, February 1822

16 Fives Court, Leicester Fields: 'the face of a racket-player is the face of a friend. There is no juggling there.'

17 Pugilists in the Fives Court: 'There was little cautious sparring – no half-hits – no tapping and trifling, none of the *petit maîtreship* of the art – they were almost all knock-down blows.'

18 William Hazlitt by William Bewick, 1825. Hazlitt was forty-six when
Bewick made this drawing. Bewick called him 'the Shakespeare prose-
writer of our glorious country'.

suspension of habeas corpus. This single, glancing reference opens up the popular discontent with the government which Hazlitt is reflecting in the articles that comprise *Political Essays*, and it shows how the life of the London streets helps to shape his writing.

Cashman had been unsuccessfully petitioning the Admiralty for pay and prize money that was owed to him. Following the riots, he was arrested on a charge of sedition for his part in an attack on a gunsmith's shop after the Spa Fields meeting, and was sentenced to death at the Old Bailey in January 1817. In March he was taken through an enormous crowd of angrily sympathetic Londoners to a wheeled scaffold outside the shop he had been convicted of looting. Cobbett's *Weekly Political Pamphlet* published a moving account of Cashman's dignified conduct throughout his trial and imprisonment:

As the sheriffs advanced, the mob expressed the strongest feelings of indignation: groans and hisses burst from all quarters, and attempts were made to rush forward. The officers, however, stood firm to their posts, and, being aided in their efforts by the wooden barriers, succeeded in preventing any encroachment. This conduct was frequently repeated before the cart had reached its destination; and Cashman joined his voice to the shouts, crying out, 'Huzza! my boys, I'll die like a man!' On his quitting the cart, and mounting the scaffold, the groans were redoubled: he seemed to enter into the spirit of the spectators, and *joined in their exclamations with a terrific shout*. He repeated his former remarks on the supposed hardship of his case. His face was placed towards Holborn Hill, but he turned his head on all sides, and greeted the mob with cries of '*Hurra, my hearties in the cause! success! cheer up!*' – The Revd Mr Cotton and Mr Devereux now ascended the platform, and endeavoured to bring the wretched man to a sense of his awful situation. Their benevolent exertions, however, were fruitless: he appeared callous to all religious exhortations, and pushing them aside, exclaimed, '*Don't bother me – it's no use: I want no mercy but from God!*' – The executioner then came forward, and put the rope round his neck. This operation excited new tumults, and fresh exclamations of disapprobation burst from the crowd. On the night-cap being put over his face, he said, '*For God's sake let me see till the last; I want no cap.*' In this he was indulged, and the cap was withdrawn. He now turned towards Mr *Beckwith's house in an angry manner*, and *shaking his head*, said, 'I'll be with you, there', meaning he would haunt the house after his death. Again turning to the people, he cried, 'I am the *last of seven* of them that fought for my

king and country; *I could not get my own, and that has brought me here.*'
The executioner having quitted the platform, the unfortunate man
addressed the crowd nearest him, and exclaimed, 'Now, you —, give me
three cheers when I trip. Hurra, you —.' And then, calling to the executioner, he cried out, 'Come Jack, you —, let go the jib-boom.' The few
remaining seconds of his existence he employed in similar addresses, and
was cheering at the instant the fatal board fell from beneath his feet. The
cap was then drawn over his face, and he died almost without a struggle.

After about ten minutes, the crowd began to shout 'Murder' at the
officials, and thousands remained until the body was cut down.

Cobbett, like Hazlitt, detested capital punishment, and for both
writers political liberty, a more humane legal system, and good
prose style are closely connected. They each compiled grammars of
the English language, and sought to articulate and codify the genius
of the language of free-born Englishmen. At the root of their art is
the belief that English liberty and a direct, passionately intelligent
prose style are identical. Cobbett speaks and thinks 'plain, broad,
downright English', and Hazlitt aims also to make his style express
the native genius of the language.

He makes this point in his robust and affectionate character
sketch of Cobbett, whose mighty pen made him a kind of 'fourth
estate' in the politics of the country. He might be said to have the
clearness of Swift, the naturalness of Defoe, and the 'picturesque
satirical description' of Mandeville, except that these comparisons
do not capture his total originality. Like all truly great writers,
Hazlitt adds, Cobbett is *sui generis*, and creates the class to which
he belongs.

The account of Cashman's execution takes us to the heart of the
popular opposition to Lord Liverpool's government. With its angry
crowds, armed militia, public scaffolds where representatives of the
State Church offer grisly consolation to those condemned to die,
this restless, violent, desperate, unpredictable urban reality seethes
in the urgency of Hazlitt's style. The state theatre of legalized murder haunted him always (nearly 7,000 men, women, and children
were executed in England and Wales during his lifetime), and like
Cobbett, he attacks the obscene English devotion to hanging.

Behind the prose of *Political Essays*, there is a life-and-death struggle going on. Southey thought he would be in danger if the cause of reform triumphed, and in September 1816 he told his friend, the conservative politician John Rickman, that he feared the danger of becoming a hired government propagandist. He knew very well what would happen to him in the event of a revolution 'were the Hunts and Hazlitts to have the upper hand'. And the following month he complained to his friend Grosvenor Bedford that 'Hunt and Hazlitt, I know, incessantly attack me'.

One of Southey's targets, as I've mentioned, was William Smith, the distinguished Unitarian MP who had defended Priestley and attacked Burke in the 1790s. Southey's *Letter to William Smith* was prompted by a debate in the House of Commons in 1817, during which Smith criticized Southey for some articles he had published in the *Quarterly Review*, and expressed his disgust at the 'settled, determined malignity of a renegado'.* In three letters to the *Examiner*, Hazlitt poured scorn on Southey's reply to Smith's attack, and defended the liberty of the press against the Poet Laureate. At the basis of his argument is the nature of the Unitarian faith, which Southey attacks in an essay, 'On the Rise and Progress of Popular Disaffection', in which he calls Hazlitt's old school 'the Socinian academy at Hackney'.

This defence of Unitarianism against Southey's polemic is particularly evident in a letter from Bristol signed 'Vindex' which was published in the *Examiner* on 6 April 1817, and which Howe convincingly attributes to Hazlitt. In the article, William Smith's remarks on 'the Renegades' are noted, and Smith is implicitly identified as a man who 'resists tyranny with Hampden, or who worships the ONE GOD AND FATHER with the Christian philosopher Locke'. This is an affirmation of Smith's Unitarian faith, and we can

---

* Five years later, Byron recalls Smith's attack in the tenth canto of *Don Juan*, which he wrote in the autumn of 1822:

> Renegados,
> Even shuffling Southey, that incarnate lie,
> Would scarcely join again the *reformados*,
> Whom he forsook to fill the laureate's sty.

feel Hazlitt rallying to that shared cause and community in the declaratory capitals which belong, I've suggested, with the image of personal integrity as a chrysolite. Waving the ONE GOD like a banner, he suggests that Coleridge and Southey would hunt the Dissenters out of the land and 'get a Unitarian in the pillory'. What we detect in Hazlitt is a type of emotional and tribal solidarity, an identification with his 'little platoon' of Rational Dissenters that is similar to Burke's anguished Catholicism. Smith was the acknowledged leader of the Dissenting cause, so his attacks on Southey reawakened memories of the earlier period.

Clearly Hazlitt felt in 1817 that there was a campaign being mounted against Unitarianism which echoed the persecutions of the 1790s, when several ministers were imprisoned and transported, and many Unitarian families emigrated to the United States. Although Hazlitt had no religious belief, and was critical of certain Protestant faults – aridity, meanness of spirit, lack of imagination – he identified in moments of crisis with Unitarian values, and more widely with Dissenting Protestantism. Locke, like Milton and Newton, was held by Rational Dissenters to be anti-Trinitarian, and his name is therefore naturally invoked after the mention of the 'ONE GOD' in Hazlitt's unsigned article. Locke was friendly with a nephew of Marvell's, the Unitarian merchant William Popple, who translated his *Letter on Toleration*. Locke denied being a Unitarian, because he did not want to be labelled with the dangerously bad name of 'Socinian', as anti-Trinitarians were often known then, though his theological work *The Reasonableness of Christianity* expresses a faith very similar to that which Hazlitt was raised in.

The douce rational style which Unitarian writers, following Locke, tend to adopt, isn't favoured by Hazlitt, who at times of particularly severe State repression unleashes an almost expressionist invective. Lambasting those writers who support Legitimacy, he becomes the prose equivalent of a political cartoonist:

now that they have restored this monstrous fiction (after twenty years of baffled, malignant opposition to human nature, long glorious and triumphant, and still to be so) you see them with their swords and pens still propping up its lethargic, ricketty form, that sits squat like a toad or ugly nightmare on the murdered corpse of human liberty, stifling a nation's breath, sucking its best blood, smearing it with the cold deadly slime of nineteen years' accumulated impotent hate, polluting the air with the stench of its nostrils, and choking up the source of man's life! And there between the dugs of this monster, dripping mingled poison and gore, that lifts its head to Heaven, and devours generations of men as its rightful prey, stands the little pert pragmatical plebeian editor of the *Times*, one of the common race of men, with his pen in his hand, ready to draw it through the names of his proscribed list of French patriots.

When he refers to the pert pragmatical editor of *The Times*, he is drawing on the phrase 'pert loquacity' which Burke employs in *Reflections*. 'Pert' is a favourite pejorative in Hazlitt's criticism: it means 'insolent, uppish, bold, over-definite, forward', and carries something of what's nowadays signified by 'yuppie', except that it describes an opinionated cast of mind. 'Petulance', which also describes an over-definite, impetuously confident style of speaking and arguing, is closely linked with it. Thomas Belsham, for example, defends the practice of religious discussion, even though it often leads to dogmatism, a 'petulance of expression' and 'a positivity of assertion'. In this period, both 'pert' and 'petulant' carry the sense of callow ideological arrogance.

Hazlitt appears to have had a particular relish for their sharp *p* and *t* sounds, as when he describes how Southey, the self-regarding polemicist, makes 'one poor effort of pert, pettifogging spite'. It's as though his prose, at least where Southey is concerned, is keyed to a rapid sequence of *p*'s and *t*'s. The sequence is there in his characterization of the old Jacobinical leaven in Southey as 'the same unimpaired desperate unprincipled spirit of partisanship', and it recurs in this description of him: 'you see the organ of vanity triumphant – sleek, smooth, round, perfect, polished, horned, and shining, as it were in a transparency'. This is what he terms the 'handle' of Southey's intellect, and at this point the aural texture of his adjectivally insistent prose establishes a strong visual presence – the glow of a transparency as well as a musical key or motif that's developed in two subsequent essays in which he gives a very thoughtful and judicious account of Southey's prose style.

It is a style which Hazlitt admires and, with characteristic dis-interest, praises, but he also identifies it with a rigid mechanical efficiency that's characterized in a series of pre-ordained plosives and dentals. In 'The Prose Style of Poets' he says that Southey is a much better prose-writer than Coleridge: his style has 'an antique quaintness, with a modern familiarity'. Southey vilifies Reform, and praises the reign of George III in 'good set terms, in a straight-forward, intelligible, practical, pointed way'. This conclusion's sharp metallic sound – the snap of its p's and t's – is echoed by the metaphor that follows: 'You may complain of a pettiness and petulance of manner, but certainly there is no want of spirit or facility of execution. He does not waste powder and shot in the air, but loads his piece, takes a level aim, and hits his mark.' Like a rifle being cocked, this terse brisk simple sentence turns the prose stylist into a kind of functionary, an efficient marksman whose move-ments are the expression of a mechanical drill which makes them rather eerily impersonal. There's something deadening in the qualities that are being identified as positive stylistic features here – *practical pointed* are echoed by *pettiness petulance pert splenetic* – and those adjectives echo the sentence in which we see the organ of vanity triumphant in Southey, like a door handle made of pol-ished bone. Taken together, those words sound like a series of dry spits.

Which is a way of recognizing that the texture, the savoured feel and relish of Hazlitt's prose, carries critical meaning, and, as we have seen in his praise of Burke, that acoustic texture can unsettle or contradict the ostensible subject of a sentence. What we realize is that this prose has both vocal tone and the self-delighting ironic playful-ness which animates speech and is also found in stage drama, espe-cially comedy. A prose which caresses itself too obviously is bound to be sterile and self-conscious, but the momentum of Hazlitt's style prevents us from dwelling on these spontaneous, but perfectly organized clusters of sound. Instead, they leave contrapuntal traces, sonic ripples, which complicate their statements.

Where Burke's prose is given characterization in the 'coign of vantage' allusion to Macbeth's castle, Southey's is made to seem simply projective or like a projectile – he is, the adjectives suggest, both a prig and a prick. In *The Spirit of the Age*, he is 'captious, dogmatical, petulant', as well as being 'sharp and angular, quaint and eccentric'. Neither gracious nor decorous, he is full of pique and self-opinion. With him everything is 'projecting, starting from its place, an episode, a digression, a poetic licence'. And in a variation on the passage which begins his discussion of Southey in 'The Prose Style of Poets', Hazlitt says that Southey's prose can scarcely be too much praised. It is 'plain, clear, pointed, familiar: perfectly modern in its texture, but with a grave and sparkling admixture of *archaisms* in its ornaments and occasional phraseology'. He is the 'best and most natural prose-writer of any poet of the day'.

The alliterating *p* sounds both praise and set a limit on the qualities of his prose, for Southey remains a poet writing prose, and so, by definition, he can never be fully attuned to the material mysteries of that art. He is still 'a government-tool' – though not always, for he can be liberal and humane. When Hazlitt asks if Southey is not 'captious, dogmatical, petulant in delivering his sentiments', the sentence has an interesting assonantal pattern which sets up a series of hard, dental *t* sounds only to pick up the *shus* in 'captious' and echo it in a series of sussurating *s*'s which create a flimsy texture that slightly softens and then diminishes the dentals. This may be to pay too much attention to prose pattern, but it fits with his use of the term 'texture' in *The Spirit of the Age*. When he speaks of the 'texture and obvious process' of Mackintosh's mind, he is using the term as a means of indicating both the quality and the feel of his ideas as they are expressed in written prose. He aims above all to give his own prose a supple sinewy texture, which is the weave of consciousness, and this means that the change from tight dentals to slushy sibilants in this clause communicates an oral relish, even if the cross-hatching of sound is just a shade too balanced and predictable. This is one expression of the sensuous manner in which Hazlitt aims to represent ideas.

We can see this effect in an unimportant sentence in the essay 'Trifles Light as Air', which is merely a piece of jobbing journalism:

It is a curious speculation to take a modern *belle*, or some accomplished female acquaintance, and conceive what her great-great-grandmother was like, some centuries ago. Who was the Mrs – of the year 200? We have some standard of grace and elegance among eastern nations 3,000 years ago, because we read accounts of them in history; but we have no more notion of, or faith in, our own ancestors than if we had never had any. We *cut the connection* with the Druids and the Heptarchy; and cannot fancy ourselves (by any transformation) inmates of caves and woods, or feeders on acorns and sloes. We seem *engrafted* on that low stem – a bright, airy, and insolent excrescence.

There is nothing especially remarkable about this passage, until Hazlitt introduces some concrete detail, and sets up a playful assonance among *acorns sloes low insolent* that culminates in the ugly word *excrescence* which completes the sentence like a bubble bursting, or like a sloe or a pustule being squeezed. The passage works towards this final, tiny, bravura performance, and we enjoy it for that almost physically affective moment. It is casual and spontaneous, but perfectly timed. From the phrase 'caves and woods' to the penultimate word in the sentence, the prose has a subtle assonance until its unity is deliberately blown and dispersed by the final ugly polysyllable, which is catapulted forward by the flick of the *t* in 'insolent', and the tiny pause that follows.

When Hazlitt, in 'The Prose Style of Poets', praises Burke's 'execution' for savouring 'of the texture of what he describes', he is drawing attention to this physical enjoyment of the medium: the pen 'slides or drags' over the ground of his subject 'like the painter's pencil'. And as we have seen, Hazlitt regarded those prose styles like Addison's that are not 'indented' and don't project from the surface as insipid. We can feel that savoured indentation in the metallic ripple of 'captious, dogmatical, petulant'. Running through the bunched adjectives is rather like dragging a stick rapidly along a line of railings to make a dry, sterile sound. Burke is the master of these effects in Hazlitt's view, nowhere more than in the Leviathan passage in *Letter to a Noble Lord*.

Southey's functional qualities are expressed in the picture of him as he walks chin erect through the London streets with an umbrella sticking out under his arm 'in the finest weather'. That umbrella, like the rifle image, succinctly figures the way his prose sticks out and annoyingly gets in the way. But Hazlitt's criticism of Southey is silently picked up and softened fourteen years later by De Quincey, who remarks that Southey's mental style naturally prompts him to adopt in conversation 'a trenchant, pungent, aculeated form of terse, glittering, stenographic sentences'. With his umbrella and metaphoric rifle, the prickly Poet Laureate is like Crusoe on his island, a plain man writing in a plain but highly effective style. He is neither decorous nor gracious; nor does he move in any given orbit, but, like a falling star, 'shoots from his sphere'. He is 'pragmatical, restless, unfixed, full of experiments, beginning everything anew'. A statement that develops the observation that he wants 'proportion, keeping, system, standard rules'.

The second term, 'keeping', is a favourite of Hazlitt's as we have seen. It derives from painting, where it means harmony of tone or composition. As Hazlitt applies the term, it signifies internal design, a steady unity of feeling. He is fond of quoting Bacon's remark that scholastic philosophy is 'fierce with dark keeping', and he employs the term many times in his critical writing. It's an aesthetic concept which perhaps best describes his manner of patterning sound in his own prose, as in his strictures on Southey, and in this sentence from a passage criticizing Percy Shelley which begins 'Egotism, petulance, licentiousness, levity of principle', where there is a dynamic keeping in the pattern of t, p, and l sounds, as well as in the matching of the two units of three words either side of the pause before 'levity'. Hazlitt employs the term in 'The Letter-Bell', where he asserts that there is at least 'a thorough *keeping* in what I write – not a line that betrays a principle or disguises a feeling'. The notion of moral integrity is obviously introduced here, while in 'The Ideal' Hazlitt gives a formal aesthetic definition when he states that keeping is not the ideal, because there may be keeping in 'the little, the mean, and the disjointed'.

The use of 'keeping' in his profile of Southey therefore carries a whole history of critical usage which informs its presence at this particular moment. Similarly, the remark that Southey is 'wild, irregular, singular, extreme' contains significant associations for

Hazlitt, which are concentrated in the adjective 'irregular'. Salvator Rosa, as we have seen, is an 'irregular genius', like Burke. This adjective can be a term of praise, but it functions negatively in the comment on Southey.

What I am arguing here is that Hazlitt's critical language has a density of associative reference, as well as a studied tonality and texture, that affects his use of particular terms. He is perhaps the only critic in English to invest his vast, complex aesthetic terminology with a Shakespearean richness. His writing is self-allusive and autotelic, and it deploys an enormous repertoire of literary allusion, often with a highly apposite complexity. Thus, in praise of Southey's persistent humanity, he quotes *Macbeth* ostensibly to reinforce his generous comment on the reactionary Laureate, remarking that at the corner of Southey's pen there hangs a 'vaporous drop profound' of independence and liberality, which falls upon its pages, and 'oozes out through the pores of the public mind'. On the surface, this sounds beautifully generous, as well as sincerely meant, but it conceals a reservation which becomes visible only when we trace the quotation back to the play, and find that it comes from Hecate's speech in which she plans Macbeth's destruction:

> Upon the corner of the moon
> There hangs a vap'rous drop profound;
> I'll catch it ere it come to ground:
> And that distilled by magic sleights
> Shall raise such artificial sprites
> As by the strength of their illusion
> Shall draw him on to his confusion.

Southey may be a liberal civic humanist on one level – the dewy purity of the vaporous drop symbolizes that side of his writing – but at a deeper level he's an artful, dangerous destroyer who is associated with lunacy, fickleness, poison, and deception, like Burke. The allusion to Hecate does not invalidate Hazlitt's praise: it just makes it more complicated, more shot through with critical antipathy or ambiguity.

Hazlitt's profile of this driven reactionary is, on a philosophic level, an account of a particular type of imaginative intellect. Southey is the best and most natural prose-writer of any poet of the day, but he has certain limitations which the age's most gifted prose-writer wishes to analyse and expose. Some of those limitations are conveyed through the acoustic texture, or keeping, of Hazlitt's prose, others by the use of allusion and association (the vaporous drop, the rifle). He also makes certain details function as symbolic signs – the umbrella, the meagre shrill dryness of Southey's actual speaking voice. Thus Southey's conversation has some resemblance to a commonplace book, and his habitual deportment is likened to a piece of clockwork. He is 'constant, unremitting, mechanical' in his studies and in the performance of his duties. Like a type of narrow autodidact, he appears to be rigidly busy, and to lack those qualities of grace and indolence which Hazlitt prized so much. His fixed aridity leads Hazlitt to conclude that this irritable but kind man is 'rather the recipient and transmitter of knowledge, than the originator of it'. He does not have the intellectual grasp to arrive at any 'great leading truth'.

This picture of Southey's limitations resembles Coleridge's argument in his conversation with Hazlitt's father that Sir James Mackintosh is a ready warehouseman of letters, who knows exactly where to lay his hand on what he wants, though the goods are not his own. Mackintosh's *Vindicae Gallicae* was a reply to Burke's *Reflections*, and was duly praised by Hazlitt's father, but Coleridge disagreed with him, arguing that Mackintosh was merely a clever 'scholastic' man who was master of certain ready-made topics. Southey is cast in the same mould here. He is 'scholastic and professional' in his ideas, which is why his conversation resembles a commonplace book (De Quincey, picking up Hazlitt's remark, prefers to call Southey's conversation 'trenchant'). What he lacks, as Hazlitt points out in *Political Essays*, is sensuality. He has a 'monarchism of the understanding' which may be traced to the over-severe prudery of his moral habits. Picking up the plosive motif, Hazlitt says that he unites the cloister's bigotry with 'its penances and privations'. In *The Spirit of the Age*, he is characterized as having a 'peaked austerity of countenance', which, with its pun on 'pique', casts a shadow on 'plain, clear, pointed, familiar', the adjectives used to praise Southey's style. His imagination lacks a 'decent mixture of the pleasurable and the sensual' – a combination that might relieve the 'morbid acrimony' of his temper. It is Southey's failure to sympathize with the enjoyments of others which makes him so antipathetic to every difference of sentiment.

Although it would be wrong to press the argument about prose texture too far, that phrase 'the pleasurable and the sensual' introduces a type of erotic susurrus that resembles Hazlitt's use of 'unctuous' as a term of praise (that image of Southey's liberality seeping through the pores of the public mind is a version of this favourite image). As we have seen, 'oily', 'unctuous', 'oozing', 'lubricated', are favourite, obviously sensual adjectives. Thus the comic actor Liston is praised for his 'oily richness', while certain paintings are 'unctuous' or 'most unctuous' in expression. The term derives, as we've seen, from his reading of Rabelais, and is one expression of the centrality of the human body to Hazlitt's criticism. Susan Sontag once remarked that in place of a 'hermeneutics we need an erotics of art', but it existed already in Hazlitt's writings, with their at times lubricious pleasure in the 'oil of humanity'. There isn't a trace of this quality in the metallic Southey.

CHAPTER EIGHT

Coleridge the Aeronaut

If Southey's style is uptight and sensuously deprived, Coleridge's is a hot air balloon that forsakes the 'plain ground of prose', a phrase that reiterates and affirms the essential strength of true prose – a strength which Coleridge lacks. Without the fire and vehemence to lift his words, the former Unitarian preacher is a flaccid, turgid balloonist whose style is not 'succinct'. There is a delicious comedy in Hazlitt's account of Coleridge's voluminous manner of overdoing everything in sentences that move over the page like a patriarchal procession, 'with camels laden, wreathed turbans, household wealth, the whole riches of the author's mind poured out upon the barren waste of his subject. The palm-tree spreads its sterile branches overhead, and the land of promise is seen in the distance.' The orientalist imagery wonderfully patronizes Coleridge, who is never satisfied with 'the simple truth'. No direct proposition 'fills up the moulds of his understanding'. By implication, Hazlitt is insisting on the virtues of plainness, directness, truth, and this leads naturally and inevitably to his contrasting praise of Southey in the next paragraph of the essay on prose style.

What he is arguing is that really good prose has a Dutch materialism, a necessary flatness and material resistance which do not accommodate metaphor and illustration easily. Here, we see Hazlitt savouring the distinctiveness, the otherness, the sheer difference, of prose as a medium – a medium that's hard to characterize or personify, because no lark or nightingale symbolizes its essential beauty. The out-and-out totality of prose is almost incommunicable as an autarkic quality, a thing in itself or a pure hard lamina, for it can be glimpsed only indirectly in his praise or criticism of various individual authors. Of course, the same is true of the poetic qualities of verse, but with the difference that poetry can be discussed formally, while prose has no metrical system of its own. Even so, prose styles can be studied using analytic categories employed in Latin prose, as Morris Croll's classic essay 'The Baroque Style in Prose' demonstrates. Such approaches to prose style have fallen out of favour in recent decades, with the result that in an age of often rebarbatively difficult critical prose the concept of a poetics of prose style appears impossible.

Though Hazlitt would have known Priestley's perceptive application of classical metrics to prose style, he significantly avoids this type of analysis. He does, however, echo Priestley's criticism of the weak final pause in one of Bolingbroke's sentences, when he remarks in 'The Prose Style of Poets' that an emphatic phrase must not be placed where the power of utterance is 'enfeebled or exhausted'. In order to constitute an 'efficient readable style', the words have to come trippingly off the tongue, and from this it seems that there is a 'natural measure of prose' in the feeling of the subject and the power of expression in the voice, as there is an 'artificial' verse measure in the number and co-ordination of the syllables. Because poets are attuned to metre, they are impeded by its 'trammels' when they come to write prose. Poetry permits a greater number of inversions, or allows latitude in the transposition of words, which is 'not conformable to the strict laws of prose'. What those laws are cannot be expressed directly, because there is a 'natural order' of words in prose composition, not an artificially formulated series of fixed principles. Here, we again notice the application of Hazlitt's obsessively held belief in 'nature' as a sovereign good. What he offers – *en passant*, in true prose vein – is a series of aesthetic terms that help to structure the idea of prose beauty (how oddly those two terms sit together). Thus he praises Southey's facility of execution, the 'ease, grace, and point' of Leigh Hunt's prose style, Dryden's 'simplicity, strength, and perspicuity' – active, vital qualities which contrast with the unnatural enervation of Johnson's prose style.

The poet writing prose – for example, Johnson or Milton – does not understand the 'precision of form' or the 'severity of composition' which good prose demands. The poet is free to be fanciful, but the prose-writer is compelled to 'extract his materials' patiently and bit by bit from his subject. Ornament in prose must be sparing and inserted judiciously, because it has a 'remote practical purpose' instead of the immediate emotional indulgence which poetic imagery has. Behind Hazlitt's definition of prose as a medium, there is a traditional idea of masculine value which becomes visible at this point, rather like Southey's organ of vanity triumphant. Poets are seen as tainted by what was termed 'effeminacy', immersed in sensual ideas, continually craving excitement, while prose-writers have a difficult journey to undertake. The poet cannot wait till the effect 'comes of itself, or arises out of the occasion', but must instead force it at every opportunity. He can never 'drift with the current' – that is, surrender to the flow of his medium and let it carry him along.

This image of prose as a sailing-boat, which Hazlitt employs in 'The Prose Style of Poets', neatly transposes the idea of its insistent materiality, and it also introduces the concept of creative indolence that is so important to Hazlitt's aesthetic. The poet is always 'hoisting sail', so prose is air-swollen canvas, like the buoyantly aeronautic Coleridge, except that the true prose-writer knows when not to force an image and instead go with the natural direction of his subject. The poet doesn't know when to strike 'fire from the flint by the sharpness of collision, by the eagerness of his blows'. Once more the image of prize-fighting and of lapiths and centaurs struggling on the Elgin Marbles informs the connection made here between prose style and the physical action of fighting bodies. Once again, stone – or, more accurately, the chisel or stylus hitting stone – is being identified with all that obstinately isn't verse.

What emerges from this unique essay is an affirmation of physicality, a sort of worked *thingness* in prose, that coexists with an exultant hammer-and-anvil rapidity and concentration. Prose, he insists, has to do with dry details, close reasoning, abstruse speculations that do not give any scope for vivid descriptions. This is inescapable, a Dutch or Whiggish virtue which means that prose is not, and cannot be, purely imaginative, because it must reject superficial ornament.

189

But how does Coleridge fit into this aesthetic scheme? His prose has been found wanting, his feet aren't on its plain ground, its Dutch flatland; yet for Hazlitt he's an even more seminal figure than Burke.

The answer is that, for all its materiality and dry, dense textual insistence, prose must always be buoyed by its origins in speech, particularly in familiar conversation. We have seen how essential to good prose are the flexible postures that the voice assumes in spirited conversation, and in his sometimes affectionate, sometimes angry or exasperated remarks on Coleridge's prose, Hazlitt presents him as a fount of pure, effortless conversational brilliance, a combination of intellect and imagination that is uniquely powerful. He characterizes him like this in a pseudonymous letter to the *Examiner* which was published in January 1817, and which generously counterbalances his criticism in the same journal. It is the seed of 'My First Acquaintance with Poets'.

There he remembers the raw January morning in 1798 when he walked ten muddy miles to hear a poet and philosopher preach. Quoting a talismanic passage from Rousseau – '*Il y a des impressions que ni le temps ni les circonstances peuvent effacer*' – he describes Coleridge's sermon as a plenary inspiration. The organ was playing Psalm 100 as he arrived in the chapel: 'Make a joyful sound unto the Lord' is the implicit allusion here.

Coleridge's text was from St John, and Hazlitt renders it 'And he went up into the mountain to pray, HIMSELF ALONE'. It's an epiphanic moment that is centrally defined by the beautifully inspired intelligence of Coleridge's voice, which is allusively compared to the Lady's voice in *Comus* that rises like 'a steam of rich distill'd perfumes'. Milton, the Bible, two sentences on youthful experience from Rousseau's *Nouvelle Héloïse*, are drawn together in an associative complex which gives Coleridge enormous inspirational power. Hearing him pronounce the last two words of his text, Hazlitt says that he thought the sounds seemed to echo from the bottom of the human heart. It was as if the prayer might have floated 'in solemn silence through the universe'. Coleridge is like John the Baptist crying in the wilderness and feeding on locusts and wild honey. He then launches into his sermon 'like an eagle dallying with the wind'.

This composite of allusions and associations fuses the creative, the religious, and the critical. Coleridge's sermon had a political message too – he spoke of a simple shepherd boy conscripted into the army. Here the style becomes suddenly fricative and constrained as the imagery shifts from an open-vowelled pastoralism to show the 'same poor country-lad, crimped, kidnapped, brought into town, made drunk at an alehouse, turned into a wretched drummer-boy, with his hair sticking on end with powder and pomatum, a long cue at his back, and tricked out in the loathsome finery of the profession of blood'. Dickens, who admired Hazlitt, employs this type of succinctly observed detail in his fiction. Indeed, there is an imaginative kinship between the two writers, who were both par-liamentary shorthand reporters in their youth: *David Copperfield* can be read as a brilliantly extended version of one of Hazlitt's autobiographical essays. With their love of inns, long country walks, inner London, and the life of the common people, they are both republican writers who are impatient with the established order.

In 'My First Acquaintance with Poets' and the letter which seeded it, Hazlitt is celebrating the republicanism of Rational Dissent in an earlier period of government repression throughout the United Kingdom, and remembering the year which witnessed the bloody uprising in Ireland that took place during a particularly hot sum-mer. Returning to Wem from Shrewsbury, the wan winter sun labouring through the sky seemed 'an emblem of the *good cause*' – that is, it appeared to symbolize English republicanism. There was a spirit of hope and youth 'in all nature' that turned everything into good. The face of nature didn't then have 'the brand of JUS DIVINUM', of Divine Right, on it. Coleridge, the young radical republican, is praised generously by Hazlitt, though with a keen sense of the betrayals, failures, and disappointments to come. In remembering Coleridge's sermon and conversation, he also elegizes his own father's career in a manner that makes the Unitarian cause appear noble but marginal.

In a sense, his essay is a study both in vocation and in missed vocations. Coleridge is described as lustrously eloquent, but in a phrenological or Shandyish joke his nose, 'the index of the will, was small, feeble, nothing – like what he has done'. Similarly, Hazlitt's father beams with rugged delight as he converses with Coleridge in their house in Wem. The prose is suffused with an ethereal light, and a footnote adds that Hazlitt the Elder was one of those who mistook their talent: his sermons were 'forced and dry', but his letters were remarkable for their 'ease, half-plays on words, and a supine, monkish, indolent pleasantry'.

That phrase 'indolent pleasantry' crucially introduces the idea of languorous, witty conversation and a relaxed letting go which resembles the idea of drifting with the current in the essay on prose style. Hazlitt is honouring both Coleridge and his father for their influence on his writing, so this essay is an epic piece of auto-biography about the formation of his mind. As in his account of the Louvre, we can feel the influence of *The Prelude* here.

In addition to vocation, the themes of the essay are style, inspir-ation, and its ashy opposite, writer's block. Buoyed on a sense of youthful discovery, like a passage from Rousseau's *Confessions*, Hazlitt moves from winter to spring, describing Llangollen Vale as 'the cradle of a new existence'. The valley is a procreant cradle, a stage in his discovery of Wordsworth's poetry, which, when he hears Coleridge recite it in his sonorous musical voice, overcomes him with the sense of a 'new style and a new spirit' in poetry. Again, vocalization is strongly emphasized: Wordsworth has a 'deep gut-tural intonation, and a strong tincture of the northern *burr*, like the crust on wine'. This is immediately followed by a description of Wordsworth making havoc of half a Cheshire cheese and then remarking that, unlike Southey, he knew 'the good things of this life'.

Wordsworth emerges as physically vigorous, not mechanically driven like Southey, though there is a subtle reserve within Hazlitt's vividly energetic portrayal of him:

There was a severe, worn pressure of thought about his temples, a fire in his eye (as if he saw something in objects more than the outward appearance), an intense high narrow forehead, a Roman nose, cheeks furrowed by strong purpose and feeling, and a convulsive inclination to laughter about the mouth, a good deal at variance with the solemn, stately expression of the rest of his face.

It's as if Wordsworth is part human being, part classical bust (Hazlitt criticizes Chantrey's bust of him in the next sentence). Perhaps we bring the bony coldness of Wordsworth's various portraits to this sentence; perhaps our reading is informed by a knowledge of his quarrel with Hazlitt; perhaps the fermented coldness of that Cheshire cheese somehow connects with the bust's marbled classicism (there's an associative link here that I can't quite trace, which must be responsible for the hint of chillness in the portrait). Yet how generously – how disinterestedly – Hazlitt writes here. This is a concentrated account of various seminal stylists (including Burke and Jeremy Taylor), and painting is also introduced when the embrowned woods near the small town of Dunster are said to look as ideally pure as any landscape of Poussin or Domenichino.

Hazlitt wants to communicate both the ideal light of imagination and style, along with the wintry deadness, rawness, and blankness before creativity, before the achievement of style and vision: 'I was at that time dumb, inarticulate, helpless, like a worm by the wayside, crushed, bleeding, lifeless.' But he owes his intellectual liberation to Coleridge, a winged expansion and soaring sense of freedom as 'the light of his genius shone into my soul, like the sun's rays glittering in the puddles of the road'. Meeting him for the first time, he listens long and silently, then ventures to say that he has always admired Burke, and that to dismiss him with contempt might be made the test of a 'vulgar democratical mind'. Coleridge is impressed, and in the next sentence Hazlitt remembers that the leg of Welsh mutton and the turnips they ate had 'the finest flavours imaginable'. This is similar to the image of Wordsworth demolishing the cheese, and it's an example of the technique of introducing sensible images into prose discourse. The sensuous relish imparted is an expression of Hazlitt's view that at the outset of life 'our imagination has a body to it'. This contrasts with his description of how he sat down shortly after he had tried to explain his concept of natural disinterestedness to Coleridge and wrote a few meagre sentences 'in the skeleton-style of a mathematical demonstration', before giving up half-way down the second page.

Style obsesses him in this essay, and when he expresses displeasure at Coleridge's antipathy to Hume, he's developing this theme. What he terms 'the excellence of Hume's general style' is important to Hazlitt, for it helped him to shape his own prose. Indeed, his remark in one of the philosophy lectures about Hume being an 'easy, indolent, good-tempered man' is refracted in his praise of his father's style and in his remark later in the same essay: 'So have I loitered my life away, reading books, looking at pictures, going to plays, hearing, thinking, writing on what pleased me best.' This follows from the sentence in which he mentions 'sauntering' on the banks of the River Bridgewater, and it expresses his idea that hanging around, indolently loitering, lazily doing nothing, is an essential part of the creative process.

The meaning of indolence as a state of rest or ease, in which neither pain nor pleasure is felt, is now obsolete, but Hazlitt would have known its usage in William Popple's translation of Locke's *Letter Concerning Toleration*, in which civil interests are defined as 'life, liberty, health, and indolency of body', as well as material possessions. This is close to the American Declaration of Independence's 'life, liberty, and the pursuit of happiness' – words which modify Jefferson's original draft and which must derive from Locke. They give a civic dimension, as we've seen, to the easy relaxed carelessness of what is now regarded as simply a personal quality. Hazlitt's use of 'loitered' chimes with the mention of his father's 'indolent pleasantry' to create another of those 'half-plays on words' for which he praises him. We begin to see how very subtle is the construction of this autobiographical essay, as if somewhere between pun and assonance lies a form of word-play which prose writing derives from the playfulness of conversation, its shifting, stroking tones. Glancing at Psalm 85 – 'Mercy and truth are met together; righteousness and peace have kissed each other' – he exultingly states: 'Poetry and Philosophy had met together. Truth and

Genius had embraced, under the eye and with the sanction of Religion.'

Coleridge's brilliance lifted the young Hazlitt into another dimension of being, and his former disciple generously pays tribute to the youthful talker and preacher. But it is Coleridge's manner of walking which betrays that 'instability of purpose or involuntary change of principle' which is to appear later: 'In digressing, in dilating, in passing from subject to subject, he appeared to me to float in air, to slide on ice ... he continually crossed me on the way by shifting from one side of the footpath to the other.' Further, Coleridge slights Hume's style, a begrudging observation which Hazlitt says betrays 'a want of taste or candour'. Here, the limitations of Coleridge's own style are being physically embodied in his manner of walking, which is like a type of locomotive aporia.

This critical view is expressed in more detail in *Political Essays*, where he attacks Coleridge as the prince of preparatory authors, a writer who is incapable of coming to a conclusion and who never lets anyone else arrive at one either. He is 'at cross-purposes' with himself, as well as with others, and in a brilliant metaphor Hazlitt characterizes his hectic criss-crossing prose as resembling seasickness. All his impulses are 'loose, airy, devious, casual'. He flies up, down, and all over the place like a demented angel (in 'My First Acquaintance with Poets' he is both the archangel Raphael and a fallen angel). Coleridge crosses everything, so his imagination becomes metaphysical, 'his metaphysics fantastical, his wit heavy, his arguments light, his poetry prose, his prose poetry, his politics turned'.

This is the reverse of Burke's prose poetry because it represents not an interstitial reality between prose and verse, but a neurotic crossing over from one genre to another. At the same time, his negative image for Coleridge's lack of will – 'lighter than the gossamer' – carries elsewhere a philosophical application that changes its critical direction entirely. In an important essay on Madame de Staël's account of German philosophy and literature, Hazlitt says that the 'fine network of the mind, the intellectual cords that bind and hold our scattered perceptions together, and form the living line of communication between them, are dissolved and vanish before the clear light of modern metaphysics, as the gossamer is dissipated by the sun'. Interestingly, he uses the image of a line of communication to characterize the Shropshire Dissenting ministers whose local and national network helped keep alive the flame of civil and religious liberty. The spider's web is his image of consciousness as an active, shaped, and shaping force, which he describes a few sentences earlier in his review of de Staël as 'one diffusive, and yet self-centred intellect, one undivided active spirit co-extended with the object, and yet ever present to itself'.

Coleridge uniquely embodies this intellect: he is god-like, 'HIM-SELF ALONE', a type of that infinite I AM which Coleridge uses as a figure for the imagination. He is a complex autonomous spirit, filmy like gossamer, but also reticulated and highly organized. Where Wordsworth at the end of *The Prelude* ascends Snowdon and sees in the moonlit sea of clouds the 'perfect image of a mighty mind', Hazlitt finds divine inspiration in the outpourings of Wordsworth's friend, as he endlessly talks about books and ideas. If Coleridge's impulses are airy and loose, his mind is also superfine like gossamer; holding forth about Berkeley's philosophy, he can make the entire material universe become 'a transparency of fine words' – that is, like a verbal colour slide illuminated on a screen. Coleridge's shining complexion, its blooming sheen – probably a version of Moses' face when he descended Mount Sinai after beholding God – is a natural figure for the pure consciousness he embodies.

If we look at Hazlitt's view of Coleridge, it's curiously similar to his view of Johnson – both are bad prose stylists, but wonderful talkers. Johnson's style of conversation has a 'muscular strength and agility' – he became a prize-fighter when he spoke. The boxing metaphor is high praise; Johnson joins Burke and Cobbett in the ring, where he is distinguished by the 'vigorous and voluntary' exercise of his faculties. Coleridge is a similarly powerful talker, and in a remarkable passage in 'The Drama', an essay published in 1820, two years before Hazlitt wrote 'My First Acquaintance with Poets', he allows us to hear Coleridge in conversation – really in critical monologue, arguing that Racine's plays are a parcel of set speeches, of epigrammatic conceits, of declamatory phrases, without any of the glow, and glancing rapidity, and principle of fusion in the mind of the poet, to agglomerate them into grandeur, or blend them into harmony. The principle of the imagination resembles the emblem of the serpent, by which the ancients typified wisdom and the universe, with undulating folds, for ever varying and for ever flowing into itself – circular, and without beginning or end. The definite, the fixed, is death: the principle of life is the indefinite, the growing, the moving, the continuous.

This is the language of Unitarian science applied to art. Hazlitt shared this critical language; indeed, he used it so pervasively that the various terms like 'fusion', 'definite', and 'fixed' don't seem novel or out of place here, with the strange result that Coleridge almost appears to be ventriloquizing for Hazlitt in this critical monologue. The idea of fusion and movement being a good, which contrasts with the negative nature of definite fixities, is a deeply Protestant idea, which, as we have seen, runs through Hazlitt's criticism, just as it does through Lawrence's. The free individual conscience aims to be fluid, not set or petrific like the Petrine rock, the pun on which the Catholic Church is founded. Where better to embody that conscience than in the free flow of conversation? As he says in *The Spirit of the Age*, few traces of Coleridge's fertile, subtle, expansive understanding are likely to remain when his voice is stilled. If he had not been the most impressive talker of his time, he would probably have been its finest writer. He is in the first class of 'general intellect', though his works do not place him there.

The account of Coleridge's intellectual odyssey in *The Spirit of the Age* has a panoramic comedy which beautifully catches his intellectual enthusiasm, its too continual, unfixed movement:

Next, he was engaged with Hartley's tribes of mind, 'ethereal braid, thought-woven', – and he busied himself for a year or two with vibrations and vibratiuncles and the great law of association that binds all things in its mystic chain, and the doctrine of Necessity (the mild teacher of Charity) and the Millennium, anticipative of a life to come; and he plunged deep into the controversy on Matter and Spirit, and, as an escape from Dr Priestley's Materialism, where he felt himself imprisoned by the logician's spell, like Ariel in the cloven pine-tree, he became suddenly enamoured of Bishop Berkeley's fairy-world, and used in all companies to build the universe, like a brave poetical fiction, of fine words. And he was deep-read in Mal-ebranche, and in Cudworth's *Intellectual System* (a huge pile of learning, unwieldy, enormous) and in Lord Brook's hieroglyphic theories, and in Bishop Butler's Sermons, and in the Duchess of Newcastle's fantastic folios, and in Clarke, and South, and Tillotson, and all the fine thinkers and mas-culine reasoners of that age; and Leibniz's *Pre-established Harmony* reared its arch above his head, like the rainbow in the cloud, covenanting with the hopes of man.

Two long sentences compose the tumbling, but rather soothing, almost stroking movement of this paragraph, in which Priestley and Clarke represent Coleridge's Unitarian interests. With its list of almost forgotten names, the paragraph shimmers with learned references. Samuel Clarke, an Anglican cleric and Newtonian philosopher who was accused of Arianism, was England's leading philosopher for the next quarter-century after Locke's death in 1704. His a priori philosophy was opposed to Locke's – Rousseau praises him in *Emile*, and Hazlitt admired his *Discourse Concerning the Being and Attributes of God*. Again, the reference to Bishop Butler is significant for Hazlitt's interests, because Butler, who joined the Anglican Church from English Presbyterianism, was a distinguished intellectual, who influenced Francis Hutcheson.

In this epic, wittily affectionate sketch of Coleridge's intellectual development in *The Spirit of the Age*, he is like Satan falling from noon to dewy eve:

And then he fell plump, ten thousand fathoms down (but his wings saved him harmless) into the *hortus siccus* of Dissent where he pared religion down to the standard of reason, and stripped faith of mystery, and preached Christ crucified and the Unity of the Godhead, and so dwelt for a while in the spirit with John Huss and Jerome of Prague and Socinus and old John Zisca, and ran through Neal's HISTORY OF THE PURITANS and Calamy's NON-CONFORMISTS' MEMORIAL, having like thoughts and passions with them.

'*Hortus siccus*', we know, is borrowed from Burke's *Reflections*. Here it signals that Coleridge's stay among the Rational Dissenters is only a stage in his progress towards a final conservative position that is similarly hostile to the Unitarian culture which is represented here by Socinus and Zisca. Like the previous paragraph, this long two-sentence waterfall of recondite references compresses in a beautifully silky manner Coleridge's intellectual development. The sentences ask not so much to be read as to be intoned like a familiar reading from the Bible or a children's story. There is a fluid anapaestic movement:

  × × / × × / × × / × × /   /
 and so dwelt for a while in the spirit with John Huss.

All is process, movement, gush; as Hazlitt says in a footnote, Coleridge's ideas are 'like a river, flowing on for ever, and still murmuring as it flows'.

 Hazlitt's fondness for repeating Burke's comparison of the Dissenters to a dried herb garden suggests that he recognizes the limitations of Nonconformist culture, but he turns the phrase in an opposite direction in an essay 'On Court-Influence', in which he praises English Presbyterianism, and states that no patriotism, no public spirit that is not reared in the 'inclement sky and harsh soil, "in the *hortus siccus* of dissent," will generally last'. Dissenters are 'the safest partisans and the steadiest friends'. What he is saying here is that they possess the prose virtues of plainness, directness, and grit. They are almost the only people who have an idea of 'abstract attachment' to a cause, or to an individual; they have it from a 'sense of fidelity' which is independent of prosperous or adverse circumstances. And, in spite of opposition, they stick to their principles, unlike Coleridge, who tumbled briefly into the dry garden of Dissenting liberty, before moving on and eventually sinking into a 'torpid, uneasy repose, tantalized by useless resources, haunted by vain imaginings, his lips idly moving, but his heart for ever still'. Like the pretender to a throne – Bonnie Prince Charlie, say – he enjoys a miserable exile, and here the adapted Miltonic phrase 'vain imaginings', which is applied to the fallen angels, underlines the monarchical reference.

 Hazlitt's theme in his criticism of Coleridge is the nature of the imagination. Coleridge's he links with Burke's monarchism, signalling this at the beginning of 'My First Acquaintance with Poets' when the young radical Unitarian preacher arrives in Shrewsbury and holds the town in 'delightful suspense' for three weeks 'fluttering the proud Salopians like an eagle in a dovecote'. The quotation from *Coriolanus*, which Hazlitt elsewhere applied to Burke's attacks on republican ideology, establishes an associative bridge with the Irish polemicist. Another link is made in Hazlitt's praise of the *Ancient Mariner*'s 'wild, irregular, overwhelming imagination', where the adjective 'irregular' carries Burkean associations, as we have seen. It is Coleridge's power of vocalization which fascinates Hazlitt, who remarks that the *Ancient Mariner*'s rich varied movement gives a distant idea of his 'lofty or changeful' tones of voice. But the problem is that this emphasis on voice then relegates all his published work to secondary status. If Coleridge's poetry is inferior to his conversation, his prose is 'utterly abortive', an exclamatory dismissive phrase that seems to leap out of Restoration comedy. He is a fountain of pure talk, all gush without any lasting substance or form.

Hazlitt then contrasts Coleridge with Godwin, in a manner which, by implication, pits the republican faculty of reason against the imagination's monarchism. Godwin, the sketch of whom is strategically placed before Coleridge's in *The Spirit of the Age*, was reared in the dry garden of Presbyterianism in the flatlands of Wisbech in Cambridgeshire (his family was friendly with the Loftuses, Hazlitt's mother's family). He is presented as less gifted, but more concentrated, diligent, and confidently centred than the gossipy, gadabout Coleridge. Godwin's faculties have 'kept at home, and plied their task in the workshop of the brain', whereas Coleridge has dissipated his genius. This contrast is slightly reminiscent of the distinction between Burke and his opponent, Mackintosh, which Coleridge makes in his conversation with Hazlitt's father. Mackintosh argues efficiently in his prose, while Godwin is a hardworking craftsman. Godwin is more naturally gifted than Mackintosh, but both writers share a certain unimaginative utile quality which is nevertheless one of the important prose virtues. Godwin has '*valves* belonging to his mind, to regulate the quantity of gas admitted to it, so that like the bare, unsightly, but well-compacted steam-vessel, it cuts its liquid way'; whereas Coleridge travels in a light poetic 'bark' whose arrival in its destined harbour we await in vain. Between the technology signalled by 'valves' (steam craft appeared in the early 1800s) and the deliberately archaic imagery applied to Coleridge, it is clear that Hazlitt is both regretting and anticipating the disappearance of a more spacious, natural imagination. Burke's age of calculators is triumphing, and Coleridge's very inability actually to give permanent expression to his genius exemplifies how the *Zeitgeist* is pushing all that he represents to one side. Taken together with the sketch of Bentham, Hazlitt's accounts of these figures resemble John Stuart Mill's famous essays on Bentham and Coleridge – the 'two great seminal minds of England in their age', as Mill calls them.

Hazlitt begins his collection with a profile of Bentham, then sketches Godwin, then Coleridge, in order to signal that this is the age of steamboats and steam central heating. He does so because, as he states at the end of his profile of Coleridge, the spirit of monarchy is at variance with the spirit of the age. The philosophers, those 'dry abstract reasoners', have armed themselves with patience to bear 'discomfiture, persecution and disgrace'. So it is that Godwin, he notes just before this observation, with less 'variety and vividness, with less subtlety and susceptibility both of thought and feeling, has had firmer nerves, a more determined purpose, a more comprehensive grasp of his subject'. This is in some ways similar to Hazlitt's description of Cassius, whose 'watchful jealousy' made him anticipate the worst that might happen, and whose 'irritability of temper added to his inveteracy of purpose, and sharpened his patriotism'. This is the vigilant, suspicious, dedicated republican spirit which refuses to be disabled by an idealistic self-esteem, and which understands the cunning of the opposition.

The textual placement and the critical comparison between Godwin and Coleridge express the struggle between the stubborn heroism of the republican philosophers and the feeble fickleness of the poets, who couldn't stand the frowns of both the king and the people. They did not like being excluded when places, pensions, critical praise, and the laureateship were about to be distributed.

Coleridge therefore sounded the retreat for them 'by the help of casuistry and a musical voice'. And so his friends in the Lake school turned back disgusted and panic-stricken from the 'dry desert of unpopularity'.

Earlier in this paragraph Hazlitt uses the same adjective – 'dry abstract reasoners' – so that when he repeats it here, this apparently dismissive term becomes charged with modern, republican virtue. In it is concentrated those harsh, inclement Presbyterian values that nourished the young Godwin. Because he is engaged in designing what we might term a 'semiotics of liberty', Hazlitt returns again and again to the *hortus siccus* of Dissent, but this process of repeated quotation differs from his obsessive citation of Burke's praise of Marie-Antoinette: he doesn't so much flog the adjective 'dry' to death as flex it into life. The parched desert, the apparently dead herb garden, now take on a fertile quality through obstinate repetition, and in a final flourish Coleridge is allowed to remain in a similar, though not identical, condition. Where the Lake school is comfortably ensconced in the walled city of Legitimacy, Coleridge has chosen not to enter with them, pitching his tent instead 'upon the barren waste without, and having no abiding place nor city of refuge!'

The exclamatory conclusion to the sketch expresses Coleridge's nomadic intellectualism and also the fact that his brilliance is a matter of being always on the move, continually offering provisional conclusions. He is all air and motion, somehow eternally about to be. He is a writer skimming over the summery surfaces of perpetual promise.

Hazlitt's quarrel with Coleridge, as with Burke, is complex, because behind the adjective 'irregular', which he applies to both writers, as well as to Southey and Salvator Rosa, lies a fundamental recognition that the gothic values which that term implies are opposed to the radical Enlightenment. It's as if he is caught between the daylight gods and those dangerous irrational forces that oppose them and which civic, utilitarian values can never accommodate. In 'The Age of Elizabeth' he remarks that English literature is 'gothic and grotesque; unequal and irregular'. The English imagination prefers the rough, the uneven, the unfinished, to the smooth and formal. In the same essay, though with a certain ironic distance, he speaks of 'worse than gothic darkness', one of many pejorative uses of the term ('gothic ignorance and barbarism' being just one further example). Sometimes – and this is Hazlitt's problem – the term is linked to Burke, and this means that it cannot be entirely dismissive, must in fact be a term of approbation on another level. This is obvious in the conclusion to 'The Age of Elizabeth', where he states that the English understanding is not a smooth thoroughfare for the commonplace, 'but full of knotty points and jutting excrescences, rough, uneven, overgrown with brambles'. This picks up the word 'jutty' in the procreant cradle speech in *Macbeth*, and therefore associates the gothic with rough, uneven castle walls and with Shakespeare's imagination. What we realize again is the richness and density of Hazlitt's highly allusive use of language, his sophisticated intertextuality. Southey isn't gothic, though: the projective qualities of his prose are metallic, not woody and apparently natural.

Later in the Elizabethan lectures, Hazlitt draws a contrast between classical elegance and gothic quaintness, but his most sustained discussion of the term is in his review of a translation of Schlegel's *Lectures on Dramatic Literature*, which was published in 1815. Though he criticizes the Germans for being 'a slow, heavy people', who lack ease, quickness, and flexibility, he concedes that Schlegel's is the best account of Shakespeare there is. Importantly, he contrasts the 'modern or *romantic* style' with the 'antique or *classical*'. This is similar, even identical, to Hazlitt's contrast between Charles James Fox's plain classical manner of expressing himself and the knottiness of the procreant cradle. In Schlegel's account, Shakespeare's descriptions are too boldly figurative, too 'profuse of dazzling images' for the 'mild, equable' tone of classical poetry. This resembles Hazlitt's remark that the French have no style of their own in serious art because they have no real force of character. The 'dark and doubtful view of things, the irregular flights of fancy' are excluded from their literalness. Hazlitt is against French formalism, but he has an anguished resistance to his own perception that modernity is gothic and romantic, barbarous and irrational – hence his hidden, even subconscious identification of Shakespeare with Milton's Satan in his lecture on Elizabethan literature, where he says that Shakespeare towered above his fellows, 'in shape and gesture proudly eminent'. He loves Shakespeare and reveres Burke, but they are gothic geniuses who tend to the arbitrary side of the question, and challenge his republican values.

Those values are often imaged as the human eye in his writing, so Southey is 'blind with double darkness' like Milton's Samson, while readers of the reactionary *New Times* 'roll their eyes in vain, and "find no dawn"; but, in its stead, total eclipse and ever-during dark surrounds them'. Milton's account of his blindness in the invocation to light which opens the third book of *Paradise Lost* held a particular appeal for Hazlitt, because he felt that after Napoleon's defeat his own situation – a radical raging against a hostile government – resembled Milton's perilous existence in the early days of the Restoration. The Masonic and Enlightenment symbol of the eye is a powerful icon for him, though it has of course a broader value than this. In 'What is the People?', which was published in the *Examiner* early in 1818, he addresses a representative Tory who might ask that question, and hurls this at him: 'you would tread out the eye of Liberty (the light of nations) like "a vile jelly," that mankind may be led about darkling to its endless drudgery, like the Hebrew Samson (shorn of his strength and blind), by his insulting taskmasters'. Here, the use of 'darkling' combines an allusion to Milton's invocation – where the nightingale sings darkling – as well as to Lear and the fool who sit darkling on the heath. The allusion to Samson completes the symbol's tragic symmetry, and makes Hazlitt's prose feel anguished, trapped in darkness, jagged, and dissonant, unlike the 'harmonious numbers' that the blind, defeated, tragically dignified Milton draws from the perpetual night he shares with his society.

CHAPTER NINE

Blind Orion

Three years after he published his attack on those Tories who would tread out the eye of liberty, Hazlitt's republican faith sustained two heavy blows. Keats, his friend and admirer, died in Rome on 23 February 1821, and his hero Napoleon died on St Helena on 5 May. The following month, Hazlitt saw a painting in the annual exhibition of Old Masters at the British Institution in London, which inspired him to compose an essay that is more than a piece of art criticism: it is an elegy for those two geniuses and for the values he shared with them.

'On a Landscape of Nicolas Poussin' has one of the finest opening paragraphs in the history of criticism, a paragraph so long and carefully moulded, so epic in its momentum, that it's like a concentrated essay in itself:

'*And blind Orion hungry for the morn.*' – KEATS

Orion, the subject of this landscape, was the classical Nimrod; and is called by Homer 'a hunter of shadows, himself a shade'. He was the son of Neptune; and having lost an eye in some affray between the gods and men, was told that if he would go to meet the rising sun, he would recover his sight. He is represented setting out on his journey, with men on his shoulders to guide him, a bow in his hand, and Diana in the clouds greeting him. He stalks along, a giant upon earth, and reels and falters in his gait, as if just awaked out of sleep, or uncertain of his way; – you see his blindness, though his back is turned. Mists rise around him, and veil the sides of the green forests; earth is dank and fresh with dews, the 'grey dawn and the Pleiades before him dance', and in the distance are seen the blue hills and sullen ocean. Nothing was ever more finely conceived or done. It breathes the spirit of the morning; its moisture, its repose, its obscurity, waiting the miracle of light to kindle it into smiles: the whole is, like the principal figure in it, 'a forerunner of the dawn'. The same atmosphere tinges and imbues every object, the same dull light 'shadowy sets off' the face of nature: one feeling of vastness, of strangeness, and of primeval forms pervades the painter's canvas, and we are thrown back upon the first integrity of things. This great and learned man might be said to see nature through the glass of time: he alone has a right to be considered as the painter of classical antiquity. Sir Joshua has done him justice in this respect. He could give to the scenery of his heroic fables that unimpaired look of original nature, full, solid, large, luxuriant, teeming with life and power; or deck it with all the pomp of art, with temples and towers, and mythologic groves. His pictures 'denote a foregone conclusion'. He applies nature to his purposes, works out her images according to the standard of his thoughts, embodies high fictions; and the first conception being given, all the rest seems to grow out of, and be assimilated to it, by the unfailing process of a studious imagination. Like his own Orion, he overlooks the surrounding scene, appears to 'take up the isles as a very little thing, and to lay the earth in a balance'. With a laborious and mighty grasp, he put nature into the mould of the ideal and antique; and was among painters (more than any one else) what Milton was among poets. There is in both something of the same pedantry, the same stiffness, the same elevation, the same grandeur, the same mixture of art and nature, the same richness of borrowed materials, the same unity of character. Neither the poet nor the painter lowered the subjects they treated, but filled up the outline in the fancy, and added strength and prominence to it: and thus not only satisfied, but surpassed the expectations of the spectator and the reader. This is held for the triumph and the perfection of works of art. To give us nature, such as we see it, is well and deserving of praise; to give us nature, such as we have never seen, but have often wished to see it, is better, and deserving of higher praise. He who can show the world in its first naked glory, with the hues of fancy spread over it, or in its high and palmy state, with the gravity of history stamped on the proud monuments of vanished empire – who, by his 'so potent art', can recall time past, transport us to distant places, and join the regions of imagination (a new conquest) to those of reality – who teaches us not only what nature is, but what she has been, and is capable of being – he who does this, and does it with simplicity, with truth, and grandeur, is lord of nature and her powers; and his mind is universal, and his art the master-art!

The painting is Poussin's *Paysage avec Orion aveugle*, and Hazlitt's intense response to it in June 1821 needs a careful, even painstaking analysis. As Richard Verdi argues, this late painting, with its 'undisciplined beauty' and vision of 'the monstrous, the irrational, and the uncanny' in nature, is one of the most daring of all Poussin's works. Verdi argues that Hazlitt showed his critical independence by choosing to write about this painting. It is impossible to over-estimate the importance of his 'highly original' and, for its time, 'wholly unorthodox' account. Hazlitt's whole life is packed into its opening paragraph, and only by examining the quotations which compose it, can we begin to glimpse the deep structure of his critical imagination.

By printing a line adapted from *Endymion* as an epigraph, Hazlitt both memorializes Keats and immediately introduces the republican classicism which he and the poet share with the painter. (As Ian Jack suggests, Keats is probably drawing on his memory of a print of *Paysage avec Orion aveugle* for the line from *Endymion*, 'Or blind Orion hungry for the morn'.) In the opening lines of the third book, Keats turns on the various reactionary, European regimes which had defeated Napoleon:

> There are who lord it o'er their fellow-men
> With most prevailing tinsel, who unpen
> Their baaing vanities to browse away
> The comfortable green and juicy hay
> From human pastures; or – oh, torturing fact –
> Who, through an idiot blink, will see unpacked
> Fire-branded foxes to sear up and singe
> Our gold and ripe-eared hopes. With not one tinge
> Of sanctuary splendour, not a sight
> Able to face an owl's, they still are dight
> By the blear-eyed nations in empurpled vests,
> And crowns and turbans. With unladen breasts,
> Save of blown self-applause, they proudly mount
> To their spirit's perch, their being's high account,
> Their tiptop nothings, their dull skies, their thrones,
> Amid the fierce intoxicating tones
> Of trumpets, shoutings, and belaboured drums,
> And sudden cannon. Ah, how all this hums

In wakeful ears, like uproar past and gone –
Like thunder clouds that spake to Babylon,
And set those old Chaldeans to their tasks.
Are then regalities all gilded masks?

These lines have some affinity with Poussin's biblical and classical battle-scenes, and their harvest imagery is part of the subtly coded, post-Peterloo politics of 'To Autumn'. Keats's radical metropolitan imagination drew both on Poussin's art and on Hazlitt's praise of it. Eulogizing Keats in an earlier essay in *Table-Talk*, in which he notes that 'Cockney' is now an abusive critical term, Hazlitt exclaims: 'Poor Keats! What was sport to the town was death to him.' The epigraph to Hazlitt's essay on Poussin is therefore much more than a decorative introductory flourish: it goes straight to the heart of his loss in 1821, and helps us begin to glimpse the DNA structure of his allusive imagination.

Poussin's political vision is discussed in Maria Graham's biography, published in 1820, shortly before Hazlitt began writing his essay. In a long footnote, he quotes from her *Memoirs of the Life of Nicolas Poussin*, in order to establish Poussin's meticulous study of nature, but he drew more from her study than just this innocuous quotation. In her preface, Graham insists on the republican cast of Poussin's mind, arguing against the idea that painting flourishes best in 'slavish countries, and in slavish times'. Those who believe this forget that poetry and painting both sprang up in 'the free cities of ancient Greece'. They also forget that the period

when the great poets of Italy wrote, and when her greatest painters were born, was one of freedom, bordering on licentiousness. Look into the annals of Italy. Michaelangelo, Raffaelle, Titian, Leonardo, Giulio, and Giorgione, were all born in the space between 1442 and 1492, while Florence was a republic, and when the Captains of Italy fought in the pay of free cities. From the moment those Captains became stationary tyrants, no great man in art was born or nurtured in the North of Italy.

This argument invisibly informs Hazlitt's essay, and the fact that he quotes from a recently published book – it was the first English study of Poussin – adds to his subject's topicality. Graham also remarks that the cities in the Papal States for a long time retained, together with the republican form of government, 'something of the republican spirit; that spirit which sleeps, but is not even yet dead in the ashes of old Rome'. And she asks if it is too much to argue that Poussin, Le Brun, and Le Sueur, emerged in France because the country was then 'more free than at any other period'. The religious wars had brought about a freedom of feeling and discussion, favourable to fostering 'every liberal art', and the 'iron age' of Louis XIV had not yet arisen to crush 'the farther rise of the very talent with which it decked itself'. Although Hazlitt does not quote Graham on the republican inspiration of great art directly, her insistence on the power of that anti-monarchical imagination in the past must have helped to inspire his 'epoch-making' essay, as Verdi calls it. But it is this very pastness which haunts him. Something is finished for ever, he's admitting here, because he knows in his bones that the republican spirit is cold, not warm, ash. The ideal republic is – now and always – only a series of antique ruins and paintings of those ruins.

If we examine his essay closely, we can see that it's constructed through a characteristic deployment of quotation, the equivalent of the borrowed materials Poussin so richly deploys. Hazlitt is using quotations as building-blocks and as intertextual links to their repetition elsewhere in his criticism. They are force fields and associative symbols which are hallowed in the way place-names sometimes are for other writers. This means that the opening sentence asserting that Orion is 'the classical Nimrod' is, for Hazlitt, both a quotation from Genesis, where Nimrod is 'a mighty hunter before the Lord', and a buried reference to a passage in one of his favourite polemics, A Letter to a Noble Lord, where Burke refers to the 'cannibal philosophers of France' who are a 'misallied and disparaged branch of the house of Nimrod'. Those republican theorists are that radical Whig, the duke of Bedford's 'natural hunters', and he is their natural game.

These remarks immediately follow the 'proud Keep of Windsor' passage which Hazlitt so much admired, and in explaining that Orion is the classical Nimrod, he is going out of his way to admit, if only to himself and a tiny number of readers alert to his critical spoor, that the blinded hunter carries associations with the dark side of republicanism – fanatical Jacobinism and murderous violence. The Homeric Nimrod – that uneasy cross between the Hellenic and the Hebraic – is like a modern republican political theorist, a shadowy hunter of shadows, a deviser of impossible constitutions like the Abbé Sieyès, another of Burke's targets. Howe, perhaps rather tenuously, links the phrase 'a hunter of shadows, himself a shade' with this passage in Pope's translation of the *Odyssey*:

> There huge *Orion* of portentous size,
> Swift thro' the gloom a giant-hunter flies;
> A pond'rous mace of brass with direful sway
> Aloft he whirls to crush the savage prey;
> Stern beasts in trains that by his truncheon fell,
> Now griesly forms, shot o'er the lawns of hell.

Lodged in Hazlitt's capaciously allusive memory, these lines describe Napoleon's deeds as they are re-enacted in the afterlife that is posterity. There he is for ever defeating giant monarchs.

But as well as Pope's lines, Hazlitt would have remembered Milton's prophecy in the last book of *Paradise Lost*, where he describes how families and tribes live peacefully in a republican state of nature until

>   one shall rise
> Of proud ambitious heart, who not content
> With fair equality, fraternal state,
> Will arrogate dominion undeserved
> Over his brethren, and quite dispossess
> Concord and law of nature from the earth,
> Hunting (and men not beasts shall be his game)
> With war and hostile snare such as refuse
> Subjection to his empire tyrannous:
> A mighty hunter then he shall be styled
> Before the Lord, as in despite of heaven,
> Or from heaven claiming second sovereignty:

And from rebellion shall derive his name,
Though of rebellion others he accuse.

In *Eikonoklastes* Milton says that Nimrod is 'the first that hunted
after Faction', and is reputed 'by ancient Tradition, the first that
founded Monarchy'. Later in the same work, he calls Nimrod 'the
first King'. For Hazlitt, this meant that Orion/Nimrod held
uncomfortable associations – associations which express his
subconscious resistance to the sway that his self-crowned hero,
Napoleon, exercised over his imagination. Dryden, in a glance at
Cromwell in *The Hind and the Panther*, is quite clear that 'diff'ring
worship of the Deity' caused religious persecution, which in turn
produced 'the mighty hunter of his race'.

Hazlitt's description of Orion's mythological pedigree becomes
interestingly evasive when he remarks in the second sentence that
Orion lost an eye 'in some affray' between the gods and men. His
briskly casual vagueness here was picked up by a reviewer of *Table-
Talk* the following year, who pointed out that Hazlitt was mistaken
in suggesting that Diana in Poussin's painting was greeting Orion.
The hunter lost his sight, the reviewer notes, 'in consequence of an
attempt on the goddess, who was avenged by an arrow of her
brother Apollo'. This is more than the correction of the kind of
mistake which literary journalists writing to a deadline are prone to
make, because it recalls accounts of the episode in Hazlitt's youth
when he had to escape from the Lake District after sexually harass-
ing a young woman. No doubt the reviewer knew the story, which
was circulated by Wordsworth years after the event in an attempt to
discredit him.

The figure of Orion, therefore, has a profoundly uncomfortable
personal connotation for Hazlitt: not only is Orion associated with
the cannibal French philosophers, but he is also a now not-so-
private symbol of a shaming episode in his youth. Then again, the
early morning misty dampness in Poussin's painting, which he celebrates so lavishly, is reminiscent of that raw dewy morning when he
set out at the age of nineteen to hear Coleridge preach, in January
1798. This buried memory is benignly idealistic and exciting, but

it's overlaid by a memory of what happened in Keswick five years later, and by the belated gossip that was provoked when the incident became common knowledge in the literary world in 1815. Blind Orion is the sexually disturbed Hazlitt, a failure in love who was always to be the victim of his neuroses.

At the same time, the painting has a particular significance for the student of Poussin's work, in that the adjective 'dry' simply cannot be applied to it. Richard Verdi, author of the catalogue for the 1995 Poussin exhibition at the Royal Academy in London, comments that the painting is one of the most pantheistic of Poussin's entire career:

With its dense undergrowth and umbrageous trees, the picture is pervaded by an intoxicating range of greens that evoke nature in its primordial state. Scarcely less visionary is the composition of the scene, which violates all the conventions of classical art in its abrupt and mysterious spatial elisions and dramatic distortions of size. These combine to conjure forth thoughts of the most wondrous and inexplicable forces in nature, and reveal the aged Poussin immersed in the mystery of creation and awed by its elemental power.

Interestingly, Verdi uses the Hazlittian adjective 'abrupt' to describe a painting which, implicitly in his account, anticipates Romantic art.

The picture spoke to the pantheism that is usually present when Hazlitt cites 'Tintern Abbey', and it must have brought back his journey down through England in the spring of 1798 to visit Coleridge and Wordsworth. Just before setting off, he went to Llangollen Vale, in order to initiate himself into 'the mysteries of natural scenery'. He calls that valley 'the cradle of a new existence: in the river that winds through it, my spirit was baptised in the waters of Helicon!'

But the associations which Hazlitt brings to Orion's dawn journey are more than personal, because they also attach to the traditional image of the blind epic poet, and blindness in turn has a more than personal significance for him, as the first quotation from *Paradise Lost* – 'grey Dawn, and the Pleiades before him danced' – makes us recognize, once we apply it to the essay's epic republican theme. Hazlitt is citing the passage in the seventh book where Raphael explains to Adam how and why God created the world, and he would have remembered how Raphael a few lines earlier says:

> Of light by far the greater part he took,
> Transplanted from her cloudy shrine, and placed
> In the sun's orb, made porous to receive
> And drink the liquid light, firm to retain
> Her gathered beams, great palace now of light.

The emphasis Milton places on the word 'now' is similar to the weight Marvell gives it in his 'Horatian Ode on Cromwell's Return from Ireland' ('The forward youth that would appear / Must now forsake his muses dear'; 'And now the Irish are ashamed'). David Norbrook, who links Marvell's use of the word with a portrait of the English republican Henry Marten which has 'NOW' inscribed on it, suggests that in Marvell it is a 'Machiavellian' – that is, republican – injunction to decisive action. Thus, by alluding to Raphael's speech, Hazlitt is summoning the ideal Commonwealth. Orion's journey towards the rising sun is symbolic of the advance of history towards republican forms of government (there is a related image in 'My First Acquaintance with Poets', where the sun labours through the damp mist like a symbol of the good old cause).

What Hazlitt is designing here is another symbolic image of his own capacity for setting out on the journey towards that ideal polity. In a review of *The Excursion*, which provoked Wordsworth to circulate the shaming story about Hazlitt and the young Keswick woman, he slightly misquotes Wordsworth's 'Immortality Ode':

But though we cannot weave over again the airy, unsubstantial dream, which reason and experience have dispelled –

> What though the radiance, which was once so bright,
> Be now for ever taken from our sight,
> Though nothing can bring back the hour
> Of glory in the grass, of splendour in the flower: –

yet we will never cease, nor be prevented from returning on the wings of imagination to that bright dream of our youth; that glad dawn of the day-star of liberty; that spring-time of the world, in which the hopes and expectations of the human race seemed opening in the same gay career with our own; when France called her children to partake her equal blessings under her laughing skies; when the stranger was met in all her villages with dance and festive songs, in celebration of a new and golden era; and when, to the retired and contemplative student, the prospects of human happiness and glory were seen ascending, like the steps of Jacob's ladder, in a bright and never-ending succession.

His imagination filled with reminiscences of *The Prelude*, he is for ever journeying like Orion to meet the rising sun. Against the historical odds, he hopes to enter the great palace *now* of light. Like Milton, he affirms the pressure of the present moment in opposition to all the traditions that oppose it. He is also remembering his youthful ambition to do a painting of that Masonic symbol Jacob's ladder, a symbol which still decorates Orange arches in the North of Ireland.

For all the elegiac sense of failure and pastness that there is in Hazlitt's essay, he aims to invest Orion with an intense, concentrated power. Here, we must follow a trail not of direct quotation from Milton, but of indirect allusion. In the Old Testament book of Amos we are told: 'Seek him that maketh the seven stars and Orion, and turneth the shadow of death into the morning, and maketh the day dark with night: that calleth for the waters of the sea, and poureth them out upon the face of the earth: The LORD is his name.' Milton takes up this verse, just after the famous comparison of the fallen angels to autumn leaves. He, too, is celebrating power as water – which is why the 'waters of the sea' figure so strongly in Hazlitt's sources for this paragraph (Poussin's picture can be read as an allegory of 'the circulation of water in nature'). Milton's subject is the defeat of an army of fallen angels, which now lies like

> scattered sedge
> Afloat, when with fierce winds Orion armed
> While with perfidious hatred they pursued
> The sojourners of Goshen, who beheld
> From the safe shore their floating carcasses

And broken chariot wheels, so thick bestrewn
Abject and lost lay these, covering the flood,
Under amazement of their hideous change.

Milton also intends this to act as an image out of recent history
which represents the defeat of the royalist armies by Cromwell's
New Model Army (Hazlitt's use of Pope's description of Orion
similarly gives a contemporary application). In comparing Poussin
to Milton, and in quoting *Paradise Lost*, Hazlitt would have
remembered that, just before this passage, Milton describes how
Satan uses his huge spear to support his 'uneasy steps' – an
uncertain movement paralleled by Poussin's giant Orion, who
stalks along 'and reels and falters in his gait'. This means that
Orion, far from being a straightforward force and value in Hazlitt's
interpretation of Poussin's painting, carries a Satanic negativity as
well as a driving power. But such possible or hinted negativity is
purged at the end of the essay, where Napoleon's death is mourned,
and his lost power asserted.

In that last sentence, Hazlitt describes certain art galleries in
England as privileged sanctuaries: 'where the eye may dote, and
the heart take its fill of such pictures as Poussin's Orion, since the
Louvre is stripped of its triumphant spoils, and since he, who collected it, and wore it as a rich jewel in his Iron Crown, the hunter of
greatness and of glory, is himself a shade!' This picks up the opening
reference to Orion being a 'hunter of shadows himself a shade', and
it also refers to 'the Iron Crown of Charlemagne', which Hazlitt in
his biography of Napoleon says the Emperor placed on his own
head.

It was the Iron Duke who stripped the Louvre of its spoils, and
Hazlitt is remembering this, to him, act of desecration at the essay's
close. In a letter to Castlereagh, which Hazlitt quotes in his celebration of the Louvre collection in his *Life of Napoleon*, Wellington
said that he had dispersed the paintings in order to teach the French
'a great moral lesson'. Throwing the phrase back at the duke,
Hazlitt celebrates Napoleon's palace of culture, calling the Louvre
'a great moral lesson' and a 'school and discipline of humanity'. As

with the phrase 'Iron Crown', this shows his method of making concentrated dialogic allusions.

The direct comparison between Orion and Napoleon is held back until the end, but it can be felt throughout the essay in its elegiac sense of an enormous power that is past. Seeing the painting in London just after his hero's death, Hazlitt faces the reality of Napoleon's defeat: that the Louvre is stripped bare is now part of the picture's meaning for him, even though *Paysage avec Orion aveugle* was never in the collection.

Hazlitt is bringing a series of personal associations to the painting. He is saturating it with memories and allusions, most notably to Milton, the blind epic poet of liberty. In the concluding essay in his *Examiner* series, 'What is the People?', he again quotes Milton's lines on his blindness, and asks if the Tories would blindfold the British people 'with the double bandages of bigotry, or quench their understandings with "the dim suffusion", "the drop serene", of Legitimacy, that "they may roll in vain and find no dawn" of liberty, no ray of hope?' Here, Hazlitt has taken Milton's apparently personal account of his blindness as a medical condition and transformed it into a metaphor for the loss of liberty and free speech.

Addressing the sun's 'sovereign vital lamp', Milton says that while he can feel the heat of light,

> thou
> Revisit'st not these eyes, that roll in vain
> To find thy piercing ray, and find no dawn;
> So thick a drop serene hath quenched their orbs,
> Or dim suffusion veiled.

This is a complex reprise of Satan's journey out of hell, and it carries a powerful tragic accent, as the blind poet confronts defeat and failure like Oedipus at Colonus.

As Alistair Fowler shows in his edition of the poem, Milton may be hesitating – probably strategically – between Trinitarian and dangerously Arian views of the Son of God in the lines before this passage, where he appears to vacillate between deciding whether Christ is begotten in time or is co-eternal with the Father. These arguments would have spoken to the anti-Trinitarianism in Hazlitt's upbringing, especially because Milton is one of the central cultural pillars of Unitarianism; to cite his poetry or prose is implicitly to affirm that faith and perpetuate it in the present. It is also to affirm solidarity with Milton's experience, because he composed his epic poem in the aftermath of the Restoration, when his life was in danger as a notorious republican and defender of regicide. He went into hiding in 1660, and was nearly condemned to death, while copies of his most notorious books were burnt by the common hangman. Hazlitt reanimates this experience of defeat in his political essays by making the Allied victory over Napoleon the equivalent of Milton's tragic disappointment at the restoration of the Stuarts. The historicity of his reading of Milton adds another dimension to Poussin's painting, by transforming Orion into the blind epic poet and polemicist who never ceased to imagine a restored Commonwealth.

In another quotation from *Paradise Lost* in the opening paragraph of the Poussin essay, Hazlitt remarks that the same dull light of early dawn 'shadowy sets off' the face of nature. This is a reference to Eve's speech in the fifth book, where she says that the moon 'with more pleasing light / Shadowy sets off the face of things'. Interestingly, the next lines of her speech – 'in vain / If none regard, heaven wakes with all his eyes' – pick up the phrase 'these eyes, that roll in vain' in the opening of the third book, to produce a complex internal allusion which identifies heavenly light with republicanism and the seeing eye. And by drawing that subtle effect into his argument, Hazlitt aims almost to paste in a unified feeling of vastness, strangeness, and 'primeval forms' that pervades the canvas and throws us back on 'the first integrity of things'. This utopian primitivism is both Miltonic and the expression of Unitarian culture's attraction to the primitive Church. Joseph Priestley revered the early Church, and in a discourse to the supporters of Hackney New College in 1791, he praised the primitive Christians, and said that institutions such as the college planted the seeds of 'genuine, unsophisticated' Christianity. In a passage in *The Confessions* which Hazlitt would have known, Rousseau describes how before he wrote his *Discourse on Inequality* he wandered deep into the forest of Saint-Germain:

Tout le reste du jour, enfoncé dans la forêt, j'y cherchais, j'y trouvais l'image des premiers temps, dont je traçais fièrement l'histoire; je faisais main-basse sur les petits mensonges des hommes; j'osais dévoiler à nu leur nature, suivre le progrès du temps et des choses qui l'ont défigurée, et comparant l'homme de l'homme avec l'homme naturel, leur montrer dans son perfectionnement prétendu la véritable source de ses misères.

Rousseau's childhood Unitarianism informs this passage, and shapes his vision of the primitive past. Orion in the wet, wild woods is the philosopher on his journey to fame and power, as well as the bloodied avatar of the republic.

Maria Graham, in her biography of Poussin, praises the 'first simplicity' of the Athenian republic, and this chimes with the vision of a primal commonwealth in Hazlitt's essay. In 'My First Acquaintance with Poets', he calls the prospect of hearing Coleridge preach 'a sort of revival of the primitive spirit of Christianity'; so it is difficult not to view the Poussin essay as also being on one level an elegy for Unitarianism with its republican idealism, faith in progress, and devotion to the primitive Church.

Even that phrase 'first integrity of things' is echoed in the late essay 'The Letter-Bell', in which he remarks on the 'unbroken integrity' of early opinions. He also describes in that essay how the

long line of blue hills near the place where I was brought up waves in the horizon, a golden sunset hovers over them, the dwarf-oaks rustle their red leaves in the evening-breeze and the road from [Wem] to [Shrewsbury], by which I first set out on my journey through life, stares me in the face as plain, but from time and change not less visionary and mysterious, than the pictures in the *Pilgrim's Progress*. I should notice, that at this time the light of the French Revolution circled my head like a glory, though dabbled with drops of crimson gore: I walked comfortable and cheerful by its side.

By an uncomfortable allusion to the Terror, the wet grass and the figure of blind Orion are being introduced almost subliminally here.

The idea of an irrefragable liberty is connected in Hazlitt's mind with youth and the Dissenting culture that nourished him. He is implicitly eulogizing the sensuous, visionary power of Puritanism when, before linking Poussin to Milton's verse, he remarks that his classicism gives the scenery in the painting of Orion an 'unimpaired look of original nature, full, solid, large, luxuriant, teeming with life and power'. It's here that Hazlitt begins to introduce the critical reservation which he has about Poussin's genius: both Milton and the painter have, he says, the same stiffness and elevation, the same 'laborious and mighty grasp'. This anticipates an observation he makes elsewhere that Poussin paints like 'a professor at a University', and is close to his observation that the paintings are 'laboured, monotonous, and extravagant', a view that implicitly backs up a hinted reservation about Milton's verse.

The view that there is something learned, starchy, pedantic, or academic in Poussin's art is hinted at in Hazlitt's use in the opening paragraph of a Shakespearean phrase – 'foregone conclusion' – which acts as an important critical term in his writings. In *Othello* the phrase 'foregone conclusion' means 'previous consummation' – that is, something which has already taken place. Lamb and Hazlitt first adapted the phrase to general usage, as in Hazlitt's remark in 'Definition of Wit' that particular ideas are either not noticed or else 'determined to a set purpose and "foregone conclusion"'. In modern usage, the phrase means a decision or opinion that is already formed before a case is argued or the full evidence known. It also means a result that might have been seen as inevitable. As Hazlitt employs it, the term is usually negative, part of a series of terms – 'set', 'fixed', 'dry as the remainder biscuit' – which contrast with his aesthetic delight in bustle and fluid energetic motion. Often he adduces Rubens as Poussin's opposite in this respect, so that, like Johnson and Goldsmith, the two painters become associatively linked (Ruben's 'glad gorgeous groups' are mentioned later in the Poussin essay). But the view that Poussin's works each denote a foregone conclusion, while not totally negative, does describe their static, frozen qualities, the sense that they are trapped in an idea of the past that is a fixed notion, not a living idea. This is amplified by Hazlitt in a footnote to *Notes of a Journey through France and*

Italy, in which he says that it cannot be denied that there is a certain 'setness and formality, a *didactic* or prosing vein' in Poussin's compositions. Yet the most troubling quality in Poussin's classicism, and in Hazlitt's contemplation of it just after Napoleon's death, lies concealed behind an unacknowledged – even secret – quotation from *Hamlet* in the last sentence of the opening paragraph, where he describes how the painter shows the world in its 'high and palmy state', with the 'gravity' of history stamped on the 'proud monuments of vanished empire'.

This is a revealing allusion to the opening scene of *Hamlet*, where Horatio reflects on the ghost's appearance on the battlements:

> A mote it is to trouble the mind's eye:
> In the most high and palmy state of Rome,
> A little ere the mightiest Julius fell,
> The graves stood tenantless, and the sheeted dead
> Did squeak and gibber in the Roman streets;
> As stars with trains of fire and dews of blood,
> Disasters in the sun; and the moist star,
> Upon whose influence Neptune's empire stands,
> Was sick almost to doomsday with eclipse.

In adapting these apocalyptic lines, Hazlitt is subconsciously registering that the classical order which Poussin celebrates has broken up, just as the attempt by revolutionary France to create a new classical empire has failed (he alludes to Horatio's speech a few years later, in *The Life of Napoleon*, saying that if 'Pope Pius VII represented the decay of ancient superstition, Buonaparte represented the high and palmy state of modern opinion').

The 'dews of blood' in Horatio's speech are picked up and adapted in the phrase 'earth is dank and fresh with dews', which in turn anticipates the road from Wem to Shrewsbury 'dabbled with drops of crimson gore' in 'The Letter-Bell'. Poussin, the interconnected phrases imply, is merely a gifted memoralist who imaginatively records a high and palmy state that is now defunct. Or, if we consider the emphasis in Hazlitt on wetness, the dewy dawn in the painting becomes symbolic of the flow of blood during the

Revolution. To admire Poussin, post Napoleon, is to recognize that his ample canvases are like stage-sets that remain after the drama has ended. Something is over and done with, finished, fated, foregone. The paintings have been made redundant by the modern gothic spirit which underpins Legitimacy, reminding Hazlitt that the French Revolution with all its classical forms, images, insignia – its Phrygian caps, paintings by David, fasces, liberty trees – has failed. After Poussin, the deluge. And now we can detect a premonition of the social inundation that was to come. It is as though Hazlitt has adapted Horatio's 'moist star' and 'Neptune's empire' to his vision of the son of Neptune setting out through the damp early morning. In deliberately creating this moist texture, he gives imaginative life to that tired phrase 'the tide of history'.

This insistence on the morning freshness of the natural world runs throughout the opening paragraph, where Hazlitt employs the terms 'nature' and 'natural' to express his critical aesthetic. In a discussion elsewhere of the literary uses of classical mythology during the Elizabethan period, he remarks that from copying artificial models we lose sight of 'the living principle of nature', a principle that is central to his criticism. Nature is an obviously puritan and romantic ethic which can easily denote only a solipsistic, inspirational vitalism that opposes any concept of aesthetic form (D. H. Lawrence at his most predictable). Quoting Maria Graham's biography, Hazlitt notes that Poussin would carry home small stones, moss, flowers, in order to copy them 'exactly from nature'. Poussin makes his scenery embody this principle of a nature that has been studied exhaustively, and he combines it with his study of the antique.

'Nature' is Hazlitt's most important – indeed, most overloaded – critical term. He defines it very subtly in a brief essay entitled 'Poetry', in which he offers an analysis of Perdita's famous flower speech in *The Winter's Tale*:

>   Daffodils,
> That come before the swallow dares, and take
> The winds of March with beauty; violets, dim,

> But sweeter than the lids of Juno's eyes,
> Or Cytherea's breath; pale primroses,
> That die unmarried ere they can behold
> Bright Phoebus in his strength, (a malady
> Most incident to maids).

In this essay, Hazlitt makes it clear that there is a patriotic emphasis in his affirmation of nature as a critical principle. This passage, he insists, 'knocks down John Bull with its perfumed and melting softness'. It is a mystery, 'an *untranslatable* language, to all France', because the French take their ideas from words, while we English, who are 'slower and heavier', are forced to look more closely at things before we can pronounce upon them. Applying this vindication of English empiricism to Poussin, we can see that Hazlitt is implicitly saying that although the artist was French, and therefore vulnerable to those faults of aridity and formality which that culture possesses, he nevertheless behaved in a practical English manner by studying nature so closely. And in his commentary on Perdita's speech, Hazlitt illustrates this type of close observation by taking the phrase 'violets dim' and asking what other adjective could recall its 'deep purple glow, its retired modesty, its sullen, conscious beauty'. In a series of rapid, exact, almost Lawrentian adjectives, he describes how the violets look 'dull, obtuse, faint, absorbed', but at the same time 'soft, luxurious, proud, and full of meaning'.

In a later essay in the same collection, 'On the Aristocracy of Letters', he picks up Perdita's lines when he insists that Keats was not 'a sycophant plant' protected from criticism:

he lay bare to weather – the serpent stung him, and the poison-tree dropped upon this little western flower: – when the mercenary servile crew approached him, he had no pedigree to show them, no rent-roll to hold out in reversion for their praise: he was not in any great man's train, nor the butt and puppet of a lord – he could only offer them 'the fairest flowers of the season, carnations and streaked gilliflowers' – 'rue for remembrance and pansies for thoughts' – they recked not of his gift, but tore him with hideous shouts and laughter,

> Nor could the Muse protect her son!

Keats's death brings back the memory of Milton's fears during the Restoration; but, as Susan Wolfson has pointed out, Hazlitt is also feminizing Keats by, among other strategies, changing 'defend' to 'protect' in the quotation from *Paradise Lost*. He has combined Perdita's speech with this passage in *Paradise Lost*:

> Standing on earth, not rapt above the pole,
> More safe I sing with mortal voice, unchanged
> To hoarse or mute, though fallen on evil days,
> On evil days though fallen, and evil tongues;
> In darkness, and with dangers compassed round,
> And solitude; yet not alone, while thou
> Visit'st my slumbers nightly, or when morn
> Purples the east: still govern thou my song,
> Urania, and fit audience find, though few.
> But drive far off the barbarous dissonance
> Of Bacchus and his revellers, the race
> Of that wild rout that tore the Thracian bard
> In Rhodope, where woods and rocks had ears
> To rapture, till the savage clamour drowned
> Both harp and voice; nor could the muse defend
> Her son.

This is Milton dictating his epic under the Restoration, and we can see how the complex associative network of allusion, quotation, and compressed biography articulates Hazlitt's experience in Lord Liverpool's Britain. He would have known that Milton is drawing on his own invective against those who in 1660 were transferring their allegiance to Charles Stuart. Our 'zealous backsliders', he says in a pamphlet published that year, must 'forethink' – anticipate – how their necks will be 'yok'd with these tigers of Bacchus', the pox-ridden monarchists.

Keats is identified with Orpheus being torn to pieces by forces which Hazlitt's symbolic code intends us to identify as vindictive royalist reviewers. This is the same mercenary, servile crew that Milton feared would literally tear him to pieces on the scaffold, as they did the regicides who were hung, drawn, and quartered according to the barbarous practices of the time.

If Hazlitt is addressing the failure of the great experiment which began with the French Revolution, he is not despondent, because the driving theme of the Poussin essay is art, especially republican art, as power. This is the purpose of the two biblical allusions in the opening paragraph, and it is made clear near the end of the same paragraph when Hazlitt quotes Prospero's phrase 'so potent art'.

Comparing Poussin to 'his own Orion', he quotes from Isaiah: 'Behold, the nations are as the drop of a bucket, and are counted as the small dust of the balance: behold, he taketh up the isles as a very little thing.' Applied to Hazlitt's text, this is Poussin as Napoleon, remoulding nature, overturning monarchs, shaping and changing nations. It's at this point that Hazlitt's prose breaks into a kind of massy free verse that continues the elevated rhythms of the Authorized Version:

> With a laborious and mighty grasp
> he put nature into the mould
> of the ideal and antique;
> and was among painters
> (more than any one else)
> what Milton was among poets.

And then he begins to note their shared stiffness, pedantry, elevation, and grandeur, a perception that issues from the almost muscle-bound opening rhythm of this sentence, with its resonantly clinking *t* sounds, its heavy antique, slightly over-emphatic, even archaic teakiness.

In the Book of Job, God is the absolute power which alone 'spreadeth out the heavens, and treadeth upon the waves of the sea. Which maketh Arcturus, Orion, and Pleiades, and the chambers of the south.' Orion is both changing sea and starry constellation for Hazlitt, just as Napoleon is both a great historical force and a mythic figure who exists as a fixed heroic pattern in the heavens. Orion, the god who could walk on the waves, is obviously a symbol of power, and if we examine Prospero's speech celebrating his 'potent art', another reference to Neptune – Orion's father – appears just at the moment when Shakespeare is exulting in his long career as a dramatist:

> Ye elves of hills, brooks, standing lakes, and groves
> And ye that on the sands with printless foot
> Do chase the ebbing Neptune, and do fly him
> When he comes back; you demi-puppets that
> By moonshine do the green sour ringlets make,
> Whereof the ewe not bites; and you whose pastime
> Is to make midnight mushrumps, that rejoice
> To hear the solemn curfew; by whose aid
> (Weak masters though ye be) I have bedimmed
> The noontide sun, called forth the mutinous winds,
> And 'twixt the green sea and the azured vault
> Set roaring war; to the dread rattling thunder
> Have I given fire and rifted Jove's stout oak
> With his own bolt; the strong-based promontory
> Have I made shake and by the spurs plucked up
> The pine and cedar; graves at my command
> Have waked their sleepers, oped, and let 'em forth
> By my so potent art. But this rough magic
> I here abjure; and when I have required
> Some heavenly music (which even now I do)
> To work mine end upon their senses that
> This airy charm is for, I'll break my staff,
> Bury it certain fathoms in the earth,
> And deeper than did ever plummet sound
> I'll drown my book.

What is particularly interesting in Hazlitt's citation of 'so potent art' from this speech – a phrase which mnemonically compresses the entire passage for him – is the way he moves to it after he has alluded to Horatio's lines in *Hamlet*. In those lines, which I quoted earlier, Horatio uses the phrase 'moist star' after he has evoked the sheeted dead in a Rome that is still republican. In *The Tempest*

Shakespeare is ventriloquizing through Prospero, and saying 'by my powers as an artist I opened graves and let the sleepers, notably the ghost of Hamlet's father, walk'. Prospero's and Horatio's speeches are closely connected, and Hazlitt's citation of them acts as an invisible textual gloss that draws attention to their relationship. We can also see that Prospero is saying that his art is finished, over and done with, and this backs on to Hazlitt's view that Poussin's paintings denote a foregone conclusion. At the same time, we can connect the 'green sour ringlets' and 'midnight mushrumps' with Hazlitt's celebration of dewy nature in Poussin. Hazlitt's Shakespeare is simultaneously celebrating the power of art and saying that, in the cases of Poussin, Prospero, and himself, it is completed, or about to be completed. Indeed, there is a last-phase feeling in this essay, as though he is anticipating the elegiac, valedictory mood of 'The Letter-Bell' and 'A Farewell to Essay-Writing'.

By tracing Hazlitt's quotations back to their sources and then considering the contexts in which he uses them elsewhere – 'procreant cradle', for example – we begin to understand how rich, detailed, creative, and powerfully synthesizing his critical intellect is. In realizing the imaginative and intellectual power he possesses – and the way in which the vigour and range of his memory articulate that intellect – we also perceive how, in his manner of uniting Poussin and Milton's strength, he acquires some of the power, the 'mighty grasp', that he's celebrating. Yet from one point of view, he offers only a rhetorical descriptiveness which is posturing and self-reflective, and which advances nothing. But precisely because this argument can be turned into one which says, 'Yes, this is the essence of the critic as performer', we see how writing as performance depends on the topicality of the act, as well as on our awareness that it is precisely an *act*, a sudden dramatic concentration of language, voice, gesture, and audience. In print this demands the use of frequent italics, because it takes place before an audience that watches the performer utter words which appear to write him into existence as they are read. Such is its momentum that by the time we reach the end of the paragraph, we believe that the critic is 'lord of nature and her powers; and his mind is universal, and his art the master-art!' When Hazlitt says that Poussin and Milton share 'the same richness of borrowed materials', we immediately recognize that he, too, is constructing an elaborate composition out of highly intelligent and apposite borrowings.

Remembering that paintings are contextual – they're exhibited in buildings – we naturally understand what Hazlitt is signifying when he links the painting of Orion with the emptied Louvre. Obviously Hazlitt wants to identify it more completely with the defeated Napoleon, but what of his apparently rather dragged-in remark about Rubens's 'prodigies of colour, character, and expression, at Blenheim'? Surely he mentions Blenheim because he intends that squat, rather theatrical palace to function as a modest Whig equivalent of Napoleon's Louvre? The country house built by a grateful nation to reward the duke of Marlborough for winning the War of the Spanish Succession is an embodiment of an earlier struggle against tyranny, because the duke's shift of allegiance from James II to William of Orange enabled the Glorious Revolution to succeed. Having helped expel James II and install William and Mary, he then went on to defeat Louis XIV at the battles of Blenheim, Ramillies and Malplaquet.

When Hazlitt concludes the next essay, 'On Milton's Sonnets', by saying that he has often wished that Milton could have lived to see the Revolution of 1688, his purpose becomes clear: this is Whig writing which centres heavily on Milton, the poet 'blind, yet bold' as Marvell called him, in a phrase also quoted in the sonnet essay. And with the reference to 1688 in its concluding paragraph, the essay on Milton's sonnets is clearly intended as compensation for the sense of failure in the conclusion to the account of blind Orion (Hazlitt wrote it the following year). Yet, how characteristically he uses the Poussin essay's final exclamation mark to triumph heroically over failure, now that 'the hunter of greatness and of glory, is himself a shade!' As in the final paragraph celebrating his father in 'On the Pleasure of Painting', the very first essay in *Table-Talk*, the exclamation triumphs rhetorically over failure, joining Napoleon to the Reverend Hazlitt, whose memory is linked inseparably for his son with the evening-star and with Napoleon's victory at Austerlitz.*

---

* Later in the same issue of the *London Magazine*, Hazlitt's readers would have found this brief notice in the deaths column: 'At St Helena, Saturday, May 5th, at 6 p.m. NAPOLEON BUONAPARTE, aged 51 years and 9 months, being born at Ajaccio in Corsica, Aug. 15, 1769. He expired after an illness of six weeks, the last fortnight only of which was considered by his Medical Attendants to be dangerous. On the body being opened, the disease was ascertained to be a cancer in the stomach, with a great extent of ulceration: although the pain he suffered must have been excruciating, he manifested no symptoms of impatience. After lying in state, he was buried, Wednesday, May 9th, with military honours, in a spot called Haines Valley about two miles distant from Longwood where a grave was made beneath some willow trees.'

CHAPTER TEN

Hazlitt *faciebat*: *The Spirit of the Age*

In the collection of what we now would term newspaper profiles which he published in 1825 under the title *The Spirit of the Age*, Hazlitt aims to communicate a momentous and insistent topicality. His prose in this, his most famous work, is impelled by the 'force of present conviction', as he terms the urgency of Cobbett's writing, and it is supported by those consistent, but never inflexible, principles which underlie all his writing. This is journalism in its purest form. Yet it is something else as well: something more lasting and durable, which was expressed eleven years after the volume's publication by a journalist who called Hazlitt 'this democratic Plutarch'. He is also writing for posterity, and when he remarks in his admiring portrait of Cobbett that there isn't a single sentence or *bon mot* in all of that mighty journalist's publications which has ever been quoted again, the implicit message is that he wants his own journalism to achieve the classic permanence created by constant citation. As a critic, Hazlitt is the supreme master of the art of quotation; so he naturally wants his own work to last. One way of wooing posterity, or at least of remaining in the memory of his current readership as a notable journalist, is by drawing attention to style, particularly prose style. Along with 'imagination', 'machinery', 'understanding' in the philosophical sense of 'intellect', style is a major theme in the collection, and one which is closely connected with fluid movement and the idea of modernity.

This fusion of a written style with motion here and now occurs in that image of the Scottish lawyer and editor of the *Edinburgh Review*, Francis Jeffrey, wielding a pen which never stands still and which therefore dazzles 'like an eye that is ever in motion'. There is a similar moment in the sketch of Godwin, where he overpraises his derivative novel *St Leon*, calling it a brightly coloured 'staring transparency' in which we cannot distinguish the application of the thin colours from the light that shines through them and gives them brilliance. Making that characteristic comparison with a relatively new visual form of popular entertainment, Hazlitt is also making a claim for the type of Whig writing which Jeffrey and Godwin practise. And in singling out Jeffrey's critical journalism as a dazzling combination of light and swift optical motion, he's anticipating the future almost like a writer of science fiction. His journalistic technique in *The Spirit of the Age* doesn't simply advance the new form of the 'serial' or profile to sudden maturity: at moments it attains a visual immediacy that is the equivalent of a television documentary. By 'transparency', Hazlitt does not mean prose that is perspicuous like a modern window-pane – Orwell's limiting comparison – but prose that glows as part of a spectacle designed to entertain a city crowd. Glossy this writing certainly is, but that does not mean that it is simply clear, static, denotative. This is because Jeffrey may be said to weave words 'into any shapes he pleases for use or ornament, as the glass-blower moulds the vitreous fluid with his breath; and his sentences shine like glass from their polished smoothness, and are equally transparent'.

Again, the adjective 'transparent' carries not simply the sense of being perspicuous, but the idea of a warmly illuminated transparency, so that the term communicates a powerful visual presence. The image of glass being blown is a version of the favourite 'bubble' image which he applies to Shakespeare's imagination: so it combines the moment of production in the theatrical and publishing senses of the term with that 'bubble reputation' which is all that even the most famous journalists can hope to have. It is an image of taut nowness that's wittily reinvented when he describes Cobbett's mind 'fermenting and overflowing', and then adds that an argument doesn't 'stagnate and muddle' in his brain, but passes immediately on to the page, so that his ideas are served up 'like pancakes, hot and hot'. This is a perfect image for the translation of copy into newsprint, for the heat of the moment which gives shape and form to the liquid pour of driven, intelligent feeling. Cobbett as polemical journalist, editor, and publisher is like someone at a fairground selling hot pancakes. It's a vigorous image for the moment of production, for the passage of idea into form, into hot metal and fresh text. Pancakes taking sudden shape, molten glass being blown, an always moving human eye – these are Hazlitt's symbols for writing and publication as a single, unified, continuous act.

'Motion', as we have seen, is one of Hazlitt's favourite critical terms. It is implicit in the various contemporary references in *The Spirit of the Age* to steam power, canals, railways, voltaic batteries, and to John MacAdam, inventor of macadamized road surfaces. It is there, too, in the remark in his *Life of Napoleon* that society is 'an electrical machine, by which good and evil, vice and virtue are communicated with instantaneous rapidity'; and it appears again in the 'electrical and instantaneous' effect produced by Mackintosh's lectures on his London audience (Mackintosh gave a series of lectures at Lincoln's Inn in 1799). At this and other similar moments, it's as though Hazlitt intuitively feels that live television and information technology are just around the corner. He relishes the excitement of modernity, but at the same time represents it as a historical process that is noisy, mechanical, driving, and intense. His prose is high on present conviction, as though fuelled by adrenalin and the strong tea he was addicted to, and it flags only in the series of double portraits that complete the volume.

Emphasizing modernity's mechanical logic, he opens with a profile of Bentham, who for the last forty years has lived in a house in Westminster like an anchorite in a cell, 'reducing law to a system, and the mind of man to a machine'. The philosopher speaks in 'shrill, cluttering accents' which reflect his reduction of human life to 'dull, plodding, technical calculation' – adjectives which are echoed in Hazlitt's rather snobbish portrait of the reactionary critic William Gifford, who merely understands the 'mechanical and instrumental' aspects of learning, and inclines to the 'technical' in style. It is also echoed in his criticism of the Scottish intelligentsia, who treat everyone 'in the light of a machine or a collection of topics'. In an aptly technological image, he says that they turn you round like a cylinder to see what 'use' they can make of you.

Against this type of rigid utilitarianism, Hazlitt sets an idea of the intellect, or 'understanding', as he habitually terms it, which is distinctively English. He praises the reformer Sir Francis Burdett as one of the few remaining types of 'the old English understanding and old English character'. This echoes his early account of Bulstrode Whitelocke in *The Eloquence of the British Senate*, in which he laments the successive changes that have taken place in the minds and characters of Englishmen within the last 200 years. As we have seen, his praise of Whitelocke's 'honest seriousness and simplicity of old English reasoning' is the source of Eliot's concept of the dissociation of sensibility.

This nativist definition of the understanding is essentially conservative, which is why it appealed so strongly to Eliot, and it underpins all Hazlitt's criticism. Thus, when he praises Cobbett as a 'very honest man', the adjective is shorthand for the type of intellect which, despite certain shortcomings, he shares with Burdett and Whitelocke. Bentham, it's hinted, is an almost Scottish figure – all law topics and scraky accents – who has taken forceful, but insensitive, occupation of the house and garden which was 'the cradle of *Paradise Lost*'. He is completely lacking in any aesthetic sense, and at one time proposed to cut down the two beautiful cotton-trees that shade the garden. Hazlitt, when he was Bentham's tenant in York Street, is supposed to have inserted in the garden wall a stone tablet inscribed 'Sacred to Milton, Prince of Poets'. By referring to *Paradise Lost* at this point in the profile, he intends not just to commemorate Milton, but to make a contrast between the poet's radical art and the philosopher's reductive logic. In a series of living cameos, he describes Bentham's time-saving running walk, negligent dress, and screaky voice, as well as his lack-lustre eye and breathlessness when he stops to point out the commemorative tablet to a foreign visitor. This type of witty documentary realism has a zany rapidity and critical delight in eccentricity that take it beyond reportage into a parallel fictional world which Smollett or Sterne might have designed.

Warming to his theme, he complains that Bentham had planned to convert the garden into a paltry 'Chrestomathic School', and to make the house into a thoroughfare for the 'idle rabble'. Then, reining in his snobbery, he exclaims that he's going too fast – 'Milton himself taught school!' A memory of Samuel Johnson's rebuke to those who sneer at schoolteachers stops him in his tracks, and he proceeds to compare Bentham's appearance to portraits of Milton:

There is something not altogether dissimilar between Mr Bentham's appearance and the portraits of Milton – the same silvery tone, a few dishevelled hairs, a peevish, yet puritanical expression, an irritable temperament corrected by habit and discipline. Or in modern times, he is something between Franklin and Charles Fox, with the comfortable double-chin and sleek thriving look of the one, and the quivering lip, the restless eye, and animated acuteness of the other. His eye is quick and lively; but it glances not from object to object, but from thought to thought.

Hazlitt is obviously aligning Bentham and Milton because they belong to the same radical tradition, but he also wants his readers to visualize Bentham clearly. The comparison is chancy – he says that the two figures are 'not altogether dissimilar', which is stretching it. But when he adds that the philosopher is like a cross between Franklin and Fox, suddenly a living Whig portrait emerges out of this radical composite. Franklin's beautifully observed sleek glossiness is reflected in the two references to moving eyes, which animate the portrait and give it its Titian-like watchfulness and sheen. Fox's restless eye is shared with another important reformer, Francis Jeffrey, though Franklin's 'sleek thriving look' has an originality and a fresh tingling accuracy which are also part of the shine and glow of present conviction. The subtle assonance *thriving quivering* helps give the sentence keeping, while 'comfortable' and 'sleek' suggest something smugly operative in Bentham's outlook.

Picking up a favourite quotation from Burke's criticism of the French revolutionaries' carelessness of human life, he says that Bentham regards the people about him 'no more than the flies of a summer'. Where Burke is referring to the way in which radical change ruptures historical continuity in a state and destroys the links between generations, Hazlitt is noticing Bentham's complete lack of interest in people as individuals and his indifference to

individual lives. Wholly insensitive to beauty, and with no awareness of the human spirit, he resembles a miller who grinds facts to
dust in his 'logical machinery'. Describing Bentham's open shirt
collar, single-breasted coat, old-fashioned boots, and ribbed stock-
ings, Hazlitt offers a concise portrait of the philosopher, whose
general appearance is a 'singular mixture of boyish simplicity and
of the venerableness of age'.

It's a moving eye which gives fluidity and cinematic presence to
what might otherwise be static descriptive writing. As Roy Park
points out in his study of Hazlitt, he employs a 'kinetic' critical
vocabulary which is most succinctly communicated in his account
of Wordsworth's enthusiasm for Poussin, whom he contrasts with
those painters who fail to express 'the time of day, the climate, the
period of the world' which the completed work is meant to illustrate. This insistence on 'wholeness', on the here-and-nowness of
atmosphere, weather, time, and place, gives buoyant immediacy to
Hazlitt's contemporary portraits, and suggests that he wants his
writing to be aligned with that of certain old masters. He mentions
Titian's picture of the meeting of Bacchus and Ariadne in his portrait of Wordsworth, and it is likely that his technique in *The Spirit
of the Age* is partly formed by his expert knowledge of the artist
whom he regarded as the greatest portrait painter ever.

As a young artist working in the Louvre on commissions for
Unitarian businessmen, Hazlitt copied Titian's *Hippolito de Medici*
and *Man with a Glove*, both of which he cherished as 'living
objects'. The portrait of the young man holding a glove was talismanic for him: two of his copies were among his most treasured
possessions, and a detail in the portrait may lie behind a simile he
applies to Godwin, who, with his success and popularity, has lost a
certain captiousness of manner, and from being 'too pragmatical,
become somewhat too careless. He is, at present, as easy as an old
glove'. Titian portrays a young nobleman who has an elegant,
worn, very thin leather glove on his left hand; the other glove lies
loosely in the almost breathy crinkles of his gloved hand. The casual, sophisticated, but at the same time innocent elegance of this
detail is beautifully caught in Hazlitt's simile.

In 'Gusto', the essay where he defines the critical term with which he is most frequently associated, Hazlitt praises Titian's colouring for its gusto, arguing that not only do his heads seem to think, 'his bodies seem to feel'. His flesh colour has *morbidezza*: it seems sensitive and alive all over. It hasn't merely the look and texture of flesh, but 'the feeling in itself'. That phrase 'sleek thriving look' is an image drawn from Titian's colouring, as well as an example of the critical body language that Hazlitt employs. Thus Titian catches that type of 'tingling sensation to the eye' which the body experiences 'within itself'. This is gusto, and it's also a description of the sheer concentrated zing and ontological atmosphere of Hazlitt's method in *The Spirit of the Age*. He wants to portray living, animated human beings, each in the present moment, not a series of posed, static figures.

As we have seen, Hazlitt often refers to Titian's signature – *Titianus faciebat* – to emphasize that the artist felt that everything falls short of nature because it's impossible to realize successive movements of expression and changes in countenance. The signature, 'Titian was working on this', means that the artist doesn't so much finish, as abandon, a particular composition. In the *Conversations* Northcote expands on this, saying that the more one knows of the art of portraiture, and indeed the better one can paint, the less one is satisfied: 'This made Titian write under his pictures *faciebat*, signifying that they were only in progress.' A portrait, Northcote says, is only 'a faint relic' of an individual. It is only a slightly better memorial than 'the parings of the nails or a lock of the hair'. This is similar to the passage in 'Whether Genius is Conscious of its Powers?', where Hazlitt contrasts the stimulus of the writing process with the 'mere waste-paper' of the printed text.

In *The Spirit of the Age*, Hazlitt wants to make his portraits somehow more than faint relics of living, breathing human subjects: he wants to communicate his pleasure in the process of composition, and to make each profile resemble something that is happening now, like a scene in a play. Indeed, the tone which he adopts often has the wit and timing of stage comedy. Thus a straightforward critical remark that Bentham has a language of his own which 'darkens knowledge' is amplified by the perfectly poised throwaway line: 'His works have been translated into French – they ought to be translated into English.' The witty put-down springs from the familiar, egalitarian tone of the portraits; we are not awed by these powerful public figures, because Hazlitt is game for them all. What we enjoy as readers is the comic process of his prose, its flexible conversational mix of ease and smartness.

This type of process, which *The Spirit of the Age* so fluidly represents, is best expressed in a passage in the essay 'On Application to Study' which develops the glass-blower image which he applies to Jeffrey:

I do not conceive rapidity of execution necessarily implies slovenliness or crudeness. On the contrary, I believe it is often productive both of sharpness and freedom. The eagerness of composition strikes out sparkles of fancy, and runs the thoughts more naturally and closely into one another. There may be less formal method, but there is more life, and spirit, and truth. In the play and agitation of the mind, it runs over, and we dally with the subject, as the glass-blower rapidly shapes the vitreous fluid. A number of new thoughts rise up spontaneously, and they come in the proper places, because they arise from the occasion. They are also sure to partake of the warmth and vividness of that ebullition of mind, from which they spring. *Spiritus precipitandus est.* In these sort of voluntaries in composition, the thoughts are worked up to a state of projection: the grasp of the subject, the presence of mind, the flow of expression must be something akin to *extempore* speaking; or perhaps such bold but finished draughts may be compared to *fresco* paintings, which imply a life of study and great previous preparation, but of which the execution is momentary and irrevocable.

He then disagrees with Cobbett's statement that the first word that occurs is always the best. In the hurry of composition three or four words may present themselves, 'one on the back of the other', and the last may be the best and right one. He grants, though, that it is hopeless trying to seek the right word by trying to arrive at it 'second-hand' or as a paraphrase of some other word: 'the proper word must be suggested immediately by the thought, but it need not be presented as soon as called for.'

The figure of the glass-blower rapidly shaping 'the vitreous fluid' takes us close to the centre of Hazlitt's critical aesthetic, and it's connected to his statement later in the same paragraph that proper expressions rise to the surface 'from the heat and fermentation of the mind, like bubbles on an agitated stream'. Significantly, he wrote this in 1823, the same year he dashed off that ecstatic account of the stimulus of writing in 'Whether Genius is Conscious of its Powers?'. The glass-blower is a dynamic image for Priestley's idea of matter as energy. Wordsworth's motion that rolls through all things similarly adapts this fusion of matter and spirit. Literally, this is the shaping spirit of the age. When Hazlitt makes *motion moving matter* part of his critical vocabulary, he is obeying Priestley's injunction not to separate reality into mind and matter, but to view the two as fused energies. The portraits in *The Spirit of the Age* are a series of 'voluntaries in composition' which aim to have the glistening sheen of fresh bubbles or moving eyes. It's almost as though this spontaneous prose has a reflecting surface that lets us see ourselves mirrored in its changing surfaces and which bonds us as audience. This is that optical tingling sensation which Hazlitt discerns in Titian. What he is aiming for is an expressive flow – a gusto – which carries the reader along as though we are participating in a conversation. And when he says that in such compositions the thoughts are worked up to 'a state of projection', the idea of an illuminated transparency is being introduced, as the collateral comparison to frescoes – that is, fixed projections on walls – makes clear.

As we have seen, the image of a bubbling stream is central to a republican poetics which aims at both 'sharpness and freedom'. The momentum of his prose aims at a totally unified composition in which everything – music, painting, writing – comes together. Interestingly, he seeks to capture moving light in his prose, not colour; there are very few colours mentioned in *The Spirit of the Age*, but this allows us to fill in colour through our appreciation of the quality of the light he describes or by activating the associations with actual paintings or engravings.

Although he was no admirer of Priestley's prose style, he would have known that spontaneity or 'unpremeditated discourse' is among the qualities that are recommended in Priestley's textbook

Lectures on Oratory and Criticism. The perfection of speaking, Priestley insists, is extempore speech, and he particularly stresses the importance of figurative expressions, which he suggests are hardly to be considered as words. Instead, they should be viewed in the same light as 'attitudes, gestures, and looks, which are infinitely more expressive of sentiments and feelings than words can possibly be'. This is to view spoken language as what Brecht terms *Gestus*, and it naturally identifies speech acts with the active human body as it moves and performs on stage.

In order to represent things true to life and so hold the reader's or the audience's attention, Priestley says that it is especially advantageous to introduce as many 'sensible images' as possible. Hazlitt follows this advice, and has at times a novelist's sense of detail – cotton-trees, Bentham's fine old organ, Hogarth prints, steam central heating, the lathe on which the philosopher turns wooden bowls 'for exercise', all the while imagining that he 'can turn men in the same manner'. That little word 'turn' resonates with the idea of 'distort, redirect, change their loyalty', even execute (hangmen were said to 'turn off' a victim). Perhaps Hazlitt knew that the philosopher had once employed a servant who was later executed at Tyburn for stealing some of his cutlery. In *Great Expectations*, there is a similarly queasy public/private atmosphere in Wemmick's house in Walworth. We may imagine what Gillray would have made of Bentham at the lathe, or how Hogarth would have portrayed him at home. In designing these sensible images, Hazlitt seems sometimes to anticipate Dickens, who shares his fascination with the criminal mind, the geography of inner London, and the gnarled contortions of legal language. With its pot-houses, lawyers' chambers, courtrooms, twisting narrow streets, and crowded sinister Newgate, where convicts wait to be hanged or sent to the hulks, London figures so strongly in both writers' work that it is difficult not to feel Dickens as a proleptic presence shadowing these glimpses of city life and institutional violence. Dickens, like Hazlitt, was a parliamentary shorthand writer, and as a young man he was friendly with some of Hazlitt's journalistic associates and with his son, for whom he wrote a number of testimonials. In 1848 he made a pilgrimage to

Winterslow Hut, the inn where many of Hazlitt's critical essays were written. I have a hunch that 'Mr Bentham' is one of the seeds of *Bleak House*, and that Hazlitt's writing exercised a profound influence on Dickens, whose account of the limitations of utilitarianism closely follows his. Again, as I suggested earlier, the portrait of Bradley Headstone in *Our Mutual Friend* – his mind is a place of 'mechanical stowage' like a 'wholesale warehouse' – is similar to Hazlitt's account of Coleridge's criticism of Mackintosh as 'the ready warehouseman of letters'. And one of Hazlitt's subjects in *The Spirit of the Age* – his friend Leigh Hunt – appears in *Bleak House* as Horace Skimpole, who is described in the list of characters as 'a brilliant, vivacious, sentimental, but thoroughly selfish man'.

It is their witty, insistent fictionality – with the social buzz that surrounds it – which gives these sketches such imaginative buoyancy. When Horne Tooke, for example, is described as resembling 'the finished gentleman of the last age', we seem to have been transposed for a moment into a Turgenev novel, where the modern and the socially archaic jostle each other. The sense of freedom which the sometimes fictive quality of the sketches releases necessarily prevents Hazlitt from appearing to be merely the servant or amanuensis of his subjects. Instead, he is the master portraitist for whom they are sitting. Like Titian, he aims to capture them in a moment of being or, rather, to link a series of such moments in the equivalent of a Hogarthian progress or narrative sequence of prints. Bentham walks and talks with a foreign visitor in his garden, plays his organ, works his lathe – actions which somehow have the woody, utile quality of Hogarth's engravings, as well as the slightly fantastical eccentricity which is also one of the artist's subjects.

Godwin's adeptly casual social grace is caught in the cleverly pictorial glove image, and by suggesting that he resembles the standard portraits of Locke, Hazlitt also places him in the heroic Whig tradition of radical reformers, as well as implying certain limitations in his philosophy. For all his acquired easy charm, Godwin emerges as both angular – his deportment is neither graceful nor animated – and lacking that 'vinous' quality of mind which Leigh Hunt possesses. But he is also characterized as 'the bold and adventurous pilot, who dared us to tempt the uncertain abyss'. The image is drawn from Dryden's portrait of Shaftesbury in *Absalom and Achitophel*:

> A daring pilot in extremity;
> Pleas'd with the danger, when the waves went high
> He sought the storms.

By picking up Dryden's lines, he invigorates the Whig tradition, just as he similarly extends it in his portrait of his father reading Shaftesbury's grandson's *Characteristics*. He also points to the element of intellectual daring and risk-taking in Whig radicalism.

Yet Godwin isn't spontaneously talented: he has succeeded by sheer will-power, by the voluntary exercise of his abilities. He therefore lacks the innate, natural genius of Coleridge, the next portrait in the series. Godwin resembles an eight-day clock that must be wound up for a long time before it can strike (this is a version of the cylinder image that is applied to Scottish conversation). His powers of conversation are therefore limited, and, like Mackintosh, he has certain mechanical qualities.

The sketches of Bentham and Godwin stand at the beginning of the volume, because they introduce Hazlitt's twin themes of modernity and style. Noticing the 'desolate monotony' of Robert Owen's model mill village of New Lanark, Hazlitt remarks a few pages later that Godwin's very originality in his fictional method tends to 'a certain degree of monotony'. Although he has been praising Godwin, the term is necessarily limiting and negative, as well as a reminder of Owen's social experiments. Modernity, Hazlitt is saying, is going to be regimented, planned, and very boring. Excitement, paradoxically, is now all in the urge towards a condition that will exclude excitement.

What obsesses him is the idea that reform – that is, the spirit of the age – is somehow out of kilter with what he terms the 'irregularities' of the human will. Owen's flat, regular parallelograms cannot encompass either the imagination or a Burkean idea of community, and, as we have seen, the adjective 'irregular' is permanently associated with Burke in Hazlitt's writings. In his sketch of Bentham he employs it as shorthand for the argument that the philosopher has 'not allowed for the wind'. His dull, plodding, technical calculation cannot admit an idea of the soul, that 'aggregating and exclusive principle' which clings obstinately to some things, and violently rejects others. This resembles Dostoyevsky's *Notes from Underground*, where the obsessive monologuist attacks 'your statisticians, sages and humanitarians' who foolishly think that they can define exactly what is in the interest of a human being. Hazlitt, who, like Dickens, was fascinated by the poor and the derelict, asks how Bentham and Members of Parliament can know anything of what passes 'in the hearts of wretches in garrets and night-cellars, petty pilferers and marauders, who cut throats and pick pockets with their own hands'. There is an underground, or underworld, quality to the prose here which anticipates the cellar-dwelling scrivener Nemo in *Bleak House*, as well as the rasping, vindictive, tortured, very honest voice of Dostoyevsky's narrator.

Hazlitt is on the same side as the reformers, but he carries the exasperated burden of knowing that they are too complacent – that snug adjective 'comfortable' applied to Bentham's double-chin anticipates this point. Hazlitt is not simply, as E. P. Thompson argues, a middle-class reformer whose style, 'with its sustained and controlled rhythms, and its antithetical movement', belongs to 'the polite culture of the essayist', but a radical who knows something of the apparently unreformable, desperate, heroic, present-centred nature of common life. Most philosophic liberals, he insists, don't understand this anarchic, essentially imaginative principle, so it's ceded to the reactionaries. But perhaps it belongs naturally to the Right?

Hazlitt's famous distinction, in his *Coriolanus* essay, between the republican, calculating understanding and the 'exaggerating and exclusive' faculty of the monarchical imagination is echoed both in his description of Bentham's plodding technical calculation and in his definition of the soul in the next paragraph as an 'aggregating and an exclusive principle'. The language is virtually identical, prompting the thought that 'aggregating' in the sketch of Bentham is a slip for 'exaggerating'. In any case, it seems to jar in a slightly contradictory manner, because Bentham notoriously presents society as an aggregate of social atoms. In fact, as Uttara Natarajan shows, the term 'aggregate' is important in Hazlitt's writing as a way of retaining, 'within a profoundly pluralistic approach, a meaningful concept of the universal'. It issues from Hazlitt's belief that human beings are free agents motivated by a power principle, not a utilitarian pleasure principle. Really, Hazlitt is setting Burke against Bentham. The adjectives 'exaggerating' and 'exclusive' evoke Burke's writings, as does the phrase 'extraordinary excitement', which Hazlitt uses to describes the 'charm' of criminal life. There is, then, a current of almost Nietzschean irrationalism which Hazlitt is aware of, and which he wants reformers to recognize – 'take account of', I nearly wrote, but that would suggest that the appeal of criminality can somehow be factored into a rational social equation.

Accompanying this distinction between the irrational nature of the imagination and a type of forensic calculation is the emphasis which Hazlitt places on style. In his analysis of defective, or not wholly adequate, styles, he may be implicitly arguing for a wholly active, plenary style – his own – except that his treatment of this subject is one of the cohesive features of this work, as well as being a consistent feature of all his critical writings. 'On the Prose Style of Poets', written three years earlier in 1822, is his most concentrated exploration of the subject, but a similar essay on the prose style of prose-writers might be extracted from these contemporary portraits.

Bentham is described as

a kind of manuscript author – he writes a cypher-hand, which the vulgar have no key to. The construction of his sentences is a curious frame-work with pegs and hooks to hang his thoughts upon, for his own use and guidance, but almost out of the reach of everybody else. It is a barbarous philosophical jargon, with all the repetitions, parentheses, formalities, uncouth nomenclature and verbiage of law-Latin; and what makes it worse, it is not mere verbiage, but has a great deal of acuteness and meaning in it, which you would be glad to pick out if you could.

Bentham has overlaid his once-vigorous style with the 'dust and cobwebs of an obscure solitude'.

How to redeem the language of Reform from this type of racked contortion is one of the problems Hazlitt sets himself to address in this work. This partly explains his fascination with the Revd Edward Irving, the Scottish preacher whom he presents as the embodiment of one of modernity's distinctive features – celebrity. The Calvinist cleric paradoxically evokes a past age, rather like Scott's fiction, which is why fashionable London finds him so irresistible. It is as if a 'Patagonian savage' were to come forward to preach evangelical religion. This is heritage modernity, provincial chic, but it appears to carry genuine power. Armed with 'modern topics and with penal fire', the preacher goes out of his way to attack Bentham and amaze the town. In a witty, eighteenth-century locution, Hazlitt adds: 'The thing was new.' This is the clever, amused language of social comedy and the coffee-house.

Commenting on Irving's attack on Bentham, Hazlitt adds a last sentence to the paragraph that has a conclusiveness and a keeping which is best ascertained by rendering it as verse:

> He thus wiped the stain
> of musty ignorance and formal bigotry
> out of his style.

The *st* patterning – *stain musty style* – as well as the *thus musty* rhyme and the bracing *t* sounds, pattern the sentence so that it sounds arresting and definitive.

Irving next lashes out at the radical politician Brougham, and glances at the reactionary Canning. Quoting *Coriolanus*, Hazlitt says that it was rare sport to see Irving 'like an eagle in a dove-cote, flutter the Volscians in Corioli'. This line, we know, is normally applied to Burke, when Hazlitt wants to praise his counter-revolutionary polemic. Though he says that Irving has found the secret of 'attracting by repelling', and though he seems both amused and bemused by the preacher's celebrity, there is also real admiration for his fire and energy in this account of a 'raw, uncouth Scotchman' whose black hair, iron-grey complexion, and firm-set features turn him into the likeness of 'a noble Italian picture'. He is a Titan out of Titian, a magnificent fulminating figure from a past age. An atavism that issues from the Calvinism of Hazlitt's paternal grandparents may be shaping this portrait of a preacher whom he imagines in a subsequent article to be a mile tall instead of six feet three inches: 'let him resemble one of earth's firstborn, Titan, or Briareus, or "blind Orion hungry for the morn" – with strength proportioned and zeal unabated.'

Irving had a marked squint, which is the immediate reason for citing Keats's line about blind Orion, but the allusion also has the larger significance of increasing Hazlitt's identification with the preacher by introducing an association, however privately comic, with Poussin's painting and with Napoleon.

The reference to Titian and Briareus is taken from the passage in *Paradise Lost* where the gigantic Satan lies 'floating many a rood' – a quotation which, as we've seen, is also taken from the famous passage in Burke's *Letter to a Noble Lord* where he imagines the duke of Bedford as the Leviathan among all the creatures of the Crown:

He tumbles about his unwieldy bulk; he plays and frolics in the ocean of the Royal bounty. Huge as he is, and whilst 'he lies floating many a rood', he is still a creature. His ribs, his fins, his whalebone, his blubber, the very spiracles through which he spouts a torrent of brine against his origin, and covers me all over with the spray – everything of him and about him is from the Throne.

Hazlitt loved this visceral, primitivist passage, and when he describes the qualities that launched Irving into the 'ocean-stream of popularity, in which he "lies floating many a rood"', he is recalling the Bedford Leviathan with amused delight, as well as quoting Milton indirectly through Burke. He is as fascinated by Irving as Dryden was by the first earl of Shaftesbury, and in praising his graceful figure, adds that he possesses a 'bold and fiery spirit'. This is another reference to Achitophel's political daring, and also suggests that Hazlitt wants to equal Dryden's poem in his prose.

The intention here is to emphasize Irving's physical attributes, his total integration of looks, voice, bodily action, and intellect. Achitophel has a puny, diseased body, but Irving's is elegant, supple, magnificent, like a boxer's – Neate is mentioned earlier in the sketch – and the preacher has the self-possession and 'masterly execution' of an experienced player or fencer.

These comparisons are more than merely decorative, because they forcibly express the central significance of the active human body in Hazlitt's critical aesthetic. If Irving is in many ways a joke figure – larger than life, all personality and theatrical surface, like a modern media personality – he is also irresistibly fascinating. In comparing him to an Italian portrait, Hazlitt may have been thinking either of Titian's *Portrait of Benedetto Varchi* or of copies of other portraits of the humanist scholar in William Roscoe's Liverpool collection (Hazlitt's family was friendly with Roscoe, the famous Unitarian banker and poet, and Hazlitt visited the city, and also copied paintings by Titian and various artists in the Louvre for another Liverpool Unitarian businessman).

The reference to Italian painting in the portrait of Irving communicates his deep joy in the process of composition – applying oils, writing prose. This utterly grounded, sensuous delight in the medium is there in that Hazlittian phrase 'the heavy, dingy, slimy effect of various oils and megilps' in Northcote's *Life of Titian*. When Northcote states that Titian may be said to have 'almost equalled Nature herself', and that his figures seem to 'move, breathe and live' – they have 'the tender pliancy of real flesh' – we can detect Hazlitt's style and his admiration for Titian in the writing. This is a version of the unctuous quality he praises in certain writers.

Titian is also notable for his portraits of powerful princes of the Church – Cardinal Bembo, Pope Paul III – and at a level that is more than comic or mock-heroic Hazlitt is implying that his own portrait of Irving, as well as his joy in the process of creating it, is to be compared with Titian's expressive genius. Part of our experience as readers here is the sense that we are watching a skilled portraitist at work: Hazlitt is re-creating Irving and making him into a living work of art. Just as he praises Homer for showing life and action, the 'bodies as well as the souls of men', so he is aiming to exemplify through his treatment of Irving that principle of 'strong, vivid, bodily perception' which he admires in Cobbett. This is a 'material intuition' whose concrete ideas are not at all abstracted. Irving becomes an exemplar of criticism as an active embodied spirit. He is a living symbol of prose style, even though he is a particularly negative, destructive critic who levels everyone and everything, until nothing is left standing but himself, 'a mighty landmark in a degenerate age'. He is monstrous, seriously ridiculous, but compelling.

If we take Irving as the extreme exemplar of the polemical critic, then William Wilberforce, who is briefly mentioned in this sketch, typifies the critic who goes with the tide: 'He leads by following opinion, he trims, he shifts, he glides on the silvery sounds of his undulating, flexible, cautiously modulated voice, winding his way betwixt heaven and earth, now courting popularity, now calling servility to his aid.' Voice is one of the leitmotifs in the collection, with Hazlitt aiming to reproduce its cadences like a critical tape recorder. Where a modern journalist can invariably assume that his audience is familiar with a particular public figure's vocal tones, Hazlitt has to describe and evaluate simultaneously. He dislikes Wilberforce's wheedling, insinuating manner, which he characterizes as a type of silvery serpent. Yet Wilberforce is probably cleverer than Irving, he concludes. But popularity, or charismatic celebrity, depends on many other qualities besides intelligence. W. J. Fox, for example, a Unitarian minister who was friendly with Hazlitt's father, is as fluent a speaker as Irving, has a 'sweeter' voice and more animated countenance, yet he doesn't attract fashionable crowds simply because he is a small man.

Hazlitt sees cultural life as a kind of fairground, where noisy crowds gape at various giants and grotesques exhibited under the flaring torches. Comparing Irving to the pugilists Neate, Cribb, and Molyneux, he transforms the preacher into a popular sportsman; but since he makes similar comparisons with Cobbett's prose, we might consider boxers as spiritual avatars for the polemicist. Neate the pugilist is to Hazlitt what Michael Robartes was to Yeats – a force to be invoked, a source of imaginative power who, rather than being a heroic shade, is a living, sweaty, active, perfectly co-ordinated body. Fuelled by his narrow puritan values, Irving thumps and bashes the modern world, which rewards him with wealth and attention. His ideas are neither complex nor original; but he has substantial entertainment value. He is a licensed moralist, who becomes a figure for Hazlitt's ideal of critical prose as action. Indeed, the best analogy is with action painting. Hazlitt wants us to regard his portrait of Irving not as a static prose description, but as an intense process in which we participate as we read.

He aims to make his own prose as different as possible from the regular, formal, sluggish, cramped manner exemplified by Samuel Johnson. Indeed, we might regard Hazlitt's prose as fighting a permanent battle with Johnson and his imitators. With his abstract and general vocabulary, his morose, singsong Latinity, that secret Jacobite is the enemy of an engaged Whig prose. And, as W. K. Wimsatt shows in his study of Johnson's prose style, Hazlitt's rushing manner is superior to Johnson's slow accumulation of adjectival triplets. Irving becomes a stylistic symbol for prose energy: he has fire in his belly, and, like Achilles, he hits hard, which is why Hazlitt warms to him, makes him into a mythic giant, and indirectly compares him both to Burke and to one of Burke's most famous targets, the whale-like duke of Bedford.

CHAPTER ELEVEN

Vehemence versus Materialism:
The Spirit in the Age

Irving the Calvinist preacher has a passionate intensity that contrasts with the qualities which Hazlitt describes in his next portrait, 'The Late Mr Horne Tooke'. The politician and philologist is a decorously spoken English gentleman who holds radical views about contemporary politics, even though he belongs to the previous period, and so resembles a museum piece. Tooke is important in the overall design of the collection, because he draws together the themes of style, language, eloquence, and liberty, as well as offsetting Irving's Scottishness. Yet, at the same time, his ideas are critically analysed, because he is a materialist who resembles Bentham in his literalness and lack of imagination. Throughout his critical writings, Hazlitt opposes the view that the mind simply reflects on a series of passively acquired sense impressions. There is a 'hard, dry materialism', he says, in the 'very texture' of Horne Tooke's understanding.

This use of the term 'texture' is interesting. In 'A Farewell to Essay-Writing', he says that his ideas, 'from their sinewy texture', have been to him in the nature of realities, and the word 'texture' is closely connected with his favourite image of the mind as a spider's web. In *The Light of Nature Pursued*, which Hazlitt admired and published in a shortened version in 1807, Abraham Tucker applies the term for the first time to a spider's web: 'Now the spider entangles the heedless fly in his texture.'

The hard-textured Tooke is a clever talker, a lawyer, an ingenious logician; but his mind has none of the 'grand whirling movements' of the French Revolution. Calling him 'full of chicane and captious objections', Hazlitt links him to Godwin as well as Southey, to whom he also applies the term 'captious'. Yet there is a fine balance in his assessment of Tooke, because of the radicalism he shared with him and their complementary work on English grammar. The literal, matter-of-fact, unimaginative nature of Tooke's understanding equipped him to strip away prejudice and illusion from the study of language. There is a distinct relish in Hazlitt's manner of characterizing that understanding as what he calls the reverse of 'effeminate'. Whig culture strongly emphasized the 'manly', and Tooke's understanding is 'hard, unbending, concrete, physical, half-savage'. *The Diversions of Purley*, his philosophical grammar, or analytic account of English, enables us to see the language in its primitive state.

At the start of his career, Hazlitt published a grammar which was significantly influenced by Tooke, and which similarly respects spoken English. As Olivia Smith shows in *The Politics of Language*, the idea that the vernacular is as 'equally genuine and pure' as the written language was a politically radical concept. At this period, various grammarians and philologists associated the vernacular with English liberty, while the values of the new American republic are reflected in Noah Webster's writings on language and in his great dictionary. Cobbett, who published *A Grammar of the English Language* in 1819, follows Tooke in refusing, as Smith notes, to see language as either a 'gentlemanly attribute or as a moral virtue'. So Tooke's arguments helped to weaken a hegemony of language which had been complete and intact until the first volume of *The Diversions of Purley* was published in that year of Demogorgon, 1798.

When Hazlitt mentions in his profile of Tooke that Lindley Murray's highly influential *English Grammar* mistakes the genius of the English language, making it 'periphrastic and literal, instead of elliptical and idiomatic', he is drawing on Tooke's concept of 'dispatch', or ellipsis – the natural tendency of speakers to abbreviate and condense expression. Hazlitt disliked Murray's grammar, which was first published in 1795, and sold millions of copies throughout the nineteenth century. The work is daunting as well as socially reactionary: in a section entitled 'Promiscuous Exercises in Etymological Parsing', the example 'In your whole behaviour, be humble and obliging' is given. This passive acceptance of the status quo is reinforced by the division of conjunctions 'into two sorts, the COPULATIVE and the DISJUNCTIVE', so that, as Olivia Smith argues, students who were not well educated already were bound to be intimidated by the work's technical complexity and formality. Tooke clearly has Murray in mind when he remarks that 'we shall get rid of that farrago of useless distinctions into *Conjunctive, Adjunctive, Disjunctive, Subdisjunctive, Copulative*'. Cobbett echoes Tooke's criticisms, mocking Murray for introducing a grammatical error on the title-page of his work.

By describing the decisive clarity which Tooke brought to the study of language, and by praising Cobbett's style, Hazlitt is aiming to identify the cause of liberty with the English language's creative vigour. There is a powerful nativist strain in the way Tooke, Cobbett, and Hazlitt think about language as they seek to overturn traditional hierarchical views of language. Hopkins has a similar enthusiasm for English's deep groundswell – Germanic, consonantal, energized, and above all spoken (the pluck and knock of the tide in Auden's 'Look, Stranger' affirms a similar nativism). The commitment to the spoken language that is at the root of this identity and aesthetic is present in the anecdote in which Tooke argues that Addison's style is without modulation, and therefore flawed, because it is physically impossible for anyone to write well who is habitually silent in company.

In addition to criticizing the aridity of Tooke's intellect, Hazlitt points to his cowardice and limitations as a politician. The hard concreteness of his legalistic mentality, that odd, appositely tusky name, conjure up an atmosphere of dusty bark and acorns, yet at the same time we appreciate Tooke's urgent sense of the thingness of words, their ontological presence and uniqueness. With his etymologies and word lists, his scorn for Samuel Johnson and delight in the 'winged' nature of language, Tooke's philosophical grammar aims to explain what English culture fundamentally derives from.

Calling Johnson's etymological derivations 'false, absurd, and impossible', he remarks that Johnson did not acknowledge 'any RIGHTS of the people; but he was very clear concerning Ghosts and

Witches, all the mysteries of divinity, and the sacred, indefeasible, inherent, hereditary RIGHTS of Monarchy'. Aiming to discredit Johnson, he attacks his derivation of the noun 'rack' as applied to clouds, for example, arguing correctly that it does not come from the Dutch *racka*, 'track', but from *reek*, meaning 'vapour, steam, inhalation'. Tooke dedicates the second volume of *The Diversions of Purley*, which was published in 1805, both to the legal counsel who acted for him at the Treason Trial in 1794 and to the jury which acquitted him and his fellow defendants. The two volumes were printed by Joseph Johnson, who had spent nine months in the King's Bench prison after being arrested and tried for selling a seditious pamphlet in 1797. A footnote to the dedication reads: 'The fears of my printer (which I cannot call unfounded, in the present degraded state of the press) do not permit me to expose (as ought to be done) the circumstances producing, preceding, accompanying, and following my strange trial of six days for High Treason.' Tooke originally wrote that England was in 'a state of siege', but because of the printer's fear of prosecution, the comment was omitted, and a blank was left. As Smith shows, the text bears 'the scars of the imposture', an imposture which is supported, Tooke claims, by genteel ideas of language.

The Diversions of Purley comprises two sumptuous, leatherbound quartos, and its argument is conducted in a series of Platonic dialogues which reinforce the leisurely, cultivated personality of the work. It has a handsome engraving of Mercury as a frontispiece, the god symbolizing the dispatch, or winged nature, of spoken language, that rapidity of execution which Hazlitt admires. The work embodies the idea of English liberty, and seeks to trace it in the very 'stamina' of the language, as Priestley terms its inherent primitive structure. Hazlitt calls *The Diversions* a 'great thing', though one that has been spun out with a lot of prolix irrelevancies. Yet it is a 'genuine anatomy of our native tongue', unlike Murray's popular and mistaken *Grammar*.

Tooke often cites Locke as an authority, and Hazlitt's criticism of the philologist reflects his view of Locke's limitations as a thinker. Locke, too, he criticizes for the 'prolixity and ambiguity of his style'; and in a sequence of adjectives which is reminiscent of his portraits of Bentham and Godwin, he notes the 'literal, matter-of-fact, unimaginative' nature of Tooke's understanding. When he criticizes Tooke's eloquence as a 'succession of drops, not a stream', he is echoing his earlier criticism of Locke's epistemology, which, in enduing human beings with only a power of sensation, allows

no room for more than an individual impression at once. Our sensations must always succeed each other. One thought must have completely passed away, before another could supply its place. Our ideas would leave no traces of themselves, like the bubbles that rise and disappear on the water, or the snow that melts as it falls.

Locke, like Tooke, has no concept of the cementing power of the understanding. Tooke's intellect, his 'determined' mind, lacks chiaroscuro: there is nothing 'hazy' or 'doubtful' in it, which is a way of saying that he is a subject more worthy of Hogarth than Rembrandt. He is rigid, constant, literal, pertinacious. He lacks momentum, and was beaten by Junius's polemics, which overcame him by mere 'force of style', even though Tooke had the best of the argument.

Tooke's inability to press home his intellectual superiority points to the relationship which exists between the force of style and the power of the understanding to make 'atomic impressions . . . club together', as Hazlitt puts it in his critique of Locke. For Tooke's eloquence to cease being a disparate succession of separate points, it needs a force to bind together this otherwise formless conglomeration. But Tooke lacks that necessary 'sacred vehemence', partly because his mind – unlike Irving's, say – has no '*religion* in it'. So in the account of style which these sketches offer, momentum and Miltonic vehemence are significant qualities that might redeem the hard dry texture of a Lockean understanding. By placing his sketch of Tooke after that of Irving, and by quoting *Comus*, Hazlitt is alluding to a distinction Milton draws in the masque between the 'dazzling fence' of wit and rhetoric and the uncontrollable value of 'this pure cause', which would, the Lady tells Comus,

> kindle my rapt spirits
> To such a flame of sacred vehemence,
> That dumb things would be moved to sympathize,
> And the brute Earth would lend her nerves, and shake,
> Till all thy magic structures reared so high,
> Were shattered into heaps o'er thy false head.

By drawing on this speech, Hazlitt introduces the theological concept of the divinely inspired free spirit, but because the terms he uses are Milton's, not his own, the question of religious faith is neatly side-stepped, though it is interesting to note that he jibs at the utterly secular cast of Tooke's mind when he surprisingly and emphatically points to its lack of religion. As a non-believer, Hazlitt could not profess belief in God, but, by quoting the Lady in *Comus*, he adopts a type of puritan camouflage in order to avoid a more abstract or theoretical mode of defining his critical meaning. He also conceals the void which a purely secular idea of the imagination might create, as well as affirming solidarity with the republican cause that Milton and he share. But, rather like Matthew Arnold repeating the Swiftian image of 'sweetness and light', he wraps himself in an arresting phrase, then disappears or moves on to the next stage in his argument.

Sir Walter Scott, whose portrait is placed after that of Tooke, also lacks a shaping and cementing imagination – what Hazlitt calls 'this creative impulse, this plastic power'. Just as Cobbett is a 'matter-of-fact reasoner', Scott is a 'learned, a literal, a *matter-of-fact* expounder of truth or fable'. It must be owned, Hazlitt insists, that in true poetry there is a power which lifts the mind from the ground of reality to a 'higher sphere', penetrates the 'inert, scattered, incoherent' materials presented to it, and by a 'force and inspiration of its own, melts and moulds them into sublimity and beauty'. But Scott does not have 'this capacity of reacting on his first impressions'. Because he is so matter of fact, he can't soar above and look down upon his subject.

The idea of plastic power is a version of the glass-blowing image, as well as of the furnace image which he applies to Milton's imagination. And when he says that Scott doesn't soar, he means that the novelist is incapable of the panoptic vision that shapes *Paradise Lost*. His speculative understanding is 'empty, flaccid, poor and dead'. He writes bad, slovenly English, and has a 'drooping' style. His muse is a 'Modern Antique': that is to say, he designs a type of polished, heritage, pseudo-rebellious modernity in verse, whose 'smooth, glossy' texture contrasts with the historical suffering in the materials of which it's composed. This removes any harshness from the world he depicts.

Yet, in the exclamatory paragraph which begins 'What a list of names! What a host of associations', Hazlitt scoops praise on Scott, asserting that his collected works are almost like a new edition of human nature. He goes on to recommend the politics of his Scottish novels, pointing to Scott's possession of 'candour', that quality which Unitarian culture valued so highly. By 'candour' is meant not simply openness or outspoken frankness, but a principle of fairness, impartiality, and justice, with the addition of kindliness and freedom from malice. Thus the 'candour' of Scott's historical writing sees fair play between Roundheads and Cavaliers, Protestants and Catholics.

Through some odd process of what Hazlitt calls 'servile logic', it seems that Scott, in restoring the Stuart claims to the throne by the 'courtesy of romance', has strengthened the House of Brunswick, and also given legitimacy to the Bourbons. His loyalty is founded on 'would-be treason'. He props up the throne by the shadow of rebellion. This paradox follows from Hazlitt's insight into the appeal of Scott's novels, which act as a relief to a mind 'rarefied' by modern philosophy and 'heated' with extreme radicalism (the Calvinist preacher Irving's sermons have a similar function). The pressures of modernity – the sheer drive and anxiety of the *Zeitgeist* – give rise to a type of escapist literary jacobitism. Scott becomes the designer of literary theme parks.

These criticisms incensed Scott's son-in-law, J. G. Lockhart, who attacked *The Spirit of the Age* in an angry review which communicates a murderous hatred of Hazlitt. Four years earlier, a friend of Lockhart's, Jonathan Christie, had challenged the radical, London-based journalist and editor John Scott to a duel over the issue of Lockhart's relationship to *Blackwood's Magazine* (Lockhart had also been seeking a duel with Scott). On 27 February 1821, John Scott died of his wounds. When Hazlitt says that the editor must have gone to his painful, premature death with 'some degree of satisfaction', because he had written the most elaborate panegyric on Scott's novels that had yet appeared, he is reminding readers of the fatal duel, as well as reminding Christie and Lockhart of the death for which they were responsible. His now almost invisible irony aims to embarrass and shame the two men.

The passage that begins 'O Wickliff, Luther, Hampden, Sidney, Somers, mistaken Whigs and thoughtless Reformers in religion and politics' is balanced by the other enormous sentence that comprises most of the final paragraph. Here, Scott's limitations are expressed through Goldsmith's lines on Burke: the novelist narrowed his mind, and 'to party gave up what was meant for mankind'. Hazlitt's supercharged sentences demonstrate the principles of momentum and vehemence which are absent from Sir Walter's detumescent prose. However, a reviewer in the *London Magazine* criticized this rhapsodic style, stating that a considerable part of the book resembled 'a translation of poetry not into sense, but into prose'.

Scott is indicted in *The Spirit of the Age* for reserving his candour for history, and venting his 'littleness, pique, resentment, bigotry, and intolerance' on his contemporaries. The adjectives link him to Southey, and strike at his association with *Blackwood's* and with other organs of conservative opinion. Scott helped to found the conservative journal the *Quarterly Review*, and he was also involved in setting up *John Bull* and the *Beacon* to counter the radical movement. It was the *Quarterly* which published the notorious attack on Keats; and when Hazlitt describes the novelist strewing the slime of 'rankling malice and mercenary scorn' on the bud and promise of genius, he is avenging his dead friend.

This furious attack on Scott's 'degraded' genius is balanced in the sketch of Byron which follows by the remark that the novelist is one of the 'greatest teachers of morality'. He emancipates the mind from narrow prejudices, while Byron pampers those prejudices by appearing to think that there is nothing else worth encouraging, except the seeds of 'the full luxuriant growth of dogmatism or self-conceit'. Byron's style is rich, cloudy, and opaque, while Scott's is 'perfectly transparent', but – the implication is – transparent like a window-pane, not an illuminated slide.

The comparison between Scott and Byron develops the theme of style in the collection; it also applies the concept of candour in a manner which favours the conservative novelist over the radical poet who seldom gets beyond 'force of style', a value that must be inferior to 'sacred vehemence'. This preference for Scott over Byron is integral to Hazlitt's critical purpose, because it demonstrates the principle of disinterestedness in practice, and suggests that his own method is superior to the partisan writing published in the *Quarterly* and other journals. This fairness is particularly evident in his portrayal of the humane, kind Southey, who is both mocked and almost cherished by Hazlitt. When he opens with a recollection of the poet in his radical youth – 'a hectic flush upon his cheek, a roving fire in his eye, a falcon glance, a look at once aspiring and dejected' – his prose technique is modelled on Hogarth's method of bringing out the 'exact feeling of the moment'. The expression, Hazlitt says in his essay on the artist, is always taken '*en passant*', and in this and other sketches he adopts this method by portraying mobile countenances or, as with Bentham in his garden, showing the subject walking and talking. He portrays Southey walking stiffly through the London streets, his umbrella projecting from under his arm. And Southey, in his wedgy, angular quaintness, is a Hogarthian figure whose faults Hazlitt seems to mark down with a precise, delineating relish.

It is the delight in pictorial images, in style and in the newly painted freshness of the present moment – a delight that's rapid and spontaneous, not lingering – which gives Hazlitt's portraits such an expressive, at times ecstatic, texture. He runs away with his subject, throwing out questions and exclamations, bashing faults and generously rewarding virtues. It's a highly concentrated performance, in which there is no marking time, no pausing to draw breath. This is a collection to be read through at one sitting, like *Dubliners*.

There is a partying quality to the style, a buzz that never lets up; but there is also a countering, witty metropolitan indolence which plays against any sense which the reader may have that the writer is trying too hard. Our reading becomes a type of complete, on-line involvement – we can feel the solid definition of the individual words, almost as though we're running a finger along a metal typeface.

It is this concentration of sensuous texture and timeliness – the moment of performance – which takes on an epic force in his sketch of Wordsworth, whom he describes as a 'pure emanation of the Spirit of the Age'. The prose rhythm is emphatic, and at the beginning of this sentence trochaic: 'This he probes, this he tampers with, this he poises, with all its incalculable weight of thought and feeling, in his hands, and at the same time calms the throbbing pulses of his own heart by keeping his eye ever fixed on the face of nature.' Wordsworth is like a cross between the divine artificer and a fell farmer building a drystone wall; the vibrating rockiness of that verb 'poises' in 'this he poises' has an exact materiality which is picked up by the subtler, but still very definite, rhythm of the remainder of the sentence. Robert Frost's image in 'Mending Wall' of his neighbour advancing with a stone grasped firmly in each hand, 'like an old-stone savage armed', similarly designs a literary creation myth. Hazlitt's poised phrase 'incalculable weight' might compress the whole world into one heavy chunk of rock.

In Hazlitt's portrait, Wordsworth is seen as a titanic innovator, whose poetry is founded on the opposition between the natural and the artificial, the spirit of humanity and the spirit of worldly fashion. Wordsworth then pushes this position 'to the utmost length'. In this he is the opposite of Tom Moore, who is portrayed as a fashionable tinselly poet who, in a clever phrase, has converted the 'wild harp of Erin into a musical snuff-box'. By contrast, Wordsworth's 'popular, inartificial style' gets rid of all the cloudy, flimsy trappings of verse, and strips everything naked: 'He gathers manna in the wilderness; he strikes the barren rock for gushing moisture.' Again he is identified with rock, and with a simplicity that is epic, biblical, original, profound, and – this is the key concept – revolutionary. His innovatory verse is magnificently of the age: 'the political

changes of the day were the model on which he formed and conducted his poetical experiments.'

The reference to experiments picks up the verbs in 'This he
probes, this he tampers with' in the previous paragraph, and it
obliquely identifies Wordsworth with science. So does the verb 'tampers', which, interestingly, is used in an earlier essay 'On Paradox
and Commonplace', in which Percy Shelley is portrayed as a
Frankenstein figure: 'He tampers with all sorts of obnoxious subjects, but it is less because he is gratified with the rankness of the
taint, than captivated with the intellectual phosphoric light they
emit.' Hazlitt greatly admired Mary Shelley's *Frankenstein*, and the
link with the novel which the word 'tampers' establishes, as well as
the criticism of Percy Shelley it introduces, brings to the surface the
underlying reservations which Hazlitt has about Wordsworth's
Jacobin ruthlessness. In the first edition of the novel, Frankenstein
describes how, as a teenager, 'my utmost wonder was engaged by
some experiments on an air-pump, which I saw employed by a
gentleman whom we were in the habit of visiting'. Hazlitt would
have noted the glance at Burke's attack, in *Letter to a Noble Lord*,
on Priestley's experiments on mice in an air-pump. It is hard not to
see Wordsworth in these opening paragraphs as another Frankenstein, a poet who is both a natural and a political scientist, and
whose 'levelling' muse seeks to reduce everything to the same
standard of equality. He strips away pretentious decorations
'without mercy', because they are 'barbarous, idle, and gothic'.

Here Wordsworth is characterized as a writer who applies his
new and highly original poetic like a republican statesman. There is
a letter which Burns finished on New Year's Day 1795 in which he
mentions the 'deserved fate' of the French king and queen, whom
he calls 'a perjured Blockhead & an unprincipled Prostitute'.
Wordsworth's muse is the expression of similarly merciless
republican logic: 'Kings, queens, priests, nobles, the altar and the
throne, the distinctions of rank, birth, wealth, power, "the judge's
robe, the marshal's truncheon, the ceremony that to great ones
'longs", are not to be found here. The author tramples on the pride
of art with greater pride.' This is an anticipation of a passage in

Notes of a Journey, in which Hazlitt remarks of an inn that it was from here that Rousseau journeyed to Paris in order to 'overturn the French monarchy by the force of style'.

The concept of style as a weighty, decisive, absolute value that is often instinct with a powerful sense of historic intervention is a complete thing, not a series of surface ornaments; and in his evocation of the actively simplifying, equalizing qualities of Wordsworth's poetry, it cuts like a heavy blade. Hazlitt's habitual technique of association means that he is also thinking of Rousseau when he describes the characteristics of Wordsworth's style. In turn, this passage anticipates another in his sixteenth conversation with Northcote, where he praises Rousseau in a manner very similar to his eulogy of Wordsworth:

But it was the excess of his egotism and his utter blindness to everything else, that found a corresponding sympathy in the conscious feelings of every human breast, and shattered to pieces the pride of rank and circumstance by the pride of internal worth or upstart pretension. When Rousseau stood behind the chair of the master of the *château* of ——, and smiled to hear the company dispute about the meaning of the motto of the arms of the family, which he alone knew, and stumbled as he handed the glass of wine to his young mistress, and fancied she coloured at being waited upon by so learned a young footman – then was first kindled that spark which can never be quenched, then was formed the germ of that strong conviction of the disparity between the badge on his shoulder and the aspirations of his soul – the determination, in short, that external situation and advantages are but the mask, and that the mind is the man – armed with which, impenetrable, incorrigible, he went forth conquering and to conquer, and overthrew the monarchy of France and the hierarchies of the earth. Till then, birth and wealth and power were all in all, though but the framework or crust that envelops the man; and what there was in the man himself was never asked, or was scorned and forgot. And while all was dark and grovelling within, while knowledge either did not exist or was confined to a few, while material power and advantages were everything, this was naturally to be expected. But with the increase and diffusion of knowledge, this state of things must sooner or later cease; and Rousseau was the first who held the torch (lighted at the never-dying fire in his own bosom) to the hidden chambers of the mind of man – like another Prometheus, breathed into his nostrils the breath of a new and intellectual life, enraging the Gods of the

259

earth, and made him feel what is due to himself and his fellows. Before, physical force was every thing: henceforward, mind, thought, feeling was a new element – a fourth estate in society.

Here, the 'modern Prometheus', Mary Shelley's phrase for Franken-stein, exercises the divine power of creating life. We're close to the levelling power of the Jacobin Wordsworth, while the reference to the fourth estate is a version of his tribute to Cobbett, who has become 'a kind of fourth estate in the politics of the country'.

These interconnections are applications of the concept of associ-ation, a concept which functions as a shaping critical principle for Hazlitt, and which is also a fundamental imaginative resource for Wordsworth, who

exemplifies in an eminent degree the power of *association*; for his poetry has no other source or character. He has dwelt among pastoral scenes, till each object has become connected with a thousand feelings, a link in the chain of thought, a fibre of his own heart. Everyone is by habit and familiar-ity strongly attached to the place of his birth, or to objects that recall the most pleasing and eventful circumstances of his life.

The road from Wem to Shrewsbury has a similar familiarity in Hazlitt's prose, but as he is a critic writing primarily about ideas and works of art, we need to substitute the literary canon for places and natural objects. Instead of mountains and lakes, he habitually dwells among the works of Shakespeare, Milton, and Burke, texts he knows minutely. Picking up a 'little musty duodecimo', he remarks in 'Reading Old Books':

not only are the old ideas of the contents of the work brought back to my mind in all their vividness, but the old associations of the faces and persons of those I then knew, as they were in their lifetime – the place where I sat to read the volume, the day when I got it, the feeling of the air, the fields, the sky – return, and all my early impressions with them.

He quotes copiously and brilliantly, often returning to the same texts, the same quotations, so that the talismanic – even the topo-graphic – feel they take on becomes a significant feature of his personality. Sometimes this appears self-indulgent (at least to readers who find *Don Quixote* tedious). But at the same time we are comforted by familiar literary landmarks: Uncle Toby in *Tristram Shandy*, the eccentric romance *John Buncle*, even that aged chestnut, Burke's hymn to Marie Antoinette.

What we respond to in Hazlitt's writing is this cherishing of certain texts, many of which he first read as a youth. In a sense those texts are like stepping-stones or signature phrases: they direct the reader, and also impart a feeling of safety and security. Though in his Wordsworth eulogy there's no trace of a wish for us to apply the concept of literary association to his own prose at this point, there is something intensely personal in the image he gives of the poet's isolation:

He has described all these objects in a way and with an intensity of feeling that no one else had done before him, and has given a new view or aspect of nature. He is in this sense the most original poet now living, and the one whose writings could the least be spared: for they have no substitute elsewhere. The vulgar do not read them; the learned, who see all things through books, do not understand them. The great despise, the fashionable may ridicule them: but the author has created himself an interest in the heart of the retired and lonely student of nature, which can never die.

Note how the sentences begin with either 'He' or 'The'. This is Wordsworth's epic simplicity transposed into passionate prose. By 'the retired and lonely student of nature', Hazlitt means himself; but it is fair that we should also see the books in his own mental library as the equivalent of the daisy, cuckoo, linnet's nest, and lichens that Wordsworth delighted in.

One of Hazlitt's recurrent examples of this capacity for spontaneous delight in natural objects is the passage in Rousseau's *Confessions* where he exclaims '*voilà de la pervenche!*' In the last essay in *The Plain Speaker*, a collection that has been out of general circulation for more than seventy years, Hazlitt says that 'all Europe has rung' to that exclamation, and the moment was obviously crucial to him:

Le premier jour que nous allâmes coucher aux Charmettes, Maman était en chaise à porteurs, et je la suivais à pied. Le chemin monte: elle était assez pesante, et craignant de trop fatiguer ses porteurs, elle voulut descendre à peu près à moitié chemin pour faire le reste à pied. En marchant elle vit quelque chose de bleu dans la haie, et me dit: Voilà de la pervenche encore en fleur. Je n'avais jamais vu de la pervenche, je ne me baissai pas pour l'examiner, et j'ai la vue trop courte distinguer à terre les plantes de ma hauteur. Je jetais seulement en passant un coup d'œil sur celle-là, et près de trente ans se sont passés sans que j'aie revu de la pervenche ou que j'y aie fait attention. En 1764, étant à Cressier avec mon ami M. Du Peyrou, nous montions une petite montagne au sommet de laquelle il a un joli salon qu'il appelle avec raison Belle-Vue. Je commençais alors d'herboriser un peu. En montant et regardant parmi les buissons, je pousse un cri de joie: *Ah! voilà de la pervenche!*

Rousseau's *pervenche* – a tiny periwinkle – is an object which inspires a sudden prose poem. It is one of the most famous episodes in the *Confessions*, and it particularly appealed to English writers. Rousseau's aim is to illustrate how he was moved by everything that relates to his youth, especially his relationship with Madame de Warens, or 'Mama'. Hazlitt is fond of citing this moment because reading it for the first time as a youth was the equivalent of Rousseau's sudden rediscovery of past time in his sighting of some blue periwinkles in a hedge.

Rousseau's passage has nothing of the power, say, which the image of frosty, snapped crocuses has, in *The Prelude*, though it clearly held intense significance for Hazlitt. It belongs to that personal anthology of key artistic moments which shape his critical discourse. Those moments belong inside texts like the *Confessions*, which are Hazlitt's equivalent of Lakeland scenery. Helvellyn, Skiddaw, Winander, are transposed into moments from books and paintings, which nourish and sustain him both for what they are and for the personal associations they hold. But Rousseau's paragraph on the *pervenche*, despite its wide appeal, is nothing spectacular. What counts in Hazlitt's citations of it is that he is invoking his youthful discovery of Rousseau's rediscovery of the blue periwinkle.

It is helpful if we see Hazlitt's response to art objects as the equivalent of this moment, and also as the equivalent of Wordsworth's treatment of natural objects. Thus his account of the poet's manner of obliterating traditional learning and superstition is more than simply descriptive, because it affirms his own critical ideal.

One of the effects of this associative critical method is that it condenses a whole train of thought and feeling. Discovering and analysing such sequences is Hobbes's purpose in his reflections on the Roman penny in *Leviathan*, and in Hazlitt's critical writings adjectives often function like coins that are encrusted with associations. They are as compact as microchips. We often talk of critics coining new critical terms – 'gusto', 'objective correlative', 'creative misprision', 'jouissance', 'intertextuality' – but adjectives in Hazlitt's writing are not fixed, static terms or flat counters. They have a history, a patina of personal associations, which means that their reiteration brings many of their past applications to bear on Hazlitt's present use of them. Sometimes he seems to be worrying an adjective to death, as if he wants to shake it off but can't.

The term 'gothic', which he uses in his account of Wordsworth stripping away fanciful decoration, is a particularly interesting case. By implication and association, it sets Wordsworth against Burke, who is frequently associated with the term. Yet Hazlitt desperately senses that the battle between republican neo-classicism and gothic conservatism is lost. Even Unitarian culture, which had been so strongly opposed to Burke's monarchism, began to register a loss of confidence in the Enlightenment as it moved away from neo-classical architecture. In the 1830s and 1840s, Unitarian congregations tended to commission gothic chapels rather than church buildings designed along the classical lines which had always been favoured by Rational Dissent (the chapel in Harris Manchester College, Oxford, which was built by Unitarians in 1893, is standard Victorian gothic). This move away from austere neo-classicism expresses the social acceptance which Unitarianism had achieved. When Hazlitt portrays Wordsworth as the enemy of gothic ornament, he is evoking the spirit of the 1790s. He knows that the mature Wordsworth is an admirer of Burke's writings and a convinced Tory.

There is a similar moment in 'What is the People?', which Hazlitt published in the *Champion* on 26 March 1818. Arguing that the 'tenaciousness' of power is the chief obstacle to progress and the cause of reactions against improvement, he states:

In America, a free Government was easy of accomplishment, because it was not necessary, in building up, to pull down: there were no nuisances to abate. The thing is plain. Reform in old Governments is just like the new improvements in the front of Carlton House, that would go on fast enough but for the vile, old, dark, dirty, crooked streets, which cannot be removed without giving the inhabitants notice to quit. Mr Burke, in regretting these old institutions as the result of the wisdom of ages, and not the remains of gothic ignorance and barbarism, played the part of *Crockery*, in the farce of *Exit by Mistake*, who sheds tears of affection over the loss of the old windows and buttresses of the houses that no longer jut out to meet one another, and stop up the way.

Notice the relished *k* sounds in this passage – *dark crooked Crockery mistake* – which design a keeping with the second syllable of *gothic*.

Writing to Albert Gallatin in February of the same year, Thomas Jefferson reflected on the questions of 'unity and trinity' which were being debated in the eastern states of the Union, and said that the argument must issue in the triumph of common sense over 'the unintelligible jargon of gothic fanaticism'. The term is often used during and after the French Revolution, but it is interesting that Jefferson, who became a Unitarian, uses it in a theological context, though he is clearly thinking of Burke, whose writings he detested. In *The Spirit of the Age*, Hazlitt aligns Wordsworth, who was much influenced by Unitarian science and republican theory in the 1790s, with Rational Dissent's hostility to that monarchical tenacity which the gothic embodies.

Hazlitt uses the term many times in his writing, and it carries an impacted, accreted series of references and associations which, as we have seen, sometimes makes it a highly ambivalent adjective that gives off a kind of atomic buzz. When Hazlitt says that our literature is 'gothic and grotesque, unequal and irregular', he is recognizing that he cannot kick against the prickly thorns of his own culture.

In the winter of 1817–18, the term seems to have been especially fashionable – Coleridge, Jefferson, and Hazlitt all employ it. In his lecture on the gothic mind Coleridge praised

the massy architecture of the Goths, as wild and varied as the forest vegetation which it resembled. The Greek art is beautiful. When I enter a Greek church, my eye is charmed, and my mind elated; I feel exalted, and proud that I am a man. But the gothic art is sublime. On entering a cathedral, I am filled with devotion and with awe; I am lost to the actualities that surround me, and my whole being expands into the infinite; earth and air, nature and art, all well up into eternity, and the only sensible impression left, is, 'that I am nothing!'

Although Hazlitt's article ante-dated Coleridge's lecture, the phrase 'gothic ignorance and barbarism' is directed at the type of swooning self-abnegation which he loathed in the admiration of the gothic. This topicality, which is part of the atmosphere of all journalism, is hard to recover in all its volatile, current detail. Nevertheless, the term vibrates with a contesting actuality.

There is a similar compactness in the several references to painters in Hazlitt's study of Wordsworth. Comparing the poet to one of Holbein's heads – 'grave, saturnine, with a slight indication of sly humour' – he recounts how Wordsworth would talk about Poussin and Rembrandt. Hazlitt points to the fact that when Wordsworth praises Rembrandt's manner of transforming the stump of a tree, a common figure, into an ideal object 'by the gorgeous light and shade' which are thrown upon it, he is drawing an analogy with his own mode of investing the minute details of nature with 'an atmosphere of sentiment'. In pronouncing Rembrandt a genius, he 'strengthens' his own claim to the title.

I have suggested that we similarly strengthen Hazlitt's claim to that title as we read his sketch of Wordsworth, though there is an impersonal, rather than a self-conscious, identification with the driving egalitarianism of Wordsworth's imagination here. That ambivalent identification is not signalled, but it is proper that we make it for him.

Hazlitt's reference to Holbein has a kind of photographic immediacy. A dark Lutheran materiality and sense of power is introduced, partly because the painter is inescapably associated with the court of Henry VIII. However, in the essay 'On Old English Writers and Speakers', which appeared in the *New Monthly Magazine* in 1825, the same year that *The Spirit of the Age* was published, he remarks that the expression in Holbein's pictures conveys a faithful but not very 'favourable' notion of the literary character of that period: it is 'painful, dry, and laboured'. By contrast, his references to Titian add colour and expressive action to Hazlitt's writing unreservedly. He also aims to give Wordsworth presence and immediacy, describing his smile and the deep 'manliness' and 'rugged harmony' in the tones of his voice. The link with Holbein intensifies those 'old English' qualities, but it also carries certain negative associations, which Titian never does. This is the moment now and *en passant*, even though it is less vivid than the portrait of Wordsworth with his brown fustian jacket and striped pantaloons in 'My First Acquaintance with Poets'.

There is a much subtler equivalent passage in his sketch of Wilberforce's creepy, snake-like voice, its manner of making pathetic appeals in a 'faltering, improgressive, sidelong way, like those of birds of weak wing'. Here, in the manner of a political caricaturist, Hazlitt gives visual representation to a 'fluctuating, time-serving principle'. Interestingly, when he proceeds to praise Thomas Clarkson, the leading anti-slavery campaigner of the day, he describes him as resembling one of the apostles in a cartoon by Raphael. Where Wilberforce is given an image from Gillray or Cruikshank, Clarkson is simultaneously associated with great art and supreme sanctity. Within a few sentences we shift from popular caricature to high art, and the sketch concludes triumphantly with the claim that Clarkson deserves 'to be added to the Twelve!'

Hazlitt's vast knowledge of the visual arts helps to structure the individual portraits in *The Spirit of the Age*. It can be regarded as the equivalent of quotation, but with an added quality of immediacy and modernity, as though he knew intuitively that in the next century photography would utterly transform journalistic practice. As a cartoonist, he has sport with Sir James Mackintosh, whose style of parliamentary oratory has an academic pointlessness, a manner of raising objections for the sake of answering them, which makes it a 'mere exercise' of the understanding without zest or spirit. Comparing Mackintosh to a 'provident' military engineer who has come to shatter the strongholds of corruption by a 'well-directed and unsparing discharge of artillery', he says that it was as though the orator had brought along with him not only his own cannon-balls, but his own 'wool-packs' to ward off the threatened mischief. The effect is to make Mackintosh ridiculous in a very concise, concrete fashion.

Such sensible images help to produce the witty, sometimes wonderfully patronizing tone of the collection. So does the Shake-spearean quotation in the next paragraph, where Hazlitt describes the success of Mackintosh's *Lectures on the Law of Nature and Nations*, delivered at Lincoln's Inn, a venue more suited to his talents than the Commons. The electrical effect of the lectures inspired Mackintosh to even greater self-confidence:

He grew wanton with success. Dazzling others by the brilliancy of his acquirements, dazzled himself by the admiration they excited, he lost fear as well as prudence: dared everything, carried everything before him. The Modern Philosophy, counterscarp, outworks, citadel, and all, fell without a blow by 'the whiff and wind of his fell *doctrine*', as if it had been a pack of cards.

By picking up the player's Marlovian speech in *Hamlet*, Hazlitt immediately disables Mackintosh with the memory of those clotted, overdone, parodic lines:

> Unequal matched,
> Pyrrhus at Priam drives, in rage strikes wide,
> But with the whiff and wind of his fell sword
> Th'unnervèd father falls. Then senseless Ilium,
> Seeming to feel this blow, with flaming top
> Stoops to his base, and with a hideous crash
> Takes prisoner Pyrrhus' ear.

The effect is amusingly muscle-bound, and the speech's echo makes Mackintosh appear to be a daft, pompous ham actor reciting someone else's resonantly hollow lines. We warm to the spectacle of Mackintosh laying about him 'like one inspired', and we eagerly participate in Hazlitt's superior intelligence. Like a savage boar, Mackintosh has 'got into the garden of the fabled Hesperides'. He is a self-caricaturing absurdity, like the Scottish preacher Irving.

Yet how does Hazlitt's deployment of quotation here and throughout his critical writing avoid the criticism that he is designing centos, not original arguments? When he remarks that Mackintosh's lectures were 'but a kind of philosophical centos' whose brilliancy and novelty were borrowed, he's reducing the distinguished jurist to the status of Rameau's nephew in Diderot's essay. Like Pangloss in George Colman's play *The Heir at Law*, Mackintosh spoke 'only in quotations'. The pith and marrow of his reasoning might be put in inverted commas.

This is similar to the charge which Hazlitt levels at the Tory politician Canning, whose language is 'a cento of florid commonplaces', and it sinks both Mackintosh and Canning under the weight of their huge lack of originality. Yet we know that Hazlitt also described Milton as a writer of centos, but one who approaches the originality of Homer. And we can see that Hazlitt's essays are intricately tessellated with quotations – phrases such as 'sacred vehemence' which he sometimes uses as a kind of critical camouflage.

So are there good and bad centos? Is he exploring an anxiety about his own critical practice? Or does the distinction lie in whether an argument thickly pasted together with quotations does or does not have vehemence, momentum, energy, vivacity? Those terms – they're among the most important in Hazlitt's critical aesthetic – describe the quickening of the otherwise inert dough of mass quotation. Where Milton melts down his sources in the furnace of his imagination – makes a new molten metal out of quotations from many texts – Mackintosh lacks the 'principle of fusion'. In a telling, very witty phrase, Hazlitt says that Mackintosh 'strikes after the iron is cold'. His style lacks 'malleability'.

The portrait of Mackintosh, whose voice, dress, and features are never described, therefore becomes a study in intellectual failure. This distinguished jurist writes in a 'composite style', which is a way of rephrasing the charge that he writes philosophical centos. Where Coleridge is fluid, Mackintosh has nothing but 'fixtures'. All his ideas may be said to be 'given preconceptions', a term that is the equivalent of 'foregone conclusion'. He is representative of those Scottish intellectuals who have a precocious ability to 'get up' school exercises on any given subject in a masterly manner, but who at the age of forty are either just where they were or 'retrograde'. There is a similar perception in the portrait of Jeffrey, where Hazlitt describes how every participant in a Scottish conversation is looked upon as a 'machine or a collection of topics'.

This criticism of the mechanical and the utile issues from Hazlitt's sense that modernity will always work to crush individual genius and spontaneity. Compared with Coleridge and Burke, Mackintosh lacks 'unforeseen' flashes of thought and invention. Although the jurist can impart all that can be said on a subject, Coleridge has an original brilliance that makes him easily superior. Mackintosh has something of the dexterity and self-possession of a political and philosophical 'juggler' – which is to say, he possesses what is termed 'mechanical excellence' in 'The Indian Jugglers'. But he is unable ever to get beyond the intellectual equivalent of the manual exhibition of skill. He belongs therefore with all the boxers, wrestlers, rope-dancers, jugglers, and racket-players whom Hazlitt admired. He is the philosopher in the fairground, a performer who is condemned to parody intellectual excellence without ever being able to achieve it. Hazlitt is therefore gloomy about the nature of progress, because modernity will more and more demand and supply fixed, routine topics, not living ideas.

In a sense, he is arguing that Mackintosh's arguments are just a series of prefabricated sound-bites. This is because Mackintosh lacks something which his Scottishness must deny him access to: the old English intellect which Bulstrode Whitelocke possessed. The reformer Sir Francis Burdett also possesses that 'old English understanding and old English character' which is one of the casualties of modernity. Cobbett's honesty attaches him to some extent to this ideal native intellect, as does his way of viewing things as they affect himself – 'close, palpable, tangible' – but he lacks the judiciousness

of this manner of thinking. Something of the almost mystical patriotism that suffuses Hazlitt's thinking about the English mind can be
felt in his emblematic image of Cobbett's capacity for always being
against the powers-that-be: 'he naturally butts at all obstacles, as
unicorns are attracted to oak-trees.' This is a perfect symbol of
Cobbett's polemical imagination, and it lets us glimpse the visionary patriotism which his fellow polemicist shares with him. When
Eric Blair abandoned his Scottish surname and Victorian first name
in order to reinvent himself as George Orwell, he raised the red-
cross flag over his writing, and signalled that he wanted to be
accounted one of the company which includes Cobbett and Hazlitt.
In dramatically portraying the *Zeitgeist* of the mid-1820s, Hazlitt
wants his readers to know that, like Cobbett and Burdett, he
embodies a uniquely English quality which he hopes will always
endure.

The collection peters out after Cobbett, and I like to think that its
real conclusion is the portrait of him in that essay's final paragraph, where he is described as looking like an eighteenth-century
gentleman-farmer or a Member of Parliament in the reign of
George I. This, at least for Hazlitt, is a securely Whig conclusion:
the Hanoverian succession is in place, and Cobbett, with his good
sensible face and ruddy complexion, has an iconic rural cheerful-
ness which reassures. There is nothing tragic about *The Spirit of the
Age*: its mode is generous comedy, and its form that of a freshly
invented classic. Though it is one of the products of 'this new-
sprung modern light' – Burke's phrase – the work is an organic
mulch of traditional, inherited ideas which the master would have
admired.

CHAPTER TWELVE

Great Plainness of Speech

Hazlitt's final collection of essays, *The Plain Speaker*, was published anonymously in 1826. Its title appears to be direct and definite, more than a shade obvious, except that, as we have seen, the Shakespearean prose-writer can take even a common word like 'dry' and pack it with complex meaning. There is more to this title than meets the eye, in part because Hazlitt wants to signal the presence of the spoken word in his writing. As he explains in the introduction to the Paris edition of the text:

I had remarked that when I had written or thought upon a particular topic, and afterwards had occasion to speak of it with a friend, the conversation generally took a much wider range, and branched off into a number of indirect and collateral questions, which were not strictly connected with the original view of the subject, but which often threw a curious and striking light upon it, or upon human life in general.

It therefore occurred to him that it might be possible to combine the advantages of the literary and the conversational styles. This promised a 'greater variety and richness', and perhaps – key phrase – a 'greater sincerity' than could be obtained by a 'more precise and scholastic method'.

He is also trying to give an illusion of coherence and unity to a collection of journalistic pieces that were written over several years. His title, which might belong to a magazine or a journal, implies continuity, as well as honesty, and is worth examining closely. Like any critic gathering disparate essays into book form, he is bound to search for an arresting title which appears to bind all the pieces into a unified argument. Where a book is a series of consecutive chapters that develop towards a conclusion, a collection of essays is less a linear progress than a framed group of animated particles in complex relation with each other. It's a team playing a game, rather than a line of soldiers heading towards a definite objective. There must be something random, chancy, sparky, *and* organized about a book of essays. It cannot lead the reader by the nose down a straight road, but neither can it hope to attract readers with a title like *Miscellaneous Prose Pieces 1821–1826*.

In this collection, the at first sight rather dull adjective 'plain', which recurs many times, acts as a dynamic centre that binds the disparate pieces together. So does 'speech', 'conversation', and that obsessive term 'style', which is often attached to those nouns, and which denotes one of his pervasive critical themes (he's particularly animated when discussing the painter Fuseli's style of conversation). What we're being offered is a printed text that aspires to the condition of rapid, direct, inspired speech. Thus the opening essay 'On the Prose Style of Poets' is answered by 'On the Conversation of Authors', and by 'The Difference between Writing and Speaking' and 'Old English Writers and Speakers'. In addition, there is a dialogue essay on envy, which helps to create the effect that these essays are in dialogue not just with their readers, but with each other. What we are being offered is a printed text that aspires to the sociable condition of animated conversation.

This aspiration is one expression of Hazlitt's puritan inheritance, and in its primary biblical source, Paul's second letter to the Corinthians, the statement 'we use great plainness of speech' refers to the hermeneutic process. Paul is arguing that under the Mosaic law the Jews were blinded by ignorance: until the coming of Christ there remained 'the same veil untaken away in the reading of the old testament'. Even to this day, he argues, when they read Moses, 'the veil is upon their heart'. This picks up Paul's statement at the beginning of the chapter that 'Ye' – the Corinthians – are 'our epistle written in our hearts'. It is a welcoming, warmly inclusive gesture which fuses the writer as speaker of plain truths with his audience, so that this emotionally charged spiritual unity contrasts with the Mosaic law, which is identified with material reality – stone, papyrus inscribed with ink. In this way, Paul posits a higher, immaterial value, which is Christian doctrine. Thus Paul's pen appears to repudiate the letters it inscribes in favour of emotive speech. The epistle of Christ 'ministered by us' is written not with ink, but with 'the Spirit of the living God; not in tables of stone, but in fleshy tables of the heart'. The letter kills, but the spirit gives life. Direct, emotional speech is therefore superior to the letter of the law. It is the spirit which strips away the veil, the text, the letter, because it expresses a glorious hope and faith.

Hazlitt, an unbeliever, replaces Christian redemption with the spirit of criticism. As we have seen, he grounds that spirit, like Paul, in speech. Many of the other essays refer to speech as a subject, so it's almost as though he wants to melt writing into conversation. Here, we should notice that in collections of essays, themes aren't so much developed as passed like batons or juggled like balls; they are leitmotifs, always in motion. Speech is a whirling theme, a conversational eddy that ripples in and out of the essays, shaping their form. Northcote, a conversational genius for Hazlitt as well as a plain-spoken fellow Unitarian, is a crucial figure, because speech and painting are twinned motifs. Hazlitt's *Conversations of James Northcote*, which was published four years later in 1830, the year of Hazlitt's death, is really a companion volume to *The Plain Speaker*, and reads like a farewell to essay writing.

Another shaping personality is Charles James Fox, whose familiar conversation Hazlitt mentions overhearing in the Louvre, when they were both visiting Paris during the Peace of Amiens in 1802. This is a double epiphany in Hazlitt's criticism, because that building is a structural motif – more, a totemic symbol. As we have seen, he states in his early essay on Fox, which was published five years later, that the politician's character was a 'plain marble slab, inscribed in plain legible characters'. In this, his final collection, he refers to Fox's 'plain, natural style', so it's clear that, by the principles of association, 'plain' is indissolubly linked to Fox and to the style of parliamentary eloquence he commanded (Fox was famously plain-spoken). The word carries authority, as well as a certain unadorned classical simplicity and lack of ostentation. It's a Whig value, because Chatham's speeches are also said to contain 'a few plain truths told home'. And when Coleridge's balloon flights are said to move away from 'the plain ground of prose', Hazlitt characteristically links the adjective to prose as well. He also notes that Fox's prose style wasn't distinguished, which is a way of implying that in his own critical writing he is trying to unite the virtues of Foxian eloquence with the active engaged medium of critical prose.

The term 'plain' has another resonance, which emerges in his remark that Chatham's parliamentary speeches were delivered 'in clear, short, pithy, old English sentences'. Similarly, in 'Old English Writers and Speakers' he discerns 'something fine, manly, and old English' in the devout seriousness of Holbein's portraits. And in the same essay he praises Hogarth and Fielding for demonstrating 'genuine English intellect' by constantly combining 'truth of external observation with strength of internal meaning'. Plain speech is the expression of that intellect, and its exponents include Cobbett, Burdett, Brougham, Tooke, and of course Hazlitt himself. Jeremy Taylor, the Anglican visionary and devout monarchist, is numbered among the old English prose-writers; so is Bacon, whose writings combine 'the gravity of prose with the fervour and vividness of poetry', and whose style is 'equally sharp and sweet, flowing and pithy'. And though he wasn't English, Burke also possesses this essentialist quality, as we would now term it. He delivered 'plain things on a plain ground', but when he rose, his style was a Coriolanian eagle.

Interestingly, this vertical/horizontal image is picked up in 'Depth and Superficiality', where the republican character of North American culture is discussed. Hazlitt contrasts the 'democratic level, the flatness of imagery' with the 'towering and artificial heights' of old monarchical states. We are back with Shenstone's distinction between prose Whigs, who are friendly with the Dutch, and Tory poets, who admire the French. The word 'plain' is therefore both adjective and noun: it carries connotations of the flatlands of Holland, even of the 'low, fat, Bedford level' in Burke's *Letter to a Noble Lord*.

Burke is a lifelong obsession, and he makes frequent appearances in *The Plain Speaker*. Hazlitt's living link to the supreme prose stylist is through Northcote, who often describes meetings with

Burke and Sir Joshua Reynolds. It's here that we approach what looks very like the holy of holies, a type of makeshift inner sanctum, where the spirit of criticism lives and breathes, in Northcote's studio – this is the shifting conversational centre of Hazlitt's critical imagination. Wearing a green velvet cap, and looking 'very like Titian', the old painter becomes a kind of Prospero figure, magically active in his cave of making. He also looks like a Roman cardinal or a Spanish inquisitor, so he resembles one of Titian's powerful subjects too. Those portraits have intense presence: 'they look you through', as if they're living human beings, he remarks in one of the essays on the Elgin Marbles, and this is echoed in the essay on Van Dyke, which is placed next to 'The Difference between Writing and Speaking', where he says that whenever you look at Titian's portraits, 'they appear to be looking at you'. This sense of Titian's eerie power is developed when Northcote says in one of the conversations that Titian was a 'fine old mouser' who gives a 'cat-like, watchful, penetrating look' to all his faces.

Northcote is the best conversationalist Hazlitt knows, because he is also the best listener. In his studio, Hazlitt is sure to get something that is to be found nowhere else:

a welcome, as if one was expected to drop in just at that moment, a total absence of all respect of persons and of airs of self-consequence, endless topics of discourse, refined thoughts, made more striking by ease and simplicity of manner – the husk, the shell of humanity is left at the door, and the spirit, mellowed by time, resides within! All you have to do is to sit and listen; and it is like hearing one of Titian's faces speak.

The language at this point in 'The Spirit of Obligations' is epiphanic: this is vision with the husk or veiling letter left outside. We're part of a continuous process, happening in the painter's workshop, not in a gallery where varnished, framed, finished works are displayed. This idea of the unfinished – *Titianus faciebat* – is linked to the extemporized and spontaneous, the casually conversational, as well as to the living, active, unsettling vigilance of Titian's subjects.

Printed conversations are of course like stage dialogue; so we have the idea that, ideally, the essay form is like an improvised one-act play taking place in a painter's studio. Talk in a workshop is

275

more intense, more familiar and relaxed, less nonchalantly self-conscious than it is in the coffee-shop; we're backstage in a bare room. And as the host is the artist, Hazlitt has to fight – or seem to fight – for his conversational chances. He doesn't take on a controlling authority, but displaces it by sharing power with the painter.

Any one of Northcote's *tête-à-têtes* would make an essay, Hazlitt says in 'The Conversation of Authors', but for the fact that the painter can't form ideas or write consecutive prose. So a lens is necessary to collect 'the diverging rays, the refracted and broken angular lights of conversation on paper'. Hazlitt's prose supplies such a lens: he is the perfect chrysolite, which unifies or centres many disparate subjects.

But conversation, he points out, isn't seamlessly unitary: contradiction is 'half the battle in talking', because you're startled by what someone else says and have to defend yourself on the spot. 'Lively sallies and connected discourse' are very different things, but there is no good style which isn't fit to be spoken or read aloud with effect. This is true, not only of emphasis and cadence, but also with regard to 'natural idiom and colloquial freedom'. In this respect, Sterne's style was the best that was ever written, because it makes us imagine that we hear his characters talking.

Hazlitt revered *Tristram Shandy*, and with his delight in a creative indolence he would have recognized that novel's subversion of Whig narrative and Lockean associationism. When Tristram says he will now be able to go on with his Uncle Toby's story and his own, in a tolerably straight line –

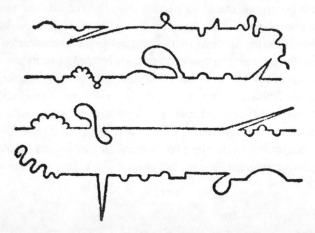

– we delight in the visual representation of the novel's anarchic vernacular, which destroys, Sterne wittily remarks, 'that necessary equipoise and balance (whether of good or bad) betwixt chapter and chapter, from whence the just proportions and harmony of the whole work results'. This is Johnson's prose crashing to the ground, or it is luxuriant speech dancing like weeds on a temple ruin painted by Poussin. A collection of essays, likewise, isn't a justly proportioned perfect form. Instead, its individual components must bunch, grapple, break, then ebb and flow like conversation. They aren't classical arches, and they don't succeed each other like chapters.

Hazlitt would naturally have been attracted to speech, because it seems to come into being naturally – doodling, doubling back, a walking line which knows when to dawdle or when to spout and gush. And he would have realized, uncomfortably perhaps, that speech, by its very unfinished, unpunctuated nature, is impatient with a fixed classical form. Perhaps speech is gothic then? All stops, starts, and sudden jagged sallies, because, unlike prose, it doesn't run in paragraphs or aim to exist as connected discourse.

What Hazlitt wants to combine, as he implies in his essay on the difference between speaking and writing, is the liveliness of conversation with the concentrated focus of connected prose. Expert speakers are lively because they do what they do 'off-hand, at a single blow'; while studious prose-writers work by a 'repetition of blows', because they have time to think and to do better. When Hazlitt uses the word 'blow' in this context, he's obviously linking prose with boxing or the blacksmith's craft: hot metal, like molten glass, is a good figure for this process. And glass is blown, so there's a pun, which makes the link with speech, with blown words. But really what he's aiming to communicate is the idea of immediacy as a powerful physical sensation. Discussing Titian's portrait of Hippolito de Medici in the accompanying essay on Van Dyck, he says that there is a 'keen, sharpened expression that strikes you, like a blow from the spear that he holds in his hand' – again, the word 'blow' picks up its use in the previous essay, and draws speaking, writing, and painting together. Because form, colour, feeling, and character seem to 'adhere' to his eye, Titian's paintings 'leave stings' in the mind.

That phrase is linked in 'Gusto' to that 'tingling sensation to the eye, which the body feels within itself', and which he elsewhere discerns in Titian, and it expresses the 'principle of motion' which a still life can never possess. What he's describing is process, the ongoingness of communication, an absence of closure. This develops the account of Burke in the previous essay on the difference between writing and speaking: his mind never became set, but was always in further 'search and progress' – a point which is illustrated by an anecdote Hazlitt tells about how the proofs of *Letter to a Noble Lord* were so pestered by Burke's corrections that the printer broke up the type and reset the copy.

When Hazlitt says that Burke is 'communicative, diffuse, magnificent', he's praising the intense process of his prose; but in a footnote to the same essay, he suggests that prose can't be a seamlessly fluent continuum, by pointing to the necessity of introducing breath-pauses. A bad style, he says, is essentially one in which the person writing seems never to stop for breath. In order to determine if the pauses it employs are natural, style must always be tested on the stomach. Good prose is like the active, supple human body – the 'bulk, and thews, and sinews of a man'.

The theme of embodied prose is wittily combined with the Napoleonic themes that empower his criticism. In an essay 'On the Qualifications Necessary to Success in Life', he praises bodily stamina, as well as the 'alacrity, the unthinking confidence' it inspires. He develops this theme, and then, in a sudden Shandyish change of tack, raises the objection that some of the most successful people

have been little men. 'A little man, but of high fancy', is Sterne's description of Mr Hammond Shandy. But then they have been possessed of strong fibres and an iron constitution. The late Mr West said, that Buonaparte was the best-made man he ever saw in his life. In other cases, the gauntlet of contempt which a puny body and a fiery spirit are forced to run, may determine the possessor to aim at great actions; indignation may make men heroes as well as poets, and thus revenge them on the niggardliness of nature and the prejudices of the world. I remember Mr Wordsworth's saying, that he thought ingenious poets had been of small and delicate frames, like Pope; but that the greatest (such as Shakespeare and Milton) had been healthy, and cast in a larger and handsomer mould. So were Titian, Raphael, and Michaelangelo. This is one of the few observations of Mr Wordsworth's I recollect worth quoting, and I accordingly set it down as his, because I understand he is tenacious on that point.

This turns into a put-down: Wordsworth's dopey observation both makes and unmakes Hazlitt's contention about Napoleon's height. This is a Shandyish technique, which releases into prose the ironic slipperiness of conversation – its tonal trills, demurrals, sliding shifts of emphasis, as well as its ways of adapting to the other person's moods and its habit of constantly rollicking around. Conversation is never in one key, or becomes deeply dull if it is.

Examining the witty shakiness of his argument, we can see that it is constructed out of a train of associated ideas that begins with Sterne, that perfect vocal stylist who both deploys and ironizes a Whiggish association of ideas:

In the case of *knots* – by which, in the first place, I would not be understood to mean slipknots – because in the course of my life and opinions – my opinions concerning them will come in more properly when I mention the catastrophe of my great-uncle Mr Hammond Shandy – a little man – but of high fancy: – he rushed into the Duke of Monmouth's affair.

Hazlitt alludes to this passage, then mentions Napoleon, then glances at Dryden's Achitophel, the Whig tempter with the frail body who prompts Monmouth to become a rebel. The theme of the body is being wittily varied here, and the defeats of Monmouth's forces at Sedgemoor and Napoleon's at Waterloo are also being touched on associatively; but devotees of Sterne will recall that Uncle Toby is given to whistling 'Lillibulero', so there's the tingling of a faint Whig triumphalism on the far fringes of the allusion.

In a passage which Hazlitt dropped from one of the footnotes when he reprinted the essay, he says that he is so sick

of this trade of authorship, that I have a much greater ambition to be the best racket-player, than the best prose-writer of the age. The critics look askance at one's best-meant efforts, but the face of a racket-player is the face of a friend. There is no juggling there. If the stroke is a good one, the hit tells. They do not keep two scores to mark the game, with Whig and Tory notches. The thing is settled at once, and the applause of the *dedans* follows the marker's voice, and seconds the prowess of the hand, and the quickness of the eye.

He then goes on to suggest, in a passage he retained, that 'the accomplishments of the body' are obvious and clear to everyone, while mental abilities, which are 'recondite and doubtful', tend to be grudgingly acknowledged, or mocked.

There are several other references to racket playing, a subject that's developed in his twentieth conversation with Northcote, where the painter responds to Hazlitt's praise of John Davies's ease as a player by saying:

every motion of that man was perfect grace: there was not a muscle in his body that did not contribute its share to the game. So, when they begin to learn the piano-forte, at first they use only the fingers, and are soon tired to death: then the muscles of the arm come into play, which relieves them a little; and at last the whole frame is called into action, so as to produce the effect with entire ease and gracefulness.

Motion and an easy grace are closely allied in Hazlitt's critical aesthetic, and these qualities are most completely expressed in racket playing and conversation. We often use terms drawn from tennis as metaphors to describe conversation, partly because spoken words, though they're all air and voice, have a rapid, spinning, engaged physicality that is often intensely enjoyable. Horne Tooke, who is celebrated in the essay on the qualifications necessary to success in life, and who was fascinated by the mercurial pitch of the spoken word, is described as a master of conversation who overflows with an 'interminable babble'. By aural suggestion, we're returned to the bubbles of Shakespeare's verse, and also catch a gleam of the glass-blower's bubble, that figure for a clear and perfect written style.

Northcote, similarly, is 'completely extempore' in 'The Old Age of Artists'. There's the same 'unconsciousness' in his conversation that there is in Shakespeare's dialogues. The painter's figure is 'small, shadowy, emaciated', but you think only of his face, which is 'fine and expressive'. His body, Hazlitt adds, is 'out of the question'.

As a critic, Hazlitt wants to represent expression as a graceful, moving body – except that 'represent' is too distanced a term. Really – and it isn't tautological to say so – he wants to incarnate the body in his prose, so that his writing takes on the body's fluid actions, its restful being or tense power. So, when he remarks in the same essay that Fuseli's conversation is more striking and extravagant, but less pleasing and natural than Northcote's, he uses the artist's face as a symbol for his style of talking:

> You are sensible of effort without any repose – no careless pleasantry – no traits of character or touches from nature – everything is laboured or overdone. His ideas are gnarled, hard, and distorted, like his features – his theories stalking and straddle-legged, like his gait – his projects aspiring and gigantic, like his gestures – his performance uncouth and dwarfish, like his person. His pictures are also like himself, with eye-balls of stone stuck in rims of tin, and muscles twisted together like ropes or wires.

The Shandyish dashes appropriately give a spoken improvisatory texture to the sentence, an extempore effect that's developed further when he suddenly makes the artist into a kind of Frankensteinian monster whose pictures are also 'like himself'. Like a modernist sculpture, a piece of *bricolage*, Fuseli lurches into a kind of artificial life.

This characterization of Fuseli is a brief, dashed-off moment in the essay, but I want to consider it at some length, because it may be another figure for Hazlitt's critical art. Like Frankenstein, like Fuseli, he seeks to make something out of pre-existing materials – books, plays, pictures, allusions, quotations, critical terms, all sorts of phrases and scraps. What he designs isn't planned a priori, but comes into existence spontaneously. His centos or critical collages are thrown together quickly from bits and pieces that are to hand.

Here it's worth considering this technique in relation to more recent accounts of the nature of literary criticism. Particularly to Gérard Genette's discussion of its relationship to Claude Lévi-Strauss's definition of mythical thought as a kind of *bricolage* that always makes use of materials and tools that, unlike those of the engineer, 'were not intended for the task in hand'. Applying this insight to the practice of literary criticism, Genette points out that literary criticism distinguishes itself formally from art or music criticism by the fact that it uses the same materials – written words – as the works with which it is concerned. It is therefore a 'metalanguage', or 'discourse upon a discourse', as Barthes terms it – which means that original writers belong to nature, critics to culture. Hazlitt's obsession with 'nature' as a critical term represents his agonized desire to cross the apparently absolute divide between the two. Fuseli, in Hazlitt's characterization of him, becomes a figure for the critic who takes, say, a sentence from Burke, a phrase from Milton, an image from Shakespeare, an account of a painting by Poussin, and binds them together into an argument about the nature of prose style. Those same images might also be applied in an essay on Indian jugglers, Kean's Iago, or the ignorance of the learned, or whatever subject he happens to be addressing where they might be appropriate – or might be made to appear appropriate.

If we set to one side the concept of the original, fixed aesthetic masterpiece, and concentrate on the critical argument's process, on the business of assembling a particular passage, we can watch the critical act taking place as a form of creativity, rather than as a subsidiary gesture. It's like pasting up a collage, or making a bowl out of papier mâché, or having a conversation in a studio.

Commenting on the concept of *bricolage*, Amit Chaudhuri describes how the plaster original of Picasso's sculpture *The She-Goat* was constructed from a wicker-basket, palm leaves, scraps of iron, and ceramic pots which represented the goat's belly, backbone, ribs, shoulder, and udder. What is remarkable, Chaudhuri notes, is that even in the 'finished' – really never finished – product, the 'materials of creation', the process of construction and making, the peculiar pathos and joy of gradual creation, are left open to view. The effect of this is to deny that the final structure came into perfect form by inspiration, genius, or 'an automatic authorial magic'. For example, when Lawrence describes a bat as having 'long, black paper ears', or a tortoise as having a mouth like 'sudden curved scissors', he's substituting improvisation and process for static description. If we compare this anti-aesthetic with Hazlitt's characterization of Fuseli, we may note that while he immediately adds that Fuseli is 'undoubtedly a man of genius', he has raised the question of improvisation in a manner which denies traditional ideas of pure, plenary inspiration. What he communicates is the hectic, driven nature of the creative process – its use of the makeshift, the ready-to-hand.

Ted Hughes similarly celebrates Shakespeare's gift for improvising language, and in a note to one of the poems in *Moortown Diary* praises his father-in-law, the farmer Jack Orchard, who was 'equal to any job, any crisis, using the most primitive means, adapting and improvising with any old bit of metal'. And we can see this all-off-the-top-of-the-head spontaneity in Lawrence's line 'I say untarnished, but I mean opaque' – a perfect iambic pentameter disguised as a sudden second-thought revision interjected immediately after the slightly sluggish lines which open 'Bare Fig Trees':

> Fig-trees, weird fig-trees
> Made of thick, smooth silver,
> Made of sweet, untarnished silver in the sea-southern air –
> I say untarnished, but I mean opaque.

Lawrence abandons the first three lines by suddenly substituting 'opaque' for 'untarnished' – this makes the poem run in a much more natural, improvised manner, while at the same time stressing the metallic, man-made, and therefore not in the least natural qualities of the fig-trees.

If we take Hughes on the way in which farmers adapt old metal scraps, Hazlitt on the tin-like Fuseli, Lawrence on silver-smooth fig-trees, as symbolic of the process of creating a work of art or a critical essay, then we can see that they share an aim to break down the barrier between criticism and artistic creation. The Dissenting culture that nurtured them is suspicious of finished or overly perfect works of art, and values instead the utile, the recycled, the improvised and economical. Hazlitt wasn't good with money, but he was able to circulate and recirculate the wealth of quotations he had banked from his early reading. The Kurt Schwitters of literary criticism, he pastes up his centos and abandons them rapidly. But he can make repeated lines from Shakespeare or Burke sound like his own signature phrases. Curiously, T. S. Eliot does something similar in *The Waste Land*, where a line from Marvell can reverberate with a snatch of overheard conversation or a fragment of stage dialogue to produce an effect that's meant to resemble an orchestra tuning up. Despite the apparently recondite or élitist nature of the references in Eliot, the cento is a highly democratic form of art, because it transforms bits and pieces of cultural scrap into a new type of broken or dissonant form, which allows the audience to participate in the process of assembling the diverse components.

In his account of Lawrence's imagination, Chaudhuri argues that the dichotomy which 'almost always' exists in Western culture between the interpretative and the aesthetic functions is often 'dissolved' in Lawrence's writing. Instead, his criticism '*enters*, textually, the work being looked at, plays with it, imitates it, takes on its characteristics', so that interpretation can't be kept separate from creativity.

Chaudhuri's comment issues from an impatience with the founding tropes of Western criticism – sight and hearing. Following Derrida, he argues that those senses are 'antithetical to desire', and naturally lend themselves to 'distancing, clarity, logic, perspective, and the ideal'. The more physically immediate senses, which are excluded as 'tropes of understanding' – touch and taste – would lend themselves to an aesthetic of 'sensation, collision, eroticism and the surface'. Hazlitt's frequent invocation of the body in his criticism, his pervasive recourse to boxing and racket playing as figures for prose style, are an attempt to put sensation and physical impact at the centre of his writing: every word should be a blow, every hit should tell. And, interestingly, Hazlitt quotes Horne Tooke in 'The Prose Style of Poets' on the defects of Addison's prose:

Its smooth, equable uniformity, and want of sharpness and spirit, arose from his not having familiarized his ear to the sound of his own voice, or at least only among friends and admirers, where there was but little collision, dramatic fluctuation, or sudden contrariety of opinion to provoke animated discussion, and give birth to different intonations and lively transitions of speech.

There then follows the statement, which I've linked to the procreant cradle image, that Addison's style was not 'indented', and did not 'project from the surface'. The sensuous texture communicates that erotics of prose style which is such a rubbed, tactile feature of Hazlitt's writing, and which links him to Hindu aesthetics. Both Chaudhuri and Hazlitt use the term 'collision' to express the at times erotic abrasiveness valued by this aesthetic. Chaudhuri points out that in Indian poetry, painting, and music, the operative critical term is *rasa*, or 'juice'. The person who responds to a work of art inevitably tastes its juice or flavour, and here 'taste' relates less to the upper-class British usage than to appetite, so this is an aesthetic that 'admits of desire'.

Interestingly, Hazlitt in his criticism of contemporary utilitarian reformers argues that their 'intellectual food does not assimilate with the juices of the mind'. Similarly, in the dialogue essay 'On Envy' he praises Northcote's manner of discussing Titian: 'your discourse has an extreme unction about it, a marrowiness like his colouring.' The idea of the unguent, the oily, the juicy, which I mentioned earlier, must have been current in Hazlitt's circle, because it's also present in an epicurean letter Charles Lamb wrote to his friend, the orientalist Thomas Manning, in which he savours 'the unctuous and palate-soothing flesh of geese wild and tame'.

Although the adjective 'unctuous' is now wholly pejorative, it once signified deep spiritual feeling, and was associated with the sacred: 'But ye have an unction from the Holy One, and ye know all things.' For Hazlitt, unctuousness is a quality that opposes the 'dry, meagre, penurious' imagination which he dislikes in 'captious and scrutinizing' Protestant culture. In the same essay, 'Hot and Cold', he contrasts North European repugnance and shame with

the dirty, dingy, greasy, sunburnt complexion of an Italian peasant or beggar, whose body seems alive all over with a sort of tingling, oily sensation, so that from any given particle of his shining skin to the beast 'whose name signifies love' the transition is but small. This populousness is not unaccountable where all teems with life, where all is glowing and in motion, and every pore thrills with an exuberance of feeling. Not so in the dearth of life and spirit, in the drossy, dry, material texture, the clear complexions and fair hair of the Saxon races, where the puncture of an insect's sting is a solution of their personal identity.

This passage is echoed in that passage in Northcote's *Life of Titian* where the 'heavy, dingy, slimy effect' of various oils and meglips is praised. We can hear Hazlitt relishing the adjectives, almost as though he is working paint with a brush.

In 'Hot and Cold', Germany is icy, Italy fiery and untidy; while in an ecstatic passage Hazlitt says that the Indian twines the 'forked serpent round his hand unharmed, copper-coloured like it, his veins as heated'. The Brahmin cherishes his life, and disregards his own person as 'an act of his religion – the religion of fire and of the sun!' In an earlier essay in *The Plain Speaker*, he remarks that seeing half a dozen Lascars wandering through the streets of London gives him a better idea of 'the soul of India, that cradle of the world, and (as it were) garden of the sun' than all the reports and statistics sent back to London. Schlegel, in his lectures on drama which Hazlitt reviewed in 1816, speaks of Indians as the people from whom 'perhaps all the cultivation of the human race has been derived'.

Hazlitt appears to have been fascinated by India, and as well as the famous essay on the Indian jugglers, there is a passage in the *Round Table* essay 'Manner' in which he discusses grace as the outward expression of the inner harmony of the soul, and says that the Hindus who are seen on the streets of London are an example of this:

They are a different race of people from ourselves. They wander about in a luxurious dream. They are like part of a glittering procession – like revellers in some gay carnival. Their life is a dance, a measure; they hardly seem to tread the earth, but are borne along in some more genial element, and bask in the radiance of brighter suns.

This is one of several visionary moments in his writing where he celebrates the idea of wandering about – walking with no aim in mind. In a rather Jack Yeats-like moment in 'The Manager', he says that wherever the strolling players come, they 'shed a light upon the day, that does not very soon pass off. See how they glitter along the street, wandering, not where business but the bent of pleasure takes them, like mealy-coated butterflies, or insects flitting in the sun.'

This is his aesthetic of motion, though he also prizes what he regards as the Oriental ability to sit and think and do nothing. Stasis is creative too, and in an uncollected essay, 'The Causes of Public Opinion', he remarks that anyone who sticks to an opinion by conviction, unmoved by ridicule and other social forces, shows no less resolution than 'the Hindoo who makes and keeps a vow to hold his right arm in the air till it grows rigid and callous'. In this comparison, we may detect a certain self-doubt lurking beneath the consistency of opinion which Hazlitt prided himself on possessing. By sticking so rigidly to his early principles, is he not like a grotesque Hindu mystic?

If the unctuous and the oily are set against the dry, they are also associated with a kind of baked or burnt umber quality that attracts him powerfully, and which is contrasted with a presumably blonde Swiss dairymaid who 'scours the very heart' out of a wooden pail. Swiss women are 'neat and clean', but they are also 'insipid'. Hogarth in his *Analysis of Beauty* defines 'insipid' as a lack of expression: 'How soon does a face that wants expression, grow insipid, though it be ever so pretty.' Earlier, in 'Hot and Cold', Hazlitt contrasts young Swiss women with a single Milanese market-girl who appeared to have 'more blood in her body, more fire in her eye (as if the sun had made a burning *lens* of it), more spirit and probably more mischief about her than all the nice, *tidy*, good-looking, hard-working girls I have seen in Switzerland'. His sexual stimulus is obvious, but what he is praising is a quality in which everything is 'baked and burnt-up, and sticks together in a most amicable union of filth and laziness'. The dirt of Italians, he observes, is 'as it were baked into them', and is so ingrained that it becomes part of them, and causes no discontinuity of their being. The idea of wholeness, of a chthonic energy where 'all is glowing and in motion', as well as a warm slippery natural *jouissance*, are being hymned here.

If he's impelled to make nature sacral, he also recognizes that an art such as literary criticism which assembles second-hand bits and pieces can never touch the green grassy slopes of what's natural. Praising the 'bold and startling outline' of Fuseli's conversational style, he makes a sudden sketch of the artist which bulges with the critic's ambivalent sense of modernity. Nature, Fuseli complains, 'puts him out', and we recognize that because that term is so central for Hazlitt, he must be dubious about an artist who wants to go beyond it into the artificial, the extreme, the camp, or the manu-factured. Dubious, because as a critic, Hazlitt is condemned to do the same thing. He dislikes the artificiality of opera, but he too designs showy surfaces, and performs enormous single-sentence arias. He wants his critical performance to have a provisional, unfinished, dominating, bravura quality.

The idea of the unfinished, as I've noted, is an important aesthetic conception in Hazlitt's criticism, and it's closely related to conversa-tion (after all, there is no such thing as a finished conversation – it's a contradiction in terms). Commenting on Reynolds's 'unfinished style' in 'Sitting for One's Picture', Hazlitt states that his best pic-tures are those of his children, who were his worst sitters. They are like the infancy of art itself – 'happy, bold, and careless'. In the next essay, on whether genius is conscious of its powers, he praises the 'unfinished state' of Hogarth's comic designs, and a few pages later remarks on the 'natural and unstudied' quality of Shakespeare's plays.

This idea of the spontaneous and incomplete is given more atten-tion in his twelfth conversation with Northcote, when the painter quotes a friend's remark that they might have made their fortunes if they'd had the foresight to lay out a few pounds on the loose sketches and sweepings of Reynolds's lumber room. Yes, Northcote says, they're more sought after than ever, because those 'imperfect hints and studies' seem to bring us more into contact with the artist, and explain the 'process' of his mind in the various stages of composition. A finished work, Northcote explains, is somehow 'detached from and independent of its author', while an unfinished sketch appears to be still in progress, still waiting to be finished. Or else our imaginations supply 'the absence of well-known excellences', so that we have a 'two-fold property' in the incomplete work.

This is an important piece of conversational criticism, because it points towards what we might see as the North American style of Hazlitt's thinking – his idea of 'further search and progress', his fascination with consciousness and conversation as process. It is closely linked to a footnote to the previous conversation, where he gives a long quotation from Kendall's *Letters on Ireland* in which Shakespeare is praised for writing his plays for the 'simple purpose of the moment' and without any ambition for the immortality they would acquire. Hazlitt also links the ephemeral and the immortal in his account of Van Dyck's manner of painting many of his finest portraits in the course of a single day – 'Oh! ephemeral works to last for ever!' The self-reference is obvious, and when we read Kendall's remark that Shakespeare imagined himself writing 'only for the day before him', we again get a powerful sense of topicality. What this constructs is a statement about the real nature of art: it should be spontaneous, like conversation, stage dialogue, and certain paintings, as well as physically expressive, graceful, natural, unfinished, and quickly executed. This last quality is described in the sixth conversation with Northcote, in which the Dissenting preacher Doddridge is quoted on his unwillingness and haste in composing: he never sat down to write until the printer's boy had called at the door for his manuscript.

Similarly, Hazlitt later tells Northcote that in his youth he hadn't been in the habit of writing, so that if he did put pen to paper, he always took a long time to finish something. It was only when he had to write for newspapers that 'the fluency came'. He often had to write a theatre review after midnight for publication next morning. Because he had to do it at once, to think 'on the spot', his ideas were fresh. Observing that 'when you are tied to time, you can come to time', he then discusses the subject of extempore speaking, which he rates below writing to tight deadlines. This is because extempore speeches can be prepared, and are on a set or agreed topic.

What he wants his prose to ride on is the surge and eddy of familiar conversation:

N. Though you do not know Sir Walter Scott, I think I have heard you say you have seen him.

H. Yes, he put me in mind of Cobbett, with his florid face and scarlet gown, which were just like the other's red face and scarlet waistcoat. The one is like an English farmer, the other like a Scotch *laird*. Both are large, robust men, with great strength and composure of features; but I saw nothing of the *ideal* character in the romance-writer, any more than I looked for it in the politician.

N. Indeed! But you have a vast opinion of Cobbett too, haven't you? Oh! he's a giant! He has such prodigious strength; he tears up a subject by the roots. Did you ever read his Grammar? Or see his attack on Mrs — — It was like a hawk pouncing on a wren. I should be terribly afraid to get into his hands. And then his homely, familiar way of writing – it is not from necessity or vulgarity, but to show his contempt for aristocratic pride and arrogance. He only has a kitchen-garden; he could have a flower-garden too if he chose. Peter Pindar said his style was like the Horse-Guards, only one story above the ground, while Junius's had all the airy elegance of Whitehall: but he could raise his style just as high as he pleased; though he does not want to sacrifice strength to elegance. He knows better what he is about.

Again, we notice the obvious point about physical robustness here; but what is especially lively about this conversational sally is the change in tone between Northcote's sidling prompt, with its rising inflection, and his subsequent decisive 'Indeed!' Here, the direct physicality of Cobbett's style – its titanic social angers and tender observation of nature – have a performative bounce and immediacy that turn criticism into theatre. Hazlitt then moves into a long reply which culminates in the account of Rousseau's career as a footman. Northcote dismisses this long 'rhapsody', and says that he is unable to express how detestable Rousseau's character is. Dismissing his pride, ambition, conceit, and 'gross affectation', he says that Rousseau's name brings back 'all the gloomy horrors of a mob-government'.

By dramatizing criticism as conversation, Hazlitt allows the provisional, contradictory nature of critical judgement to fissure in front of our eyes, like the sudden star-pattern that happens when a stone hits a pane of glass. Criticism can leap like a spark between opposite poles, it can be on both sides of the street at the same time, it can dance contradictions. Dramatic and intense, it must aim never to be fixed or finished. Provisional, exploratory, mercurial, eagerly engaged, it can also be decisive and downright – the Johnsonian 'Out upon it, sir!' is an essential gesture in the critic's conversational repertoire.

As we have seen, it's with walking rather than dancing that Hazlitt identifies his critical style. In the essay on genius and its powers, he suddenly begins a paragraph with the Shandyish statement 'I am not in the humour to pursue this argument any farther at present, but to write a digression'. This is because his readers should be aware of the fact, if they don't know it already, that he is writing this at Winterslow. And this direct, here-and-now immediacy is a version of the sense of climate and time of day that Wordsworth praised in Poussin's paintings. Fifteen years earlier, our critic 'trod the lengthened greensward by the low wood-side', and now he does so again. At Winterslow, his style is apt to be 'redundant and excursive', while elsewhere it may be 'cramped, dry, abrupt'. From the fusillade of those impacted adjectives, he moves to a liberating wetness, asserting that here his prose flows 'like a river, and overspreads its banks'. His style now has an exulting plenitude and a sense of flowing power. He doesn't have to seek out thoughts or hunt images – they come of themselves. 'I inhale them with the breeze', he says triumphantly. In its movement from dry fixity to natural flow, this is like his praise of Thomson's colours in *The Seasons*: they are 'yet wet and breathing, like those of the living statue in the *Winter's Tale*' – a comparison that significantly builds the bridge between art and nature which he wants to cross in his criticism.

To digress is to wander about the countryside, loll on Salisbury Plain, and draw nourishment from the associations which the place has. Here, he's drawing on nature poetry, and on the years he's known the village of Winterslow, in order to give his critical prose both a physical alacrity and an ontological confidence. The imagery of Romantic poetry is being applied to critical prose in what we would now term an 'ontological' discovery. We can feel the critic flexing his muscles as he repeats mockingly that he is not 'a government-tool' – a phrase he playfully and exultantly beats to death in the paragraph.

Of course, Hazlitt is writing at a desk or a table: he isn't moving about like an actor – though in a famous passage describing the view from his window just after a rain shower he seems to suddenly throw his body into a formal posture: 'Mr Blackwood, I am yours – Mr Croker, my service to you – Mr T. Moore, I am alive and well – Really, it is wonderful how little the worse I am for fifteen years' wear and tear.' Here he bows, ready for any duel. We are watching a stage performance in which voice and physical movement are perfectly co-ordinated. This is prose which positions itself confidently, and glows with chipper good health. Like the expressive face of the comic actor Liston, this passage is oily with a perfect enjoyment of its art.

This gracefulness is lovingly embodied in the motion picture he draws of Sir Charles Bunbury

as he saunters down St James's Street, with a large slouched hat, a lack-lustre eye, and aquiline nose, an old shabby drab-coloured coat, buttoned across his breast without a cape, – with old top-boots, and his hands in his waistcoat or breeches' pockets, as if he were strolling along his own garden-walks, or over the turf at Newmarket, after having made his bets secure, – presents nothing very dazzling, or graceful, or dignified to the imagination; though you can tell infallibly at the first glance, or even a bow-shot off, that he is a gentleman of the first water (the same that sixty years ago married the beautiful Lady Sarah L-nn-x, with whom the king was in love). What is the clue to this mystery? It is evident that his person costs him no more trouble than an old glove. His limbs are, as it were, left to take care of themselves.

Perhaps the studied negligence of this sketch in 'The Look of a Gentleman' inspired Wilde to reinvent the Bunburying pleasure principle for the 1890s. Though Sir Charles has a lack-lustre eye, this is a portrait out of Titian: the old glove makes a reappearance, and Hazlitt uses the adjective 'old' three times to design a keeping, or unity, of shade and texture. Contemplating these sentences, I'm caught here, as elsewhere, by wanting to characterize them as resembling both a sketch and a portrait. This may be because, remembering a remark in Northcote's life of Titian, Hazlitt, like the painter, possesses the power of uniting the 'clearness' of water-colours with the 'depth and solidity' of oils.

There's a sauntering, slouchy, perfectly easy quality to the prose, which is best expressed by the dialect word 'soodling', which John Clare uses to describe a particular way of rambling which country people have. Because their gait isn't made rigid or mechanical by ambition, men and women who walk like this are 'at home' – an important phrase – among any kind of people anywhere. Actors, the natives of non-industrial countries, often possess that lazy rest-fulness of gesture which E. M. Forster admired in convivial Indians. Such a way of walking or writing articulates what Heidegger, the notorious Black Forest walker, terms *Dasein*; and of course the verb 'articulate' applies to the body's joints, as well as to speech and writing. Hazlitt the journalist penning an article is trying to articu-late various 'members', as clauses used to be termed. Praising Kean's acting of Richard III, he says that he cannot imagine any character who is 'more perfectly *articulated* in every part'. It's as though his emphatic italics represent the union of the prose-writer's pen with the actor's supple body. In 'The Look of a Gentleman', where he describes Sir Charles Bunbury's walk, Hazlitt states that a man who possesses that look does so because he manifests 'in his air and manner a voluntary power over his whole body'. He 'looks and does as he likes', and is never confused or awkward. Likewise with prose sentences and actors, the implication is.

Later in the essay, he contrasts this easy, voluntary movement with the plebeian, London walk: 'a quick flexibility of movement, a smart jerk, an aspiring and confident tread, and an air, as if on the alert to keep the line of march'. But – and the critical qualification seems a shade unfair – there is not much 'grace or grandeur' in this cockney 'local strut'. Though this is hardly the easy dawdle of the *flâneur*, it's sufficiently close to the Belfast dander to make me think that Hazlitt's close observation of the semiotics of the cockney walk is admiring as well as dismissive. It differs from his curt remark in the next essay that, as a youth, he thought that Johnson's style was 'walking on stilts', by comparison with Burke's. The elevated, wooden progress of Johnson's predictable sentences is a type of anxiously stiff strut which needs to be seen in relation to the critical or aesthetic concept of the walk which Hazlitt outlines in these essays.

Introducing his major symbol for perfect prose, the Elgin Marbles, he says in 'Madame Pasta and Mademoiselle Mars' that we English also like 'the sway of the limbs and negligent grandeur' of those sculptures. They have the 'buoyancy of a wave of the sea, with all the ease and softness of flesh'. This in turn is another version of Thomson's wet colours resembling Hermione's breathing statue. Once again he's emphasizing physical expression and praising the mobility of the body, or 'tender pliancy of real flesh' as he terms it in the *Life of Titian*. Behind his intermittently anapaestic sentence – 'of a wave of the sea' – is that passage in *The Winter's Tale* where Florizel says to Perdita: 'When you do dance, I wish you / A wave o' th' sea.' Everything is drawn loosely but precisely together.

Yet that adjective 'negligent' in the phrase 'negligent grandeur' isn't a simple statement of value for the critic, because it carries aristocratic associations that disturb him. Discussing the type of person who lacks ease and self-confidence, he says in 'The Look of a Gentleman' that there is another sort who has too much 'negligence of manner and contempt for formal punctilios'. And then he offers a sketch of the notorious Foreign Secretary Castlereagh, who may be thought to possess a 'bold, licentious, slovenly, lounging character'. It might be said of him

without disparagement, that he looks more like a lord than like a gentleman. We see nothing petty or finical, assuredly, – nothing hard-bound or reined-in, – but a flowing outline, a broad free style. He sits in the House of Commons, with his hat slouched over his forehead, and a sort of stoop in his shoulders, as if he cowered over his antagonists, like a bird of prey over its quarry – 'hatching vain empires'. There is an irregular grandeur about him, an unwieldy power, loose, disjointed, 'voluminous and vast' – coiled up in the folds of its own purposes – cold, death-like, smooth and smiling, – that is neither quite at ease with itself, nor safe for others to approach!

This sketch complements Bunbury's – both men wear slouched hats. In its style it also aims to catch that particular negligent aristocratic quality which Hazlitt both deplores and admires. Thus the flowing outline and broad free style which Castlereagh possesses are both descriptive of the aristocratic politician and self-reflexive as regards Hazlitt's enjoyment of the process of prose composition. This is another portrait by Titian – or preliminary sketch – and when Hazlitt goes on to remark that Castlereagh may be compared to 'a loose sketch in oil, not properly hung', he is signalling the comparison. In 'loose' there is also the idea of the unfinished, which is important, as we have seen, to his critical aesthetic. But, as he says later in the same essay, a habit of plain speaking is 'totally contrary to the tone of good breeding'. Looseness, negligence, ease of carriage, run counter to honesty and directness. Hazlitt is caught in a contradiction.

His portrayal of Castlereagh is studied, but very spontaneously executed, with a beautiful transition from 'stoop in his shoulders' to the image of a hawk – in falconry 'stoop' means 'swoop'. The use of 'cowered' to describe the hovering movement cleverly catches the vindictive cowardice that informs this reactionary's exercise of power. This is like a moment out of Dante or Milton, and in a marvellously clever development of the image, he moves naturally to evoke Beelzebub addressing the parliament of fallen angels and trying to 'hatch' or plot vain empires. The adjective 'irregular', as we have seen, evokes the gothic, the Burkean, the monarchical and imaginative, as well as the romantic and unfinished. Hazlitt is attracted, as well as repelled, by this figure who changes in the quotation from *Paradise Lost* into the serpent-like monster before the gates of hell:

> The one seemed woman to the waist, and fair,
> But ended foul in many a scaly fold
> Voluminous and vast, a serpent armed
> With mortal sting.

Hazlitt's sketch of Castlereagh is both *bricolage* and a step towards a full portrait. It is complemented by a 'half-length', anonymous portrait of the reactionary reviewer and secretary to the Admiralty, John Wilson Croker, which Hazlitt published anonymously in the *Examiner* in 1824. Hazlitt, as we have seen, links Croker and Castlereagh in his obituary for John Cavanagh, the Irish racket-player, and in this sketch, whose authorship was established only ten years ago, we catch Hazlitt's loathing for Croker's politics and person:

Who is it that you meet sauntering along Pall Mall with fleering eyes, and nose turned up, as if the mud and the people offended him, – that has the look of an informer, or the keeper of a bagnio, or a dealer in marine stores, or an attorney struck off the list – a walking nuisance, with the sense of smell added to it, a moving *nausea*, with whose stomach nothing agrees, and that seeks some object to vent its spleen and ill-humour upon, that turns another way, afraid to express it –

'A dog, in forehead; and in heart, a deer;'

that stops to look at a print shop with a supercilious air of indifference, as if he would be thought to understand, but scorned to approve any thing – that finds fault with Hogarth, and can see no grace in Raphael; with his round shoulders, *hulking* stoop, slouching great-coat, and unwashed face, like the smut of his last night's conversation – that's let in and out of [Carlton] House, like a night-cart, full of filth, and crawling with lies – the Thersites of modern politics, the ring-leader of the Yahoos of the Press, the *ghoul* of the Boroughmongers; that preys on the carcase of patriot reputation; the Probert of the Allies, that 'bags the game' of liberty in the *Quarterly* that Duke Humphrey slew in the field – a Jack-pudding in wit, a pretender to sense, a tool of power, who thinks that a nick-name implies disgrace, as a title confers honour, that to calumniate is to convince, and whose genius is on an exact par with the taste and understanding of his employers – whose highest ambition is to be a *cat's-paw*, whose leading principle is to advocate his own interest by betraying his country and his species; to whom the very names of LIBERTY, HUMANITY, VIRTUE, PATRIOTISM, are a bye-word from the want of a single generous or manly feeling in his own breast; whose only pleasure is in malignity, and whose only pride is in degrading others to his own level; who affects literature, and fancies he writes like Tacitus, by leaving out the conjunction *and*; who helps himself to English out of Lindley Murray's Grammar, and maintains, with a pragmatical air,

that no one writes it but himself; who conceals his own writings and publishes those of other people, which he procures from his relations at a
lodging-house; who frightens elderly gentlewomen who ask him to dinner,
by pleasantly offering to carve a 'Holy-Ghost Pye,' that is, a Pigeon-Pye,
and gallantly calling for a bit of the 'Leg of the Saviour,' that is, a leg of
Lamb; who afterwards props the Bible and the Crown with ribaldry and
slander, but who has no objection to the Pope, the Turk or the Devil, provided they are on the side of his LEGITIMATE Patrons, and who keeps a
fellow even more impudent than himself, who, whenever the cause of
humanity is mentioned, sticks his hands in his sides, and cries HUMBUG,
and while nations are massacring, and the hopes of earth withered, plays a
tune on the salt-box for the amusement of the Ladies and Gentlemen of
Great Britain, and in honour of the Great Fûm?

This is the Hazlitt who so influenced Dickens: his portrait of Croker
might be a particularly malign version of Krook in *Bleak House*,
and the sketch shares with that novel a viscid, faecal, fetid atmosphere, whose nauseous texture communicates the squalor of the
legal and political institutions that dominate London. Probert was a
notorious criminal – 'a slippery malefactor', Stanley Jones, who discovered the portrait, calls him. A murderer, he was executed for
horse-stealing the following year, and the mention of his name again
lets us glimpse the fascination with the criminal underworld which
Dickens and Hazlitt shared.

Virginia Woolf's remark that Hazlitt's essays aren't 'independent
and self-sufficient' in the way we expect of the form, but fragments
broken off from 'some larger book', catches the unfinished, promis-
ing quality he seeks to impart to his writing. We have to construct
from a paragraph here, an essay there, an image, a stray remark, the
idea of an unwritten or unfinished epic of his times. Perhaps what
we need is an anthology of his writings that breaks open individual
essays and books in order to present fragmentary passages that
point to the entire Parthenon frieze on which he worked all his life.
Shorn of critical commentary, those panels and reliefs and abraded
statues might answer and relate to each other so completely that
they become ideally perfect – but with a perfection that is determined by the way in which each individual reader gives these
broken, unfinished pieces the diffused glow of passing form.

Epilogue

Early in 1830, Hazlitt moved into a rooming-house in Frith Street, Soho. He was given a back room on the third floor, and soon became seriously ill. He wrote an essay entitled 'The Sick Chamber', which was published unsigned in the August issue of the *New Monthly Magazine*. In it he describes and analyses his fatal illness:

It is amazing how little effect physical suffering or local circumstances have upon the mind, except while we are subject to their immediate influence. While the impression lasts, they are everything: when it is gone, they are nothing. We toss and tumble about in a sick bed; we lie on our right side, we then change to the left; we stretch ourselves on our backs, we turn on our faces; we wrap ourselves up under the clothes to exclude the cold, we throw them off to escape the heat and suffocation; we grasp the pillow in agony, we fling ourselves out of bed, we walk up and down the room with hasty or feeble steps; we return into bed; we are worn out with fatigue and pain, yet can get no repose for the one, or intermission for the other; we summon all our patience, or give vent to passion, and petty rage; nothing avails; we seem wedded to our disease, 'like life and death in disproportion met', we make new efforts, try new expedients, but nothing appears to shake it off, or promise relief from our grim foe: it infixes its sharp sting into us, or overpowers us by its sickly and stunning weight: every moment is as much as we can bear, and yet there seems no end of our lengthening tortures; we are ready to faint with exhaustion, or work ourselves up to frenzy: we 'trouble deaf Heaven with our bootless prayers': we think our last hour is come, or peevishly wish it were, to put an end to the scene; we ask questions as to the origin of evil and the necessity of pain; we 'moralize our complaints into a thousand similes'; we deny the use of medicine *in toto*, we have a full persuasion that all doctors are mad or knaves, that our object is to gain relief, and theirs (out of the perversity of human nature, or to seem wiser than we) to prevent it; we catechize the apothecary, rail at the nurse, and cannot so much as conceive the possibility that this state of things should not last for ever; we are even angry at those who would give us encouragement, as if they would make dupes or children of us; we might seek a release by poison, a halter, or the sword, but we have not strength of mind enough – our nerves are too shaken – to attempt even this poor revenge – when lo! a change comes, the spell falls off, and the next moment we forget all that has happened to us.

In a sentence whose length reminds us of the famous description of Coleridge tumbling from one intellectual fad to another, or the epic account of Scott's fiction, he enacts the drawn-out agony of his illness, and gives us a few images from his last days on earth. He wakes out of a short, uneasy doze, and sees 'a golden light shine through my white window-curtains on the opposite wall'. 'Is it the dawn of a new day, or the departing light of evening?' He is so drugged with opium, he can't tell. By puzzling over his doubt about what time of day it is, his attention is drawn 'a little out of myself to external objects', and he begins to consider whether it would not 'administer some relief to my monotonous languor, if I should call up a vivid picture of an evening sky I witnessed a short while before, the white fleecy clouds, the azure vault, the verdant fields and balmy air. In vain! The wings of fancy refuse to mount from my bed-side.'

The routine adjectives and predictable cadencing deny imagination. And what is outside has nothing in common 'with the closeness within'. The clouds disappear; the sky is 'instantly overcast and black'. He goes out for a walk in this scene – scene, not place, he doesn't tell us where – soon after he recovers, and with these favourite objects – clouds, sky, fields, air – interposed, he can no longer recall 'the tumbled pillow, the juleps or the labels, or the unwholesome dungeon' in which he was confined.

Though this is a piece of journalism hacked out by a dying man who needs a cheque to pay for his rent and his doctor's bills, the prose energy he spent his life affirming is still fitfully present, and those details of the pillow, juleps, and labels act like concrete facts in a Crabbe poem. Describing a brief remission in his illness, he says that in returning to life 'with half-strung nerves and shattered strength, we seem as when we first entered it with uncertain purposes and faltering aims'.

But he soon became ill again. A friend describes him lying 'ghastly, shrunk and helpless', unable to lift his hand from the coverlet, his voice 'diminished to a hoarse whisper, resembling the faint scream that I have heard from birds'. It was then he dictated his last letter. It was to Francis Jeffrey, the editor of the *Edinburgh Review*, whose intellect he had celebrated in *The Spirit of the Age*:

Dear Sir,

I am dying; can you send me 10£, and so consummate your many kindnesses to me?

W. Hazlitt

Jeffrey at once sent a cheque for £50, but it arrived after Hazlitt's death on 18 September 1830. His last words are reported to have been: 'Well, I've had a happy life.' His son, William, and Charles Lamb were at his side when he died. He was buried in St Anne's churchyard, a few yards from Shaftesbury Avenue, and this memorial, which stood until 1870, was erected:

Here rests

WILLIAM HAZLITT

Born April 10th, 1778, died Septr 18th, 1830.
He lived to see his deepest wishes gratified
as he has expressed them in his Essay
'On the Fear of Death.'
Viz:
"To see the downfall of the Bourbons,
And some prospect of good to mankind:"
(Charles X
was driven from France 29th July, 1830).
"To leave some sterling work to the world:"
(He lived to complete his 'Life of Napoleon').

His desire
That some friendly hand should consign
him to the grave was accomplished to a
limited but profound extent; on
these conditions he was ready to depart,

and to have inscribed on his tomb,
"Grateful and Contented."

He was
The first (unanswered) Metaphysician of the age.
A despiser of the merely Rich and Great:
A lover of the People, Poor or Oppressed:
A hater of the Pride and Power of the Few,
as opposed to the happiness of the Many;
A man of true moral courage,
Who sacrificed Profit and present Fame
To Principle,
And a yearning for the good of Human Nature.
Who was a burning wound to an Aristocracy,
That could not answer him before men,
And who may confront him before their Maker.

He lived and died
The unconquered Champion
of
Truth, Liberty, and Humanity,
"Dubitantes opera legite."

This stone
is raised by one whose heart is
with him, in his grave.

Biographical and Subject Appendix

Abernethy, John (1680–1740) Northern Irish Dissenting clergyman, leader of the non-subscribing Presbyterians (Unitarians). Opponent of the Test Act.

Adams, Henry (1838–1918) American historian and man of letters. Author of *The Education of Henry Adams* (1907).

Addison, Joseph (1672–1719) Essayist, poet, dramatist, and politician. A leading contributor, with Richard Steele, to *The Tatler* and *The Spectator*.

Aikin, John (1713–80) Unitarian scholar and tutor at the Warrington Academy, which lasted from 1757 to 1786, and has been termed the 'cradle of Unitarianism'.

Aikin, Lucy (1781–1864) Unitarian poet and novelist. Niece of Anna Letitia Barbauld.

Amory, Thomas (1691[?]–1788) Unitarian writer and scholar. Author of *The Life of John Buncle* (2 vols, 1756 and 1766).

Anti-Trinitarianism Several Christian churches rejected the doctrine of the Trinity in the Middle Ages, and several sects in the post-Reformation period also denied the Trinity. This denial of Christ's divinity and assertion of the oneness of God, contributed to the idea of scientific law.

Arianism Christian heresy first proposed by the fourth-century Alexandrian presbyter Arius, who affirmed that Christ is not a truly divine but a created being.

Bacon, Francis: Baron Verulam (1561–1626) Lawyer, statesman, philosopher, scientist. Hazlitt revered his *Essays*.

Bailly, Jean-Sylvain (1736–93) French philosopher and revolutionary politician.

Barbauld, Anna Letitia (1743–1825) Daughter of John Aikin. Unitarian writer, poet, and editor.

Bedford, duke of: Francis Russell (1765–1802) Whig politician attacked by Burke in *Letter to a Noble Lord* (1796) after he criticized Burke being given a pension.

Belsham, The Revd Thomas (1750–1829) Unitarian divine. Professor of divinity and resident tutor at Hackney New College.

Bentham, Jeremy (1748–1831) Utilitarian philosopher, economist, and theoretical jurist.

Biddle, John (1616–62) Father of English Unitarianism.

Blackwood, William (1776–1834) Scottish publisher and founder of *Blackwood's Edinburgh Magazine*.

Bolingbroke, Viscount: Henry St John (1678–1751) Leading Tory politician in the reign of Queen Anne (1702–14). Historian, philosopher, and libertine.

Bridgewater, Isabella (1791–1869) Hazlitt's second wife. She married him in 1824, and left him in 1827.

Brougham, Henry Peter: Baron Brougham (1778–1868) Lawyer, Whig politician, reformer, and orator.

Browne, Sir Thomas (1605–82) Baroque English prose stylist, physician, and antiquarian, best known for *Religio Medici*.

Burdett, Sir Francis (1770–1844) Reforming politician. Gaoled in 1810 for attacking the imprisonment of William Cobbett.

Burke, Edmund (1729–97) Irish statesman and political thinker. His *Reflections on the Revolution in France* (1790) attacked the Revolution, and prompted a pamphlet war.

Butler, Joseph (1692–1752) Anglican bishop and moral philosopher.

Canning, George (1770–1827) Foreign Secretary 1822–7. Prime Minister for four months during 1827.

Cashman (?–1817) Irish sailor executed for his alleged part in looting a London gun shop during the Spa Fields Riots in 1816.

Castlereagh, Viscount: Robert Stewart, second marquess of Londonderry (1769–1822) Reactionary Anglo-Irish politician who suppressed the 1798 rebellion in Ireland. British Foreign Secretary 1812–22. Architect of the Grand Alliance against Napoleon.

Cellini, Benvenuto (1500–71) Florentine sculptor, goldsmith, and writer. Published his famous *Autobiography* in 1562.

Charles I: Charles Stuart (1600–49) King of England, Scotland, and Ireland, 1625–49. Defeated in the Civil War (1642–6), convicted of treason, and beheaded.

Charles II: Charles Stuart (1630–85) Son of Charles I. With the restoration of the monarchy in 1660, Charles succeeded to the throne. His Roman Catholic sympathies and close links with France alienated many of his subjects. Between 1679 and 1681, the Whigs in Parliament sought to exclude his Roman Catholic brother James from succeeding to the throne.

Chatham, Lord: William Pitt the Elder (1708–88) Statesman, Prime Minister 1756–61 and 1766–8. Known as 'the Great Commoner', Pitt transformed Britain into an imperial power in the mid eighteenth century.

Christie, Thomas (1761–96) Co-founder with Joseph Johnson of the *Analytical Review*. Zealous Unitarian and political writer.

Cicero, Marcus Tullius (106–43 BC) Roman statesman, scholar, lawyer, writer, and orator.

Clare, John (1793–1864) Leading Romantic poet whose work, neglected for many decades, is beginning to receive significant critical attention.

Clarendon, first earl of: Edward Hyde (1609–74) Royalist statesman and historian. Exiled to France in 1667.

Clarke, Samuel (1675–1729) Theologian, philosopher, Anglican cleric, and exponent of Newtonian physics. Accused of Arianism.

Clarkson, Thomas (1760–1846) Leading abolitionist, who joined with William Wilberforce to fight the slave trade.

Claude Lorraine (1600–82) French landscape painter, one of the great masters of ideal landscapes.

Cobbett, William (1763–1835) English popular journalist who founded the *Political Register* in 1802. Brought up on a farm in Surrey, he championed rural England against changes brought about by the Industrial Revolution.

Coligny, Gaspard II de: Seigneur de Chatîllon (1519–72) Admiral of France and leader of the Huguenots (French Protestants) during the early years of the Wars of Religion. Murdered in the St Bartholomew's Day Massacre, 24 August 1572.

Colman, George, the Younger (1762–1836) Playwright and theatre manager.

Condillac, Étienne Bonnot de (1715–80) French philosopher and leading advocate of Locke's philosophy.

Crabbe, George (1754–1832) Late Augustan poet. *Peter Grimes* (1810) is his most famous verse tale.

Croker, John Wilson (1780–1857) Irish politician, essayist, and reviewer. A convinced Tory. Appointed Secretary to the Admiralty by Spencer Perceval.

Cruikshank, George (1792–1878) Artist, caricaturist, and illustrator. Rivalled and surpassed James Gillray, the leading caricaturist of the previous generation.

Davy, Humphrey Sir (1778–1829) Leading chemist, who discovered several chemical elements and invented the miner's safety lamp.

De Quincey, Thomas (1785–1859) Essayist and critic. *Confessions of an English Opium-Eater* (1822) is his most famous work.

Diderot, Denis (1713–84) French man of letters, philosopher, and chief editor of the *Encyclopédie*.

Doddridge, Philip (1702–51) Nonconformist divine.

Drennan, William (1754–1820) Ulster Presbyterian radical, poet, doctor, and pamphleteer. One of the founders of the United Irishmen.

Edgeworth, Maria (1767–1849) Anglo-Irish writer and founder of the regional novel in English. *Castle Rackrent* (1800) is her most famous novel.

Eldon, first earl of: John Scott (1751–1838) Reactionary lawyer and Lord Chancellor for much of the period between 1801 and 1827.

Ellenborough, Baron: Edward Law (1750–1818) Lord Chief Justice 1802–18. Reactionary, overbearing, and intolerant, he was humiliated by the two acquittals of William Hone in 1817.

Emlyn, Thomas (1663–1741) Presbyterian minister and writer who first publicly took the Unitarian name.

Emmet, Robert (1778–1803) Anglo-Irish republican who led the abortive 1803 uprising in Dublin.

Erskine, Thomas (1750–1823) Distinguished lawyer who defended various politicians and reformers against charges of treason, and helped check repression by the British government in the wake of the French Revolution.

Fawcett, Joseph (1758–1804) Unitarian preacher, poet, and writer who influenced Wordsworth and Hazlitt.

Fawkes, Guy (1570–1606) Roman Catholic conspirator who aimed to blow up the houses of parliament in November 1605.

Finnerty, Peter (1766–1822) Irish journalist, sentenced to the pillory and to two years' imprisonment for publishing a letter attacking the execution in 1797 of William Orr, an Ulster Presbyterian farmer, for administering the United Irish oath. In 1811, Finnerty was sentenced to 18 months' imprisonment for libelling Castlereagh. Shelley helped him financially. Described in the *DNB* as 'an eccentric Irishman, extremely quick, ready and hot-headed', he was a friend of Hazlitt.

Flaxman, John (1755–1826) Neoclassical sculptor, illustrator, and designer.

Fox, Charles James (1749–1806) Leading Whig politician who opposed George III's policies. Briefly Prime Minister in 1783. Supported the French Revolution, and helped to end the British slave trade and to restore rights to trial by jury in libel cases.

Franklin, Benjamin (1706–90) American author, inventor, scientist, and diplomat. Helped frame the Declaration of Independence and the US Constitution. Invented the lightning rod.

Frend, William (1757–1841) Reformer and scientific writer. Unitarian. Influenced Coleridge at Cambridge, where he was a Fellow until his expulsion in 1793.

Fuseli, Henry (1741–1825) Swiss painter who spent most of his working life in London.

Gallatin, Albert (1761–1849) US politician who worked closely with Thomas Jefferson.

Gay, John (1685–1732) Poet and dramatist. *The Beggar's Opera* (1728) is his most famous work.

George III (1738–1820) King of Great Britain and Ireland 1760–1820. Politically inept, he alienated the American colonies, and opposed Pitt's proposals for the emancipation of Irish Catholics in 1801. By 1811 he had become violently insane, and his son was made Regent.

George IV (1762–1830) Became Regent in 1811 and King in 1820. Lazy, louche, and profligate, he was highly unpopular.

Gifford, William (1756–1826) Chiefly remembered as editor of the *Quarterly Review*, founded by John Murray to combat the liberalism of the *Edinburgh Review*. Attacked by Hazlitt in *A Letter to William Gifford Esq.* (1819).

Gillray, James (1757–1815) Leading caricaturist. His political cartoons were immensely popular and influential.

Godwin, William (1756–1836) Social philosopher, novelist, and political journalist. His principal work is *An Enquiry concerning Political Justice* (1793). His *Caleb Williams* (1794) is the first political novel in English. Married Mary Wollstonecraft in 1797.

Goldsmith, Oliver (1730[?]–74) Anglo-Irish essayist, poet, novelist, and dramatist. His poem *The Deserted Village* (1770) and his play *She Stoops to Conquer* are his best-known works.

Gordon, Lord George (1751–93) Instigator of the anti-Catholic 'Gordon Riots' in 1780.

Graham, Maria (1785–1842) Author and traveller. Wrote the first biography of Poussin in English – *Memoirs of the Life of Poussin* (1820).

Hampden, John (1594–1643) Parliamentary leader who vigorously opposed Charles I's policies. Fought at the Battle of Edgehill (1642), and died in a skirmish with Royalist troops the following year.

Hardy, Thomas (1752–1832) Radical politician and shoe-maker. With a number of friends, he founded the London Corresponding Society in 1792, with the aim of promoting parliamentary reform.

Harrington, James (1611–77) Political philosopher. His major work, *The Commonwealth of Oceana* (1656), influenced Thomas Jefferson and other American presidents.

Haydon, Benjamin (1786–1846) Historical painter and writer.

Hazlitt, Grace (née Loftus, 1746–1837) Hazlitt's mother. Married The Revd William Hazlitt in 1766.

Hazlitt, John (1767–1837) Hazlitt's brother. Portrait painter and miniaturist.

Hazlitt, Margaret (1770–1841) Hazlitt's sister. Her journal, *The Journal of Margaret Hazlitt: Recollections of England, Ireland, and America*, was published in 1967.

Hazlitt, The Revd William (1732–1820) Hazlitt's father. Born in Shronell, Co. Tipperary, he studied at the University of Glasgow, and ministered to Unitarian congregations in England, Ireland, and the United States. He held uncompromising radical political views, and published several books of sermons.

Hazlitt, William III (1811–93) Hazlitt's son. Writer and lawyer.

Hazlitt, William Carew (1834–1913) Hazlitt's grandson. Writer.

Heidegger, Martin (1889–1976) German philosopher and Nazi. *Sein und Zeit* (1927) is his most famous work. His ontological philosophy is generally held to be separate from his politics.

Helvétius, Claude-Adrien (1715–71) French Enlightenment philosopher.

Hobbes, Thomas (1588–1679) Philosopher and political theorist. *Leviathan* (1651) is his most famous work.

Holcroft, Thomas (1745–1809) Radical novelist, journalist, and actor. Hazlitt was employed by his widow to edit his autobiography. *The Memoirs of the Late Thomas Holcroft* was published in 1816.

Hone, William (1780–1842) Radical publisher, satirist, and journalist. Tried and acquitted three times in 1817 for publishing pamphlets attacking the government.

Hume, David (1711–76) Scottish philosopher, historian, economist, and essayist. *A Treatise of Human Nature* (1739–40) is his most important work.

Hunt, Leigh (1784–1859) Essayist, journalist, editor, poet, and critic.

Launched the weekly *Examiner* with his brother John in 1808. A friend of Keats, Shelley, and Hazlitt.

Hutcheson, Francis (1694–1746) Ulster-Scots philosopher. Father of the Scottish Enlightenment. His *Inquiry into the Original of our Ideas of Beauty and Virtue* (1725) founded aesthetics as a subject.

Irving, The Revd Edward (1792–1834) Church of Scotland minister who was called to the Caledonian Chapel in London in 1822. An immensely popular preacher, he was excommunicated by the London presbytery in 1830.

James II: James Stuart (1633–1701) King of Great Britain 1685–8. Overthrown by the Glorious Revolution of 1688.

Jefferson, Thomas (1743–1826) Third President of the United States (1801–9) and first Secretary of State. Principal author of the Declaration of Independence.

Jeffreys, George (1645–89) Notoriously cruel judge who presided over the 'Bloody Assizes' of 1685, following the failure of the duke of Monmouth's rebellion.

Johnson, Joseph (1738–1809) Radical publisher known as 'the father of the book trade'. Co-founded the *Analytical Review* with Thomas Christie in 1788. Published Blake, Wordsworth, Coleridge, Joseph Priestley, Maria Edgeworth, as well as Hazlitt's first book, *An Enquiry into the Principles of Human Action*.

Joyce, The Revd Jeremiah (1763–1816) Unitarian minister and writer.

Junius: pseudonym of Sir Philip Francis (1740–1818) Author of a series of letters that appeared in the *Public Advertizer* (Jan. 1769–Jan. 1772). The letters, written from a Whig standpoint, bitterly attacked the duke of Grafton, Lord Mansfield, and George III.

Kean, Edmund (1789–1833) Great tragic actor, his innovative naturalistic style relied on agility rather than static posing.

Kippis, Andrew (1725–95) Unitarian divine and biographer. Tutor at Hackney New College.

Lamb, Charles (1775–1834) Essayist and critic, best known for *Essays of Elia* (1823, 1833). Unitarian background.

Lindsey, Theophilus (1723–1803) Unitarian cleric and reformer.

Liverpool, Lord: Robert Banks Jenkinson (1770–1828) After the assassination of Prime Minister Spencer Perceval in 1812, Liverpool became Prime Minister, and remained in office until 1827. He suspended the Habeas Corpus Act in Britain in 1817, and imposed other repressive measures in 1819.

Locke, John (1632–1704) Philosopher, physician, and political theorist. A committed and influential Whig, Locke was close to Anthony Ashley Cooper (later first earl of Shaftesbury). *An Essay Concerning Human Understanding* (1690) and *Two Treatises of Government* (1690) are among his most important works. Regarded as a Unitarian.

Lockhart, John Gibson (1794–1854) Critic, novelist, and biographer. Best known for his *Life of Sir Walter Scott* (1837–8). One of the main contributors to the Tory *Blackwood's Magazine*. His essay 'On the Cockney School of Poetry', published in *Blackwood's*, was the first of a series of attacks on Keats, Shelley, and Leigh Hunt.

Louis XIV (1638–1715) Absolutist King of France, known as the 'Sun King'. He succeeded to the throne in 1643, but until 1661 was subject to a regency under Cardinal Mazarin. Fought a series of wars with other European powers between 1667 and 1697.

Mackintosh, Sir James (1765–1832) Lawyer and politician who replied to Burke's *Reflections on the Revolution in France* (1790) in *Vindiciae Gallicae* (1791). He later renounced the principles expounded in that work, and became an admirer of Burke.

Macready, Charles (1793–1873) Actor-manager, a leading figure of the nineteenth-century stage.

Malthus, Thomas Robert (1766–1834) Economist and demographer, best known for *An Essay on the Principle of Population* (1795), which was attacked by Hazlitt and Cobbett. Unitarian background.

Mandeville, Bernard de (1670–1733) Prose-writer and philosopher who settled in England. Best known for *The Fable of the Bees* (1714).

Marat, Jean-Paul (1743–93) Leading French revolutionary. Assassinated by Charlotte Corday.

Marie-Antoinette (1755–93) Queen Consort of King Louis XVI of France (ruled 1774–93). Her political intrigues and extravagant court expenditure helped to discredit the French monarchy.

Marlborough, duke of: John Churchill (1650–1722) General who led British and Allied armies to important victories over Louis XIV of France. Transferred his allegiance from James II to William of Orange in 1688.

Martineau, James (1805–1900) Unitarian theologian and philosopher.

Mill, John Stuart (1806–73) Philosopher and political economist.

Molesworth, Viscount: Robert Molesworth (1656–1725) Anglo-Irish politician and scholar.

Monmouth, duke of: James Scott (1649–1685) Illegitimate son of Charles II. Championed by Anthony Ashley Cooper, first earl of Shaftesbury, as a Protestant successor to Charles, he led an unsuccessful rebellion against James II in 1685. Captured after the Battle of Sedgemoor, he was executed.

Montagu, Basil (1770–1851) Legal and miscellaneous writer and philanthropist. A friend of Hazlitt, Wordsworth, and Coleridge.

Moore, Tom (1779–1852) Irish poet and musician. Friend of Byron and Shelley. Moore's *Irish Melodies* (1807–34) are his most famous work.

Murray, John (1778–1843) Publisher and friend of Byron. With Sir Walter Scott he set up the Tory *Quarterly Review* in 1809.

Murray, Linley (1745–1826) American grammarian who settled in England in 1784. He published an *English Grammar* in 1795, a *Reader* in 1799, and a *Spelling Book* in 1804, all of which were widely used in schools. Cobbett and Hazlitt detested his classically based view of English grammar.

Newton, Isaac (1643–1727) Physicist and mathematician, author of *Principia* (1687). Regarded as a Unitarian.

Northcote, James (1746–1831) Portraitist and historical painter. A pupil of Sir Joshua Reynolds and later a friend of Hazlitt. Unitarian background.

Owen, Robert (1771–1858) Welsh manufacturer and social reformer. Set up New Lanark Mills in Lanarkshire, and introduced many improvements into the lives of the mill-workers. New Lanark became a place of pilgrimage for politicians and social reformers.

Paine, Tom (1737–1809) Radical political journalist and pamphleteer. His *Rights of Man* (1791) is a reply to Burke's *Reflections on the Revolution in France* (1790).

Patmore, Peter George (1786–1855) Journalist and friend of Hazlitt and Lamb. Many of the letters in *Liber Amoris* are addressed to him.

Phidias (fl. *c.* 490–430 BC) Athenian sculptor who directed the construction and design of the Parthenon. Carved the sculptures known as the Elgin Marbles.

Pindar (*c.* 518–*c.* 438 BC) Greatest of the Greek choral lyricists, master of the odes celebrating athletic victory.

Popple, William (1701–64) London merchant and dramatist. A nephew of Andrew Marvell and close associate of Locke, whose *Letter on Toleration* (1689) he translated from Latin.

Poussin, Nicolas (1594–1665) French classical painter.

Price, The Revd Richard (1723–91) Welsh Presbyterian (therefore Unitarian) minister, moral philosopher, and expert on insurance and finance. A friend of Joseph Priestley. His sermon 'A Discourse on the Love of our Country' (1789) angered Burke, who wrote *Reflections on the Revolution in France* (1790) in reply.

Priestley, Joseph (1733–1804) Unitarian cleric, scientist, political theorist, and educator. A supporter of the French Revolution, he emigrated to the United States in 1793 when a Birmingham church-and-king mob burned his church and laboratory.

Prince Regent: see George IV.

Pym, John (1583–1643) Leading puritan parliamentarian who organized the victorious parliamentary army in the first phase of the Civil War.

Reynolds, John Hamilton (1796–1852) Poet and friend of Keats.

Rickman, John (1771–1840) Statistician and friend of Southey.

Rogers, Samuel (1763–1855) Unitarian poet and banker.

Rosa, Salvator (1615–73) Italian painter, poet, satirist, and musician. Remembered for his wildly romantic landscapes.

Roscoe, William (1753–1831) Liverpool Unitarian, banker, poet, and historian. Hazlitt painted his portrait. His son married a sister of Sarah Walker.

Rousseau, Jean-Jacques (1712–78) Swiss-born philosopher and political theorist, whose novels and treatises inspired the French Revolution and the Romantic movement. Unitarian background.

Rubens, Peter Paul (1577–1640) Flemish baroque painter whose dynamic, sensuous paintings Hazlitt admired.

Russell, Lord William (1639–83) Whig martyr to English liberty. Executed, after a trial presided over by Judge Jeffreys, for his alleged part in the Rye House plot to assassinate Charles II and his brother James, duke of York (afterwards James II). Ancestor of Lord John Russell and Bertrand Russell.

Schlegel, August Wilhelm von (1767–1845) German romanticist, critic, and philosopher. Became famous for his lectures *Über dramatische Kunst und Literatur* (1809–11), translated by John Black as *Lectures on*

Dramatic Art and Literature (1815). Hazlitt reviewed the lectures favourably and at length in the *Edinburgh Review*.

Scott, John (1783–1821) Editor of the *London Magazine* in which De Quincey, Hazlitt, Lamb, Keats, and Clare were published. His attacks on *Blackwood's Magazine* culminated in a duel with J. H. Christie, a close friend of Lockhart, in which Scott was killed.

Shaftesbury, first earl of: Anthony Ashley Cooper (1621–83) Whig politician who held office after the restoration of Charles II, and then fought against the King's pro-Roman Catholic policies. The model for Dryden's Achitophel in *Absalom and Achitophel* (1681).

Shaftesbury, Lord, third earl of: Anthony Ashley Cooper (1671–1713) Moral and aesthetic philosopher. Like Francis Hutcheson, he opposed Hobbes's selfish theory of human conduct, and held that human beings were capable of holding disinterested views and ideas. His principal work is *Characteristics* (1711).

Shelburne, Lord: William Petty Fitzmaurice (1737–1805) Whig statesman prominent during the age of the American Revolution. Prime Minister July 1782–February 1783. A patron of Joseph Priestley, he was interested in science, and hated by Burke.

Shenstone, William (1714–63) Poet, essayist, and landscape gardener.

Sheridan, Richard Brinsley (1751–1816) Anglo-Irish actor-manager, playwright, and leading Whig politician. A friend of Charles James Fox, and Edmund Burke. A brilliant orator, he played a central part in the impeachment of Warren Hastings. *The School for Scandal* and *The Rivals* are his best-known plays.

Siddons, Sara (1755–1831) Leading tragic actor.

Sidney, Algernon (1622–83) Whig politician and martyr to English liberty executed for his alleged part in the Rye House plot to assassinate King Charles and James, duke of York. His *Discourses Concerning Government* (1698) is often seen as a work of republican political theory, though it argues for a limited monarchy. Sidney met his death like a classical Roman republican.

Smith, Adam (1723–90) Social philosopher and political economist. *The Wealth of Nations* (1776) is his best-known work. Taught Hazlitt's father at Glasgow University.

Smith, William (1756–1835) Distinguished Unitarian politician and businessman, acknowledged leader of the Dissenting cause while MP for Norwich. Grandfather of Florence Nightingale.

Socinianism Sixteenth-century religious group which rejected the doctrine of the Trinity and viewed Jesus as a man, not the son of God. The movement originated in Italy with the work of Lælius Socinus and his nephew, Faustus Socinus. The sect flourished principally in Poland. Socinian ideas influenced John Biddle, the father of English Unitarianism. For writers like Southey, 'Socinian' is a pejorative term for Unitarian.

Somers, Baron: John Somers (1651–1716) Statesman, chief minister to King William III from 1696 to 1700.

Southey, Robert (1774–1843) Poet and prose-writer associated with Wordsworth and Coleridge. A youthful supporter of the French Revolution, he became an influential Tory writer and an early advocate of the Welfare State. Attacked by Hazlitt and Byron.

Stanhope, Charles: third earl (1753–1816) Radical politician and scientist. Chairman of the Revolution Society (founded 1788).

Stoddart, John (1773–1856) Journalist, brother of Hazlitt's first wife. Founded and edited The *New Times*. Known as 'Dr Slop'. A convinced Tory.

Stoddart, Sarah (1774–1840) Hazlitt's first wife. Separated from him in 1819, divorced in 1822, they remained friends until his death.

Taylor, Jeremy (1613–67) Anglican cleric and royalist. Admired for his prose style. *The Rule and Exercises of Holy Living* (1650) and *The Rule and Exercises of Holy Dying* (1651) are his best-known works.

Taylor, John (1781–1864) A partner in the publishing firm of Taylor and Hessey, he published Clare, Keats, and Hazlitt. Edited the *London Magazine* 1821–4.

Taylor, William (1756–1836) Unitarian author and translator. Contributed over 800 reviews, essays, and translations to the *Monthly Magazine*, an influential radical publication founded in 1796 by Richard Phillips, a Jacobin and friend of Paine. Its first editor was the Unitarian John Aikin. In a footnote to 'Mr Jeffrey' in *The Spirit of the Age*, Hazlitt says: 'The style of philosophical criticism, which has been the boast of the *Edinburgh Review*, was first introduced into the *Monthly Magazine* about the year 1796 in a series of articles by Mr William Taylor of Norwich.'

Test Act and Corporation Acts Required those who held civil or military positions to prove their loyalty to the State Church by receiving the sacrament of the Lord's Supper in the Church of England. The first Test Act was passed in 1673, and the combined Test and Corporation Acts were finally repealed in 1823.

Thelwall, John (1764–1834) Radical writer and editor. One of the defendants in the 1794 Treason Trials.

Thomson, James (1700–48) Scottish poet. His poem *The Seasons* (1726–30) was immensely popular and influential.

Titian (*c.* 1487–1576) Great Italian painter whose handling of oil paint is unrivalled.

Tone, Wolfe (1763–98) Irish republican, one of the leaders of the 1798 rebellion.

Tooke, John Horne (1736–1812) Radical politician and philologist. One of the defendants in the 1794 Treason Trials. His philological work *The Diversions of Purley* (1786–1805) attacks Samuel Johnson's and Lindley Murray's views of the English language.

Unitarianism Unitarians deny the divinity of Christ and believe that God is one, not triune. They trace their beliefs to certain unorthodox theological views in the early Christian Church and the Reformation period. Unitarian churches were established in Hungary, Romania, and Poland in the sixteenth century and in England, the United States, and other countries in the eighteenth and nineteenth centuries. Unitarianism does not begin with the idea of God, or a church, but with the study of human nature. It dreads to be 'artificial' or 'insincere', and has no obligatory rites, ceremonies, or dogmas. It rejects the traditional doctrines of the Atonement, the Trinity, original sin, vicarious punishment, and eternal hell, and regards evil as having no substance. Unitarianism is closely associated with social and political reform, educational theory, science, economics, journalism, and periodical literature. Historically, it has been a significant and influential force in British culture: Unitarians have been described as 'an intellectual aristocracy in the ranks of Dissent', and are often known as 'Rational Dissenters'. Persecuted in the 1790s, Unitarians became powerful and respected members of the middle class in the nineteenth century.

Wakefield, Gilbert (1756–1801) Classical scholar and controversial Unitarian. Tutor at Warrington Academy, then at Hackney New College. Gaoled for two years for publishing a pamphlet attacking the bishop of Llandaff.

Walker, Sarah (1800–78) Daughter of the family with whom Hazlitt lodged in Southampton Buildings, near Chancery Lane, after his separation from Sarah Hazlitt in 1817. He fell obsessively in love with her, describing his passion in *Liber Amoris* (1823).

Wellington, duke of: Arthur Wellesley (1769–1852) Anglo-Irish soldier and politician. Defeated Napoleon at the Battle of Waterloo (1815).

A member of Tory anti-reform cabinets 1818–27. Prime Minister 1828–30.

Whitelocke, Bulstrode (1605–75) Politician and diplomat. On the parliamentary side during the Civil War.

Wilberforce, William (1759–1833) Politician and philanthropist, prominent from 1787 in the struggle to abolish the slave trade.

William of Orange (also William III of Great Britain) (1650–1702) Ruler who governed the United Provinces of The Netherlands as Stadtholder from 1672 and reigned in Great Britain from 1689. He accepted an invitation from opponents of the Catholic James II, and landed in England in 1688.

Windham, William (1750–1810) Politician and statesman. A friend of Johnson and Burke, and an associate of Cobbett.

Wollstonecraft, Mary (1759–97) Writer and journalist who worked closely with Joseph Johnson. Married William Godwin in 1797, died shortly after giving birth to a daughter, Mary, who married Percy Shelley.

Wyclif, John (c. 1324–84) Theologian, philosopher, church reformer, and promoter of two translations of the Bible. A forerunner of the Reformation.

Wyvill, Christopher (1740–1820) Advocate of parliamentary reform.

Hazlitt's Publications

An Essay on the Principles of Human Action (1805)
Free Thoughts on Public Affairs: or, Advice to a Patriot (1806)
Preface to an Abridgment of Abraham Tucker's Light of Nature Pursued (1807)
Advertisement and Biographical and Critical Notes from *The Eloquence of the British Senate* (1807)
A Reply to Malthus's Essay on Population (1807)
Prospectus of a History of English Philosophy (1809)
A New and Improved Grammar of the English Tongue (1810)
Lectures on English Philosophy (delivered 1812–13, first published in *Literary Remains of the Late William Hazlitt,* 1836)
Memoirs of Thomas Holcroft (1816)
The Round Table (1817)
Characters of Shakespear's Plays (1817)
Lectures on the English Poets (delivered and published 1818)
A View of the English Stage (1818)
Lectures on the English Comic Writers (delivered 1818, published 1819)
A Reply to 'Z' (1818, published 1923)
Political Essays (1819)
Lectures on the Dramatic Literature of the Age of Elizabeth (delivered 1819, published 1820)
A Letter to William Gifford, Esq. (1819)
Table-Talk (1821)
Prefatory Remarks to Oxberry's *New English Drama* (1818–25)
Liber Amoris; or, The New Pygmalion (1823)
Characteristics (1823)
Preface and Critical List of Authors from *Select British Poets* (1824)
Sketches of the Principal Picture Galleries in England (1824)
The Spirit of the Age (1825)
Notes of a Journey through France and Italy (1826)
The Plain Speaker (1826)

Conversations of Northcote (1830)
The Life of Napoleon Buonaparte (1828–30)

Volumes XVI–XX of Howe's Collected edition comprise:
  Contributions to the *Edinburgh Review*
  Uncollected Essays
  Art Criticism
  Dramatic Criticism
  Literary Criticism
  Political Criticism
  Miscellaneous Writings

Bibliography

Abrams, M. H., *The Mirror and the Lamp: Romantic Theory and the Critical Tradition* (New York: Oxford University Press, 1953).

Adams, M. Ray, *Studies in the Literary Backgrounds of English Radicalism: With Special Reference to the French Revolution* (Lancaster, Pa.: Franklin and Marshall College Studies, 1947).

Addison, Joseph, *The Miscellaneous Works*, ed. A. C. Guthkelch, 3 [*recte* 2] vols (London: G. Bell and Sons, 1914).

Aikin, Arthur (ed.), *The Annual Review, and History of Literature; for 1803*, vol. II (London: Printed for T. N. Longman and O. Rees by T. Gillet, 1804).

[Aikin, J.], *An Address to the Dissenters of England on their Late Defeat* (London: Printed for J. Johnson, 1790).

– *Letters from a Father to his Son, On Various Topics Relative to Literature and the Conduct of Life. Written in the Years 1792 and 1793* (London: Printed for J. Johnson, 1793).

– *Letters from a Father to his Son, On Various Topics Relative to Literature and the Conduct of Life. Vol. II. Written in the Years 1798 and 1799* (London: Printed for J. Johnson, 1800).

Albrecht, W. P., *Hazlitt and the Creative Imagination* (Lawrence, Kan.: University of Kansas Press, 1965).

[Amory, Thomas], *The Life of John Buncle, Esq.; Containing Various Observations and Reflections, Made in Several Parts of the World; and Many Extraordinary Relations*, 2 vols (London: Printed for J. Noon and printed for J. Johnson and B. Davenport, 1756, 1766).

The Analytical Review, or History of Literature Domestic and Foreign, on an Enlarged Plan. Containing Scientific Abstracts of Important and Interesting Works, Published in English; A General Account of Such as are of Less Consequence, with Short Characters; Notices, or Reviews of Valuable Foreign Books; Criticisms on New Pieces of Music and Works of Art; and the Literary Intelligence of Europe, &c. Vol. I *From May to August, Inclusive, 1788* (London: Printed for J. Johnson, 1788).

Anderson, R. G. W., and Lawrence, Christopher (eds), *Science, Medicine and Dissent: Joseph Priestley (1733–1804) – Papers Celebrating the 250th Anniversary of the Birth of Joseph Priestley together with a Catalogue of an Exhibition held at the Royal Society and the Wellcome Institute for the History of Medicine* (London: Wellcome Trust/Science Museum, 1987).

Andrews, Jeanne, 'Bacon and the "Dissociation of Sensibility"', *Notes and Queries*, vol. 199 (Nov. 1954): 484–6.

Anonymous, 'Cashman', *Cobbett's Weekly Political Pamphlet*, 32/11 (15 Mar. 1817): 334–46.

Anonymous, 'Joseph Hunter on the Hazlitts', *Notes and Queries*, vol. 202 (June 1957): 265–6.

Anonymous, 'Review of Wm. Hazlitt, Table-Talk; or Original Essays (Vol. II)', *The London Museum; or Record of Literature, Fine Arts, Science, Antiquities, The Drama, &c.*, no. 12 (13 July 1822): 177–9.

The Anti-Jacobin Review and Magazine; or, Monthly Political and Literary Censor (1799).

Arnold, Matthew, *The Complete Prose*, ed. R. H. Super (Ann Arbor: University of Michigan Press, 1960–77).

– *A Matthew Arnold Prose Selection*, ed. with introduction and notes by John D. Jump (London: Macmillan; New York: St Martin's Press, 1965).

Art, 'Review of Edmund Burke, *Reflections on the Revolution in France, &c.*, *Analytical Review*, 8 (Dec. 1790): 408–14.

– 'Review of Edmund Burke, *Reflections on the Revolution in France, and on the Proceedings in Certain Societies in London Relative to that Event. In a Letter Intended to have been sent to a Gentleman in Paris'*, *Analytical Review*, 8 (Nov. 1790): 295–307.

Auden, W. H., *The English Auden: Poems, Essays and Dramatic Writings 1927–1939*, ed. Edward Mendelson (London: Faber and Faber, 1977).

Bacon, Francis, *The Advancement of Learning*, ed. G. W. Kitchin, introduction by Arthur Johnston (1605; repr. London: J. M. Dent & Sons, 1973).

Baker, Herschel, *William Hazlitt* (Cambridge, Mass.: Belknap Press of Harvard University Press; London: Oxford University Press, 1962).

Barrell, John, *The Political Theory of Painting from Reynolds to Hazlitt: 'The Body of the Public'* (New Haven and London: Yale University Press, 1986).

Bate, Jonathan, *Shakespearean Constitutions: Politics, Theatre, Criticism 1730–1830* (Oxford: Clarendon Press, 1989).

Belsham, Thomas, *Discourses, Doctrinal and Practical; Delivered in Essex*

Street Chapel, 2 vols (London: Printed for R. Hunter, 1826–7).
- *Elements of the Philosophy of the Mind, and of Moral Philosophy. To which is Prefixed a Compendium of Logic* (London: J. Johnson, 1801).
- *Freedom of Enquiry, and Zeal in the Diffusion of Christian Truth, Asserted and Recommended in a Discourse Delivered at Bristol, July 9, 1800, before the Society of Unitarian Christians, Established in the West of England, for Promoting Christian Knowledge and the Practice of Virtue, by the Distribution of Books* (London: G. Woodfall; London: J. Johnson, 1800).
- 'Memoir of the Reverend Theophilus Lindsey, M.A.', in *idem, Sermon*, pp. 51–70.
- *Memoirs of the Late Reverend Theophilus Lindsey, M.A. Including a Brief Analysis of his Works; together with Anecdotes and Letters of Eminent Persons, his Friends and Correspondents: Also a General View of the Progress of the Unitarian Doctrine in England and America* (London: J. Johnson and Co., 1812).
- *A Sermon, Occasioned by the Death of the Rev. Theophilus Lindsey, M.A., Preached at the Chapel in Essex Street, Strand, November 13th, 1808* (London: J. Johnson, 1808).
- *The Sufferings of Unitarians in Former Times, Urged as a Ground of Thankfulness for their Recovered Liberties: A Discourse Preached at Essex Street Chapel, July 25, 1813, Being the First Sunday after 'The Act to Relieve Persons who Impugn the Doctrine of the Trinity' had Received the Royal Assent* (London: J. Johnson and Co., 1813).
Bennet, George, *The History of Bandon, and the Principal Towns in the West Riding of County Cork*, enlarged edn (Cork: Francis Guy, 1869).
Biddle, John, *The Apostolical and True Opinion concerning the Holy Trinity, Revived and Asserted: Partly by Twelve Arguments Levied against the Traditional and False Opinion about the Godhead of the Holy Spirit. Partly by a Confession of Faith Touching the Three Persons. Both which having been formerly set forth, were much Altered and Augmented, with Explications of Scripture, and with Reasons: And Finally, with Testimonies of the Fathers, and of Others. All Reprinted, Anno 1653. And Now Again with the Life of the Author Prefixed, Anno Dom. 1691* (n. pl.: n. imp., 1691).
- *A Brief Scripture-Catechism for Children. Wherein, Notwithstanding the Brevity thereof, All Things Necessary unto Life and Godliness are Contained* (London: Printed by Ja: Cottrel, for Rich. Moone, 1654).
[–] *A Confession of Faith Touching the Holy Trinity, According to the Scripture* (London: n. imp., 1648).

[– (ed.)], *The Testimonies of Irenæus, Justin Martyr, Tertullian, Novatianus, Theophilus, Origen, (Who Lived in the Two First Centuries after Christ was Born, or thereabouts): As also, of Arnobius, Lactantius, Eusebius, Hilary, and Brightman; Concerning that One God, and the Persons of the Holy Trinity. Together with Observations on the Same* (London: n. imp., n.d.).

Blake, William, *Writings*, ed. G. E. Bentley, Jr., 2 vols (Oxford: Clarendon Press, 1978).

Bloom, Harold (ed.), *Modern Critical Views: William Hazlitt* (New York: Chelsea House Publishers, 1986).

Bowra, C. M., Introduction to Pindar, *The Odes*, pp. ix–xviii.

Boyce, D. George, *et al.* (ed.), *Political Thought in Ireland since the Seventeenth Century* (London and New York: Routledge and Kegan Paul, 1993).

Brett, R. L., *The Third Earl of Shaftesbury: A Study in Eighteenth-Century Literary Theory* (London: Hutchinson's University Library, 1951).

Bromwich, David, *Hazlitt: The Mind of a Critic* (New York and Oxford: Oxford University Press, 1983).

– (ed.), *Romantic Critical Essays* (Cambridge: Cambridge University Press, 1987).

Brown, Peter, *The Chathamites: A Study in the Relationship between Personalities and Ideas in the Second Half of the Eighteenth Century* (London: Macmillan; New York: St Martin's Press, 1967).

Burke, Edmund, *Reflections on the Revolution in France and on the Proceedings of Certain Societies in London Relative to that Event*, ed. with introduction by Conor Cruise O'Brien (1790; repr. Harmondsworth: Penguin Books, 1969).

– *The Writings and Speeches*, gen. ed. Paul Langford (Oxford: Clarendon Press, 1981–).

Burns, Robert, *The Letters*, ed. J. De Lancey Ferguson, 2nd edn, ed. G. Ross Roy, 2 vols (Oxford: Clarendon Press, 1985).

Butler, Marilyn, 'Satire and the Images of Self in the Romantic Period: The Long Tradition of Hazlitt's *Liber Amoris*', in Rawson (ed.), *English Satire*, pp. 209–25.

Butterfield, H., *The Whig Interpretation of History* (London: G. Bell and Sons, 1931).

Byron, Lord, *Don Juan*, ed. T. G. Steffan *et al.* (2nd var. edn, 1971, with mds; repr. Harmondsworth: Penguin Books, 1973).

Carlyle, Thomas, and Welsh, Jane, *The Collected Letters*, gen. ed. Charles Richard Sanders, ed. Clyde de L. Ryals and Kenneth J. Fielding (Durham, NC, and London: Duke University Press, 1970–).

Carnall, Geoffrey, 'Letter to the Editor: A Hazlitt Contribution', *Times Literary Supplement*, no. 2,681 (19 June 1953): 397.

Cassirer, Ernst, *The Philosophy of the Enlightenment*, trans. Fritz C. A. Koelln and James P. Pettegrove (1932; Princeton, NJ: Princeton University Press, 1951).

Cellini, Benvenuto, *The Autobiography*, trans. with introduction by George Bull (1728; repr. Harmondsworth: Penguin Books, 1956).

Chandler, George, *William Roscoe of Liverpool*, with introduction by Alfred Shennan, preface by Vere E. Cotton (London: B. T. Batsford, 1953).

Chard, Leslie F. II, *Dissenting Republican: Wordsworth's Early Life and thought in their Political Context* (The Hague and Paris: Mouton, 1972).

– 'Joseph Johnson: Father of the Book Trade', *Bulletin of the New York Public Library*, 79/1 (Autumn 1975): 51–82.

Chaudhuri, Amit, 'Text and Intertextuality in the Poetry of D. H. Lawrence' (University of Oxford D. Phil. thesis, 1993).

Clare, John, *John Clare by Himself*, ed. Eric Robinson and David Powell, wood engraving by John Lawrence (Ashington: The Mid-Northumberland Arts Group; Manchester: Carcanet Press, 1996).

– *John Clare*, ed. Eric Robinson and David Powell (Oxford and New York: Oxford University Press, 1984).

– 'To the Cowslip', *London Magazine*, 5/29 (May 1822): 444.

Clark, G. Kitson, *The English Inheritance*: *An Historical Essay* (London: SCM Press, 1950).

Cobban, Alfred, *Edmund Burke and the Revolt against the Eighteenth Century*: *A Study of the Political and Social Thinking of Burke, Wordsworth, Coleridge and Southey*, 2nd edn (London: George Allen & Unwin, 1960).

Cobbett, William, *The Autobiography*: *The Progress of a Plough-Boy to a Seat in Parliament*, ed. William Reitzel, new edn (London: Faber and Faber, 1947).

– *A Grammar of the English Language, In a Series of Letters; Intended for the Use of Schools and of Young Persons in General; but More Especially for the Use of Soldiers, Sailors, Apprentices, and Plough-Boys. To which are Added Six Lessons, Intended to Prevent Statesmen from Using False Grammar, and from Writing in an Awkward Manner*, new edn (London: Ward, Lock, and Co., n.d. [1880]).

– *Selections from Cobbett's Political Works*: *Being a Complete Abridgement of the 100 Volumes which Comprise the Writings of 'Porcupine' and the 'Weekly Political Register' with notes, historical and explanatory*, by John M. Cobbett and James P. Cobbett, 4 vols (London: Anne Cobbett; Edinburgh: W. Tait; Manchester: W. Willis, n.d.).

Coleridge, Samuel Taylor, *Lay Sermons. I. The Statesman's Manual. II. Blessed are Ye that Sow Beside All Waters*, ed. with the author's last corrections and notes by Derwent Coleridge, 3rd edn, 4 vols (London: Edward Moxon, 1852).

– *The Literary Remains*, collected and ed. by Henry Nelson Coleridge, 4 vols (London: William Pickering, 1836–9).

Colley, Linda, *Britons: Forging the Nation 1707–1837*, corrected pbk edn (London: Pimlico, 1994).

Cook, B. F., *The Elgin Marbles* (London: Published for the Trustees of the British Museum by British Museum Press, 1984).

Cooper, Anthony Ashley, third earl of Shaftesbury, *Characteristics of Men, Manners, Opinions, Times, &c.* (1711).

Coote, Stephen, *John Keats: A Life* (London: Hodder & Stoughton, 1995).

Cranston, Maurice, *John Locke: A Biography* (London: Longmans, Green and Co., 1957).

Croll, Morris W., 'The Baroque Style in Prose', in Kemp Malone and Marten B. Ruud (eds), *Studies in English Philology* (1929), pp. 427–56.

Cunningham, Valentine, *Everywhere Spoken Against: Dissent in the Victorian Novel* (Oxford: Clarendon Press, 1975).

Davis, Richard W., *Dissent in Politics 1780–1830: The Political Life of William Smith, MP* (London: Epworth Press, 1971).

Deane, Seamus, *The French Revolution and Enlightenment in England 1789–1832* (Cambridge, Mass.: Harvard University Press, 1988).

– *Strange Country: Modernity and Nationhood in Irish Writing since 1790* (Oxford: Clarendon Press, 1996).

– (gen. ed.), *The Field Day Anthology of Irish Writing*, ed. Andrew Carpenter and Jonathan Williams, 3 vols (Derry: Field Day Publications, 1991).

De Quincey, Thomas, *Recollections of the Lakes and the Lake Poets*, ed. with introduction by David Wright ([1834–40]; repr. Harmondsworth: Penguin Books, 1970).

Dickens, Charles, *Our Mutual Friend*, ed. with introduction by Stephen Gill (1865; repr. Harmondsworth: Penguin Books, 1971).

Diderot, Denis, 'Rameau's Nephew' and 'D'Alembert's Dream', trans. with introductions by L. W. Tancock (repr. Harmondsworth: Penguin Books, 1966).

Dostoyevsky, Fyodor, *Notes from Underground*, in *idem*, 'Notes from Underground', pp. 90–203.

– 'Notes from Underground', 'White Nights', 'The Dream of a Ridiculous Man', and Selections from 'The House of the Dead', trans. with foreword by Andrew R. MacAndrew (1864, 1848, 1877, 1859–61; repr. New York and Toronto: New American Library; London: New English Library, 1961).

Drennan, William, 'The Intended Defence (1794)', in Deane (gen. ed.), Field Day Anthology, III. 319–26.

Dryden, John, The Poems and Fables, ed. James Kinsley (London and Oxford: Oxford University Press, 1962).

Dunn, John, Locke (Oxford and New York: Oxford University Press, 1984).

Eagleton, Terry, 'William Hazlitt: An Empiricist Radical', New Blackfriars (Mar. 1973): pp. 108–17.

[Edgeworth, Maria], Castle Rackrent, An Hibernian Tale. Taken from Facts, and from the Manners of the Irish Squires, before the Year 1782 (London: Printed for J. Johnson by J. Crowder, 1800).

– Castle Rackrent, ed. with introduction by George Watson (1800; repr. Oxford and New York: Oxford University Press, 1980).

Eliot, T. S., Selected Essays, 3rd enlarged edn (London: Faber and Faber, 1951).

Emmet, Thomas Addis, Memoir of Thomas Addis and Robert Emmet, with their Ancestors and Immediate Family, 2 vols (New York: Emmet Press, 1915).

Enfield, William, The Speaker: Or, Miscellaneous Pieces, Selected from the Best English Writers, and Disposed under Proper Heads, with a View to Facilitate the Improvement of Youth in Reading and Speaking. To which is Prefixed an Essay on Elocution (London: J. Johnson, 1774).

Fawcett, Joseph, Sermons Delivered at the Sunday-Evening Lecture, For the Winter Season, at the Old Jewry, 2 vols (London: printed for J. Johnson, 1795).

Fearn, John, An Essay on Consciousness; Or, A Series of Evidences of a Distinct Mind, 2nd edn (London: Longman, Rees, Orme and Brown, 1812).

Foot, Michael, Debts of Honour (London: Davis Poynter, 1980).

Fraser, Antonia, Cromwell: Our Chief of Men (London: Weidenfeld and Nicolson, 1973).

Friel, Brian, Philadelphia, Here I Come! (London: Faber and Faber, 1965).

Frost, Robert, The Poetry, ed. Edward Connery Lathem (1969; repr. London: Jonathan Cape, 1971).

Genette, Gérard, Figures of Literary Discourse, trans. Alan Sheridan with introduction by Marie-Rose Logan (Oxford: Basil Blackwell, 1982).

Gibbon, Edward, *The Letters*, ed. J. E. Norton, 3 vols (London: Cassell and Company, 1956).

Godwin, William, *St Leon*, ed. with introduction by Pamela Clemit, 4th edn (1831; repr. Oxford and New York: Oxford University Press, 1994).

Goldsmith, Oliver, *Selected Writings*, ed. with introduction, notes, and foreword by John Lucas (Manchester: Fyfield Books, 1988).

Gordon, Ian A., *The Movement of English Prose* (London: Longmans, 1966).

Graham, Maria, *Memoirs of the Life of Nicolas Poussin* (London: Longman, Hurst, Rees, Orme, and Brown; Edinburgh: A. Constable and Co., 1820).

Gravil, Richard, and Lefebure, Molly (eds), *The Coleridge Connection: Essays for Thomas McFarland* (Basingstoke and London: Macmillan, 1989).

Hackwood, Frederick William, *William Hone: His Life and Times* (London and Leipsic: T. Fisher Unwin, 1912).

Hazlitt, Margaret, *The Journal: Recollections of England, Ireland, and America*, ed. and annotated by Ernest J. Moyne (Lawrence, Kan.: University of Kansas Press, 1967).

Hazlitt, W., Sr., *Sermons for the Use of Families*, 2 vols (London: printed for J. Johnson, 1808).

Hazlitt, W. Carew, *Four Generations of a Literary Family: The Hazlitts in England, Ireland, and America – their Friends and their Fortunes 1725–1896*, prts repr. from minutes by John Hazlitt, 2 vols (London and New York: George Redway, 1897).

– *The Hazlitts: An Account of their Origin and Descent – With Autobiographical Particulars of William Hazlitt (1778–1830), Notices of his Relatives and Immediate Posterity, and a Series of Illustrative Letters (1772–1865)* (Edinburgh: Printed by Ballantyne, Hanson & Co., 1911).

– *The Hazlitts: Part the Second – A Narrative of the Later Fortunes of the Family – With a Survey of the Western and Other Suburbs of London as they were Sixty Years Since* (Edinburgh: Printed by Ballantyne, Hanson & Co., 1912).

– *Memoirs of William Hazlitt. With Portions of his Correspondence*, 2 vols (London: Richard Bentley, 1867).

Hazlitt, William, *The Complete Works*, ed. P. P. Howe, aft. edn A. R. Waller and Arnold Glover, 21 vols (London and Toronto: J. M. Dent & Sons, 1930–4).

– *The Eloquence of the British Senate* (London: Thomas Ostell, 1807).

- *Hazlitt Painted by Himself*, prs. Catherine MacDonald MacLean (London: C. and J. Temple, 1948).
- *The Letters*, ed. Herschel Moreland Sikes, with Willard Hallam Bonner and Gerald Lahey (New York: New York University Press, 1978).
- 'On the Elgin Marbles', *London Magazine*, 5/29 (May 1822): 445–55.
- 'On the Elgin Marbles. By the Author of "Table-Talk"', *London Magazine*, 5/26 (Feb. 1822): 153–6.
- *The Plain Speaker*, with notes by A. R. Waller and Arnold Glover and an introduction by P. P. Howe (1826; repr. London and Toronto: Published by J. M. Dent & Sons; New York: E. P. Dutton & Co. [1928]).
- 'On the Punishment of Death', Folger Shakespeare Library, T.6.18, fols 17–36.
- 'To the Editor of the Monthly Magazine. Proposal for the Basis of a New System of Metaphysical Philosophy', *Monthly Magazine*, 27/181 (1 Feb. 1809): 15–19.
- *The Spirit of the Age or Contemporary Portraits*, ed. E. D. Mackerness, gen. ed. Mark Roberts, 2nd edn (1825; repr. Plymouth: Northcote House, 1991).
- 'Table-Talk. No. XI. On a Landscape of Nicolas Poussin', *London Magazine*, 4/20 (Aug. 1821): 176–9.
- Healy, Thomas, and Sawday, Jonathan (eds), *Literature and the English Civil War* (Cambridge: Cambridge University Press, 1990).
- Heidegger, Martin, *Basic Writings from 'Being and Time' (1927) to 'The Task of Thinking' (1964)*, ed. with general introduction and introduction to each selection by David Farrell Krell (London and Henley: Routledge & Kegan Paul, 1978).
- Hobbes, Thomas, *Leviathan*, with introduction by K. R. Minogue (1651; repr. London: Dent; New York: Dutton, 1973).
- Hogarth, William, *The Analysis of Beauty. Written with a View of Fixing the Fluctuating Ideas of Taste* (London: Printed by J. Reeves for the Author, 1753).
- Holcroft, Thomas, 'Hazlitt's Death Bed', *Monthly Magazine and British Register* (Mar. 1833): 257–8.
- Holt, Raymond V., *The Unitarian Contribution to Social Progress in England*, 2nd rev. edn (London: Lindsey Press, 1952).
- Hone, William, *The Political House that Jack Built* (London: William Hone, 1819).
- Hopkins, Gerard Manley, *Further Letters: Including his Correspondence with Coventry Patmore*, ed. with notes and introduction by Claude

Colleer Abbott, 2nd edn, rev. and enl. (London: Oxford University Press, 1956).
- *The Letters to Robert Bridges*, ed. with notes and introduction by Claude Colleer Abbott, 2nd (rev.) imp. (London: Geoffrey Cumberlege; Oxford University Press, 1955).
- *The Poetical Works*, ed. Norman H. MacKenzie (Oxford: Clarendon Press, 1990).
Houck, James A., *William Hazlitt: A Reference Guide* (Boston, Mass.: G. K. Hall & Co., 1977).
Howe, P. P., *The Life of Hazlitt*, introduced by Frank Swinnerton (1932; repr. with introduction, Harmondsworth: Penguin Books in association with Hamish Hamilton, 1949).
Howell, T. B. (compiler), *A Collection of State Trials* (1–9, R. Bagshaw; 10–33, Longman & Co.: London, 1820).
Hughes, Ted, *Moortown Diary* (London and Boston: Faber and Faber, 1989).
Hunt, Leigh, *The Poetical Works*, ed. H. S. Milford (London: Humphrey Milford and Oxford University Press, 1923).
Hutcheson, Francis, *An Inquiry into the Original of our Ideas of Beauty and Virtue: In Two Treatises. I. Concerning Beauty, Order, Harmony, Design. II. Concerning Moral Good and Evil*, 5th edn cr. (London: Printed for R. Ware, J. and P. Knapton, T. and T. Longman, C. Hitch and L. Hawes, J. Hodges, J. and J. Rivington and J. Ward, 1753).
- *A Short Introduction to Moral Philosophy, in Three Books; Containing the Elements of Ethicks and the Law of Nature. Translated from the Latin* (Glasgow: Printed and Sold by Robert Foulis, 1747).
- *A Short Introduction to Moral Philosophy, in Three Books; Containing the Elements of Ethicks and the Law of Nature. Translated from the Latin*, 2nd edn (Glasgow: Printed and Sold by Robert and Andrew Foulis, 1753).
- *A Short Introduction to Moral Philosophy, in Three Books; Containing the Elements of Ethicks and the Law of Nature. Translated from the Latin*, 3rd edn (Glasgow: Printed by Robert and Andrew Foulis, 1764).
- *A System of Moral Philosophy, in Three Books; Published from the Original Manuscript, by his Son Francis Hutcheson, M.D. To which is Prefixed Some Account of the Life, Writings, and Character of the Author, by the Reverend William Leechman, D.D., Professor of Divinity in the same University*, 2 vols (Glasgow: Printed and Sold by R. and A. Foulis Printers to the University; London: Sold by A. Millar and by T. Longman, 1755).

– *On Human Nature*: '*Reflections on our Common Systems of Morality*', '*On the Social Nature of Man*', ed. Thomas Mautner (1724, 1730; repr. Cambridge: Cambridge University Press, 1993).

Jack, Ian, *Keats and the Mirror of Art* (Oxford: Clarendon Press, 1967).

Jefferson, Thomas, *The Writings*, ed. Andrew A. Lipscomb and Albert E. Bergh (Washington, D.C.: Thomas Jefferson Memorial Association, 1907).

Johns, John, *The Season of Autumn, As Connected with Human Feelings and Changes, A Sermon Occasioned by the Death of William Hazlitt* (London: Exeter, 1830).

Jones, Stanley, 'First Flight: Image and Theme in a Hazlitt Essay', *Prose Studies*, 8/1 (May 1985): 35–47.

– *William Hazlitt: A Life – From Winterslow to Frith Street* (Oxford: Clarendon Press, 1989).

– 'Three Additions to the Canon of Hazlitt's Political Writings', *Review of English Studies: A Quarterly Journal of English Literature and the English Language*, n.s. 38/151 (Aug. 1987): 355–63.

Joyce, James, *A Portrait of the Artist as a Young Man: Text, Criticism, and Notes*, ed. Chester G. Anderson (repr. Harmondsworth: Penguin Books, 1977).

Junius, *The Letters*, ed. John Cannon (Oxford: Clarendon Press, 1978).

Keats, John, *The Poems*, ed. Miriam Allott, 3rd impression with corrections (London: Longman, 1975).

Kippis, Andrew, *A Sermon Preached at the Old Jewry, on Wednesday the 26th of April, 1786, on the Occasion of a New Academical Institution, among Protestant Dissenters, for the Education of their Ministers and Youth* (London: H. Goldney, for T. Cadell; London: J. Johnson, 1786).

Kivy, Peter, *The Seventh Sense: A Study of Francis Hutcheson's Aesthetics and its Influence in Eighteenth-Century Britain* (New York: Burt Franklin & Co., 1976).

Knight, Joseph Elwood, 'Hazlitt's Use of the Character Tradition: His Philosophy and his Aesthetics in *The Spirit of the Age*' (University of Oregon Ph. D. thesis, 1972).

Lamb, Charles, *Charles Lamb and Elia*, ed. with introduction and notes by J. E. Morpurgo (Manchester: Fyfield Books, 1993).

Landseer, Thomas (ed.), *Life and Letters of William Bewick (Artist)*, 2 vols (London: Hurst and Blackett, 1871).

Lawrence, D. H., *The Complete Poems*, collected and edited with an introduction and notes by Vivian de Sola Pinto and Warren Roberts, 2 vols (London: Heinemann, 1964).

– *The Letters*, ed. Harry T. Moore (London: Heinemann, 1962).

Leechman, William, 'The Preface, Giving some Account of the Life, Writings, and Character of the Author', in Hutcheson, *A System of Moral Philosophy*, pp. i–xlviii.

Lindop, Grevel, 'Lamb, Hazlitt and De Quincey', in Gravil and Lefebure (eds), *The Coleridge Connection* (1990), pp. 111–32.

Locke, John, *A Letter Concerning Toleration* (1689), in *idem*, *Locke on Politics, Religion, and Education*, pp. 104–46.

– *A Letter Concerning Toleration: Latin and English Texts*, rev. and ed. with vrs. and introduction by Mario Montuori (1689; 2nd edn 1690; repr. The Hague: Martinus Nijhoff, 1963).

– *Locke on Politics, Religion, and Education*, ed. with introduction by Maurice Cranston (New York: Collier Books; London: Collier-Macmillan, 1965).

– *A Paraphrase and Notes on the Epistles of St Paul to the Galatians, 1 and 2 Corinthians, Romans, Ephesians*, ed. Arthur W. Wainwright, 2 vols (1705–7; Oxford: Clarendon Press, 1987).

[Lockhart, J .G.], 'Works of the First Importance. No. II. *The Spirit of the Age*', *Blackwood's Edinburgh Magazine*, 17/98 (Mar. 1825): 361–5.

McBride, Ian, 'The School of Virtue: Francis Hutcheson, Irish Presbyterians and the Scottish Enlightenment', in Boyce *et al*. (ed.), *Political Thought in Ireland*, pp. 73–99.

Mackerness, E. D., 'Preface' to Hazlitt, *The Spirit of the Age*, pp. 11–16.

McLachlan, H., *English Education under the Test Acts: Being the History of the Non-Conformist Academies 1662–1820* (Manchester: Manchester University Press, 1931).

– *The Unitarian Movement in the Religious Life of England: 1. Its Contribution to Thought and Learning 1700–1900* (London: George Allen & Unwin, 1934).

Maclean, Catherine MacDonald, *Born under Saturn: A Biography of William Hazlitt* (London: Collins, 1943).

Malone, Kemp, and Ruud, Martin B. (eds), *Studies in English Philology: A Miscellany in Honor of Frederick Klaeber* (Minneapolis: University of Minnesota Press, 1929).

Marvell, Andrew, *The Complete Poems*, ed. Elizabeth Story Donno (Harmondsworth: Penguin Books, 1972).

– *Andrew Marvell*, ed. Frank Kermode and Keith Walker (Oxford and New York: Oxford University Press, 1990).

Mill, John Stuart, *The Earlier Letters 1812–1848*, ed. Francis E. Mineka, introduced by F. A. Hayek, 2 vols (London and Toronto: University of Toronto Press, 1963).

- *Mills on Bentham and Coleridge*, introduced by F. R. Leavis (London: Chatto & Windus, 1950).

Milton, John, '*Areopagitica*' *and* '*Of Education*', ed. K. M. Lea (1644; repr. Oxford: Clarendon Press, 1973).

- *The Complete Prose Works*, general editor Don M. Wolfe, 8 vols (New Haven: Yale University Press, 1953–82).

- *The Complete Shorter Poems*, ed. John Carey, pbk edn (London: Longman, 1971).

- *Paradise Lost*, ed. Alastair Fowler, corrected pbk edn (2nd edn, 1674; repr. Harlow: Longman, 1971).

Montuori, Mario, Introduction to Locke, *Letter Concerning Toleration* (1963), pp. xv–l.

Motion, Andrew, *Keats* (London: Faber and Faber, 1997).

Moyne, Ernest J., 'The Reverend William Hazlitt: A Friend of Liberty in Ireland during the American Revolution', *William and Mary Quarterly*, 3rd ser., 21/2 (Apr. 1964): 288–97.

Murray, Lindley, *An English Grammar: Comprehending the Principles and Rules of the Language, Illustrated by Appropriate Exercises, and a Key to the Exercises*, 2 vols, new edn (London: Longman, Hurst, Rees, and Orme for Darton and Harvey; York: Wilson and Son for R. and W. Spence; Edinburgh: Constable and Co., 1808).

Natarajan, Uttara Valli, 'Hazlitt and the Reach of Sense, Criticism, Morals, and the Metaphysics of Power' (University of Oxford D. Phil. thesis; 1995).

Norbrook, David, 'Marvell's "Horatian Ode" and the Politics of Genre', in Healy and Sawday (eds), *Literature and the English Civil War*, pp. 147–69.

Northcote, James, *The Life of Titian: With Anecdotes of the Distinguished Persons of his Time*, 2 vols (London: Henry Colburn and Richard Bentley, 1830).

O'Brien, Conor Cruise, 'Introduction: "The Manifesto of a Counter-Revolution"', in Burke, *Reflections*, pp. 9–76.

- *The Great Melody: A Thematic Biography and Commented Anthology of Edmund Burke* (London: Sinclair-Stevenson, 1992).

- and Vanech, William Dean (eds), *Power and Consciousness* (London: University of London Press; New York: New York University Press, 1969).

O'Brien, P., *Warrington Academy 1757–86: Its Predecessors and Successors* (Wigan: Owl Books, 1989).

Paine, Thomas, *The Rights of Man* (1791; repr. London: J. M. Dent, 1944).

Park, Roy, *Hazlitt and the Spirit of the Age: Abstraction and Critical Theory* (Oxford: Clarendon Press, 1971).

Patmore, P. G., *My Friends and Acquaintances: Being Memorials, Mind-Portraits, and Personal Recollections of Deceased Celebrities of the Nineteenth Century: With Selections from their Unpublished Letters*, 3 vols (London: Saunders and Otley, 1854).

Paulin, Tom, *Ireland and the English Crisis* (Newcastle upon Tyne: Bloodaxe Books, 1984).

– *Minotaur: Poetry and the Nation State* (London and Boston: Faber and Faber, 1992).

Pindar, *The Odes*, tr. with introduction by C. M. Bowra (Harmondsworth: Penguin Books, 1969).

Plato, *Phaedrus*, tr. with introduction and commentary by R. Hackforth (Cambridge: Cambridge University Press, 1952).

Plutarke of Chaeronea, *The Lives of the Noble Grecians and Romaines, Compared Together by that Grave Learned Philosopher and Historiographer[s] Plutarke of Chaeronea: Translated out of Greeke into French by James Amiot Abbot of Bellozane, Bishop of Auxerre, one of the Kings privie Counsell, and great Almner of France: With the lives of Hannibal and Scipio African: translated out of Latine into French by Charles de l'Esclvse, and out of French into English, By Sir Thomas North Knight. Hereunto are also added the lives of Epaminondas, of Philip of Macedon, of Dionysius the elder, tyrant of Sicilia, of Augustus Caesar, of Plutarke, and of Seneca: with the lives of nine other excellent Chieftaines of warre: collected out of Aemylius Probus, by S. G. S. and Englished by the aforesaid Translator* (London: Printed by Richard Field, 1612).

Pope, Alexander, *The Poems*, ed. John Butt (London: Methuen, 1965).

– (tr.), *The Odyssey of Homer* (repr. London: Methuen; New Haven: Yale University Press, 1962).

P. P., 'Letter from an Absent Contributor on Hazlitt's *Spirit of the Age*', *London Magazine and Review*, n.s. 2/6 (1 June 1825): 182–9.

Price, Richard, *The Correspondence*, gen. eds W. Bernard Peach and D. O. Thomas (Durham, NC: Duke University Press; Cardiff: University of Wales Press 1983–94).

– *A Discourse on the Love of Our Country, Delivered on Nov. 4, 1789, at the Meeting-House in the Old Jewry, to the Society for Commemorating the Revolution in Great Britain. With an Appendix, Containing the*

Report of the Committee of the Society; An Account of the Population of France; and the Declaration of Rights by the National Assembly of France, 2nd edn (London: Printed by George Stafford for T. Cadell, 1789).

– *Political Writings*, ed. D. O. Thomas (Cambridge: Cambridge University Press, 1991).

– *A Review of the Principal Questions in Morals*, ed. D. Daiches Raphael (3rd edn, 1787; repr. Oxford: Clarendon Press, 1948).

Priestley, Joseph, *A Course of Lectures on Oratory and Criticism* (London: Printed for J. Johnson, 1777).

– *A Course of Lectures on the Theory of Language and Universal Grammar* (Warrington: Printed by W. Eyres, 1762).

– *A Discourse to the Supporters of New College, Hackney, With a Prayer by Thomas Belsham Subjoined* (London: J. Johnson, 1791).

– *Disquisitions Relating to Matter and Spirit. To which is Added, The History of the Philosophical Doctrine concerning the Origin of the Soul, and the Nature of Matter; with its Influence on Christianity, Especially with Respect to the Doctrine of the Pre-existence of Christ* (London: Printed for J. Johnson, 1777).

– *Disquisitions Relating to Matter and Spirit. To which is Added: The History of the Philosophical Doctrine concerning the Origin of the Soul, and the Nature of Matter; with its Influence on Christianity, especially with respect to the Doctrine of the Pre-existence of Christ*, 2nd edn, ipd. and enlarged (Birmingham and London: J. Johnson, 1782).

– *An Essay on the First Principles of Government; and on the Nature of Political, Civil, and Religious Liberty* (London: Printed for J. Dodsley, T. Cadell, and J. Johnson, 1768).

– *An Essay on the First Principles of Government, and on the Nature of Political, Civil, and Religious Liberty, including Remarks on Dr Brown's 'Code of Education', and on Dr Balguy's Sermon on Church Authority*, 2nd edn, corrected and enlarged (London: Printed for J. Johnson, 1771).

– *A General View of the Arguments for the Unity of God; and Against the Divinity and Pre-Existence of Christ, from Reason, from the Scriptures, and from History*, 2nd edn (Birmingham: Printed by Piercy and Jones for J. Johnson, 1785).

– *Heads of Lectures on a Course of Experimental Philosophy, particularly including Chemistry, Delivered at the New College in Hackney* (London: Printed for J. Johnson, 1794).

– *Letters to the Right Honourable Edmund Burke, Occasioned by His 'Reflections on the Revolution in France', &c.* (Birmingham: Thomas Pearson; London: J. Johnson, 1791).

- *Letters to the Right Honourable Edmund Burke. Occasioned by His 'Reflections on the Revolution in France', &c.*, 3rd edn, corrected (Birmingham: Thomas Pearson; London: J. Johnson, 1791).
- *The Proper Objects of Education* (London: Printed for J. Johnson, 1791).
- *Theological and Miscellaneous Works*, ed. J. T. Rutt, 25 vols (Hackney: George Smallfield, 1815–31).
- *Tracts in Controversy with Bishop Horsley: To which is Annexed an Appendix, Containing a Review of the Controversy, in Four Letters to the Bishops, By the Same Author, Never before Published*, ed. with notes by T. Belsham (London: Printed by Richard and Arthur Taylor for the London Unitarian Society and sold by J. Johnson and Co., 1815).

Rabelais, François, *The Histories of Gargantua and Pantagruel*, trans. with introduction by J. M. Cohen (1564; repr. Harmondsworth: Penguin Books, 1955).

Rae, John, *Life of Adam Smith* (London and New York: Macmillan & Co., 1895).

Rawson, Claude (ed.), *English Satire and the Satiric Tradition*, assisted by Jenny Mezciems (Oxford and New York: Basil Blackwell, 1984).

Reid, Loren, *Charles James Fox: A Man for the People* (London and Harlow: Longmans, 1969).

Robbins, Caroline, *The Eighteenth-Century Commonwealthman: Studies in the Transmission, Development and Circumstance of English Liberal Thought from the Restoration of Charles II until the War with the Thirteen Colonies* (Cambridge, Mass.: Harvard University Press, 1959).

Robinson, A., *A Short History of the Persecution of Christians, by Jews, Heathens, & Christians. To which are Added an Account of the Present State of Religion in the United States of America, and Some Observations on Civil Establishments of Religion* (Carlisle: Printed for the Author by F. Jollie and Sold by J. Johnson, n.d. [1793]).

Roe, Nicholas, *John Keats and the Culture of Dissent* (Oxford: Clarendon Press, 1997).
- *Wordsworth and Coleridge: The Radical Years* (Oxford: Clarendon Press, 1988).
- (ed.), *Keats and History* (Cambridge: Cambridge University Press, 1995).

Roper, Derek, *Reviewing before the 'Edinburgh': 1788–1802* (London: Methuen & Co., 1978).

Rose, R. B., 'The Priestley Riots of 1791', *Past & Present*, 18 (Nov. 1960): 68–88.

Rousseau, Jean-Jacques, *Les Confessions* (London, 1782).

- *The Confessions*, trans. with introduction by J. M. Cohen (repr. Harmondsworth: Penguin Books, 1971).
- *Les Confessions*, ed. Jacques Voisine (Paris: Editions Garnier Frères, 1964).
- *The Social Contract*, trans. and introduced by Maurice Cranston (Harmondsworth: Penguin Books, 1968).
Ruskin, John, *The Works*, ed. E. T. Cook and Alexander Wedderburn, 39 vols (London: George Allen; New York: Longmans, Green, and Co., 1903–12).
Rutt, John Towill, *Life and Correspondence of Joseph Priestley, LL.D., F.R.S., &c.*, 2 vols (London: R. Hunter, M. Eaton, and C. Fox, 1831–2).
Saavedra, Miguel de Cervantes, *The Adventures of Don Quixote*, trans. J. M. Cohen (1604–14; repr. Harmondsworth: Penguin Books, 1950).
Saintsbury, George, *A History of English Prose Rhythm* (London: Macmillan & Co., 1912).
- *A Short History of English Literature* (London: Macmillan & Co., 1898; 1962).
- 'William Hazlitt', *Macmillan's Magazine*, 55/330 (Apr. 1887): 429–41.
Salvesen, C. G., 'The True Jacobin: Pastoral and Politics in a Hazlitt Essay', Angol Filólogiai Tanulmányok/Hungarian Studies in English, 20 (Dec. 1989): 67–76.
Schlegel, Augustus William, *A Course of Lectures on Dramatic Art and Literature*, trans. John Black, 2 vols (London: Baldwin, Cradock, and Joy; Edinburgh: William Blackwood; Dublin: John Cumming, 1815).
Schneider, Elisabeth, *The Aesthetics of William Hazlitt: A Study of the Philosophical Basis of his Criticism*, corrected 2nd printing (Philadelphia: University of Pennsylvania Press for Temple University Publications, 1952).
Scott, William Robert, *Francis Hutcheson: His Life, Teaching and Position in the History of Philosophy* (Cambridge: Cambridge University Press, 1900).
Seed, John, 'The Role of Unitarianism in the Formation of Liberal Culture 1775–1851: A Social History' (University of Hull Ph.D. thesis, 1981).
Shakespeare, William, *The Complete Signet Classic Shakespeare*, gen. ed. Sylvan Barnet (San Diego: Harcourt Brace Jovanovich, 1972).
[Sharp, Richard], *Letters and Essays in Prose and Verse* (London: Edward Moxon, 1834).
Shelley, Mary, *Frankenstein; or, The Modern Prometheus*, ed. D. L. Macdonald and Kathleen Scherf (1818; repr. Ontario: Broadview Press, 1994).
Shenstone, William, *Letters to Particular Friends from the Year 1739*

to 1763 (Dublin: H. Saunders, W. Sleater, D. Chamberlaine, J. Potts, J. Williams, and W. Colles, 1770).

Sidney, Algernon, *Discourses concerning Government: With his Letters, Trial, Apology, and Some Memoirs of his Life* (1698; repr. augmented, London: A. Millar, 1763).

Smith, Barbara (ed.), *Truth, Liberty, Religion: Essays Celebrating Two Hundred Years of Manchester College* (Oxford: Manchester College, 1986).

Smith, Olivia, *The Politics of Language 1791–1819* (Oxford: Clarendon Press, 1984).

Sontag, Susan, *Against Interpretation and Other Essays* (1966; repr. with new preface, London: Eyre & Spottiswoode, 1967).

Southey, Charles Cuthbert (ed.), *The Life and Correspondence of Robert Southey*, 6 vols (London: Longman, Brown, Green, & Longmans, 1849–50).

Southey, Robert, *Essays, Moral and Political*, 2 vols (London: John Murray, 1832).

Stephen, Leslie, *History of English Thought in the Eighteenth Century*, 2 vols (London: Smith, Elder, and Co., 1876).

Stephenson, H. W., *William Hazlitt and Hackney College* (London: Lindsey Press, 1930).

Sterne, Laurence, *The Life and Opinions of Tristram Shandy, Gentleman*, ed. Graham Petrie, introduction by Christopher Ricks (1759–67; repr. Harmondsworth: Penguin Books, 1967).

Stevenson, Robert Louis, *The Letters*, ed. Bradford A. Booth and Ernest Mehew, 8 vols (New Haven and London: Yale University Press, 1994–5).

Stewart, A. T. Q., *A Deeper Silence: The Hidden Roots of the United Irish Movement* (London and Boston: Faber and Faber, 1993).

Thackeray, William Makepeace, *The Letters and Private Papers*, 4 vols, collected and edited by Gordon N. Ray (London: Oxford University Press, 1945–6).

Thomas, D. O., *The Honest Mind: The Thought and Work of Richard Price* (Oxford: Clarendon Press, 1977).

Thompson, E. P., 'Disenchantment or Default?: A Lay Sermon', in O'Brien and Vanech (eds), *Power and Consciousness*, pp. 149–81.

– 'Hunting the Jacobin Fox', *Past & Present*, 142 (Feb. 1994): 94–140.

– *The Making of the English Working Class* (London: Victor Gollancz, 1963).

Thomson, James, *'The Seasons' and 'The Castle of Indolence'*, ed. James Sambrook (1746; 2nd edn 1748; repr. Oxford: Clarendon Press, 1972).

Tomalin, Clare, *The Life and Death of Mary Wollstonecraft*, rev. edn (London: Penguin Books, 1992).

– 'Publisher in Prison: Joseph Johnson and the Book Trade', *Times Literary Supplement*, no. 4,783 (2 Dec. 1994): 15–16.

Tooke, J. Horne, *ΕΠΕΑ ΠΤΕΡΟΕΝΤΑ. Or, The Diversions of Purley*, 2nd edn (London: Printed for the Author at J. Johnson's, 1798–1805).

Tyson, Gerald, *Joseph Johnson: A Liberal Publisher* (Iowa City: University of Iowa Press, 1979).

Verdi, Richard, 'Hazlitt and Poussin', *Keats–Shelley Memorial Bulletin Rome*, 32 (1981): 1–18.

– *Nicolas Poussin 1594–1665*, ed. Pierre Rosenberg (London: Zwemmer in association with the Royal Academy of Arts, London, 1995).

Voltaire, *Letters on England*, trans. with introduction by Leonard Tancock (1734; Harmondsworth: Penguin Books, 1980).

Wakefield, Gilbert, *An Address to the Inhabitants of Nottingham, Occasioned by a Letter Lately Sent to the Mayor and Some Other Members of the Corporation of that Town. With an Appendix, On the Subject of the Test-Laws* (London: Printed for J. Johnson, 1789).

– *A Reply to Some Parts of the Bishop of Landaff's Address to the People of Great Britain*, 2nd edn (London: Sold for the Author by J. Cuthell, 1798).

– *The Spirit of Christianity, Compared with the Spirit of the Times in Great Britain*, new edn with corrections and additions (London: Sold by Kearsley, 1794).

– 'Trial for Seditious Libel, 21 February, 1799', in Howell (comp.), *Collection of State Trials*.

Watts, Michael R., *The Dissenters: From the Reformation to the French Revolution*, corrected pbk edn (Oxford: Clarendon Press, 1985).

Wellek, René, *A History of Modern Criticism 1750–1950*, 8 vols (Cambridge: Cambridge University Press, 1983).

Wharam, Alan, *The Treason Trials, 1794* (Leicester and London: Leicester University Press, 1992).

Wills, Gary, *Inventing America: Jefferson's Declaration of Independence* (New York: Doubleday & Co., 1978).

Wimsatt, W. K., Jr., *The Prose Style of Samuel Johnson*, 2nd printing with a new preface (New Haven and London: Yale University Press, 1963).

Wolfson, Susan J., 'Keats Enters History: Autopsy, *Adonais*, and the Fame of Keats', in Nicholas Roe (ed.), *Keats and History*, (1995), pp. 17–45.

[Wollstonecraft, Mary], *A Vindication of the Rights of Men, in a Letter to the Right Honourable Edmund Burke; Occasioned by his 'Reflections on the Revolution in France'*, (London: J. Johnson, 1790).

Woolf, Virginia, *Collected Essays* (London: Hogarth Press, 1966–7).

Wordsworth, William, *The Excursion* (London: Longman, Hurst, Rees, Orme and Browne, 1814).

– *Thanksgiving Ode, January 18, 1816. With Other Short Pieces, Chiefly Referring to Recent Public Events* (London: Printed by Thomas Davison, Whitefriars, for Longman, Hurst, Rees, Orme and Brown, 1816).

Wright, Conrad, *The Beginnings of Unitarianism in America* (Boston: Starr King Press, 1955).

Wright, William C., 'Hazlitt, Ruskin, and Nineteenth-Century Art Criticism', *Journal of Aesthetics and Art Criticism*, 32/4 (Summer 1974): 509–23.

Wyvill, Christopher, *A Defence of Dr Price, and the Reformers of England* (London: Printed by W. Blanchard for J. Johnson; London: J. Stockdale; York: J. Todd, 1792).

Yeats, W. B., *The Poems: Revised*, ed. Richard J. Finneran, 2nd edn (Basingstoke and London: Macmillan, 1991).

Notes

Indented quotations in the text are keyed by the last two or three words of the quotation, run-on quotations by the first two or three words. Where a series of run-on quotations follow from the same passage in a text I have not listed them. References to P. P. Howe's *Complete Works of William Hazlitt* are cited as, e.g., H v. 32 (i.e. vol. 5, p. 32). For *The Spirit of the Age* I have used E. D. Mackerness's edition rather than Howe's.

Introduction

1 **'dumb, inarticulate, helpless'** 'My First Acquaintance with Poets', H XVII. 107
2 **the speaking voice** see 'Lamb's unpublished review of *Table-Talk*' in Robert Ready, *Hazlitt at Table* (1981), 111
 'an Irishman' W. Carew Hazlitt, *The Hazlitts: An Account of their Origin and Descent* (1911), 345
 'somewhat Celtic' ibid., 321
 'sympathy and tie' ibid., 338
 'an ultra-Dissenter' quoted in Anon., 'Joseph Hunter on the Hazlitts', *Notes and Queries* (June 1957), 265
 'of Irish extraction' George Saintsbury, *A Short History of English Literature* (1960; first published 1898), 701
 'would have been' Margaret Hazlitt, *The Journal: Recollections of England, Ireland, and America*, ed. Ernest J. Moyne (1967), 43
3 **'never disguised'** ibid., 41
 'AN UNCHANGING WHIG' Ernest J. Moyne, 'The Reverend William Hazlitt', *William and Mary College Quarterly* (1964), 290
 'Paddy' Conrad Wright, *The Beginnings of Unitarianism in America* (1955), 214
 'radical incapacity' W. Carew Hazlitt, *Four Generations of a Literary Family* (1897), I, 216

4 'British Cassius' James Thomson, *The Seasons* (from 'Summer' 1528)
   English republicans Caroline Robbins, *The Eighteenth-Century Commonwealthman* (1959), 7
5 'was Shaftesbury's *Characteristics*' H VIII. 12
   'a poor Irish lad' H XVII. 110
6 'a very honest' Richard Price, *The Correspondence* (1983–94), II. 126–7
   'And be not' W. Hazlitt, *Sermons for the Use of Families* (1808), I. 338
   'inviolably attached' ibid., I. 354
   'On the Wisdom' ibid., I. 35
7 'the gradual and' Thomas Belsham, *The Sufferings of Unitarians in Former Times* (25 July 1813), 43
   'their primitive simplicity' Thomas Belsham, *Tracts* (1814), 148
   'the mass of' Thomas Belsham, *Memoirs of the Late Reverend Theophilus Lindsey, M.A.* (1812), 305
   'sociality' Thomas Belsham, *Elements of the Philosophy of the Mind, and of Moral Philosophy* (1801), 220
   'the voice of' Thomas Belsham, *Discourses, Doctrinal and Practical* (1826), 58
   'that infinite mass' ibid., 5
8 'good of others' Richard Price, *A Review of the Principal Questions in Morals* (1948), 151
   'gradual and accelerated' Belsham, *Discourses, Doctrinal and Practical*, I. 383
   'inert and sluggish' ibid., II. 83
   'discourse' Belsham, *Sufferings of Unitarians in Former Times*, 43
   'a process theology' R. G. W. Anderson and Christopher Lawrence (eds), *Science, Medicine and Dissent: Joseph Priestley (1733–1804)* (1987), 13
9 'confused jargon' Edmund Burke, *Reflections on the Revolution in France* (1968), 115
   'diffusion' ibid., 157
   'bigotry mark out' Hazlitt, *The Letters* (1978), 57
10 'the muster-roll' T. B. Howell (compiler), *A Collection of State Trials* (1820), XXVII. 698
   'I see the' Richard Price, *A Discourse on the Love of Our Country* (1789), 50
11 'a larger society' Joseph Priestley, *A Discourse to the Supporters of New College, Hackney* (1791), 10

11 'God save the King' quoted in H. W. Stephenson, *William Hazlitt and Hackney College* (1930), 11
'treasonable practices' ibid., 34
Thomas Hardy Hazlitt, *Letters*, 131

12 'I am sinking' quoted in Alan Wharam, *The Treason Trials, 1794* (1992), 65

13 'possibly saved' Hazlitt, *The Spirit of the Age*, ed. E. D. Mackerness (1991), 50
'souse' see below pp. 135 and 137.

15 'un-interested in him' Extract from a letter at Keats House, KH 521, John Hamilton Reynolds to Mary Leigh, 28 Apr. 1817. I owe this excerpt to Duncan Wu, who generously gave it to me.

16 'more a genius' John Clare *John Clare by Himself* (1996), 141–2

CHAPTER ONE A State of Projection

17 'mighty impulse' H VI. 182

18 'old English' H VI. 179
'putty paper' see Tom Paulin, *Ireland and the English Crisis* (1984), 171
'in a state' H VI. 182

19 'Shakespeare prose-writer' Thomas Landseer (ed.), *Life and Letters of William Bewick (Artist)* (1871) I. 42
'The passions are' H V. 51

20 'to *extempore* speaking' H XII. 62
'a *mind* to' H VI. 182

21 'strong and nervous' Algernon Sidney, *Discourses concerning Government* (1763), 45

22 'detestable doctrine' H XIX. 180
'engine at the door' H XVII. 325
'villainous' engine Andrew Marvell, *The Rehearsal Transposed* (in *Andrew Marvell*, 1990, p. 158)
'one great lever' H XVII. 329
'remote but inevitable' H XIII. 38
'principle of cohesion' H II. 153

23 'cemented' H VI. 182
'cementing together' Andrew Kippis, *A Sermon Preached at the Old Jewry on Wednesday the 26th of April, 1786* (1786), 61. The pamphlet includes 'Resolutions and Proceedings, Relating to the Establishment of a New Academical Institution among Protestant Dissenters, in the vicinity of London in the Year 1786', from which the quotation is taken.

23 'line of communication' 'My First Acquaintance with Poets', H XVII.
   107
   'mere puppet' H II. 116
   'more refined pulsations' H II. 117
24 'whatever colouring' H I. 108
   'far-fetched or abrupt' H I. 111
   'of charges, committals' H XIV. 137
   'not the cause' H I. 128
25 'had none of the' H VII. 325
   'fog and haze' H VII. 323
   'in the fog' Burke, *Reflections*, 136
26 'clambers up by' H XII. 10
   'gradual and pieced' H XVIII. 166
   'in variety, speed' Bowra, Introduction to Pindar, *The Odes* (1969),
   p. xiii
   'by position or' H XVIII. 166
   'faultless regularity' H I. 111
   'grand and daring' H VI. 203
   'more weight' H VI. 257
27 'honest abruptness' H V. 112
   'glad to leap' H XVIII. 166
   'I have run' H XVII. 274
   'Not so' H XVII. 272
28 'new shape' H I. 157
   'ready warehouseman' H XVII. 111
   'place of mechanical' Charles Dickens, *Our Mutual Friend* (1971),
   266
   'no feelings connected' H VII. 328
   'masterly and unanswerable' H I. 112
   'quickness or elasticity' H I. 157
29 'hard words' H X. 241
   'literal, dry, incorrigible' H V. 112
   'too wedgy' H V. 339
   'the flinty and' Shakespeare, *Othello*, I. iii. 227–8; H V. 339
30 'constantly clings to' H X. 243n.
   'Stung with wounds' H X. 241–2
   'ill-visaged cursing' G. M. Hopkins, 'The Summer Malison' and 'Yes.
   Why do we all, seeing of a soldier, bless him? bless'
   'wooden walls' H XIV. 17
   'hardness and setness' H IV. 49

31 'nature a materialist' H II. 116
   'light, vigorous, elastic' H XVII. 81
   heard Wordsworth recite see H I. 373
   'the bodily sense' Wordsworth, *The Excursion* (1814), 10 (I. 148–55)

32 'sentimental refinement' H I. 147
   'Pain puts life' H X. 242

33 'the mind itself' *Monthly Magazine* (Feb. 1809); see also Geoffrey Carnall, *Times Literary Supplement* (19 June 1953)
   'of something extended' H II. 208
   'endless diversity' H VI. 182

34 'free play' H IX. 51
   'common, discursive' H IX. 54
   'there are none' H IX. 58
   'This sensible warm' Shakespeare, *Measure for Measure*, III. i. 119

35 'Devoid of sense and motion' Milton, *Paradise Lost*, II. 151
   'No motion' Wordsworth, 'A Slumber'
   'project' H IX. 58
   'social joy' see Francis Hutcheson, *On Human Nature* (1993), 137
   'simple sensation' H XX. 359
   'into the process' ibid.

36 'the force of' H IX. 58
   'the good which' Francis Bacon, *The Advancement of Learning* (1973), 156
   'scarce any cheerful' Francis Hutcheson, *A Short Introduction to Moral Philosophy* (1763), 15–16

37 'diffused the doctrines' Belsham, *Memoirs of the Late Reverend Theophilus Lindsey*, 303
   'liberal discussion' ibid., 296
   'electrical machine' H XIV. 133
   'conductors' H XVI. 189
   'The Letter-Bell' H XVII. 380

38 'to expand' H XVI. 403
   Jonathan Bate *Shakespearean Constitutions* (1989), 139
   Priestley and Marat see P. O'Brien, *Warrington Academy 1757–86* (1989), 71

39 'crowned, and crested' H IV. 214

40 'is thy Daughter!' Wordsworth, 'Ode. The Morning of the Day Appointed for a General Thanksgiving' (1816), 17
   'mitigated, sceptical, liberalized' H XX. 103

343

40 'downright, rooted' H xx. 102
41 'a lord' H xx. 127
'a mere machine' H xix. 246
'power of fascination' H xx. 45
'toys of desperation' Shakespeare, *Hamlet*, i. iv. 75
42 manuscript of the essay Hazlitt, 'On the Punishment of Death', Folger
Shakespeare Library, T. b. 18, fols 17–36.
43 Patmore I owe this point to Duncan Wu, who has edited *Liber
Amoris* from the manuscript
44 'my charmer' H ix. 103
'sovereign grace' H ix. 101
'reserved and modest' H ix. 107
'common lodging-house' H ix. 106
'wanton' Shakespeare, *Othello*, iv. i. 73
a poisonous serpent H ix. 153
'I took her' H ix. 154
'talismans and love-tokens' H vi. 182
45 'Intolerable conviction!' H ix. 132
'so I told *her*!' W. M. Thackeray, *The Letters and Private Papers*, ii.
245–6
'naked shivering nature' Burke, *Reflections*, 171
46 'or wished to' Thomas Carlyle and Jane Welsh, *The Collected Letters*
(1973), iii. 139
'I dare venture' H xx. 112

CHAPTER TWO Republican Poetics

47 'barely acknowledged' Stanley Jones, *Hazlitt: A Life* (1989), 272
Waterloo veterans see E. P. Thompson, *The Making of the English
Working Class* (1963), 748
48 'importunate chink' Burke, *Reflections*, 181
'Mr Godwin' quoted in Jones, *Hazlitt*, 305n.
49 'THE AUTHOR' H vii. 5
Political Essays (1819)
50 'stubborn, rude skill' Jones, *Hazlitt*, 274–6
51 'patrician drawl' Thompson, *Making of the English Working Class*,
821–2
'suffered in the cause' Jones, *Hazlitt*, 241, and J. S. Mill, *The
Collected Works*, xii. 359
52 'each tucked string tells' Hopkins, 'As Kingfishers Catch Fire'

52 'Dear Hazlitt' Leigh Hunt 'To William Hazlitt'
'as I could' H VII. 7
'plenary consciousness' H XII. 73
'turbulent contentious cities' Sidney, *Discourses concerning Government*, 207
'this free writing' John Milton, '*Areopagitica*' and '*Of Education*' (1973), 37
'present thought' Joseph Priestley, *A Course of Lectures in Oratory and Criticism* (1777), 111

53 'sacred vehemence' Milton, *Comus*, 795
'bubbles, sparkles' H VI. 39
'the crust of formality' Milton, *Of Reformation*, 1. 522; H VI. 38

54 'glossiness' H VIII. 244
his first publications H II. 99
'the most remarkably' Priestley, *Lectures in Oratory and Criticism*, 309

55 'easy and graceful' ibid., 310
'inward unction' H VIII. 245
'most juicy books' François Rabelais, *The Histories of Gargantua and Pantagruel* (1955), 38

56 'of marrow' H V. 113
'strong, vivid' H XIX. 96
'to induce you' H XX. 236
'a body to it' H XVII. 116
'bold happy texture' H XII. 58-9
'oily richness' H XVIII. 197
'his pencil was' H XVIII. 403
'large share' Virginia Woolf, *Collected Essays* (1966), I. 164
'strong toil' Shakespeare, *Antony and Cleopatra*, V. ii. 347
'complete thing' H XVII. 86

57 'modern legal oration!' H I. 147-8
'dissociation of sensibility' T. S. Eliot, 'The Metaphysical Poets', in *Selected Essays* (1951), 288 (I subsequently discovered a very helpful article by Jeanne Andrews ('Bacon and the "Dissociation of Sensibility", *Notes and Queries* (Nov. 1954)) which makes the link between Eliot and Hazlitt)
Henry Adams Margaret Hazlitt, *The Journal*, 63 and 148n. 49

58 'Milton and Dryden' T. S. Eliot, 'Metaphysical Poets', in *Selected Essays* (1951), 287

58 **Eliot** 'A Sceptical Patrician', *Athenaeum* (23 May 1919), 361–2
 'a bit of' Eliot, *Selected Essays*, 17
59 **'no change by fusion'** Joseph Priestley, *Heads of Lectures on a Course of Experimental Philosophy* (1794), 85
 'perhaps the most' Eliot, 'John Dryden', in *Selected Essays*, 309
 'more simple, sensuous' Milton, 'On Education', 55 (Hazlitt quotes from this pamphlet in H VI. 43)
 'the liberal provision' Belsham's prayer is added to Priestley, *Discourse to the Supporters*, 44
 'no perfect enjoyment' Joseph Priestley, *An Essay on the First Principles of Government* (1768), 68
 'evil tendency' Joseph Priestley, *Disquisitions Relating to Matter and Spirit* (1777), 338 and 343
60 **'the greatest happiness'** Francis Hutcheson, *An Inquiry into the Original of our Ideas of Beauty and Virtue* (1753), 164
 'of the greatest' John Towill Rutt, *Life and Correspondence of Joseph Priestley* (1832), II. 485–6
 'doth buckle and bow' Bacon, *Advancement of Learning*, 83: Hazlitt quotes an earlier part of the passage in which this phrase appears in H V. 3–4
 'pomp and copiousness' H VI. 333
 'imposthumations' Bacon, *Advancement of Learning*, ed. Kitchin, 114
 'the powers of' H II. 125
61 **'weight and consequences'** H VI. 327–8
62 **'transparent brilliancy'** H VI. 342
63 **'as the blower's'** H IV. 226
 'at present are!' H VIII. 283
 'all glossy, spruce' H VIII. 257

CHAPTER THREE Celebrating Hutcheson

64 **'an affair'** H II. 221
 'celebrated' H I. 161
 'constant propensity to' Francis Hutcheson, *A System of Moral Philosophy*, 5th edn (1755), I. 21
65 **'following upon it'** ibid., I. 22
 'an immediate pleasure' ibid., I. 16
 'done with a' H X. 26
66 **'immediate evidence'** Hazlitt, *Spirit of the Age*, 252

66 'usefulness of the' Hutcheson, *Inquiry*, 10
Peter Kivy see Peter Kivy, *The Seventh Sense* (1976), 1–36
'the degree in' Hutcheson, *System of Moral Philosophy*, II. 118
67 philosophical discipline Kivy, *Seventh Sense*, 119–20
'the friend and' in Seamus Deane (ed.), *The Field Day Anthology of Irish Writing* (1991), III. 119
Sarah Swanwick corroborated by A. T. Q. Stewart in *A Deeper Silence* (1993), 188
68 'private virtue' David Bromwich, *Hazlitt: The Mind of a Critic* (1983), 49
'a serious departure' ibid., 54
'a passive power' Hutcheson, *Inquiry*, 74–5
'disinterested' Bromwich, *Hazlitt*, 87
'sense and candour' H VII. 305
69 'impulse to action' Hutcheson, *System*, 21
'power or passion' H IV. 77
'growing round us' H V. 87
'the time of' H XI. 93
'life and motion' H V. 3
'not only looks' H XX. 9
70 'in motion' H XII. 287
'kinetic vocabulary' Roy Park, *Hazlitt and the Spirit of the Age* (1971), 154 (I have used a number of Park's examples from Hazlitt in this paragraph)
'immediate appeal to' H V. 69
'communication of art' H XVIII. 145
'enjoyments' Hutcheson, *System*, 118
'as a whole' Park, *Hazlitt and the Spirit of the Age*, 194
71 Leslie Chard see Leslie F. Chard, II, *Dissenting Republican* (1972), 151–2
'life of things' *The Poetical Works of William Wordsworth*, ed. E. de Selincourt (1952), II. 260
72 'have their being' Joseph Fawcett, *Sermons Delivered at the Sunday-Evening Lecture, for the Winter Season, at the Old Jewry* (1795), I. 32–3
'pleasure and pain' H XII. 290
73 'Rolled round' Wordsworth, 'A Slumber'
'entirely unknown' *Monthly Magazine* (Feb. 1809), 19
74 'fixed repose' H XX. 300
'of the past' D. H. Lawrence, *The Complete Poems* (1964), I. 183

74 'allotropic' D. H. Lawrence, *The Letters* (1965), II. 183
'the immediate energy' Belsham, *Discourses, Doctrinal and Practical*, II. 81

75 'through all things' H II. 268
'microscopic impressions' H II. 153

76 'convenient repository' H II. 147
'prolixity and ambiguity' H II. 162
'decomposed and crumbled' H II. 152

77 'have to show' H XX. 76
'body is homogeneal' Milton, *Areopagitica*, 33
'solitary, poor, nasty' Thomas Hobbes, *Leviathan* (1976), 65
'magistral and peremptory' H VI. 332 and Bacon, *Advancement of Learning*, 34
'easy, indolent' H II. 260

78 'secret thoughts' Hobbes, *Leviathan*, 34
'this wild ranging' ibid., 9
'not live well' ibid., 80
'The heaven' ibid., 57
'These giant sons' H IV. 161–2
'sensible images' Priestley, *Course of Lectures*, 64
'they came in' Hobbes, *Leviathan*, 15

79 'tacit reason' H VIII. 33
'thought is quick' Hobbes, *Leviathan*, 9
'drops the intermediate' H VIII. 35

80 'not well within' H VIII. 34
'sluggish moroseness' H VI. 30; see also Hazlitt's preface to *Characters of Shakespear's Plays*, H IV. 171–8

81 'in the fine' H VIII. 32
'an *associating* principle' H XII. 51
'infinite fund' H III. 158 and see H XII. 273
'very like Mr Windham' H XVII. 85
'merited a statue' William Cobbett, *The Autobiography*, ed. William Reitzel (1947), 80

82 'none of the' H XVII. 82
'stalk of a' H VII. 313
'enslaves the country' *The Letters of Junius*, ed. John Cannon (1978), 283

83 'thus unmercifully beaten' 'Mr Cobbett's Taking Leave of his Countrymen', in *Selections from Cobbett's Political Works*, (n.d.), v. 200

83 'necessary to convey' H IX. 31
84 'it could go' H VIII. 41
   'Gribelin's etchings' H VIII. 12
85 'the moment' D. H. Lawrence, *Complete Poems*, I. 83
86 'standing resource' H XVII. 320; for Salvesen's essay see C. G.
   Salvesen, 'The True Jacobin', *Angol Filógiai Tanulmányok/Hungarian
   Studies in English* (Dec. 1989)
   'If to do' Shakespeare, *The Merchant of Venice*, I. ii. 12–14
87 'the philosophic mind' H VII. 370; Salvesen notes that Hazlitt has
   dropped Wordsworth's line 'In the faith that looks through death',
   possibly because it is too Christian
   'Cobbett and Junius' H VIII. 87
   'not indeed' H VIII. 12
88 Anna Laetitia Barbauld H V. 147
89 'of our efforts' H XII. 125
   'rapidity of execution' H XII. 62 ('On Application to Study' was
   written at Winterslow in the autumn of 1823; 'Whether Genius is
   Conscious of its Powers?' was published in the *New Monthly Magazine*
   in December 1823, and was probably composed that autumn. Both
   essays are included in *The Plain Speaker*)
   'if her waters' Milton, *Areopagitica*, 29

CHAPTER FOUR Sheer Plod: Whig Prose

91 'the Dutch' William Shenstone, *Letters to Particular Friends* (1770),
   85; quoted by Hazlitt, H VIII. 51
92 'the real plodding' H II. 162
   'jerks, the breaks' H V. 12
   'everlasting prosing tragedy' H VIII. 307
93 'plodding, persevering' H II. 261
   'belonging technic' Gerard Manley Hopkins, *Further Letters* (1956),
   380
   'the whole mass' Hazlitt, *Spirit of the Age*, 23–4
   'powerful art' Milton, *Paradise Lost*, III. 602–3
   'petrific mace' H I. 127
   'aggregated soil' ibid., X. 293–4
   'petrific pencil' H X. 201
   'Dutch interiors' H XI. 166
94 'will sooner thaw' Burke, *Reflections*, 371
   'rich, impetuous' H I. 111

94 'most contradictory materials' H v. 58
95 Cellini see p. 27; H XVII. 274; and Benvenuto Cellini, *The Autobiography* (1956), 342–50
96 'fixed essence' H v. 51
'decomposition' G. M. Hopkins, *The Letters to Robert Bridges* (1955), 157
'a chaos of' H XI. 23
'*inert*' Priestley, *Disquisitions Relating to Matter and Spirit*, 1st edn, xxviii
'the turn which' H v. 51
97 'best prose-writer' H XII. 409
'warmth and vigour' H XII. 201
lines on Shaftesbury John Dryden, *Absalom and Achitophel* (1681), 156–62
'the bold and adventurous' Hazlitt, *Spirit of the Age*, 40
'is never at' ibid., 216
98 'motion' H v. 3
'the natural movements' H x. 173
'flowing, varied prose' H x. 168–9
99 'the perfection of style' H XVI. 352
'yet wet and' H v. 87
'a principle of' H XVI. 353
100 'divine truth' quoted in B. F. Cook, *The Elgin Marbles* (1984), 63
June 1816 H XVIII. 100–3, and see H XVIII. 430 for details of the other article
'every the slightest' H XVI. 353
'negligent grandeur' H XII. 329
'the entire, undoubted' H XVI. 207
101 'Art lifted up' H XVIII. 100
'a blow' H XII. 11
'project' H XII. 6
'gradual' H XVIII. 166
102 'living moving body' H XVIII. 152
'mouldering, imperfect state' H x. 28
103 'Grecian grandeur' John Keats, 'On Seeing the Elgin Marbles'
'In the most' John Ruskin, *The Works* (1903–12), x (2). 203
'the same form' ibid., 200
'property in it' H XI. 251
'in form like' H x. 168
104 like a boxer H XVI. 155

104 'modern Ajax' H XVII. 81
'absolute intuition' Hazlitt, *Spirit of the Age*, 246
'thorough prize-fighter' H XVI. 155
'free-spoken' H XVII. 77
105 'the same thing' H XVIII. 145
'floating in his' H XVIII. 163
106 'which is especially' Plato, *Phaedrus* (1952), 23
'a piece of' H II. 166
107 'bright consummate flower!' quoted in H XVIII. 151
108 'not carpenter's work' H XVIII. 161; Addison's poem is 'Milton's Style Imitated'
'by communicating' John Milton, *Complete Prose Works* (1962), VII. 460
109 'line of communication' H XVII. 107
'telegraphs that lately' H XVII. 382
'importunate chink' Burke, *Reflections*, 181
'non-conductor' H IX. 213
'conductors to the imagination' H V. 15
'the mail coaches' H XVII. 381
110 'frank, communicative, unreserved' H XIV. 99
'a remarkable example' John Seed, 'The Role of Unitarianism in the Formation of Liberal Culture 1775–1851', 134
'the Prime Minister' ibid., 134–5
'communications network' Ian McBride, 'The School of Virtue', in Boyce *et al.*, *Political Thought in Ireland since the Seventeenth Century* (1993), 89
111 'diffused and communicated' Hutcheson, *Short Introduction to Moral Philosophy*, 3rd edn, 14
'sincere, ingenuous, candid' ibid., I. 66
'curiosity, communicativeness, desire' Hutcheson, *System of Moral Philosophy*, I. 34
'natural immediate dislike' ibid., II. 2
'an immediate approbation' ibid., II. 28
'happiness' Hutcheson stated 'that action is *best*, which accomplishes the greatest happiness for the greatest numbers' (*Inquiry*, 164)
'communicate knowledge' Belsham, *Discourses, Doctrinal and Practical*, II. 56
'in the highest' ibid., I. 23
'a cheap and' Priestley, advertisement in *A General View of the Arguments for the Unity of God* (1785)

111 'a liberal public' Seed, 'Role of Unitarianism', 309
112 'unchristian rituals' ibid., 150
'Merry England' H XVII. 152–62
'exalt the good' Bacon, *Advancement of Learning*, 156
'a sincerity' Thomas Amory, *The Life of John Buncle, Esq.* (1756), I. 10
'calm, or turbulent' Hutcheson, *Short Introduction to Moral Philosophy*, I. 20
'constant propensity to' Hutcheson, *System of Moral Philosophy*, I. 21
113 'dynamic, hortatory classroom' McBride, 'School of Virtue', 88
'plods' Kivy, *Seventh Sense*, 36
'serious, plodding, minute' H VI. 42
'plodding tenaciousness' H XVII. 158
'truth, not beauty' H XII. 10
'dry plodding art' H XX. 276
'plodders' see H X. 121, H XX. 150
114 'features of nature' H XVII. 379
'furtive, sidelong glances' H XVII. 380
115 'even by the' H XVI. 289
'the stump of' Hazlitt, *Spirit of the Age*, 149
116 'life of things' quoted in H XVII. 379
'the ONE GOD' H XIX. 197
'What I have' H XVII. 379
117 'rotten core' H XX. 234

CHAPTER FIVE The Serbonian Bog

118 'lost for ever' Burke, *Reflections*, 313
'Of fierce extremes' Milton, *Paradise Lost*, II. 592–9
119 'abyss for ever!' H XX. 234
'are destroyed together' Price, *Discourse on the Love of our Country*, 50
'catching and spreading' ibid.
120 'a context of' Conor Cruise O'Brien, *The Great Melody: A Thematic Biography and Commented Anthology of Edmund Burke* (1992), 395
'talked of a' Hansard, XXVIII. 438–9
'the general principles' Hansard, XXXIX. 1393
'Old Jewry' Burke repeats the name 'Old Jewry' *Reflections* (93,

180), and (ibid., 138) refers to 'money-jobbers, usurers, and Jews'. Lord George Gordon, who converted to Judaism, he calls 'our protestant Rabbin' (ibid., 180)

121 **the Revd Hugh Peters** see ibid., 94 and 158
'**and frothy surface**' ibid., 90
'**organic** *moleculae*' ibid., 106
'**this new-sprung modern light**' ibid., 168
'**sluggish, inert**' ibid., 140, and see ibid., 145 and 181

122 '**remove the** *odium*' Priestley, *Disquisitions Relating to Matter and Spirit*, 2nd edn, I. 23
'**evidences, and titles**' Burke, *Reflections*, 121
'**the strain of**' Hopkins, *Further Letters*, 380

123 '**his back upon**' H IV. 105
'**too bad, Jason**' Maria Edgeworth, *Castle Rackrent* (1980), 76

124 **emotive, thrilling language** see Ian A. Gordon, *The Movement of English Prose* (1966), 147–50, for a discussion of Burke's style

125 '**one fell swoop**' H XII. 12 (Hazlitt is quoting *Macbeth*, IV. III, 219)
'**of Admiral Keppel**' H VII. 186

126 '**a pleader for**' Alfred Cobban, *Edmund Burke and the Revolt against the Eighteenth Century* (1960), 55
' "**in Corioli**" ' H XII. 228
'**familiar, inimitable, powerful**' H XVI. 222

127 '**the dull English understanding**' Edmund Burke, *The Writings and Speeches of Edmund Burke*, IX. 177
'**epistolary intercourse**' Burke, *Reflections*, 92

128 '**is furious**' H IV. 104

129 '**most eloquent**' Edward Gibbon, *The Letters*, ed. J. E. Norton (1956), III. 229
'**abused metaphysics**' H IV. 105
'**coherence of understanding**' H IV. 104
'**cube of light**' I discuss this image in 'Philip Larkin', in *Minotaur: Poetry and the Nation State* (1992), 245–9
'**half poet**' H IV. 105
'**half-English**' H XIX. 167

130 '**Murray the bookseller**' H VIII. 89
Peter Finnerty see Jones, *Hazlitt*, 74–5

131 '**like great whales**' H XII. 163

132 '**all society**' H VII. 320
'**composition**' H V. 149 ('the decomposition of prose is substituted for the composition of poetry')

132 'directs the storm' Joseph Addison, 'The Campaign'
    'Gazette in rhyme' H v. 13
    'whirling career' see Hazlitt on Burke, *Letter to a Noble Lord*, quoted
    on p. 126 above
133 'madest it pregnant' Milton, *Paradise Lost*, I. 19–22
    'double prize' H XII. 227
    'the dreaded name' H XVII. 106
    'various mouths' Milton, *Paradise Lost*, II. 965–7
134 in her journal Margaret Hazlitt, *Journal*, 43
    'manly behaviour' H III. 202
135 'Old father' James Joyce, *A Portrait of the Artist as a Young Man*
    (1977), 253
    'power of execution' H VIII. 87
    'blank and dreary void' H IX. 58
136 'posthumous fame' H IV. 96
    'grandeur' Hazlitt, *The Eloquence of the British Senate*, II. 215 and
    H. VII. 313 (from the 'Character of Mr Burke', repr. in *Political
    Essays*)
137 'beneath his rage' ibid., II. 83–4
    'at another vast' H I. 101 (Howe also notes the allusion)
    'flutter over our' Burke, *Writings and Speeches*, IX. 156
138 'one of the great' see H I. 144, 149, 152
    'sense and candour' H VII. 305
    'fit of extravagant' H VII. 301
139 'whole compass' ibid.
140 'of their motion' H VII. 309–10
    'as in a furnace' H v. 58
    'the most opposite' H VII. 310
    '*set* or formal' ibid.

CHAPTER SIX The Poetry in Prose

142 daughter of memory see William Blake's 'A Descriptive Catalogue', in
    Writings (1978), II. 830
    'decaying sense' Hobbes, *Leviathan*, 5
    'general vividness' H VII. 312
    'not musical' H VII. 313 (Howe speculates that the friend was
    Fawcett, H VII. 405n.)
143 'dishevelled' Seamus Deane, *Strange Country* (1997), 23
    'no style properly' G. M. Hopkins, *Further Letters*, 380

143 'all its grossness' Burke, *Reflections*, 169–70
'the Royal favour?' Burke, *Writings and Speeches*, IX. 164

144 'indolent' see H II. 260, H. v. 86, H XVII. 238 for Hazlitt's use of this term
'the proud Keep' see H XII. 11–12 and Burke, *Writings and Speeches*, IX. 172–3

145 'kinetic emotions' Joyce, *Portrait of the Artist as a Young Man*, 205
'naturally falls in' H IV. 214
'question or department' H XIV. 274

146 'public weal' ibid.
'that he did' H VII. 318
'plain, downright English honesty' Hazlitt, *Spirit of the Age*, 88
'finished gentleman' ibid., 82

147 'procreant cradle' Shakespeare, *Macbeth*, I. vi. 6–8
'but little calculated' H IV. 214
'age of sophisters, economists' Burke, *Reflections*, 170
'glossy neatness' H VII. 312
' "fat, Bedford level" ' H XII. 12

148 'At one fell swoop' Shakespeare, *Macbeth*, IV. iii. 216–19
'a rocky cliff' H XII. 10

149 'suspended on nothing' ibid.
'Mr Burke was' H XIX. 273
'The light of' H XIX. 271
'one entire and' H XVII. 377 (the phrase is taken from *Othello*, v. ii. 145)

150 Wordsworth, Southey, Coleridge I owe this point to Steven Roberts
'every feature' H X. 79

151 George Saintsbury see George Saintsbury, *A History of English Prose Rhythm* (1912), 361

152 'start a hare!' Shakespeare, *Henry IV, Part 1*, I. iii. 186–96

153 'all we hate' H VII. 229 (the quotation is adapted from Pope's 'Epistle to a Lady', 51)
'the most unpromising materials' H XII. 10
Coriolanian eagle H XII. 228 (comparing Burke's style to an eagle in a dovecote, Hazlitt quotes *Coriolanus*, v. vi. 113–4)
'accustomed to produce' Godwin, *St Leon*, 82–3

154 'continual beauty' H XII. 10

155 'halts, totters' H XII. 5
'continual excitement' H XII. 9
'desultory vacillation' H XII. 5

157 'never do' H XIV. 274
'exaggerating and exclusive' H IV. 214
'should be a blow' H XII. 11
'There was little' H XVII. 82
'by the force' H X. 182
'something Pindaric' H XVIII. 166

158 'great, but irregular' H III. 158n.
'flaming imagination' H XIX. 271
'not a nation' ibid.
'our half-English' H XIX. 167

159 'such sweet thunder' Shakespeare, *A Midsummer Night's Dream*, IV.
i. 113–19 (for Hazlitt's discussion of the passage in his lecture on the
play, see H IV. 247)

160 'contradict even themselves' H VIII. 51
'great melody' Yeats 'The Seven Sages' ('American colonies, Ireland,
France and India / Harried, and Burke's great melody against it')

161 'dry, cold, formal' Hazlitt, *Spirit of the Age*, 159
'hackled and torn' Burke, *Reflections*, 314
'hackled & mangled' Plutarch, *The Lives of the Noble Greeks and
Romans* (1612), 741
'final settlement' Burke, *Reflections*, 376 (Burke is quoting from
'Eternity! thou pleasing dreadful thought! / Through what variety of
untry'd being, / Through what new scenes and changes must we pass!'
(*Cato* V. 1) O'Brien discusses this passage in *Reflections*, 398, and see
also Bromwich, *Hazlitt*, 87
'un-English' Matthew Arnold, 'The Function of Criticism at the
Present Time', in R. H. Super (ed.), *Lectures and Essays in Criticism*
(1962), 268 and 267

162 'Panoptic and Chrestomathic' H XII. 247

163 'in our bosoms' Burke, *Reflections*, 182
'dry, meagre, penurious' H XII. 177
'at present beautify' Burke, *Reflections*, 95–6
'the *hortus siccus*' Hazlitt, *Spirit of the Age*, 60
'hard, dry materialism' ibid., 81
'the ancient permanent' Burke, *Reflections*, 275
logical machine' Hazlitt, *Spirit of the Age*, 42
'glass bee-hive' ibid., 31

164 'the haunts of' H VII. 228
'savours of the' H XII. 12
'familiarity' H VII. 229

165 'principle of composition' H XII. 11
'each tucked string' G. M. Hopkins, 'As Kingfishers Catch Fire'
'simplicity of our' Burke, *Reflections*, 186
'good sound English' H I. 155
166 'simplicity, strength' H XII. 17
'paladins et prodiges' (knights and monsters) Joseph Priestley,
Theological and Miscellaneous Works (1831), XXI. 594
'on whom we' Joseph Priestley, *Letters to the Right Honourable
Edmund Burke* 3rd edn (1791), p. iv
'this most intemperate' ibid., 46
'evidently heated' ibid., 2
'please to change' ibid., 139
'numerous and respectable' H XIII. 52
167 'and you mourn' Mary Wollstonecraft, *A Vindication of the Rights of
Men* (1790), 144
'false and fraudulent' Christopher Wyvill, *A Defence of Dr. Price, and
the Reformers of England* (1792), 15
'looseness of style' *Analytical Review* (Sept.–Dec. 1790), 412
'too undisciplined' Richard Sharp, *Letters and Essays in Prose and
Verse* (1834), 3
'our style of' H XIX. 272
168 'a sort of' Hazlitt, *Spirit of the Age*, 221
'aëronauts of France' Burke, *Reflections*, 376
'capricious caricature' H XII. 273
'communicative, diffuse, magnificent' H XII. 275
'frank, communicative, unreserved' H XIV. 99
'rapid', 'impetuous' H XII. 275
'It is now seventeen' H VIII. 17
169 'pilgrimage to thee!' H VIII. 15–16
' "*un beau jour*" ' Burke, *Reflections*, 162 (Howe notes the allusion, H
VIII. 336)

CHAPTER SEVEN Southey's Organ of Vanity

171 'ride in the' H XIX. 274 (Howe points out the allusion to Addison's
'The Campaign' and the undercutting reference to Pope's *The
Dunciad*, III. 264 – 'On grinning dragons Cibber mounts the wind')
'implicitly trusted' H XIX. 276
172 the French monarchy see Hazlitt, 'Sketch of the History of the Good
Old Times', H XIX. 182–202

172 'one of our' H XIX. 191 (and see note H XIX. 358)
  'That in the massacres' H XIX. 192
173 'shrill eunuch's voice' H XIX. 190
  'the triple tyrant' Milton, 'On the Late Massacre in Piedmont'
  (Hazlitt quotes a version of the sonnet's title; his prose rhythm also
  picks up Milton's cadences)
  'her fires' H VII. 94 (*Examiner*, 14 July 1816)
174 'petrific even to' H XIX. 356
  'double darkness' H VII. 255 (see Milton, *Samson Agonistes*, 594
  'suspended Cashman' H XIX. 186; see Thompson, *Making of the
  English Working Class*, 663–4
176 'almost without a struggle' Cobbett's *Weekly Political Pamphlet*, (15
  Mar. 1817), 344–5
  'plain, broad, downright' Hazlitt, *Spirit of the Age*, 244
177 'were the Hunts' Charles Cuthbert Southey (ed.), *The Life and
  Correspondence of Robert Southey* (1850), IV. 212
  'Hunt and Hazlitt' ibid., IV. 217
  'settled, determined malignity' quoted in Robert Southey, *Essays,
  Moral and Political* (1832) II. 3
  'the Socinian academy' ibid., II. 79
  'the Renegades' H XIX. 197
178 'little platoon' Burke, *Reflections*, 135
179 'of French patriots' H XIX. 180–1
  'pert loquacity' Burke, *Reflections*, 182
  'petulance of expression' Thomas Belsham, *Freedom of Enquiry, and
  Zeal in the Diffusion of Christian Truth* (1800), 26
  'one poor effort' H VII. 186
  'the same unimpaired' H VII. 87
  'you see the' H VII. 187
  'an antique quaintness' H XII. 16
181 'captious, dogmatical, petulant' Hazlitt, *Spirit of the Age*, 130
  'plain, clear, pointed' ibid., 135
  'a government-tool' ibid., 134
182 'and insolent excrescence' H. XX. 282
183 'in the finest' ibid., 130–1
  'a trenchant' Thomas De Quincey, *Recollections of Lakes and the
  Lake Poets* ([1970]), 232
  'shoots from his' Hazlitt, *Spirit of the Age*, 131
  'fierce with dark keeping' H II. 125
  'Egotism, petulance' H VIII. 150

183 'a thorough *keeping*' H XVII. 378
'the little' H XX. 306
'wild, irregular' Hazlitt, *Spirit of the Age*, 130
184 'irregular' H VIII. 45
'vaporous drop profound' Hazlitt, *Spirit of the Age*, 134
'to his confusion' Shakespeare, *Macbeth*, III. v. 23–9
185 'constant, unremitting, mechanical' H XI. 85
'rather the recipient' Hazlitt, *Spirit of the Age*, 138
'scholastic' H XVII. 111
'scholastic and professional' Hazlitt, *Spirit of the Age*, 136
'trenchant' De Quincey, *Recollections*, 232
'monarchism of the' H VII. 202
'peaked austerity' Hazlitt, *Spirit of the Age*, 137
186 'plain, clear, pointed' ibid., 135
'decent mixture' H VII. 202
'oily richness' H XVIII. 197
'unctuous' H X. 127
'most unctuous' H X. 7
'hermeneutics we need' Susan Sontag, *Against Interpretation and other Essays* (1967), 14
'oil of humanity' H XX. 300

CHAPTER EIGHT Coleridge the Aeronaut

187 'plain ground' H XII. 15
188 'The Baroque Style in Prose' Morris W. Croll, in Malone and Ruud (eds), *Studies in English Philology* (1929), 437–43
'enfeebled or exhausted' H XII. 8
'precision of form' ibid.
189 'fire from the flint' H XII. 10
190 'Il y a' quoted in H VII. 128
'And he went up' H VII. 128 As Grevel Lindop points out, no such biblical text exists – see Lindop 'Lamb, Hazlitt and De Quincey', in Richard Gravil and Molly Lefebure (eds), *The Coleridge Connection* (1990), 111–32. Lindop suggests Coleridge's text was John 6: 15, and that he is also recalling Mark 6: 46 or Luke 6: 12
'a steam of' Milton, *Comus*, 556; quoted in H VII. 128
192 'the index of' H XVII. 109
'new style' H XVII. 6
193 'of his face' H XVII. 118

194 'easy, indolent, good-tempered' H II. 260
'So have I' H XVII. 116
'life, liberty, health' John Locke, *A Letter concerning Toleration*
(1963), 15
Psalm 85 I owe this point to Clare Costley
195 'at cross-purposes' H VII. 116
'loose, airy, devious' H VII. 117
'fine network' H XX. 29
196 'HIMSELF ALONE' Lindop suggests that this irresistibly calls to mind
the 'I AM THAT I AM' of Exod. 3: 14, which is 'so often referred to in
Coleridge's writings' (Lindop, 'Lamb, Hazlitt', 119)
'perfect image' Wordsworth, *The Prelude* (1805), XIII. 69
'a transparency' H XVII. 114
'muscular strength' H XVI. 155
197 'the continuous' H XVIII. 371
'general intellect' Hazlitt, *Spirit of the Age*, 63
198 'hopes of man' ibid., 59
199 'inclement sky' H VII. 240
'torpid, uneasy repose' Hazlitt, *Spirit of the Age*, 62
'vain imaginings' cf. 'Hatching vain empires' (Milton, *Paradise Lost*,
II. 378)
'delightful suspense' H XVII. 107
200 'wild, irregular' Hazlitt, *Spirit of the Age*, 62
'kept at home' ibid., 64
201 'two great seminal' J. S. Mill, *Mill on Bentham and Coleridge* (1950),
40
'dry abstract reasoners' Hazlitt, *Spirit of the Age*, 67
'watchful jealousy' H IV. 198
202 'by the help' Hazlitt, *Spirit of the Age*, 67
English literature H VI. 192
'worse than gothic' H VI. 177
203 'gothic ignorance' H VII. 280
'but fully of knotty' H VI. 192
'a slow, heavy' H XVI. 58
'modern or *romantic*' H XVI. 60
'profuse of dazzling' H XVI. 62
'dark and doubtful' H XVI. 89
204 'in shape and' H VI. 180 (see Milton, *Paradise Lost*, I. 590)
'blind with double' H VII. 255 (Milton, *Samson Agonistes*, 593)
'roll their eyes' H VII. 289

204 'you would tread' H VII. 259
    'harmonious numbers' Milton, *Paradise Lost*, III. 38

CHAPTER NINE Blind Orion

206 'the master-art!' H VIII. 168 (the exhibition of Old Masters took
    place in June and July 1821, and Hazlitt's essay was first published in
    the *London Magazine* of August 1821, so it is likely he saw Poussin's
    painting early in the exhibition)
207 'highly original' Richard Verdi, 'Hazlitt and Poussin', *Keats–Shelley
    Memorial Bulletin* (1981), 15
    Ian Jack suggests Ian Jack, *Keats and the Mirror of Art* (1967),
    156
208 'all gilded masks?' Keats, *Endymion*, III. 1–22
    'Poor Keats!' H VIII. 99 ('On Living to One's-Self', also included in
    Table-Talk)
    'slavish countries' Maria Graham, *Memoirs of the Life of Nicholas
    Poussin* (1820), p. ix
209 'something of the' ibid., p. x
    'a mighty hunter' Gen. 10: 9
    'cannibal philosophers' Burke, *Writings and Speeches*, IX. 174
210 'a hunter of' see H VIII. 353
    'lawns of hell' Alexander Pope (tr.), *The Odyssey of Homer* (1962),
    XI. 703–8
211 'others he accuse' Milton, *Paradise Lost*, XII. 24–37
    'the first that' Milton, *Eikonoklastes*, in *Complete Prose Works*, III.
    446–7
    'the first King' ibid., III. 598
    'Diff'ring worship' Dryden, 'The Hind and the Panther', I. 283–4
    'in consequence of' *London Museum* (13 July 1822)
212 'its elemental power' Richard Verdi, *Nicolas Poussin 1594–1665*
    (1995), 310
    'the mysteries of' H XVII. 115
    'grey Dawn' Milton, *Paradise Lost*, VII. 373–4
213 'now of light' ibid., VII. 359–63
    'Machiavellian' David Norbrook, 'Marvell's "Horatian Ode" and
    the Politics of Genre', in Thomas Healy and Jonathan Sawday (eds),
    Literature and the English Civil War (1990), 147 (the painting of
    Henry Marten is reproduced in Antonia Fraser's study, *Cromwell:
    Our Chief of Men* (1973) between pp. 220 and 221)

213 'splendour in the flower' Wordsworth, 'Ode on the Intimations of Immortality'

214 'and never-ending succession' H xix. 18
'Seek him' Amos 5: 8
'the circulation of' Verdi, *Nicolas Poussin*, 310

215 'their hideous change' Milton, *Paradise Lost*, i. 304–13
'uneasy steps' ibid., i. 295
'the Iron Crown' H xiv. 243
'a great moral' H xiii. 213 and 361

216 'with the double' H vii. 277 (and see H vii. 289)
'dim suffusion veiled' Milton, *Paradise Lost*, iii. 22
Alastair Fowler see Milton, *Paradise Lost*, ed. Alastair Fowler (1971), 142

217 'with more pleasing' Milton, *Paradise Lost*, v. 42–3
'these eyes' ibid., iii. 23
'genuine, unsophisticated' Joseph Priestley, *The Proper Objects of Education* (1791), 8

218 'de ses misères' Jean-Jacques Rousseau, *Les Confessions*, ed. Jacques Voisine (1964), 460
'first simplicity' Maria Graham, *Memoirs*, 165
'a sort of' H xvii. 108
'unbroken integrity' H xvii. 378
'by its side' H xvii. 377

219 'a professor at' H xx. 125
'laboured, monotonous' H x. 110
'foregone conclusion' Shakespeare, *Othello*, iii. iii. 425
'determined to a' H xx. 356
'dry as the' Hazlitt is fond of employing this phrase from Shakespeare, *As You Like It*, ii. vii. 39, as a negative critical term

220 'setness and formality' H x. 110
'doomsday with eclipse' Shakespeare, *Hamlet*, i. i. 112–25
'Pope Pius VII' H xiv. 243

221 'the living principle' H vi. 187

222 'incident to maids' Shakespeare, *The Winter's Tale*, iv. iv. 118–25
'knocks down John Bull' H xx. 209
'protect her son!' H viii. 211

223 feminizing Keats see Susan J. Wolfson, 'Keats Enters History: Autopsy, *Adonais*, and the Fame of Keats', in Nicholas Roe (ed.), *Keats and History* (1995), 28
'Her son' Milton, *Paradise Lost*, vii. 23–38

223 'zealous backsliders' John Milton, *The Readie And Easyie Way to Establish a Free Commonwealth*, 2nd edn (1660), in *Complete Prose Works*, VII. 452

224 'so potent art' Shakespeare, *The Tempest*, v. i. 50
'Behold, the nations' Isaiah 40: 15
'spreadeth out' Job 9: 8–9

225 'drown my book' Shakespeare, *The Tempest*, v. i. 33–57

227 'prodigies of colour' H VIII. 172
'On Milton's Sonnets' H VIII. 174–81
'blind, yet bold' Andrew Marvell, 'On Mr Milton's "Paradise Lost"'

CHAPTER TEN Hazlitt *faciebat*: The Spirit of the Age

229 'force of present' Hazlitt, *Spirit of the Age*, 246
'this democratic Plutarch' *Tait's Edinburgh Magazine* (3 Dec. 1836), 758–68 (quoted in James A. Houck, *William Hazlitt: A Reference Guide* (1977), 74)
'like an eye' Hazlitt, *Spirit of the Age*, 216

230 'staring transparency' ibid., 48
'into any shapes' ibid., 217
'bubble reputation' Shakespeare, *As You Like It*, II. vii. 152
'fermenting and overflowing' Hazlitt, *Spirit of the Age*, 254

231 'an electrical machine' H XIV. 133
'electrical and instantaneous' Hazlitt, *Spirit of the Age*, 155
'reducing law to' ibid., 20
'mechanical and instrumental' ibid., 193
'in the light' ibid., 219

232 'the old English' ibid., 229
'honest seriousness' H I. 148
'very honest man' Hazlitt, *Spirit of the Age*, 251
'the cradle of' ibid., 21
'Sacred to Milton' see Catherine MacDonald Maclean, *Born under Saturn* (1943), 293; Stanley Jones doubts this story (Jones, *Hazlitt*, 98)

233 'thought to thought' Hazlitt, *Spirit of the Age*, 21
'no more than' ibid. and Burke, *Reflections*, 193

234 'kinetic' Park, *Hazlitt and the Spirit of the Age*, 154
'the time of' Hazlitt, *Spirit of the Age*, 149
'living objects' P. G. Patmore, *My Friends and Acquaintance* (1854), III. 105; see Howe's Titian note, X. 322 and Patmore, III. 105.
Maclean (*Born under Saturn*, 591n.) says that one of Hazlitt's copies

of *Young Man with a Glove* is in the Maidstone Museum, but it is not listed there

234 'too pragmatical' Hazlitt, *Spirit of the Age*, 52

235 'his bodies seem' H IV. 77
'This made Titian' H XI. 314
'a faint relic' H XI. 315
'mere waste-paper' H XII. 125

236 'darkens knowledge' Hazlitt, *Spirit of the Age*, 33
'momentary and irrevocable' H XII. 62

237 'unpremeditated discourse' Priestley, *Course of Lectures in Oratory and Criticism*, 111

238 'attitudes, gestures, and looks' ibid., 77
'sensible images' ibid., 84
'for exercise' Hazlitt, *Spirit of the Age*, 35

239 'mechanical stowage' Dickens, *Our Mutual Friend*, 266
'the ready warehouseman' H XVII. 111
'the finished gentleman' Hazlitt, *Spirit of the Age*, 82
'vinous' ibid., 282
'the bold and' ibid., 40

240 'sought the storms' Dryden, *Absalom and Achitophel*, 159–61
'desolate monotony' Hazlitt, *Spirit of the Age*, 32
'a certain degree' ibid., 49
'irregularities' ibid., 23

241 'your statisticians, sages' Dostoyevsky, *Notes from Underground* (1961), 106
'in the hearts' Hazlitt, *Spirit of the Age*, 28
'with its sustained' Thompson, *Making of the English Working Class*, 822
'exaggerating and exclusive' H IV. 214
'aggregating and an exclusive' Hazlitt, *Spirit of the Age*, 24

242 'within a profoundly' Uttara Natarajan, 'Hazlitt and the Reach of Sense' (1995), 175
'extraordinary excitement' Hazlitt, *Spirit of the Age*, 31–2
'if you could' ibid., 33–4

243 'Patagonian savage' ibid., 69
'modern topics' ibid., 72
'The thing' ibid.
'raw, uncouth' ibid., 71

244 'let him resemble' H XX. 223
'floating many a rood' Milton, *Paradise Lost*, I. 196

244 'from the Throne' Burke, *Writings and Speeches*, IX. 164
'ocean-stream' Hazlitt, *Spirit of the Age*, 70
245 'the self-possession' ibid., 80
'the heavy, dingy' James Northcote, *Life of Titian* (1830), I. 61
'almost equalled Nature' ibid., I. 219
'bodies as well' H v. 16
'strong, vivid' H XIX. 96
'material intuition' ibid.
246 'a mighty landmark' Hazlitt, *Spirit of the Age*, 73
'He leads' ibid., 75
247 W. K. Wimsatt Wimsatt, *The Prose Style of Samuel Johnson* (1941), 30

CHAPTER ELEVEN Vehemence versus Materialism

248 'hard, dry materialism' Hazlitt, *Spirit of the Age*, 81
'from their sinewy' H XVII. 320
'Now the spider' cited in *OED*
'grand whirling movements' Hazlitt, *Spirit of the Age*, 89
'full of chicane' ibid., 89
249 'hard, unbending, concrete' ibid., 91
'equally genuine' Olivia Smith, *The Politics of Language 1791-1819* (1986), 148
'gentlemanly attribute' ibid.
'periphrastic and literal' Hazlitt, *Spirit of the Age*, 95n.
'dispatch' J. Horne Tooke, *The Diversions of Purley* (1798), I. 27
'Promiscuous Exercises' Lindley Murray, *An English Grammar* (1808), II. 32
250 'we shall get' Tooke, *Diversions of Purley*, I. 111
mocking Murray William Cobbett, *A Grammar of the English Language* (1880), 117
'winged' Tooke, *Diversions of Purley*, I. 28
'false, absurd' ibid., II. 5
251 'the scars of' see Smith, *Politics of Language*, 139
'stamina' Joseph Priestley, *A Course of Lectures on the Theory of Language and Universal Grammar* (1762), 289
'great thing' Hazlitt, *Spirit of the Age*, 90
'genuine anatomy' ibid., 96
'prolixity and ambiguity' H II. 162
252 'succession of drops' Hazlitt, *Spirit of the Age*, 87

252 'as it falls' H II. 154
'determined' Hazlitt, *Spirit of the Age*, 92
'atomic impressions' H II. 152
'sacred vehemence' Hazlitt, *Spirit of the Age*, 86
'*religion* in it' ibid., 81
253 'thy false head' Milton, *Comus*, 793-8
'this creative impulse' Hazlitt, *Spirit of the Age*, 99
'matter-of-fact' ibid., 99n.
'learned, a literal' ibid.
'this capacity' ibid.
254 'empty, flaccid' ibid., 96
'Modern Antique' ibid., 99
'What a list' ibid., 106
J. G. Lockhart see *Blackwood's Edinburgh Magazine* (1825),
361-5
255 'some degree of' Hazlitt, *Spirit of the Age*, 99
'O Wickliff' ibid., 109
'to party gave' Oliver Goldsmith, 'Retaliation'
'a translation' see *London Magazine* (1825), 182
'rankling malice' Hazlitt, *Spirit of the Age*, 112
'greatest teachers' ibid., 117
256 'a hectic flush' ibid., 127
'exact feeling' H VI. 145
257 'pure emanation' Hazlitt, *Spirit of the Age*, 138
'wild harp' ibid., 279
258 'He tampers' H VIII. 149
'my utmost wonder' Mary Shelley, *Frankenstein; or, The Modern
Prometheus* (1994), 69
'deserved fate' Robert Burns, *The Letters*, 2nd edn, ed. G. Ross Roy
(1985) II. 334
259 'overturn the French' H X. 182
260 'estate in society' H XI. 278-9
'a kind of' Hazlitt, *Spirit of the Age*, 244
'of his life' ibid., 142
'impressions with them' H XII. 222
261 'can never die' Hazlitt, *Spirit of the Age*, 143
262 '*voilà de la pervenche!*' H XII. 372n., and Rousseau, *Les Confessions*,
ed. Voisine, 260-1
crocuses Wordsworth, *The Prelude* (1805), I. 308-9 ('The frost, and
breath of frosty wind had snapped / The last autumnal crocus . . .')

264 'up the way' H VII. 280
'unity and trinity' Thomas Jefferson, *The Writings* (1907), XIX. 259
'gothic and grotesque' H VI. 192
265 ' "I am nothing!" ' Samuel Taylor Coleridge, *The Literary Remains*
(1836), I. 71 (Coleridge's lecture is dated 30 Jan. 1818; Hazlitt's
article 'What is the People?' was published in Oct. 1817)
'grave, saturnine' Hazlitt, *Spirit of the Age*, 146
266 'favourable' H XII. 314
'faltering, improgressive, sidelong' Hazlitt, *Spirit of the Age*, 243
267 'mere exercise' ibid., 154
'Pyrrhus' ear' Shakespeare, *Hamlet*, II. ii. 478–84
268 'a cento of' Hazlitt, *Spirit of the Age*, 181
'principle of fusion' ibid., 163
269 'machine or a' ibid., 219
'mechanical excellence' H VIII. 83
'old English understanding' Hazlitt, *Spirit of the Age*, 229
'close, palpable, tangible' ibid., 252
270 'this new-sprung' Burke, *Reflections*, 168

CHAPTER TWELVE Great Plainness of Speech

271 'life in general' quoted in William Hazlitt, *The Plain Speaker*,
introduced by P. P. Howe (1928, Everyman edition), p. vii
272 'we use great' 2 Cor. 3: 12
273 'plain marble slab' H VII. 318
'plain, natural style' H XII. 46
'a few plain' H XII. 269
274 'the plain ground' H XII. 15
'in clear, short' H XII. 269
'something, fine, manly' H XII. 315
'genuine English intellect' H XII. 322–3
'truth of external' H XII. 322
'the gravity of' H VI. 327
'equally sharp and' H VI. 328
'plain things on' H XII. 228
'democratic level' H XII. 359
'low, fat, Bedford' Burke, *Writings and Speeches*, IX. 172
275 'very like Titian' H XI. 193
'they look you' H XVIII. 162
'they appear to' H XII. 286

275 'fine old mouser' H XI. 201
'cat-like, watchful' H XI. 202
'Titian's faces speak' H XII. 85–6

276 'the diverging rays' H XII. 40
Sterne's style H XI. 41
tolerably straight line Lawrence Sterne, *The Life and Opinions of
Tristram Shandy, Gentleman* (1967), VI. 40

277 'that necessary equipoise' ibid., IV. 35
'off-hand, at' H XII. 263
'keen, sharpened expression' H XII. 286

278 'tingling sensation' H IV. 77
'principle of motion' H XII. 288
'search and progress' H XII. 275
footnote to the same essay H XII. 277
'bulk, and thews' H XII. 201

279 'on that point' H XII. 203
'of Monmouth's affair' Sterne, *Tristram Shandy*, III. 10

280 'of the eye' H XII. 409
'ease and gracefulness' H XI. 305
'interminable babble' H XII. 198
'completely extempore' H XII. 91

281 'ropes or wires' H XII. 94

282 'were not intended' Gérard Genette, *Figures of Literary Discourse*
(1982), 3
'metalanguage' ibid., 4
'finished' Amit Chaudhuri, 'Text and Intertextuality in the Poetry of
D. H. Lawrence', 89

283 'long, black paper' D. H. Lawrence, 'Man and Bat' (and see
Chaudhuri, 'Text and Intertextuality', 109)
'equal to any job' Ted Hughes, *Moortown Diary* (1989), p. 87.
'I say untarnished' Lawrence, 'Bare Fig Trees'

284 'almost always' Chaudhuri, 'Text and Intertextuality', 168
'antithetical to desire' ibid., 165

285 'transitions of speech' H XII. 6
rasa Chaudhuri, 'Text and Intertextuality', 165
'intellectual food' H XII. 248
'your discourse has' H XII. 103
'the unctuous' Charles Lamb, letter to Thomas Manning, 27 Dec.
1800, in J. E. Morpurgo (ed.), *Charles Lamb and Elia* (1993), 99–100
'But ye have' 1 John 2: 20

285 'dry, meagre, penurious' H XII. 177
286 'their personal identity' H XII. 172 (in the quoted phrase 'whose name signifies love', Hazlitt is alluding to Shakespeare, *Merry Wives of Windsor*, I. i. 15–21:

> SLENDER. They may give their dozen white luces in their coat.
> SHALLOW. It is an old coat.
> EVANS. The dozen white louses do become an old coat well. It agrees well, passant; it is a familiar beast to man, and signifies love.
> SHALLOW. The luce is the fresh fish. The salt fish is an old coat.

Hazlitt has just been discussing how Italians pick lice from each others' 'tangled locks' without shame)
'heavy, dingy, slimy' Northcote, *Life of Titian*, I. 61
'the soul of' H XII. 51
Schlegel Augustus William Schlegel, *A Course of Lectures on Dramatic Art and Literature* (1815), I. 25
'of brighter suns' H IV. 46
287 'shed a light' H XVIII. 296
'the Hindoo' H XVII. 311
'scours the very' H XII. 177
'How soon' William Hogarth, *The Analysis of Beauty* (1753), VI. 36
'more blood' H XII. 170
'baked and burnt-up' H XII. 169
'as it were' H XII. 172
288 'bold and startling' H XII. 94
'unfinished style' H XII. 111
'unfinished state' H XII. 118
'natural and unstudied' H XII. 120
'imperfect hints' H XI. 251
289 'further search' H XII. 275
'simple purpose of' H XI. 248
'Oh! ephemeral works' H XII. 111
Doddridge H XI. 222
'the fluency came' H XI. 288
290 'he is about' H XI. 276–7 (Howe suggests (H XI. 369) that Hannah More is 'Mrs —')
291 'I am not' H XII. 121
'yet wet and' H V. 87
292 'care of themselves' H XII. 211

293 **'clearness'** Northcote, *Life of Titian*, I. 61
   'soodling' Clare, 'Rural Morning'
   Dasein Martin Heidegger, *Basic Writings* (1978), 21
   'more perfectly *articulated*' H IV. 298
   'in his air' H XII. 209
   'a quick flexibility' H XII. 217
294 **'walking on stilts'** H XII. 228
   'the sway of' H XII. 329
   'tender pliancy' Northcote, *Life of Titian*, I. 219 (Hazlitt wrote the
   book for Northcote)
   'When you do' Shakespeare, *The Winter's Tale*, IV. iv. 140-1
   'negligence of manner' H XII. 214
295 **'totally contrary to'** H XII. 218
   'With mortal sting' Milton, *Paradise Lost*, II. 650-3
297 **'the Great Fûm'** see Stanley Jones, 'Three Additions to the Canon of
   Hazlitt's Political Writings', *Review of English Studies* (1987), 362
   'independent and self-sufficient' Virginia Woolf, *Collected Essays*, I.
   160

Epilogue

298 **back room** Thomas Holcroft, 'Hazlitt's Death Bed', *Monthly
   Magazine and British Register* (Mar. 1833). The manager of Hazlitt's
   Hotel says that the room where Hazlitt died is on the third, not the
   second floor as Holcroft states
299 **'has happened to us'** H XVII. 372-3
300 **'ghastly, shrunk'** quoted in Howe, *The Life of William Hazlitt*
   (1949), 418
   'W. Hazlitt' ibid., 378
301 **'in his grave'** see ibid., 420-1 and Maclean, *Born under Saturn*,
   581-2

Index

Adams, Henry, 57; *The Education of Henry Adams*, 58
Addison, Joseph, 101, 108, 156, 182, 250, 284–5; 'The Campaign', 132, 171; *Cato*, 161
Aeschylus: *Agamemnon*, 109
Aikenhead, Thomas, 8
American Declaration of Independence, 60, 194
American Enlightenment, 65
American Revolution, 119
American War of Independence, 2, 3
Amory, Thomas: *The Life of John Buncle*, 112, 261
Analytical Review, 167
Anglican Church, 120
anti-Trinitarianism, 178, 217
Arianism, 216
Arnold, Matthew, 161, 253; 'The Function of Criticism at the Present Time', 69
association, 55, 78, 80, 81, 84, 94, 104, 115, 130, 183–4, 191, 211, 216, 254, 259, 260, 263, 276, 279, 291, 294
Auden, W. H.: 'Look, Stranger', 260

Bacon, Francis, 36, 56, 60–61, 77, 112, 183, 274; *The Advancement of Learning*, 60
Baillie, Joanna, 88
Bailly, Jean-Sylvain, 94
Bandon, Co. Cork, 2
Barbauld, Anna Laetitia, 88
Barthes, Roland, 282
Bate, Jonathan, 38
Battle of Austerlitz, 5, 85, 87, 170, 228
Battle of the Nile, 30
Battle of Sedgemoor, 279
Battle of Waterloo, 40, 170, 172, 279
Beacon, 255

Beaumont, Francis, 26
Bedford, Duke of, 144, 209, 244, 247, 274
Belsham, Revd Thomas, 6, 7, 8, 10, 37, 59, 74, 111, 179
Benevolence, 6, 7, 9, 35, 39, 68, 111
Bentham, Jeremy, 18, 42, 51, 60, 91, 93, 94, 162, 163, 201, 231–6, 238–43, 248, 252, 256
Berkeley, George, 29, 196, 197
Bewick, William, 15, 19
Bible, the, 19–23, 33, 190, 199, 224, 272
Blackwood's Magazine, 255
Blake, William, 142
Blenheim, 227
body, 21, 33, 55, 56, 60, 61, 77, 87, 97, 98, 104, 112, 122, 186, 193, 245, 278–81, 284, 285–6, 293, 294
Bolingbroke, Henry St John, Viscount, 44, 55, 188
Boston, Massachusetts, 57
Boswell, James, 14
Bourbons, 172, 254, 300
Bowra, Maurice, 26
boxers/boxing, 31, 56, 81, 82, 104, 105, 112, 131, 157, 189, 196, 245, 246, 269
Brecht, Bertolt, 238
bricolage, 27, 281, 282, 296
Bridgewater, Isabella, *see* Hazlitt, Isabella
Bristol, 149, 150
British Institution, 205
British Museum, London, 100, 101, 102
Bromwich, David, 67, 68, 69
Brook, Lord, 198
Brougham, Henry, 1st Baron, 243, 274
Browne, Sir Thomas, 60
Browning, Robert, 21, 57, 150–51

Bunbury, Sir Charles, 292, 293, 295
Bunyan, John, *The Pilgrim's Progress*, 218
Burdett, Sir Francis, 232, 269, 270, 274
Burke, Edmund, 46, 48, 53, 68, 69, 80, 95, 115, 180, 184, 193, 196, 199, 201–4, 233, 240, 243, 247, 255, 260, 264, 269, 270, 284, 295; and Bentham, 242; and Christian rationalists, 23; counter-revolutionary polemics, 132, 133; defection to the Tory cause, 117, 166; as an enemy of Unitarian culture, 120; hatred of science, 120; and imagination, 125, 135, 138, 145, 148, 149, 158, 160, 161, 164, 166, 171; inspires H, 133, 135; and Junius, 13, 82, 136–7; and liberty, 121, 123, 124, 161; and Milton, 134, 135; monarchism, 117, 134, 140, 171, 199, 263; perception of, 119; and Pitt, 159; and Priestley, 120, 166, 167; principles, 149–50; and the Revolution Society, 120; Romanticism, 141, 146; Smith attacks, 177; style, 122–8, 136, 139–45, 147–50, 152–4, 156, 160–61, 162, 164–8, 274; and Windham, 81; and Wordsworth, 263; *A Letter to a Noble Lord*, 125, 126, 127, 137, 168, 182, 209, 244, 258, 274, 278; prose aria on Marie Antoinette, 150, 168, 202, 261; *Reflections on the Revolution in France*, 9, 10, 11, 25, 48, 94, 109, 118–24, 126, 127, 133, 134, 147, 161, 162–3, 166, 167, 168, 179, 185, 198; *Thoughts on French Affairs*, 161
Burns, Robert, 258
Butler, Bishop, 198
Byron, George, Gordon, 6th Baron Byron of Rochdale, 50, 155; *Don Juan*, 177

Cadogan Morgan, Revd George, 10
Calamy, Edmund: *Non-Conformists' Memorial*, 198
Calvinism, 243, 244, 254
Cambridgeshire, 2, 158
Campbell, Thomas: *The Pleasures of Hope*, 88
Candour, 7, 55, 68, 111, 138, 195, 254

Canning, George, 81, 243, 268
Carlyle, Thomas, 17, 45–6
Cashman, John, 174–6
Castlereagh, Robert, Viscount, 130, 172, 215, 294–6
Catholic Relief Act, 120
Catholics/Catholicism, 41, 126, 127, 172, 173–4, 178, 197
Cavanagh, John, 87, 129, 130, 131, 162, 296
Cellini, Benvenuto, 27, 95, 96, 142
Centos, 27, 94, 95, 100, 148, 268, 269, 281, 284
Cervantes Saavedra, Miguel de: *Don Quixote*, 260
Champion, 263
Chantrey, Sir Francis, 193
Chapman, George, 57, 59
Chard, Leslie, 71, 72, 73, 75
Charles I, King, 22
Charles X, King of France, 300
Chatham, William Pitt, Earl of, 138, 139, 273, 274
Chaucer, Geoffrey, 96
Chaudhuri, Amit, 282, 284, 285
Christianity, primitive, 217, 218
Christie, Jonathan, 254–5
Christie, Thomas, 167
Church of England: and capital punishment, 176; and Unitarianism, 8, 111–12; Wakefield attacks, 10
Cicero, Marcus Tullius, 28, 141, 147
Clare, John, 15–16, 293; *Poems Descriptive of Rural Life and Scenery*, 107; 'To the Cowslip', 107; *Village Minstrel*, 107
Clarendon, Lord, 83–4
Clarke, Samuel, 198; *Discourse Concerning the Being and Attributes of God*, 198
Clarkson, Thomas, 266
classicism, 99, 104, 108, 141, 148, 159, 162, 203, 220, 221
Claude Lorraine, 74, 81
Co. Cork, 2, 3, 134
Co. Tipperary, 2, 5, 158
Cobban, Alfred, 126
Cobbett, William, 50, 51–2, 56, 66, 80–3, 87, 104, 129, 131, 160, 175, 229–32, 236, 245, 250, 253, 260, 269–70, 274; *A Grammar of the English Language*, 249; his

imagination, 270; and liberty, 176; his style, 290; and the United States, 81, 82, 174

Coleridge, Samuel Taylor, 28, 116, 130, 150, 164, 178, 180, 185, 212, 239, 240, 269, 273, 299; and Godwin, 200, 201; H meets, 13, 134, 193; and Hume, 194, 195; and imagination, 139, 195, 196, 197, 199, 200; intellectual odyssey, 197–8, 199; on Pitt, 28–9; as a preacher, 190–91, 199–200, 211–12, 218; as a republican, 191; and Revd Hazlitt, 192; as a seminal figure, 190; his style, 187; Unitarian period, 163, 198; Wakefield influences, 10; *Ancient Mariner*, 200; 'Frost at Midnight', 134; lecture on the Gothic mind, 265

Coligny, Admiral de, 172

Colman, George: *The Heir at Law*, 268

communication, 8, 23, 36, 37, 101, 107, 108, 109–12, 151, 196, 278

Condillac, Etienne Bonnot de, 94

Congregationalism, 74

consciousness: plenary, 52; revolutionary, 10

conversation, 7, 185, 196, 271, 272, 273, 275, 276, 277, 280, 289, 290

Cork, 3, 134

Correggio, Antonio da, 107

Crabbe, George, 93, 299

Crediton, Devon, 3

critical terms: abrupt, 25–8, 53, 101, 212, 291; aggregate, 117, 241, 242; diffusion, 9, 36, 37, 111, 119; disinterested, 69, 70, 35, 36, 39, 41, 43, 55, 66–71, 85, 111, 112, 168, 194; dry, 29, 55–6, 142, 151, 163, 201, 202, 212, 219, 271, 285, 291; elasticity, 29, 155; energy, 8, 22, 37, 76, 101; enjoyment, 70, 87; expression, 63, 72, 101, 281, 294; flexible, 70, 101; gothic, 101, 102, 103, 146, 147, 148, 202, 203, 204, 221, 258, 263, 264–5, 277, 295; gusto, 8, 33, 66, 69, 87, 159, 160, 235, 237, 263, 278; happiness, 7, 8, 60, 70, 111; immediate, 65, 66, 101, 111; importunate, 48, 109, 121; indolence, 77, 78, 144, 192, 194, 257, 276; irregular, 26, 146, 183, 184,

202, 240, 264, 295; keeping, 95, 183; momentum, 53, 101, 155; motion, 34, 35, 63, 66, 69–72, 98, 99, 101, 122, 151, 229, 230, 231, 237, 278, 280, 286, 287, 288; nature, 34, 70, 95, 98, 99, 106, 107, 115, 116, 188, 191, 206, 207, 214, 221–2, 224, 245, 282, 288, 291; nervous, 21, 108; pert, 179, 180; *petit-maître*, 82, 98, 142, 157; petrific, 93; petulance, 179–83; plain, 146, 147, 186, 187, 272, 274; plodding, 66, 76, 91, 92–3, 113, 115, 231; sensuous, 58, 59, 66; sluggish, 8, 60, 80, 121, 122, 247; texture, 101, 181, 248, 254, 285, 286; unctuous, 55, 56, 186, 245, 285–6, 287; vehemence, 53, 88, 91, 101

Croker, John Wilson, 130, 296–7

Croll, Maurice: 'The Baroque Style in Prose', 188

Cromwell, Oliver, 211, 215

Crown and Anchor Tavern, 47

Cruikshank, George, 51, 266

Cudworth, Ralph: *The True Intellectual System of the Universe*, 198

Dante Alighieri, 118, 295

David, Jacques Louis, 221

Davies, John, 280

Davy, Sir Humphry, 109

De Quincey, Thomas, 183, 185

Deane, Seamus, 143

Defoe, Daniel, 92, 138, 176

Derrida, Jacques, 284

Dickens, Charles, 28, 43, 45, 191, 238–9, 241, 297; *Bleak House*, 239, 239, 241, 297; *David Copperfield*, 191; *Great Expectations*, 238; *Our Mutual Friend*, 239

Diderot, Denis, 268

Dissent/Dissenters: and Burke's defection to the Tory cause, 117, 166; debates on toleration for, 125; Dissenting counter-culture, 68; Dissenting culture, 6, 151, 218, 283; Dissenting imagination, 131; Dissenting liberty, 199; Dissenting rationalism, 119; Dissenting science, 122; structure of Dissent, 124; *see also* Rational Dissent

Doddridge, Philip, 289

Domenichino, Zampieri, 193

Donne, John, 57; 'The Second Anniversary', 58
Dostoyevsky, Fyodor, 43; *Notes from Underground*, 241
Drennan, William, 67
Dryden, John, 5, 58, 97, 137, 166, 188, 244, 279; *Absalom and Achitophel*, 240; *The Hind and the Panther*, 211
Dunster, 193
Dutch, 91, 92, 93, 113, 190, 274
Dutch painting, 114

Edgeworth, Maria: *Castle Rackrent*, 123–4, 128
Edinburgh Annual Register, 40
Edinburgh Review, 97, 229, 300
Edwards, Jonathan, 92–3, 113
electricity, 37, 38, 109, 158
Elgin Marbles, 26, 70, 98–107, 165, 169, 170, 189, 275, 294
Eliot, T. S., 57–60, 83, 96, 232; 'Tradition and the Individual Talent', 58, 140; *The Waste Land*, 284
Eliot, William Greenleaf, 59
Elizabethan literature, 17, 18, 20, 21, 26, 33, 34, 45, 47
Ellenborough, Lord, 50
Emmet, Catherine, 2
Emmet, Robert, 2
Enfield, William: *The Speaker*, 88
English Civil War, 150
English language, 165, 174, 176, 249, 250
English, the, 158; character, 30, 113, 121, 269
Enlightenment, 5, 74, 101, 110, 173, 202, 204, 263
Erskine, Thomas, 12
Examiner, 40, 49, 100, 171, 172, 177, 190, 204, 216, 296

Fawcett, Joseph, 71, 73, 75; 'Reflections Drawn from the Consideration that God is our Creator', 71–2, 119
Fawkes, Guy, 41, 43, 44, 46, 47, 47
Fielding, Henry, 274; *The History of Tom Jones, a Foundling*, 95
Finnerty, Peter, 129, 130, 131
Flaxman, John: *Lectures on Sculpture*, 99, 100
Fletcher, John: *Two Noble Kinsmen*, 26
Forster, E. M., 293

Fowler, Alastair, 216
Fox, Charles James, 25, 81, 120, 132, 133, 138, 145–6, 147, 157, 170, 203, 233, 273, 274
Fox, W. J., 246
France: 1830 revolution, 37, 109; British interference, 158; Burke on, 161; formalism, 203, 222; freedom in, 209; French national character, 30, 31; the French as 'plodding', 92; invasion of Ireland (1798), 134; Protestants massacred (1816), 172; revolutionary, 118, 137, 170, 220
Francis, Sir Philip, 136
Francis I, King of France, 172–3
Franklin, Benjamin, 4, 38, 109, 158, 233
free play, 33–4, 54
Freemasons, 4, 5, 204, 214
French National Assembly, 166, 169, 171
French Revolution, 5, 10, 22, 25, 119, 120, 125, 132, 133, 146, 157, 161, 167, 169, 170, 218, 220–21, 224, 248, 264
Friel, Brian: *Philadelphia Here I Come*, 143
Frost, Robert: 'Mending Wall', 257
Fuseli, Henry, 272, 281–2, 283, 288

Gay, John: *The Beggar's Opera*, 119, 164
Genesis, 34, 65, 75
Gennette, Gérard, 282–3
Gentleman's Magazine, 11
George III, King, 136, 180
George IV, King (as Prince Regent), 50, 173
Germany, and the Reformation, 20, 23
Gibbon, Edward, 129
Gifford, William, 33, 83, 231
Gillray, James, 238, 266
Giorgione, 208
Giulio Romano, 208
glass-blowing, 62, 63, 89, 90, 91, 99, 103, 127, 230, 236–7, 253, 280
Glorious Revolution, 119, 120, 132, 227
Godwin, William, 13, 48, 51, 91, 97, 163, 200, 201, 202, 234, 239–40, 248, 252; *Caleb Williams*, 71;

Cloudesley, 37–8; *St Leon*, 153–4, 229–30
Goldsmith, Oliver, 80–81, 114, 129–31, 219, 255
Gordon, Lord George, 120
Gordon Riots, 120, 125, 126
Grafton, Duke of, 136
Graham, Maria: *Memoirs of the Life of Nicholas Poussin*, 208–9, 218, 221
Greek signal-fires, 112, 116, 119
Gribelin (etcher), 5, 84

Habeas Corpus Act, 174
Hackney, London, 6–7
Hackney New College, 4, 7, 10–11, 23, 37, 38, 47, 48, 52, 59, 67, 74, 111, 166, 217
Halifax, 73, 75
Hampden, John, 12, 116, 177
Hardy, Thomas, 11, 12
Harrington, James, 4
Harris Manchester College, Oxford, 263
Hartley, David, 55, 197
Hastings, Warren, 136
Haydon, Benjamin, 45, 100; *Christ Entering Jerusalem*, 100
Hazlitt, Grace (née Loftus; H's mother), 2, 158
Hazlitt, Harriet (H's niece), 14
Hazlitt, Isabella (née Bridgewater; H's second wife), 16, 46
Hazlitt, John (H's brother), 13, 14, 48
Hazlitt, Margaret (H's sister), 2–3, 14, 134
Hazlitt, Sarah (née Stoddart; H's first wife), 16, 18, 62
Hazlitt, William: affair with Sarah Walker, 18, 43; appearance, 1, 15, 16; as an artist, 2, 4–5, 6, 14, 84–5, 234; attends Hackney New College, 4, 7, 10, 37, 47, 48, 52, 59, 67, 74; basis of his critical imagination, 142; birth (Maidstone, Kent, 1778), 2; concept of prose writing, 88–89, 91; death (Soho, London, 1830), 14, 18, 300; divorces Sarah, 16, 18; final illness, 298–300; influences Keats, 60; interest in criminality, 43–4, 163, 238, 242, 297; Isabella leaves (1826), 16, 46; Lake District story, 211, 212, 213; *Letters on the English Poets*,

136; marries Isabella Bridgewater, 16, 46; marries Sarah Stoddart, 16; meets Coleridge (1798), 13, 134, 193; memorial, 300–01; obsession with Sarah Walker, 16; personality, 2, 46; republicanism, 117, 134, 140; self-portrait, 1, 2, 6, 14; sense of inferiority as a prose-writer, 92
sources of inspiration, 95, 105–6, 107, 133; visits Wordsworth, 31; writing method, 20
WORKS: 'The Age of Elizabeth', 202–3; 'Arguing in a Circle', 149, 171; on Bentham, 231–4, 235–6, 239, 240–42, 252; on Burke (1807), 142, 171; on Byron, 255–6; 'Capital Punishments', 41–3; on Castlereagh, 294–6; 'The Causes of Public Opinion', 287; 'Character of Mr Burke', 82, 147, 152–3; *Characters of Shakespear's Plays*, 40–41, 106; on Cobbett, 160, 176, 229; 'The Conversation of Authors', 276; *Conversations with James Northcote*, 96, 103, 235, 259–60, 273, 280, 288–90; on *Coriolanus*, 39–40, 91, 145, 146–7, 241; 'The Court Journal – A Dialogue', 119; on Croker, 296–7; 'Definition of Wit', 35–6, 219; 'The Difference between Writing and Speaking', 272, 275; 'The Drama', 196–7; on the Elgin Marbles, 100–01, 104, 106, 107–9, 275, 294; Elizabethan lectures, 17, 18, 20, 26, 33, 34, 203, 204; *The Eloquence of the British Senate*, 32, 56–7, 136, 140, 165, 232; *An Essay on the Principles of Human Action*, 33, 158; 'A Farewell to Essay Writing', 226, 248; 'The Fight', 31, 81–2, 85, 104–5, 157; on Flaxman's *Lectures on Sculpture*, 99, 100; on Fox, 132, 134, 273; *Free Thoughts on Public Affairs*, 28, 137; on Fuseli, 272, 281–2, 283, 288; on genius and its powers, 291; on Godwin, 229–30, 239–40, 252; 'Gusto', 235; on Guy Fawkes, 40, 43, 46; 'Hot and Cold', 285–6, 287–8; 'The Ideal', 183; 'The Indian Jugglers', 87, 105, 129–30,

269, 282, 286; 'The Influence of
Books', 22; on Irving, 243–7; on
Jeffrey, 97–8, 229, 230, 269, 300;
on Johnson, 294; 'The Late Mr
Horne Tooke', 239, 248–53; lecture
on *A Midsummer Night's Dream*,
159; lecture on Locke, 106;
*Lectures Chiefly on the Dramatic
Literature of the Age of Elizabeth*,
17, 18, 20, 26, 33, 34, 48, 61;
*Lectures on the English Comic
Writers*, 53–4, 106; *Lectures on the
English Poets*, 106; *A Letter to
William Gifford*, 33–4, 36, 135;
'The Letter-Bell', 37, 109, 114,
115–16, 149, 183, 218, 220, 226;
letters, 12, 73, 86–7; *Liber Amoris*,
16, 43, 44–5; *Life of Holcroft*, 81;
Life of Napoleon Buonaparte, 1–2,
22, 24, 37, 146, 215, 220, 231,
300; 'The Look of a Gentleman',
292–4; on Mackintosh, 266–9; on
Madame de Staël, 195–6; 'Madame
Pasta and Mademoiselle Mars',
294; 'The Manager', 287; 'Merry
England', 112, 113; 'Mind and
Motive', 41; 'My First
Acquaintance with Poets', 28, 133,
190–96, 199–200, 213, 218, 266;
*A New and Improved Grammar of
the English Tongue*, 54; *Notes of a
Journey through France and Italy*,
29, 98, 100, 219–20, 258–9; 'The
Old Age of Artists', 280–1; 'On a
Landscape of Nicolas Poussin',
205–22, 224–8; 'On Application to
Study', 19–20, 89, 236; 'On Court-
Influence', 199; 'On Depth and
Superficiality', 274; 'On Envy',
272, 285; 'On Familiar Style', 54;
'On Genius and Common Sense',
79–80, 84; 'On Good-Nature',
128; 'On Liberty and Necessity',
74–5; 'On Milton's Sonnets', 227;
'On Old English Writers and
Speakers', 266, 272, 274; 'On
Paradox and Common-Place', 91,
258; on the periodical press, 126;
'On Poetry in General', 92, 109;
'On the Aristocracy of Letters',
222; 'On the Conversation of
Authors', 272; 'On the Fear of
Death', 300; 'On the Knowledge of
Character', 92–3; 'On the Living
Poets', 87–8; 'On the Pleasure of
Painting', 5, 84–6, 170, 227; 'On
the Prose Style of Poets', 25–6, 27,
101, 115, 147–9, 151, 154–7, 164,
180, 181, 182, 187, 188, 189, 242,
272, 284–5; 'On the Qualifications
Necessary to Success in Life', 97,
278–80; 'Personal Identity', 27;
'Pitt and Buonaparte', 28; *The
Plain Speaker*, 261, 271–97;
'Poetry', 221–2; *Political Essays*,
17, 18, 28, 47, 48–49, 51, 52, 53,
59, 138, 164, 171, 172, 175, 177,
185, 195; 'Proposal for the Basis of
a New System of Metaphysical
Philosophy', 33; *Prospectus of a
History of English Philosophy*, 23,
32–3; 'Reading Old Books', 126,
133, 260; review of Schlegel's
Lectures on Dramatic Literature,
203, 286; review of *The Excursion*,
213–14; *Round Table* essays,
286–7; 'Shakespeare and Milton',
94, 140; 'The Sick Chamber',
298–9; 'Sitting for One's Picture',
288; *The Spirit of the Age*, 13, 97,
115, 163, 181, 185–6, 197–200,
229–47, 248–70, 300; 'The Spirit
of Obligations', 275; *Table-Talk*,
84, 85, 208, 211, 227; on *Tom
Jones*, 95; 'Trifles Light as Air',
181–2; on Van Dyke, 72, 73–4,
275, 277, 289; *A View of the
English Stage*, 40; 'What is the
People?', 204, 216, 263–4;
'Whether Genius is Conscious of its
Powers?', 88–9, 131, 235, 237; on
Wilberforce, 266; on Wordsworth,
257–65

Hazlitt, William Carew (H's grandson):
*The Hazlitts: An Account of their
Origin and Descent*, 2, 3

Hazlitt, Revd William (H's father), 8,
185, 194, 227, 246; Adam Smith
teaches, 5, 68; background, 2, 5, 158;
birth (1734), 3; and Coleridge, 192;
death (1820), 3, 84; exchange of
ideas, 23; forced to return to Ireland,
2; founds the Unitarian church in
Boston, 57; H's portrait of, 4–5, 6, 14,

84–5; and Hutcheson, 65, 113;
Margaret on, 2–3, 134; and
Napoleon, 228; personality, 3, 5–6;
politics, 2–3, 4, 6; and Sterne, 129;
Unitarian minister, 2, 3, 5, 13, 17, 23,
57, 86, 108–9, 110, 191; *Sermons for
the Use of Families*, 6, 12
Hazlitt, William (H's son), 16, 238, 300
Hazlitt family, 2–5, 134
Hazlitt's Hotel, Frith Street, Soho,
London, 13–14
Heidegger, Martin, 293
Hellenism, 110, 124, 210
Helvétius, Claude-Adrien, 94
Henry VIII, King, 125, 266
Herbert of Cherbury, Lord, 57
Hindus, 286, 287
Hobbes, Thomas, 30, 32, 35, 60, 76,
77–8, 93, 114, 142; *Leviathan*, 79,
263
Hogarth, William, 105, 107, 151, 238,
239, 252, 256, 274, 288, 296;
Analysis of Beauty, 287; *Marriage à la
Mode*, 150
Holbein, Hans, 265–6, 274
Holcroft, Thomas, 11, 13, 134
Holub, Miroslav, 83
Homer, 94, 95, 205, 210, 245, 268;
Odyssey, 210
Hone, William, 49, 50–51; *The Political
House that Jack Built*, 51
Honest Whigs club, 4
Hopkins, Gerard Manley, 30, 52, 96,
122, 143, 165; 'The Windhover', 93
House of Brunswick, 254
Howe, P. P., 172, 177, 210
Hughes, Ted: *Moortown Diary*, 283
Huguenots, 172
Hume, David, 77, 113, 194, 195
Hunt, John, 48–50
Hunt, Leigh, 48–52, 177, 188, 239
Hunter, Revd Joseph, 2
Huss, John, 198
Hutcheson, Francis, 34, 35, 60, 63, 84,
85, 198; and aesthetics, 66–7; and
America, 110; and children, 64, 65,
66, 69, 89, 112–13; and
disinterestedness, 66, 67; influence on
H, 68; and intenseness, 69, 70; and
motion, 90; republicanism, 113; and
Revd Hazlitt, 65, 113; *An Inquiry
into the Original of our Ideas of*

Beauty and Virtue, 66–7, 68; *A Short
Introduction to Moral Philosophy*,
36–7, 110–11; *A System of Moral
Philosophy*, 64–5, 66, 111

Ilissos, 105–6, 107
imagination, 34, 35, 36, 38–45, 56, 58,
61, 70, 81, 91, 92, 109, 131, 141,
146, 147, 157, 193, 201, 206, 229,
289; anti-monarchical, 209; Burke
and, 125, 135, 138, 145, 148, 149,
160, 161, 164, 166, 171; Cobbett
and, 270; Coleridge and, 139, 195,
196, 197, 199, 200; the disinterested,
68–69; the English, 30, 202; H's
imagination, 20, 27, 77, 98, 117, 142,
207, 211, 214, 275; irrational nature
of, 242; Keats and, 208; Milton and,
94–5, 108, 140, 253–4, 268; and
monarchism, 157, 200, 241; and
Protestantism, 163; republican, 60;
Scott and, 253; Shakespeare and, 96,
203, 230; Unitarian, 59; Wordsworth
and, 265
India, 286
intellect, 32–3, 55
intuition, 95, 104
Ireland: the army in, 3; French invasion
of (1798), 134; H on the Irish, 128;
the Hazlitt family as Irish, 2; and
'Protestant violence', 125; uprising
(1798), 67, 133, 134, 191
Irish Rebellion (1798), 2
Irish Volunteers, 134
Irving, Revd Edward, 243–7, 248, 252,
254, 268

Jack Tars, 29, 30, 31, 33
Jacobin Club, Paris, 120
Jacobinism/Jacobins, 9, 86, 125, 164,
171, 172, 179, 258, 260
Jacobites/Jacobitism, 55, 247, 254
Jacob's ladder, 4–5, 214
James II, King, 22, 84, 227
Jefferson, Thomas, 60, 194, 264
Jeffrey, Francis, 97–8, 229, 230, 236,
269, 300
Jeffreys, Judge, 4
Jerome of Prague, 198
John Bull, 255
Johnson, Joseph, 6, 33, 71, 72–3, 109,
124, 167, 251

Johnson, Dr Samuel, 15, 29, 80–81, 104, 126, 131, 140, 151, 168, 188, 196, 219, 233, 247, 250–51, 277, 291, 294
Jones, Stanley, 47, 50, 130, 297
Jonson, Ben, 53, 81; *The Silent Woman*, 113
Joyce, James, 128, 135, 145; *Dubliners*, 256
Joyce, Revd Jeremiah, 11, 12
Junius, 13, 82, 87, 126, 129, 130, 131, 136–7, 142, 252, 290

Kant, Immanuel, 22, 75–6
Kean, Edmund, 29, 38, 105, 282, 293
Keats, John, 130, 205, 222–3, 244, 255; admiration for Grecian urns, 106; and the Elgin Marbles, 100, 103; H influences, 60; his imagination, 208; *Endymion*, 107, 207–8; *Lamia*, 107; 'To Autumn', 47–8, 208
Kendall, Edward: *Letters on Ireland*, 289
Keswick, 212, 213
Kinsale, American prisoners in, 3, 4
Kippis, Andrew, 110
Kivy, Peter, 66, 67

Lake District, 31, 211, 262
Lake school, 201–2
Lamb, Charles, 50, 55, 219, 285, 300
Lamb, Mary, 50
Larkin, Philip, 129
Lawrence, D. H., 108, 197, 221, 282–3; 'Bare Fig Trees', 283; *New Poems*, 74; 'Poetry of the Present', 74
Le Brun, Charles, 209
Le Sueur, Eustache, 209
Leibniz, Gottfried, 106; *Pre-established Harmony*, 198
Leonardo da Vinci, 208
Lévi-Strauss, Claude, 281–2
liberty, 8, 202, 204, 205, 214, 218; Burke and, 121, 123, 124, 161; civil, 109; Cobbett and, 176; Defoe and, 138; Dissenting, 199; English, 127, 249, 251; and English radical journalism, 51–2; H and, 20, 22, 25, 54, 135, 177, 178, 296, 301; Jefferson and, 60, 194; and John Hunt, 48–9; Milton and, 216; Price on, 119; Priestley on, 11, 59, 60; radical Whig

idea of, 122; religious, 109; Revd Hazlitt and, 3, 6, 23
Lindsey, Theophilus, 110
Linen Hall Library for the Promotion of Knowledge, 36
Liston, John, 56, 292
Liverpool, Lord, 176, 223
Llangollen Vale, 192, 212
Locke, John, 8, 23, 24, 28, 30–31, 55, 60, 75, 77, 84, 93, 108, 116, 117, 177, 198, 239, 276; and Leibniz, 106; as 'plodding', 91, 92; prose style, 87, 251–2; *Essay concerning Human Understanding*, 32, 76; *Letter concerning Toleration*, 178, 194; *The Reasonableness of Christianity*, 178
Lockhart, J. G., 254
Loftus family, 2, 200
London, 52, 75, 238, 243, 297
London Corresponding Society, 11, 12
London Magazine, 100, 106–7, 228, 255
Louis XIV, King, 209, 227
Louvre, Paris, 100–01, 102, 168, 169, 170, 215, 216, 227, 234, 245
Lovelace, Richard, 44

MacAdam, John, 231
Macaulay, Thomas Babington, lst Baron, 17
McBride, Ian, 110, 113
Mackintosh, Sir James, 28, 161, 181, 185, 200, 231, 239, 240, 266–9; *Vindicae Gallicae*, 185
Mackintosh, Sir James, *Lectures on the Law of Nature and Nations*, 267
McLachlan, H., 67
Macready, Charles, 29–30
Maidstone, Kent, 2, 13
Maidstone Museum and Art Gallery, 2, 4, 14, 85
Malebranche, Nicolas, 198
Mandeville, Bernard, 176
Mansfield, Lord, 136
Marat, Jean-Paul, 38
Marie-Antoinette, 150, 168, 202, 261
Marlborough, Duke of, 132, 134, 171, 227
Marlowe, Christopher: *Dr Faustus*, 26
Marten, Henry, 213
Marvell, Andrew, 22, 178, 227, 284;

'Horatian Ode on Cromwell's Return from Ireland', 213
Michelangelo, 208, 279
Mill, James, 51
Mill, John Stuart, 51, 201
Milton, John, 4, 8, 17, 21, 34–5, 36, 44, 52, 53–4, 58, 59, 60, 65, 93, 96, 102, 117, 127, 134, 142, 148, 174, 188, 199, 206, 219, 226, 260, 279; and Bentham, 232, 233; and Burke, 134, 135; centos, 94, 95, 100; his imagination, 94–5, 108, 140, 253–4, 268; inspires H, 95, 133; and liberty, 216; and Utilitarianism, 217; *Areopagitica*, 52, 77, 89; *Comus*, 53, 190, 252–3; *Eikonoklastes*, 21, 211; *Lycidas*, 22; *Paradise Lost*, 93, 94, 107, 118, 132–4, 204, 210–17, 223, 232, 244, 254, 295; *The Ready and Easy Way to Establish a Free Commonwealth*, 108; sonnet on the massacre of the Waldensians, 173
modernity, 148, 229, 231, 240, 243, 254, 269
Molesworth, Viscount, 85
Monarchy, 101, 171, 201, 211, 295; anti-monarchical imagination, 209; Burke as a monarchist, 117, 134, 140, 171, 199, 263; French, 157, 172, 259; imagination, 157, 200, 241; Johnson and, 250–51; Milton on monarchists, 223; monarchical culture, 109; monarchist art, 100; Rousseau and, 157; Southey as a monarchist, 171, 172
Monmouth, James, Duke of, 279
Montague, Basil, 45
Monthly Magazine, 33, 73
Moore, Tom, 50, 257
Morning Chronicle, 13, 86, 130, 171
Murillo, Bartolomé: *Spanish Beggar Boys*, 65–6
Murray, Lindley, 251; *English Exercises*, 174; *English Grammar*, 249–50, 296

Napoleon Bonaparte, 5, 13, 17, 38, 39, 40, 47, 85, 86, 87, 100, 101, 110, 137, 168, 170, 172, 174, 205, 207, 210, 211, 215, 216, 217, 220, 224, 227, 228, 244, 278, 279

Natarajan, Uttara, 242
Neal, Daniel: *History of the Puritans*, 198
neo-classicism, 141, 146
New Lanark, 164, 240
New Statesman, 38
New Times, 204
Newcastle, Duchess of, 198
Newton, Sir Isaac, 8
Nietzsche, Friedrich Wilhelm, 40, 242
Norbrook, David, 213
Northcote, James, 96, 103, 119, 235, 259, 273–6, 280–81, 285, 288–90; *Life of Titian*, 245, 286, 293, 294
Norwich, 73, 75

O'Brien, Conor Cruise, 120, 126, 161
Old Jewry meeting-house, London, 10, 23, 71, 119, 120
Orchard, Jack, 283
Orr, William, 130
Orwell, George, 230, 270
Ossian, *Poems*, 156
Owen, Robert, 164, 240; *New View of Society*, 163

Paine, Thomas, 11, 120; *The Rights of Man*, 11, 167
Paisley, Revd Ian, 18
Park, Roy, 70, 234
Patmore, 43
Paul, St, 53, 272–3
Peace of Amiens (1802), 170, 273
Peterloo massacre (1819), 47, 48, 51, 208
Peters, Revd Hugh, 121
Picasso, Pablo: *The She-Goat*, 282
Pindar, 26, 157, 158
Pindar, Peter, 290
Pitt, William, the Younger, 23 5, 26, 28–31, 80, 81, 159
Plato: *Phaedrus*, 106
Platonism, 71, 251
Plutarch, 161, 229
Political Register, 50, 174
Pope, Alexander, 210, 215, 279
Popple, William, 178, 194
Poussin, Nicolas, 48, 193, 208, 209, 215, 219, 222, 224, 244, 277; and nature, 221, 226; Wordsworth and, 234, 291; *Paysage avec Orion*

aveugle, 206–7, 211, 212, 214, 216, 217, 220–21
Presbyterianism, 18, 36–7, 64, 199, 200, 202
Price, Revd Richard, 4, 6, 8, 10–11, 12, 110, 120, 121; *Discourse on the Love of our Country*, 10, 11, 119–20
Priestley, Joseph, 4, 7, 8–11, 18, 37, 38, 58–9, 73, 75, 77, 85, 96, 109, 110, 111, 119, 158, 188, 197, 198, 217, 251; and Burke, 120, 166, 167; *Lectures on Oratory and Criticism*, 237–8; prose style, 93, 237; Smith defends, 177; and soda-water, 121, 122; *A Course of Lectures in Oratory and Criticism*, 52–3; *Essay on the First Principles of Government*, 59–60; 'Of Harmony in Prose', 54–5
prize-fighting, *see* boxers/boxing
Probert (criminal), 296, 297
Projection, 18–19, 20, 101
Protestant Association, 120
Protestantism/Protestants, 36, 45, 119, 125, 126, 129, 163, 172–3, 178, 197, 285
Public Advertiser, 135
Puritanism/Puritans, 30, 43, 45, 53–4, 59, 108, 156, 165, 219, 221, 246, 253, 272
Pym, John, 138

Quakers, 30
Quarterly Review, 33, 177, 255, 256, 296

Rabelais, François, 55, 56, 60, 112, 186
Racine, Jean, 196–7
Racket-playing, 46, 87, 96–7, 112, 131, 269, 279–80, 296
Raphael, 208, 266, 279, 296
Rational Dissent, 6, 35, 37, 39, 57, 59, 64, 66, 71, 73, 75, 108, 110, 112, 121, 148, 163, 178, 191, 198, 263, 264
Real Whigs, 3, 4
Reformation, 17–20, 23
Reformist's Register, 50
Rembrandt van Rijn, 114, 115
Repeal of Certain Penal Statutes Respecting Religious Opinions, 120
Republicanism/Republicans, 21, 100, 102, 108, 109, 111, 113, 117, 134, 140, 145, 150, 157, 170, 171, 174, 191, 200, 201, 202, 204, 205, 209, 210, 212–13, 217, 218, 224, 225, 237, 241, 264
Restoration, 204, 217, 223
Revolution Society, 11, 120, 121, 169
Reynolds, John Hamilton, 14–15
Reynolds, Sir Joshua, 37, 103, 206, 275, 288
Richardson, Samuel: *Clarissa*, 44
Rickman, John, 177
Robert, Etienne, 19
Robbins, Caroline, 4
Rochester, John Wilmot, Earl of, 44
Rockingham, Charles Wentworth, Marquis of, 110
Rogers, Samuel, 88
Romanticism, 27, 141, 146, 153, 164, 203, 212, 221, 292, 295
Rosa, Salvator, 115, 164, 184, 202
Roscoe, William, 245
Rousseau, Jean-Jacques, 45, 153, 154, 157, 173, 190, 218, 259, 290; *Confessions*, 192, 217–18, 261–2; *Discourse on Inequality*, 218; *Emile*, 198; *Nouvelle Héloïse*, 190
Rubens, Peter Paul, 74, 81, 219, 227
Ruskin, John, 103
Russell, Lord William, 12

St Anne's Church, Wardour Street, London, 14, 300
St Bartholomew's Day Massacre (1572), 172
Saintsbury, George, 2, 151
Salisbury Plain, 291
Salveson, Christopher, 86
Schlegel, August von: *Lectures on Dramatic Literature*, 203
Scotland, culture, 113
Scots, 77, 231, 269
Scott, John, 254–5
Scott, Sir Walter, 155, 243, 253–6, 290
Scottish Enlightenment, 64
Seed, John, 110, 111–12
Shaftesbury, Anthony Ashley Cooper, 3rd Earl of, 68; *Characteristics of Men, Manners, Opinions, Times*, 4, 5, 84, 85, 156, 240
Shaftesbury, Anthony Ashley Cooper, 1st Earl of, 5, 83–4, 97, 240, 244
Shakespeare, William, 19, 40, 56, 81,

98, 104, 117, 154–5, 204, 260, 271, 279, 280, 284, 288, 289; humour, 53, 63; his imagination, 96, 203, 230; and society, 96; *Coriolanus*, 39, 91, 200, 243; *Hamlet*, 41–2, 220, 225, 267; *Henry IV, Part I*, 152; *Macbeth*, 146–7, 148, 154, 184, 203; *Measure for Measure*, 34; *The Merchant of Venice*, 86; *A Midsummer Night's Dream*, 159–62; *Othello*, 116, 219; *The Tempest*, 225–6; *A Winter's Tale*, 99, 221–2, 291, 294

Sharp, Richard, 167
Shaw, George Bernard, 128
Shelburne, William Petty, 2nd Earl of, 4, 110, 120, 126
Shelley, Mary, 38, 260; *Frankenstein*, 37, 38, 109, 258
Shelley, Percy Bysshe, 38, 50, 77, 183, 258; *Prometheus Unbound*, 162
Shenstone, William, 91, 92, 157, 274
Shepherd, Revd William, 12
Sheridan, Richard Brinsley, 25, 81, 129
Shrewsbury, 133, 191, 200, 218, 220, 260
Shrewsbury Chronicle, 9
Shronell, Co. Tipperary, 3
Shropshire, 23, 108–9, 134, 196
Siddons, Sarah, 99
Sidney, Algernon, 4, 12, 21, 52, 112, 138; *Discourses concerning Government*, 21
Sieyès, Abbé, 210
Smith, Adam, 5, 68, 113
Smith, Olivia, 249, 250, 251
Smith, William, 125, 174, 177
Smollett, Tobias, 232
Society for the Diffusion of Knowledge, 111
Society for Promoting Constitutional Information, 11
Socinus, Faustus, 198, 199
Soho, London, 14, 18, 298
Sontag, Susan, 70, 186
souse, 135, 137
South, Robert, 198
Southampton Buildings, Holborn, 18
Southey, Robert, 51, 116, 125, 126, 150, 171, 173, 174, 178, 180–84, 188, 189, 202, 203, 204, 248, 256; limitations, 185, 192; prose style,

179–80, 181, 186, 187; *Letter to William Smith*, 177; *Wat Tyler*, 116
Southwark Friends of the People for the Diffusion of Political Knowledge, 36
Spa Fields Meeting (1815), 174, 175
Spenser, Edmund, 44, 173
Spinoza, Baruch, 75
Staël, Madame Anne de, 195, 196
Stanhope, Charles, 3rd Earl, 11, 121
Sterne, Laurence, 232, 276, 278, 279; *Tristram Shandy*, 129, 261, 276–7
Stewart, Prince Charles, 199, 223
Stoddart, Sarah, *see* Hazlitt, Sarah
Stormont parliament, Belfast, 123, 128
style, 99, 229, 240, 242, 243, 256, 259, 272, 278
Swanwick, Joseph, 67
Swanwick, Sarah, 67
Swift, Jonathan, 27, 29, 55–6, 128, 129, 176, 253

Tacitus, 296
Taylor, Jeremy, 56, 60, 193, 274; *Holy Dying*, 61–3, 87
Taylor, John, 16
Taylor and Hessey, 106
Tennyson, Alfred, Lord, 57
Terror, the, 132, 158, 218
Test Acts, 120
Thackeray, William Makepeace, 45–6
Thelwall, John, 11, 12, 79–80, 82, 83, 84
Thompson, E. P., 51, 241
Thomson, James, 69, 99, 294; *The Seasons*, 4, 291
Tillotson, John, 198
The Times, 174, 179
Titian, 15, 85, 89, 159, 169, 170, 208, 233, 234, 235, 237, 239, 243, 266, 275, 277–8, 279, 285, 292, 295; *Hippolito de Medici*, 234; *Man with a Glove*, 234; *Portrait of Benedetto Varchi*, 245; portrait of Hippolito de Medici, 277
Tone, Wolfe, 134
Tooke, John Horne, 11, 12, 146, 163, 239, 248–53, 274, 280, 284–5; *The Diversions of Purley*, 249, 251
Tories, 91, 92, 117, 157, 204, 205, 216, 263, 274
transparency, 16, 62, 63, 179, 196, 230, 237, 256

Treason Trials (1794), 11–13, 47, 79, 251

Trinitarianism, 216

Tucker, Abraham: *The Light of Nature Pursued*, 248

Turgenev, Ivan Sergeevich, 239

Ulster, Scottish-trained students, 110

understanding, 55, 91, 117, 127, 146, 157, 165, 185, 187, 203, 229, 232, 252, 284

Unitarian Society for the Promoting of Christian Knowledge, 7, 37

Unitarianism/Unitarians, 3, 7–10, 23, 35, 52, 58, 59, 63, 67, 68, 71, 72, 108–9, 111–12; Burke and, 120; culture, 110, 120, 135, 198–9, 217, 254, 263; emigration to America, 11, 178; H defends, 177–8; Milton and, 217; Rousseau and, 218; Unitarian science, 197, 264; writing style, 178

United Irishmen, 67, 134

United States of America: Cobbett and, 81, 82, 174; a free Government, 264; Hazlitt family in, 3, 5; Hutcheson's philosophy and, 110; Unitarians emigrate to, 11, 178

University of Glasgow, 5, 67, 68, 110

Utility/Utilitarianism, 24, 94, 232, 239, 285

Van Dyck, Sir Anthony, 72, 73, 275, 277, 289

Van Goyen, Jan, 114

Verdi, Richard, 206–7

Virgil: *Aeneid*, 137

Voltaire, 173

Wakefield, Gilbert, 10

Walker, Sarah, 16, 18, 43, 44–5, 47

Warens, Madame de, 262

Webster, Noah, 249

Weekly Political Pamphlet, 175–6

Wellington, Duke of, 170, 173, 215

Wem, Shropshire, 5, 9, 13, 63, 191, 192, 218, 220, 260

West, Benjamin, 100, 278

Whigs: characteristics, 3, 5, 22, 97; classicism of high Whig politics, 148; culture, 172, 249; elected (1830), 51;

H as a true Whig, 138; history, 38, 172; idea of liberty, 122; prose-writers as radical Whigs, 157; radicalism, 239, 240; Real, 3, 4; and Sterne, 129; triumphalism, 126; the Whig line, 84, 85; Whig narrative, 276; Whig prose, 91–117, 227, 230, 247

White terror, 172

Whitelocke, Bulstrode, 32, 56, 57, 58, 232, 269

Whitman, Walt, 65, 96, 108

Wilberforce, William, 246, 266

Wilde, Oscar, 159, 292

Wilkes, John, 136

Wilkie, David, 56

William III, King (William of Orange), 138, 227

Wimsatt, W. K., 247

Windham, William, 31, 33, 80, 81, 82, 85, 104, 168

Winterslow, Hampshire, 14, 17, 34, 47, 115, 191, 291

Winterslow Hut, 239

Wisbech, Cambridgeshire, 200

Wolfson, Susan, 223

Wollstonecraft, Mary: *A Vindication of the Rights of Men*, 167

Woolf, Virginia, 56, 297

Wordsworth, William, 35, 74, 76, 86, 105, 115, 130, 150, 173, 211, 212, 278–9; and Burke, 263; and Fawcett, 71; H on, 69, 192–3, 257–65, 266; H visits, 31; his imagination, 265; and Poussin, 234, 291; and Rational Dissent, 73, 75; vision of nature, 75; *Descriptive Sketches*, 73; *An Evening Walk*, 73; *The Excursion*, 31–2, 71, 213; 'Immortality Ode', 86–7, 213; *The Prelude*, 170, 192, 196, 214, 262; 'Thanksgiving Ode', 40; 'Tintern Abbey', 71–5, 116, 119, 122, 212

Wyvill, Christopher, 167

Yeats, Jack, 287

Yeats, W. B., 128, 160, 162, 163, 170, 246

York Street, London, 17, 18

Zisca, John, 198, 199